Cooking Basics
FOR
DUMMIES®
4TH EDITION

by Bryan Miller, Marie Rama,
and Eve Adamson

WILEY

Wiley Publishing, Inc.

Cooking Basics For Dummies®, 4th Edition

Published by
Wiley Publishing, Inc.
111 River St.
Hoboken, NJ 07030-5774
www.wiley.com

Copyright © 2011 by Wiley Publishing, Inc., Indianapolis, Indiana

Published by Wiley Publishing, Inc., Indianapolis, Indiana

Published simultaneously in Canada

For general information on our other products and services, please contact our Customer Care Department within the U.S. at 877-762-2974, outside the U.S. at 317-572-3993, or fax 317-572-4002.

For technical support, please visit www.wiley.com/techsupport.

Wiley also publishes its books in a variety of electronic formats. Some content that appears in print may not be available in electronic books.

Library of Congress Control Number: 2010939968

ISBN: 978-0-470-91388-8

Manufactured in the United States of America

10 9 8 7 6 5 4 3 2

WILEY

About the Authors

Bryan Miller is a food and wine writer and a former restaurant critic for *The New York Times*. He has written and co-written 11 books. In the past 25 years he has received numerous awards, including three writing awards from the James Beard Foundation, and the organization's prestigious Lifetime Achievement Award.

Marie Rama grew up in the restaurant business surrounded by a large Italian family of food professionals and entrepreneurs. She has worked as a pastry chef, a recipe tester, and an account executive and spokesperson for national companies and associations such as Tabasco Sauce, The United Fresh Fruit and Vegetable Association, Korbel Champagne, and Sunkist Growers. In addition to *Cooking For Dummies,* Ms. Rama also wrote *Grilling For Dummies* (with John Mariani) and is working on a cookbook that celebrates the many uses and irresistible enticement of bacon. Ms. Rama has two sons, Nicholas and William, and lives in Yonkers, New York with her husband and literary agent Mark Reiter. When she's not in the kitchen testing and researching new recipes, Ms. Rama is either volunteering for her favorite foundation, Yonkers Partners in Education, or playing golf.

Eve Adamson is a *New York Times* best-selling author who has written or coauthored over 50 books on food, cooking, dieting, and lifestyle subjects, including several other *For Dummies* guides, several books on the Mediterranean diet, and a book on craft beer. Eve is a member of the International Association of Culinary Professionals and a self-taught home cook who loves to travel and sample the cuisines of different regions and cultures. She lives in Iowa City with her family, where she spends her days writing, cooking, planning her next trip, and contemplating remodeling her kitchen (pretty much in that order). To find out more, visit her Web site at www.eveadamson.com.

Publisher's Acknowledgments

We're proud of this book; please send us your comments at http://dummies.custhelp.com. For other comments, please contact our Customer Care Department within the U.S. at 877-762-2974, outside the U.S. at 317-572-3993, or fax 317-572-4002.

Some of the people who helped bring this book to market include the following:

Acquisitions, Editorial, and Media Development

Project Editor: Joan Friedman
  (Previous Edition: Alissa Schwipps)

Acquisitions Editor: Stacy Kennedy

Assistant Editor: David Lutton

Technical Editor: Larry D. Martin, C.C.

Senior Editorial Manager: Jennifer Ehrlich

Editorial Supervisor: Carmen Krikorian

Editorial Assistant: Jennette ElNaggar

Art Coordinator: Alicia B. South

Cover Photos: ©iStockphoto.com/Ernesto Diaz; T.J. Hine Photography

Cartoons: Rich Tennant (www.the5thwave.com)

Composition Services

Project Coordinator: Sheree Montgomery

Layout and Graphics: Claudia Bell, Christin Swinford

Proofreaders: Melissa Cossell, Betty Kish

Indexer: BIM Indexing & Proofreading Services

Special Art: Elizabeth Kurtzman

Photographer: T.J. Hine Photography

Food Stylist: Lisa Bishop

Publishing and Editorial for Consumer Dummies

  Diane Graves Steele, Vice President and Publisher, Consumer Dummies

  Kristin Ferguson-Wagstaffe, Product Development Director, Consumer Dummies

  Ensley Eikenburg, Associate Publisher, Travel

  Kelly Regan, Editorial Director, Travel

Publishing for Technology Dummies

  Andy Cummings, Vice President and Publisher, Dummies Technology/General User

Composition Services

  Debbie Stailey, Director of Composition Services

Contents at a Glance

Recipes at a Glance

Salads

Main Dishes

Vegetables and Side Dishes

Sauces, Dressings, and Garnishes

Sweets and Desserts

Beverages

Table of Contents

Introduction

Whether you fancy yourself a hotshot home cook or someone who wouldn't know a whisk from a Weimaraner, *Cooking Basics For Dummies,* 4th Edition, can help you.

Unlike most cookbooks, this one is more than a compilation of tasty recipes. We also focus on cooking techniques like broiling, steaming, braising, and roasting, as well as ingredients like different kinds of grains, cuts of meat, and types of pasta. You learn the best way to mince garlic, peel a tomato, and truss a chicken (if you want to!). After you master these techniques, you're no longer a slave to recipes. You can cook with imagination and creativity — and that's the sign of a skilled cook.

Furthermore, this book is structured around the way you live. For example, it includes information about cooking economically, making a delicious meal when you don't even have time to get to the market, and throwing a party or celebrating a holiday when you've got all the time in the world.

Most of all, you actually have fun as you explore the endless pleasures of cooking. And that, after all, is what this book is all about.

About This Book

We start at the very beginning: your kitchen and your equipment. What basic tools do you need? How do you use these things? We help you stock your pantry, refrigerator, and freezer with basic staples so you know what to have on hand. Then we move on to cooking techniques to get you up and running as soon as possible. Doing simple things well offers great personal satisfaction, as you will see.

Depending on your needs and cooking skills, you can start at the beginning of the book and work your way through, go straight to the chapters that interest you most (the table of contents and index point you in the right direction), or read the book backwards, if that's your thing.

Conventions Used in This Book

Here are some non-recipe conventions you should keep in mind to get the most out of this book:

- *Italic* is used for emphasis and to highlight new words or terms that are defined.

- **Boldfaced** text is used to indicate the action part of numbered steps.

- `Monofont` is used for Web addresses.

Before charging ahead to make any of the recipes in this book, you should know a few things about the ingredients and instructions:

- **Milk is always whole.** You can substitute lowfat or skim milk, or even soy or rice milk, but these products give soups and sauces a thinner, less creamy consistency and may influence the texture in other dishes (although not necessarily in an undesirable way).

- **Butter is unsalted so you can control the amount of salt in a dish.** We don't recommend substituting margarine, which has just as many calories and just as much fat as butter, unless you are avoiding dairy products. Margarine's flavor is generally inferior to butter.

- **Unless otherwise noted, all eggs are large.**

- **All dry ingredient measurements are level.** Brown sugar is measured firmly packed.

- **All measured salt is common table salt, and pepper is freshly ground.** We don't mind if you use sea salt or kosher salt when a recipe calls for salt "to taste."

- **All oven temperatures are Fahrenheit.**

And keep the following general tips in mind:

- Read through each recipe at least once — including any tips at the end — to make sure that you have all the necessary ingredients and tools, understand all the steps, and have enough preparation time. You can also consider whether you want to try any variations.

- Be sure to use the proper size pan when a measurement is given.

- Preheat ovens and broilers at least 10 minutes before cooking begins and preheat grills for at least 15 minutes. Place all food on the middle rack of the oven unless the recipe says otherwise.

- If you're looking for vegetarian recipes, you can find them in the Recipes in This Chapter list, located at the beginning of every chapter. Vegetarian recipes are marked by the tomato bullet shown here.

What You're Not to Read

We've written this book so that you can 1) find information easily and 2) easily understand what you find. And although we'd like to believe that you want to pore over every last word between the two yellow-and-black covers, we actually make it easy for you to identify "skippable" material. This information is the stuff that, although interesting and related to the topic at hand, isn't essential for you to know. In other words, it won't be on the test!

- ✔ **Text in sidebars:** The sidebars are the shaded boxes that appear here and there. They offer personal observations and fascinating facts, but they aren't necessary reading.

- ✔ **The stuff on the copyright page:** No kidding. You'll find nothing here of interest unless you're inexplicably enamored by legal language and Library of Congress numbers.

- ✔ **Our extraordinary biographies:** You don't need to know who we are to know that this is the best cookbook out there. After all, all *For Dummies* authors are considered experts in their fields. Still, aren't you curious?

Foolish Assumptions

We wrote this cookbook with some thoughts about you in mind. Here's what we assume about you, our reader:

- ✔ You love the *idea* of cooking. You're a crackerjack at boiling water. But you just aren't quite sure how to actually organize a meal, make lots of things at once, or combine foods or flavors in ways that make your family members sigh with satisfaction after they put down their forks.

- ✔ You've cooked before. Sometimes it was pretty darn good. Sometimes you were glad you didn't have company. Sometimes the fire department had to be called. But really, sometimes it *was* pretty darn good! You're almost positive you have potential.

- ✔ You sometimes daydream about going to cooking school or impressing people with the way you chop garlic with your very expensive chef's knife. But you don't yet own a very expensive chef's knife.

- ✔ You have basic kitchen equipment on hand, including pots and pans and measuring cups, but you aren't sure whether you have all the right things you need for efficient cooking, and you probably don't know what all those different pots and pans are called.

✔ You bought this cookbook for yourself so you can finally gain the skills you need to earn the title of "really great cook." Or somebody gave you this cookbook as a gift, and you assume that it was a hint somehow related to that interesting casserole-type thing you attempted last week.

How This Book Is Organized

This book is organized around cooking techniques and real-life situations. Major sections are called *parts*. Within each part are chapters that address specific subjects. Following is a rundown of each part and what you can read about there.

Part I: Go On In — It's Only the Kitchen

What is this strange room? It's the most popular room in the house, where friends hang out as they help themselves to your food and drinks, where parties inevitably gravitate, and where couples have their best arguments. This part is designed to help you get over your apprehension about your kitchen and what goes on in there. It touches on kitchen design and organization, helping you to arrange your appliances, kitchen space, counters, and cabinets for maximum efficiency. It also covers in detail necessary equipment like pots, pans, knives, and all kinds of gadgets. You find out which basic supplies you need to stock up on. Plus, we get you cooking right away in this part, with a simple recipe guaranteed to whet your appetite to cook more.

Part II: Know Your Techniques

Part II is where the fun really begins. We start out with a whole chapter devoted to knife skills because they're so crucial to cooking success. Then we introduce essential cooking techniques: boiling, poaching, steaming, sautéing, braising, stewing, roasting, grilling, broiling, and baking. For each technique, we provide a number of recipes that show you how to put your newfound knowledge to work with confidence and skill.

Part III: Expand Your Repertoire

Part III focuses on meals and types of food, from breakfast, soup, salad, pasta, and grains on through to fancy sauces and luscious sweets. Here, you can read about how to make the perfect omelet, how to mix a balanced vinaigrette, and how to use seasonal fruits to create delectable desserts.

Also included are illustrations and charts — like the one identifying different types of pastas (so that you know cannelloni from linguine) — and, of course, dozens of delicious recipes.

Part IV: Now You're Cooking! Real Menus for Real Life

Part IV injects another dose of reality into the cooking experience. Most glossy cookbooks assume that you have all the time in the world to prepare a dish. Some books also assume that price is no object — "now take that loin of veal and sprinkle it with black truffles" — and that everybody lives next door to a gourmet market. In the real world, you have 45 minutes, if you're lucky, to prepare dinner while a 2-year-old is clinging to your leg and the cat is coughing up hairballs. And the local supermarket may be closing in 5 minutes. Now that's real-life cooking—making one-pot meals, economy meals, meals out of leftovers, and even those meals when you suddenly (without warning) have to impress someone. And, because life is also about holidays and fun, you get specific instructions on throwing a summer party and cooking for the winter holidays — because somebody's got to do it.

Part V: The Part of Tens

Just when you thought that we had covered everything, we give you more! These quick chapters cover kitchen disasters and what to do about them, tips on how to think like a chef, and tips for cooking (and eating) for good health. Before you know it, you've got this cooking thing *down*.

We round out the book with two helpful appendixes. This straightforward reference section gives you a glossary of more than 100 cooking terms, as well as common equivalents and substitutions for those emergency situations when you discover that you don't have the ingredient you need.

Icons Used in This Book

Icons are those nifty little pictures in the margin of this book. They each grab your attention for a different reason, and we explain those reasons here.

When there's an easier way to do something, a step you can take to save money, or a shortcut you can take to get yourself to the dinner table faster, we let you know by marking the tip with this icon.

The kitchen can be a dangerous place. This icon, like a flashing yellow light, steers you clear of potentially dangerous mishaps.

We hope that you remember every valuable piece of information in this book, but if your brain can hold only so much, make sure that you hang on to the tidbits marked by this icon.

When we describe cooking techniques, we often refer to recipes later in the chapter that put them to the test. This chef's hat lets you know that a related recipe awaits!

Where to Go from Here

You can start enjoying *Cooking Basics For Dummies,* 4th Edition, with any chapter you like. Even if you know your way around a kitchen pretty well, we recommend that you start by reading Chapter 2, just to be sure you really do have all the equipment to cook the recipes in this book, and Chapter 3, which talks about all the basic ingredients every well-stocked kitchen pantry, freezer, and refrigerator should contain.

If you're in the process of buying a house, remodeling a kitchen, or just dreaming about your perfect kitchen, check out Chapter 1, where you can read all about kitchen design. Wary about safety? Check out the end of Chapter 1, or skip on over to Chapter 22 for a list of ten common kitchen disasters and how to avoid them. Or, maybe you just want to start cooking. In that case, check out any of the other chapters in this book. Some are arranged around techniques; others are arranged around menus for parties, for economy, or for times when you need to prepare a meal on short notice. But all these chapters are chock-full of delicious recipes with simple instructions.

One place to check out that *isn't* in this book is www.dummies.com/go/cooking. The site features lots of cooking-related videos, many of them that are directly connected with what we discuss in this book. So if you're reading our instructions for how to carve poultry or how to mince garlic and can't quite figure out what we're trying to say, be sure to check out the Web site for videos that bring the steps to life.

We know you'll enjoy cooking with us. Cooking doesn't have to be complicated, as long as you know the basics. So come on in to the kitchen, grab a pot (we tell you which one), and get cooking. We're getting hungry just thinking about it!

Part I

Go On In — It's Only the Kitchen

"I'm sure there are some canned staples in the food pantry. That's what it's there for. Just look next to the roller blades, below the bike helmets above the backpacks, but under the tennis balls."

In this part . . .

There's no doubt about it: If you want to learn to cook, you have to go into the kitchen. But never fear! The kitchen may seem like it's full of strange appliances, oddly shaped tools, and bottles and jars and packages of ingredients you know nothing about, but as a beginning cook, this is where the fun begins! We help you navigate, utilize, and even enjoy your kitchen with organizational strategies, explanations about essential equipment, lists of must-have supplies, and even a few remodeling tips, if you should need them. You'll even try your hand at an easy recipe — that's right! You, actually cooking!

Chapter 1

Cooking with Confidence

In This Chapter

▶ Taking a good look at your kitchen

▶ Familiarizing yourself with some basic cooking techniques

▶ Figuring out your menus

▶ Making your kitchen safe and user-friendly

▶ Trying your hand at a simple recipe

So you want to find out how to cook? Good for you! Cooking is fun, interesting, and can be relaxing, exciting, even therapeutic. Cooking is a life skill, but it can also be a hobby and a passion. When you cook at home, you can eat for less money than you would spend ordering take-out or dining in a restaurant every night, and *you* control the ingredients, flavors, and health profile of your food so you know exactly what you're eating.

Cooking gives you options. Adapt your meals to suit your own nutritional and taste preferences, whether you're a gourmet or prefer simple tastes, whether you're a confirmed carnivore or a vegetarian, whether you prefer to eat light or low-carb, explore ethnic cuisines, or stick to all-American classics. When you cook, you can always get exactly the food you want. Plus, cooking the food you eat makes you more aware of your food, your health, and your environment. Yes, cooking can be that powerful!

We love to cook, and we're excited to share our knowledge with you, but we remember what it was like to be a beginning cook. Sometimes you may not feel confident enough to try what looks like a complicated recipe, let alone figure out which equipment and supplies you need and how you should set up a kitchen that works for you.

In this chapter, we begin at the beginning with the place where the magic happens: your kitchen. Whether you have a cramped apartment kitchen with counter space the size of a cereal box, or a sprawling country kitchen with a commercial stove and a work island, this chapter helps you set up your kitchen in a way that will allow you to become a more productive cook. Knowing how to use what you have efficiently is even more important than square footage. You'd be surprised to see how small some restaurant kitchens are; they work, however, because everything is in its place and is easily accessible. Have you ever ricocheted around the kitchen desperately searching for a spatula while your omelet burned in the skillet? We want to ensure that you're never in that situation again.

To do that, in this chapter, we give you a broad overview of what you need to know to be an effective cook. We talk about how to set up your cooking space, introduce you to the major appliances of a kitchen, and give you a glimpse of some basic cooking techniques. Then we discuss menu planning and kitchen safety, and we even help you to get started with a nice, easy, practical recipe.

Warming Up to Your Kitchen

There it is: the kitchen. Maybe you don't go in there very much, or maybe you like to hang around watching other people cook. Or maybe you cook dinner in there every night, but you don't enjoy it very much — it's a chore. Never fear. Your kitchen can easily become a place you *love* to cook in and be in. It's all a matter of organization.

Setting up your cooking space

You don't need a fabulous kitchen to prepare fabulous food, but a well-designed workspace sure makes cooking easier and more pleasurable. Chances are, you aren't in the process of remodeling your kitchen, and you have to make do with the basic kitchen design you have. However, if you are at liberty to shift some things around or you are designing your cooking space, consider the concept of *access*. If you want to spend the day running, join a health club. If you want to enjoy an efficient and pleasurable cooking experience, consider where your main appliances are located and where you store the equipment and ingredients you use the most. Do you have to walk 10 feet from the stove to get the salt? That's not efficient. Although nothing is wrong with a large, eat-in kitchen, the design of the cooking area in particular should be practical.

You should be able to move from your working counter space to the stove/ oven, refrigerator, and sink in a smooth, unobstructed fashion. This working space actually has a name: the *kitchen triangle* (see Figure 1-1). It applies whether you have a long narrow kitchen, a U-shaped kitchen, or an L-shaped kitchen. Consider the positioning of these three major appliances and jettison any obstacles — if a table, plant, or small child is blocking the way, move it. Even if you can't redesign your kitchen space or move your refrigerator to another wall, there are other ways to arrange what you need in a way that works for you. Here's how to do that. (For more information about designing your kitchen, check out *Kitchen Remodeling For Dummies,* by Donald R. Prestly [Wiley].)

Figure 1-1:
One
example of
an efficient
kitchen
triangle.

Decluttering your countertops

You can't chop vegetables, slice meat, or whip up a cake batter if you can't even fit a cutting board or a mixing bowl on your counter, so take a good look at your countertops. What's on them? Coffeemakers, blenders, food processors, racks of spice jars or canisters of flour and sugar, stacks of bills, permission slips, and grade school art projects? Is your countertop doubling as a magazine rack, plant holder, wine rack, or phone book shelf? Consider this: Your kitchen counters are not meant to be storage units. They are meant to be *food preparation areas.* A clean, clear counter space can inspire the creation of a great meal. A cluttered one is more likely to inspire a call to the pizza delivery guy. If your kitchen counter is cluttered with paraphernalia beyond usefulness, that's a problem you can fix.

The most important key for organizing your counter space is to keep it clear of most stuff. The ultimate test for whether something should be allowed valuable countertop real estate is how often you use it. If you use an appliance or food ingredient (like coffee or flour) *almost every day,* then go ahead and give it hallowed ground. Otherwise, stow it. Be ruthless. Put away the mixer, the food processor, the bread machine, and the rice cooker. Away with the herb and spice rack, the bottles of nut oil and fancy vinegar. Find a better spot for the phone book, the mail, the bills. As you rid your counters of this clutter, you'll also be getting rid of your excuses for not having the space to cook dinner.

In addition to keeping your countertops clutter free, take steps to care for them. Use cutting boards for cutting and trivets for hot pots and pans, and wipe up spills quickly to prevent stains. The nicer your counters look, the more you'll enjoy being in the kitchen. (Flip ahead to Chapter 22 for more information about countertop care.)

Let there be lighting

Efficient kitchens should be well lit so you can see what you are doing, whether it's chopping or sautéing or checking whether your cake is done. Poor lighting increases mistakes, especially over the workspaces and stove. Lights under the stovetop hood can really help when stirring sauces or browning meat, and a nice bright oven light makes it much easier to assess the state of doneness of your casserole or cookies. You haven't replaced those burned-out bulbs in years? Time to do it! Get out your screwdriver and remove the panel over the lights. Unscrew the bulbs and take them with you to the store so you are sure to get the right replacement. No more procrastination!

Another option is to have special lighting for the cooking area, either inset into overhead cabinets or in the ceiling. If your kitchen is poorly lit over the cooking area, the least expensive solution is a wall-mounted supplementary light.

Staple city: Organizing your pantry

The pantry is the place where you store your basic cooking staples, as well as other dry goods. (*Dry goods* are foods that aren't refrigerated or frozen, including staples like flour and sugar, and packaged foods like crackers, cookies, pasta, and rice.) If you're lucky enough to have an entire room or closet dedicated to a pantry, keep it well organized so that you can see and easily reach the staples you use most, like flour, sugar, and cooking oil. Even if you have only a cabinet or two for your pantry, organization is the key to efficiency. (For tips on what to keep in your pantry, turn to Chapter 3.)

The first thing to consider in organizing your pantry is the kind of closet or cabinet you decide to use and whether the food you store inside of it is easily accessible.

We've seen many ingenious kitchen cabinets on the market, such as those that have extra storage shelves on swing-out doors; Lazy Susan–type cabinets that rotate for full access to round shelves; and cabinets with shelves, drawers, and baskets that roll out on tracks so you can easily reach even those things you store at the back. If your cabinets don't have these convenient features, you can improvise by mounting racks on the inside of the doors or installing those handy roll-out shelves yourself. Look for such kits in hardware or kitchen stores.

A good cabinet or closet system enables you to see exactly what's in your pantry, thus helping to inspire your culinary creativity and allowing you to grab what you need without knocking over vinegar bottles and stacks of spice jars. Store dried beans, pasta, different kinds of rice, flour, sugar, tea, and coffee in large glass or clear plastic jars with lids, or in containers with clear labels — it's practical and looks professional, too.

If you use something all the time, consider taking it out of the pantry and storing it closer to your stove or workstation, in a "satellite" pantry like a cabinet or shelf. You may want to do this with your cooking oils and sprays, your spice rack, or (if you like to bake) your baking supplies such as baking soda, baking powder, and vanilla.

 Kitchen islands are efficient food preparation stations, and they can also house considerable storage space. Moreover, they can double as a kitchen table or a place to serve party food. If you don't have an island (and you have the space), consider buying a butcher block–style table to act as one — with shelving underneath to store your stuff for easy access

Introducing major appliances: Friends, not foes

There they are, those formidable appliances that make your kitchen into a room custom-made for food preparation and storage. Your major appliances are capable of producing the most exquisite gourmet meals or the most horrible, burned disasters; of yielding fresh, dewy produce or slimy bags of who-knows-what-that-used-to-be.

Major appliances are your allies in good cooking if you work with them, not against them. Until you make friends with your stove, oven, refrigerator, and small appliances (which we discuss in Chapter 2), you'll never really feel at home in the kitchen. To know your appliances is to love them, and knowing each appliance's relative strengths and weaknesses can help you make the most of what they can do for you.

Stovetop and oven

Whether you have an old gas stove that looks like it belonged to your grandma or a fancy space-age-looking glass cooktop, your stovetop may be the cooking appliance you use the most. Right under it, or sometimes over it, or possibly off to the side, is your oven, which you'll probably use almost as much for baking, roasting, and warming up leftovers. Your stove and oven are your best friends in the kitchen, and if you're buying new ones, you have all kinds of new technology to choose from. Even if you won't be going appliance shopping any time soon, knowing exactly what kind of stovetop and oven you have and how to use them may help your cooking efforts.

Gas

Most serious cooks prefer gas stoves because the gas flame is ultimately adjustable, allowing you to turn the heat up or down quickly and to make minute variations in the size of the flame. Commercial gas ranges can cut your cooking time by as much as one-fourth, but simple home ranges work just fine for most purposes. New cooks may feel intimidated by gas because they fear the presence of gas in the kitchen, and that cooking flame is *actual fire*. Because gas stoves can produce higher heat than some electric stoves, they take a little more practice to use; it's easier to burn the food when you cook with gas. However, when you know what you are doing, there is no substitute for gas. When you can confidently proclaim, "Oh, I much prefer my gas stove," you know you've reached a whole new level of culinary prowess.

Newer gas ranges should not smell of gas from flaming pilot lights. Newer models no longer have standing pilots. They ignite electronically; therefore, gas doesn't flow through the system unless the range is turned on. If you do smell gas, you have a leak in your system. This situation is dangerous — call your gas company immediately. Do not use the stove or any other electrical appliances, even your lights, because doing so can spark an explosion. This situation is rare but possible. Older gas ranges smell like gas, but the smell shouldn't be overpowering. Have your gas range serviced periodically to guard against any problems.

Electric heat

After all our fancy-shmancy talk about gas stoves, you may be eyeing your electric range with suspicion: Can it really produce anything worth eating? Of course! If you have an electric range, you can still love your stove and cook anything on it. You just have to realize that the burners will warm up (and cool down) more slowly and you may not be able to get quite the heat intensity you could on gas. But that's no big deal if you are used to cooking on electric.

Electric ranges became all the rage after World War II. They were considered clean, easy to use, and modern. The drawback to electric ranges is their slow response time. Reducing heat from high to low can take a minute; gas can do it in seconds. However, many professional chefs prefer electric ovens, especially for baking, because they're very accurate and consistent. Today's gas and electric ovens generally hold and maintain oven temperature within a variance of about 5 degrees. If you have a choice, gas is slightly preferable for stoves and electric slightly preferable for ovens.

Induction

Some professional chefs prefer *induction* heat, and some even predict it will soon replace all other systems. Whether that is true or not, induction cooking is pretty cool. Basically, it works on a *magnetic transfer* principle — heat passes via magnetic force from the burner to the pan. If you place a paper towel between the burner and the pan, the towel does not get hot. For that matter, neither will your hand — an induction burner turned on high will not burn you. Induction is just as adjustable and quick as gas, if not more so. A 2-quart pot of water comes to a boil in about a minute.

An induction cooktop uses only selected metal pans to which a magnet adheres, such as stainless steel. Copper and glass cookware, for example, do not work. Induction cooktops run on electricity, so they are a great option when you want precision in your range but don't want to install a gas line. They are expensive, however, and can cost twice as much as an equivalent standard electric or gas cooktop. Even so, plenty of home cooks say they are worth every penny.

Convection ovens

Convection ovens cook food more rapidly and evenly than standard gas or electric ovens due to a small fan in the rear of the oven that circulates air all around the food. This efficient circulation means that your cooking time and/or temperature setting may be reduced. For example, a cake meant to bake for 30 minutes may be done after 20, or you may be able to set that 350-degree oven to 325 degrees. You always adjust recipes according to the manufacturer's instructions for your individual unit (and check for doneness at least 15 minutes earlier than you would have in a standard oven). Some oven manufacturers offer both regular and convection cooking at the flick of a switch. Do you need a convection oven? No. But if you bake often, you may learn to love one.

If a convection wall oven is over your budget, consider the smaller, less expensive convection toaster oven, especially if you're cooking for one or two. It can toast, bake a cake, broil a burger, and roast a small chicken. And cooking times are shorter than in conventional ovens. Small convection ovens can cost as little as a few hundred dollars, while larger, full-sized convection ovens can range from a couple thousand dollars to $10,000 or more, depending on the model and brand.

Microwave ovens

Microwave cooking is unlike any other kind of conventional cooking. You must follow a different set of cooking rules. Although over 90 percent of American kitchens have a microwave, most people use the microwave only as a reheating and defrosting device — and maybe to make popcorn. If this is your intention, you don't need an expensive, fancy microwave with a lot of different settings. If you're short on counter or wall space, consider a microwave–convection oven combination that allows you to cook by using either method.

Microwaves can't pass through metal, so you can't cook with traditional metal cookware. You can, however, use flameproof glass, some porcelain and ceramic, paper, and some plastics. (Be sure the plastic container or plate says "microwave safe"; recent research suggests that plastics can leach chemicals into the food and should not be used in the microwave.) Some microwaves permit you to use aluminum foil to cover dishes, as long as the foil doesn't touch the oven walls or the temperature probe. Check your operating manual to see whether your appliance allows using foil in this way.

A microwave is not a replacement for conventional cooking of grilled meats, baked breads, cakes and cookies, and other foods that need browning — unless it has a browning unit. Use your microwave for what it does best in combination with other appliances. For example, you can precook chicken in minutes in the microwave and finish it under the broiler or on an outdoor grill. Following are some other microwave tips:

- Recipes that require a lot of water, such as pasta, don't work as well in a microwave and probably cook in less time on your stovetop, although microwave rice cookers are efficient.

- Foods must be arranged properly to cook evenly. Face the thickest parts, like broccoli stalks, outward toward the oven walls. Arrange foods of the same size and shape, such as potatoes, in a circle or square or like the spokes of a wheel.

- Covering dishes eliminates splattering, and it also cuts down on cooking time. Use paper towels or waxed paper. Frequently stirring, turning, and rotating foods ensures an even distribution of heat.

- As with conventional cooking, cutting foods into smaller pieces shortens cooking time.

- Before cooking, pierce with a fork any foods that have skins, like potatoes, hot dogs, and sausages. Doing so releases steam that can lead to sudden popping and splattering (or a hotdog with an exploded end like a firecracker).

- A number of variables, including the type of microwave, can affect a recipe's cooking time, so check for doneness after the minimum cooking time. You can always cook food longer. Also, always observe the recipe's "standing" time, because microwaved food continues to cook after you remove it from the oven.

- Be sure to use the defrost power setting (30 to 40 percent of full power) when thawing food to ensure slow and even defrosting; otherwise, the outside of the food may start to cook before the inside is thoroughly thawed.

Read your microwave manual carefully before using it. One woman we know ruined her microwave oven because she used the cooking-time button as a kitchen timer, not realizing that you should never run an empty microwave — a warning found in just about every manual.

Most major appliance companies have Web sites and toll-free customer service numbers with appliance experts on hand to answer questions about using and caring for any major appliance.

How does a microwave cook?

Every microwave has an energy box called a *magnetron,* which produces microwaves (from electricity). The microwaves pass through materials like glass, paper, china, and plastic to convert to heat when they come in contact with food molecules. The microwaves cause the water molecules in the food to rotate so rapidly that they vibrate, creating friction and heat.

A major misconception is that microwaves cook from the inside out. They do not. Microwaves penetrate primarily the surface and no farther than 2 inches into the food. The heat spreads by conduction to the rest of the food.

Refrigerator

Refrigerators are the black holes of the kitchen — objects drift in and are never seen again, at least until the next thorough cleaning. At that time, your leftovers may resemble compost. And what's in this little ball of aluminum foil? *Do not open!*

Refrigerators come in many sizes and shapes. A family of four needs a minimum of 16 cubic feet and should probably buy one that's at least 18 cubic feet (unless you have a teenage boy, in which case you need a second refrigerator). If you use the freezer a great deal, having the freezer compartment on the top or to the side is more convenient. If you are more of an "open the fridge and see what looks good in there" type, you may prefer a model with a bottom freezer, maybe even with expansive French doors. Make sure that the doors open in the most convenient way for your kitchen. If the entrance to the kitchen is blocked every time you open the refrigerator door, you are going to get irritated. Also check the door compartments to see whether they can hold a bottle of wine or a jug of milk. Door space should be spacious, not cluttered with little compartments that just eat up space.

Try not to pack the refrigerator too densely. Cold air needs space to circulate around and cool the food. Store foods in the same spot each time so that you don't have to search for that little jar of mustard or jelly every time you open the door. Most refrigerator shelves are adjustable, so play around with the spacing until it works for the items you generally keep on hand. Transparent shelves and bins make it even easier to see where everything is.

The bottom drawers are usually the coldest and should be used for storing meat, poultry, and fish. Fresh vegetables are usually stored in the *crisper* drawer, which is often located just above the meat bin. Salad greens and leafy herbs can be washed, thoroughly dried, and wrapped in paper towels to extend their storage life. Other vegetables, like broccoli and cauliflower, should be washed just before serving. Excess water on any vegetable in storage can hasten its deterioration.

Liberate old food from the refrigerator every two weeks or so, and give the fridge a good soap-and-water bath every few months. An open box of baking soda at the back of a shelf soaks up odors. Remember to replace the baking soda every few months, when you do your major clean-out. Keeping your refrigerator clean, organized, and filled with fresh food you love is one of the most effective and inspiring ways to get excited about cooking.

Freezer

Most of us buy more at the store than we can eat in a week. What you won't eat this week, your freezer can keep for you until later. It can also keep leftovers fresh longer so you can reheat them on days when you want a home-cooked meal but don't have time or energy to make one from scratch. Package your leftovers in individual serving-sized containers or in freezer-friendly baking pans you can slide straight into the oven.

If you're lucky enough to have a stand-alone freezer, you can take advantage of sales on meat, frozen vegetables, and fruits. You can also cook in bulk, freezing leftover soups, stews, sauces, and desserts. You'll always have food handy at the touch of the microwave's defrost button.

Not everything freezes well (milk, lettuce, and block cheese are poor candidates for the freezer, for example), but many things do, especially if they are properly sealed or wrapped to keep out oxygen. To get the most use of the freezer space you have, stack things neatly and use bins to keep things organized. If you just toss everything in there randomly, you may not find things again until they have been in there for too long and are freezer burned or stale.

Finally, while you want your refrigerator/freezer within easy reach of your workspace, you can store a stand-alone freezer in another room off the kitchen or even in the basement or the garage.

Dishwasher

Because you probably have better things to do with your evening than wash the dishes, you likely want a dishwasher, especially if you cook for more than one or two. Your dishwasher may be built in, or it may be portable. You can even buy tabletop dishwashers for modest dishwashing needs. Dishwashers use a lot of water and electricity, but for people who would rather load the dishwasher and then relax with their families after a good meal, the expense is probably well worth it.

Garbage disposal

Garbage disposals are handy for the home cook. These grinders, housed in the underbelly of your sink drain, grind up the food that goes down the drain. If all you eat are frozen dinners and take-out, you probably won't need a disposal very often, but if you're always peeling, chopping, and wiping counters of the residue of cooking a good meal, you'll appreciate the convenience of a garbage disposal.

To keep your garbage disposal smelling good, grind up a few orange or lemon peels every so often. To keep the drain clean, once a month pour ½ cup baking soda down the drain, followed by 1 cup white vinegar. Let it sit, bubbling and foaming for 15 or 20 minutes, and then pour a pot of boiling water down the drain.

Getting Acquainted with Basic Cooking Techniques

Recipes are full of terminology and techniques that new cooks may not be familiar with. At the heart of most recipes are some basic techniques, which we expand upon throughout this book in various sections. As a warm-up, however, here are the basic cooking techniques and what they involve. Become familiar with these terms, practice the techniques, and you'll realize that many recipes aren't as complicated as you thought.

- ✔ **Boiling, poaching, and steaming:** These terms involve cooking with water. *Boiling* is heating water so that it bubbles vigorously. *Poaching* is cooking fish, eggs, or vegetables in gently simmering water — water that is just beginning to bubble but not yet boil. *Steaming* is cooking food over, but not in, boiling or simmering water. We describe these techniques in detail in Chapter 5.

- ✔ **Sautéing:** This term refers to cooking food in a skillet or sauté pan quickly over high or medium-high heat, in oil or butter. Chapter 6 tells you all about sautéing.

- ✔ **Braising and stewing:** To *braise* is to cook food in a small amount of liquid, such as water or broth, for a long period of time. This technique results in particularly succulent meat. *Stewing* is cooking food (usually meat and veggies) in liquid flavored with herbs, broth, and sometimes wine until it is absorbed, to create a delectable, too-thick-to-be-soup concoction. For more on braising and stewing, check out Chapter 7.

- ✔ **Roasting:** *Roasting* involves cooking food, uncovered, in a pan in the oven. This technique is usually used to describe cooking large pieces of meat, such as a pot roast or a turkey, or vegetables. Chapter 8 has lots more details about roasting.

- ✔ **Grilling and broiling:** If you like to spend as much time as possible outdoors, *grilling* — cooking on a grate over hot charcoal or another heat element — is for you. Grill varieties include charcoal, gas, and electric. *Broiling* imitates the action of grilling, but it occurs indoors, with the heat coming from above instead of below. Chapter 9 goes into more detail about grill choices and grilling techniques, as well as broiling.

✔ **Baking:** Baking is cooking in the oven. For the purposes of this book, we use the word *baking* to mean the process of preparing bread, cake, cookies, and other flour-based concoctions. Baking is alchemy: A batter or dough transforms into something deliciously different than it was when you put it in the oven. To make batter or dough, you need to know lots of other techniques like stirring, folding, whipping, creaming, beating, kneading, rolling, and more. Chapter 10 covers baking basics.

Planning Your Menu

It's one thing to cook a recipe. It's quite another thing to plan a whole meal or a whole week's worth of meals! Menu planning may sound intimidating to the cook-in-training, but it's actually fun and a great way to experiment with new recipes and techniques. There is no right or wrong way to plan a menu. Some people like to scan cookbooks or cooking magazines for ideas, make a list of meals for the week, and then make their complete shopping list. Others may plan meals based on that week's sales at the supermarket. However you do it, planning ahead will save you time, money, and frustration, and it will minimize the chances that you'll give up and get take-out. After all, you *already planned dinner.* But how do you know what to make? Just because chicken is on sale at the grocery store doesn't mean you'll know what to do with it. And what do you serve with it?

Formal dinners typically have several courses, including appetizers, salad, soup, a main course, a dessert, and sometimes even courses such as a cheese course, a pasta course, and a casserole course. It all depends on how fancy you want to get.

For most families, however, a simple meal with a main course (a meat or vegetarian dish), accompanied by soup or a salad, some form of starch (bread, rice, pasta, or some other grain), another vegetable, and a simple dessert (or not), is plenty. Examples:

✔ Roast chicken, yellow rice, green beans with butter, and strawberries with whipped cream

✔ Salmon filets, macaroni and cheese, green salad, and homemade vanilla pudding

✔ Ratatouille, pasta salad, and a loaf of crusty bread

✔ A vegetable stir fry, brown rice, and a big green salad with Asian-style dressing

The possibilities are limited only by your imagination and (if you browse cooking Web sites the way we do) the Internet. Which is to say, they are unlimited.

This book is full of ideas to help inspire you, too. You can find ideas for breakfast in Chapter 11, soups and salads in Chapter 12, and main dish recipes in many chapters, such as the roasting chapter (Chapter 8), the grilling chapter (Chapter 9), and the chapter on one-pot meals (Chapter 16). Find side-dish recipes in the grain chapter (Chapter 13) and sweet desserts in Chapters 10 and 15.

Holidays and special events offer opportunities to plan fancier or more elaborate meals or meals with a theme — look to Chapters 18, 20, and 21 for special-occasion ideas.

But don't let yourself be limited, even by this book. This is just a beginning, and we hope you will use this launching pad to plan your own meals based on what you and your family already love, and on a sense of adventure as you get more comfortable in the kitchen trying new foods and new techniques.

Kitchen Safety 101

Cooking is fun, but it also requires certain precautions. You may think that the biggest danger in the kitchen is serving a meal that has guests roaring hysterically with laughter on their way home ("Can you believe he called that fiasco *dinner?*"). As humiliating as that scenario would be, home cooks should be aware of other perils as well, so they can take the proper precautions and cook with no worries.

Do you remember Dan Akroyd's classic skit on *Saturday Night Live,* in which he impersonates world-renowned chef Julia Child? In the middle of his cooking demonstration, he pretends to accidentally cut off his fingers: "Just a flesh wound," he warbles and continues cooking. Then he severs his wrist, his hand falling to the ground. Blood spurts everywhere. Pretty funny, huh?

That wildly exaggerated scene carries a cautionary note about razor-sharp knives: Always pay attention to what you're doing because one slip can cause great pain. (Keep in mind that dull knives can be even more dangerous because they force you to apply too much pressure, and you can lose control of the blade.) For more on kitchen safety and preventing or dealing with kitchen disasters, check out Chapter 22. Some basic rules of safety include the following:

✔ Store knives in a wooden block or on a magnetic bar mounted out of reach of children, not in a kitchen drawer. For more information about knives and knife safety, see Chapter 4.

✔ Never cook in loose-hanging clothes that may catch fire, and keep long hair tied back for the same reason (not to mention keeping hair out of the food!).

✔ Never cook while wearing dangling jewelry that can get tangled around pot handles.

✔ Professional chefs have hands like asbestos from years of grabbing hot pots and pans. You probably do not. Keep potholders nearby and use them.

✔ Turn pot handles away from the front of the stove, where children may grab them and adults can bump into them.

✔ Don't let temperature-sensitive foods sit out in your kitchen, especially in warm weather. Raw meat, fish, and certain dairy products can spoil quickly, so refrigerate or freeze them right away. Put away hot foods within two hours after a meal.

✔ Wipe up floor spills immediately so that no one slips and falls, and wipe up counter spills to keep counters sanitary (and unstained).

✔ Don't try to cook if your mind is elsewhere, because your fingers may wind up elsewhere as well.

✔ Separate raw meat, especially poultry, from produce and other items in your refrigerator to avoid cross-contamination of harmful bacteria from one food to another. Never put cooked food or produce on a cutting board where you were just cutting raw meat.

✔ Wash your hands before handling food. Hands can be a virtual freight train of bacteria, depending, of course, on what you do during the day. Also wash thoroughly after handling meat or poultry.

✔ To avoid panic-stricken searches, always return utensils to the proper place. Always return a knife to its holder when you're finished with it.

✔ Clean up as you work. We know people who can make a tuna salad sandwich and leave the kitchen looking as if they had just served a lunch to the Dallas Cowboys (we aren't naming any names). Put away dirty knives, wipe down counters, and return food to the refrigerator between steps in a recipe — doing so keeps you thinking clearly and keeps your kitchen neat and organized. Plus, cleaning up as you go frees up that spatula or whisk for the next step of the recipe, so you don't have to use a new one and double the dirty dishes.

✔ Every kitchen needs a fire extinguisher. It is inexpensive (about $20), easy to use, and mounts on the wall (or can be stowed under the sink). This device may not do much for your cherries jubilee, but it can avert a disaster.

Now Get Crackin'!

If you're eager to jump in and start cooking, try your hand at this quick and easy recipe for scrambled eggs, which you can enjoy for breakfast, lunch, or dinner. Eggs are a healthy and nutritious protein source, and cooking them is easy (see Chapter 11 for more egg recipes). If you know how to cook scrambled eggs, then you *know how to cook*. At least, a little.

 If you want to make excellent scrambled eggs, don't overbeat the eggs before you cook them. Some scrambled egg recipes call for cream, which adds a nice smoothness to the eggs; others call for water, which increases the volume by stimulating the whites to foam. You can use either ingredient, or milk, or nothing but the eggs. Try it different ways and see which you prefer. This recipe can be doubled or halved.

Scrambled Eggs

Prep time: About 5 min • **Cook time:** About 4 min • **Yield:** 4 servings

Ingredients	*Directions*
8 eggs	*1* Break the eggs into a medium bowl. With a fork or a wire whisk, beat the eggs just until they're blended to incorporate the yolks and whites.
¼ cup light cream, half-and-half, milk (whole or low-fat), or water	*2* Add the cream (or milk or water) and chives, salt, and pepper (if desired), and beat a few seconds to blend.
2 tablespoons chopped chives (optional)	*3* Heat a 10-inch (preferably nonstick) skillet or omelet pan over medium heat. Add the butter. As it melts, tilt the pan to cover the surface with butter. Pour in the egg mixture.
½ teaspoon salt (optional)	
Few dashes black pepper (optional)	
2 tablespoons butter	*4* Stir the eggs, pulling them gently across the bottom and sides of the pan with a spatula or wooden spoon as they set. Cook to desired doneness (from creamy to dry). Taste just before serving to determine whether you need more salt and/or pepper.

Per serving: Calories 228 (From Fat 167); Fat 19g (Saturated 8g); Cholesterol 450mg; Sodium 133mg; Carbohydrate 2g (Dietary Fiber 0g); Protein 13g.

Vary It! For a lower-fat option, eliminate the butter and spray the pan with cooking spray. You can dress up this basic scrambled eggs recipe by adding to the liquid egg mixture: try 2 tablespoons of chopped fresh herbs like parsley or basil, a dash of Tabasco sauce, or a sprinkling of shredded cheese (¼ to ½ cup).

Chapter 2

Investing in the Essential Tools

*O*wning kitchen equipment is like having a car. When you first get your driver's license, a dented 10-year-old Honda Civic is nirvana. But as you become a more experienced driver, you start dreaming of something better, maybe a Lexus. When you enter the wonderful world of cooking, you can do fine with just a few basic tools — the ride may not be as luxurious, but you'll get to the prom on time. You can always upgrade later.

This chapter is all about the kitchen equipment you really need, and how to use it correctly. Learning how to use kitchen equipment properly is time well spent.

If you are getting started or are on a tight budget, we suggest some essential tools. As you become more proficient, you may want to expand your repertoire — and, for that reason, we let you know about more luxurious equipment, too.

Note that the one type of equipment we don't cover in detail here is knives. That's because they're so important that we gave them their own chapter: Chapter 4.

Collecting Your Cookware Basics

Here is our short list of bare-bones-all-I-can-spend-now kitchen equipment. (You can find more detailed descriptions of some of these items later in this chapter.) See Chapter 1 for information on appliances. This is our list of pots, pans, and other tools no home cook should be without:

- ✔ **10-inch chef's knife:** You can perform more than 80 percent of all cutting and slicing chores with this knife.

- ✔ **9- to 12-inch serrated bread knife:** Invaluable for cutting slices of fresh bread without squishing the loaf, and also for slicing other delicate foods like fresh tomatoes.

- ✔ **Paring knife:** For peeling, coring, and carving radish roses and miniature replicas of the Eiffel Tower from rutabagas. (Or just for peeling and coring.)

- ✔ **10-inch nonstick skillet:** Your go-to pan for sautéing or frying just about anything.

- ✔ **3-quart saucepan:** For cooking vegetables, rice, soups, sauces, and small quantities of pasta.

- ✔ **10-quart stockpot with lid:** For making stocks or large quantities of soup, pasta, and vegetables. You'll be surprised by how often you use this pot.

- ✔ **Heavy-duty roasting pan:** For cooking everything from beef brisket to your Thanksgiving turkey. Roasting pans have high sides to keep in all those juices you can use to make gravy.

- ✔ **Liquid and dry measuring cups and measuring spoons:** So you don't botch recipes by using too much or too little of something.

- ✔ **Strainer:** Essential for straining sauces and soups, rinsing pasta, or cleaning and draining lettuce and fruit.

- ✔ **Meat thermometer:** Why guess?

- ✔ **Vegetable peeler, heatproof rubber spatula, and a few wooden spoons:** Don't go off the deep end buying little kitchen gizmos; these tools are all you need to get started.

Picking Pots and Pans

Have you ever wondered what the difference is between a pot and a pan? If it has two opposite-set handles and a lid, it's classified as a *pot*. *Pans* have one long handle and come with or without lids. This section gives a rundown of important pots and pans and how to evaluate them, including the must-haves listed in the previous section and lots of other types of fancy pots and pans you don't need but may decide to acquire anyway.

Doing some comparison shopping

Pots and pans come in all kinds of materials, from aluminum with a nonstick coating to heavy-duty stainless steel to expensive copper to muscle-building cast iron coated with enamel. The more you cook, the more uses you'll find for different kinds of pots and pans, and the more you'll develop your own tastes and preferences for different types of pots and pans and different materials.

Here are some things to keep in mind when buying cookware:

- ✔ **Consider going the nonstick route.** Nonstick coatings are the best aid to novice cooks since grocery stores started selling spaghetti sauce in jars. If you do a lot of fat-free and lowfat cooking, you want to invest in a high quality nonstick skillet, which can drastically reduce the amount of butter or oil you need during cooking. Nonstick pans don't brown foods as well as regular pans do, but they're easier to clean, and the convenience may be worth it.

  In recent years, nonstick pans have improved tremendously, and the linings last longer than before — as long as you don't use metal utensils with them. A few new varieties even work with metal utensils and have lifetime guarantees. So many brands exist that keeping track of them all is difficult.

  Nonstick aluminum is light, durable, and a great conductor of heat. Look in restaurant supply stores where you can buy a nonstick 10-inch sauté pan for as little as $15. It won't last as long as its pricier cousins (after two or three years the nonstick coating tends to wear out), but the price makes it easy to replace.

  If you decide to invest more money in longer-lasting pieces, consider your choice of materials. Copper (lined with stainless steel or tin) provides the best heat control of all metals. That control is the secret of well-textured sauces. Stainless steel with copper or aluminum sandwiched in the base works very well, too, and is less expensive than the all-copper variety.

- ✔ **Think twice about purchasing whole sets, even if they're on sale, unless you can use every piece.** Sets are limited to one type of material and one style, whereas you may be better off with various styles and materials — for example, a nonstick skillet, a cast iron stockpot, and a stainless steel saucepan.

- ✔ **Grasp the handle of the pan in the store.** It should sit comfortably in your hand. Ask yourself whether having a heat-resistant handle is important, or whether you will always remember to grab the handle with a potholder. Also consider whether the handle is ovenproof. Some recipes, such as frittatas, require both stove time and oven time. Look for a pan that can do it all.

✔ **Don't assume that the higher the price tag, the better the choice for you.** Want to know a secret? Restaurant cooks don't always use expensive equipment. They do, however, insist on quality. No loose handles or spatulas that bend and break! You want a strong pot or pan with a comfortable handle, a thick base, and if nonstick, a durable coating with a guarantee. Restaurant supply stores can be your best source for affordable, high quality cookware. As you get more experienced, you can spend more based on the way you like to cook. For example, you might try stainless steel pots and pans with a copper core for superior heat distribution, which can lead to a better texture in fancy sauces. For now though, just go for quality and the basics as you build your skills.

Buying the essentials

The following list of different kinds of pots and pans is not exhaustive, but it will get you started. These are the pots and pans we think you'll use the most.

Nonstick skillet or sauté pan

You'll probably use this skillet all the time, so get a good, heavy-duty one. (See the preceding section for tips on what to buy.) If you prefer, try a heavier and very durable nonstick stainless steel pan. The choice is yours, but nonstick is also easier to clean (although not always made for the dishwasher).

You may wonder, as you browse through your options, why some skillets have rounded, curved sides and some have straight sides. To be more specific, a *sauté pan* has straight sides, while a *frying pan* or *skillet* has rounded sides. You may prefer one or the other. The rounded sides facilitate fast cooking and flipping food around (like when those fancy chefs flip the food into the air by shaking the handle). The curved sides help you turn the food. The straight sides of a sauté pan are better for enclosing liquids like hot oil and broth so they won't slosh over the sides, and they're good for braising and stewing. Sauté pans are also more likely to come with lids.

Your skillet or sauté pan (see Figure 2-1) should be at least 10 or 12 inches in diameter and 2 inches deep, which is ideal for sautéing, braising, frying, and making quick sauces.

Figure 2-1:
A nonstick skillet or sauté pan helps you cook with very little fat.

saute´ pan

Don't buy an inexpensive pan (whether nonstick or regular) that is thin and light — it will warp over time. A good skillet should have some heft to it. Purchase pots and pans from a major manufacturer that stands behind its products and will quickly replace or repair damaged goods.

Heavy-gauge cast-iron skillet

The cast-iron skillet, shown in Figure 2-2, has been a standard in American and European kitchens for hundreds of years and still outperforms contemporary cookware in some respects (for example, browning, blackening, and searing). Better yet, a cast-iron skillet is one of the most inexpensive pans you can find, and it will outlast most other skillets as well. Tag sales and antique shops are loaded with them.

Figure 2-2:
You use a cast-iron skillet for browning, searing, and more.

cast-iron skillet

Before using a cast-iron skillet for the first time, season it by wiping it with vegetable oil and then heating it on the range on a medium setting for about 2 minutes. In addition, you must thoroughly wipe the skillet dry after washing it to prevent rust. Clean the skillet gently with water and a plastic scrubber. Never scour with metal pads, and never put soap into a cast iron skillet, as it can penetrate the coating and affect the flavor of the food you cook in it later. Look for a skillet with a spout for pouring off fat, if you think you will use it for frying. Before storing, wipe the skillet with a few drops of vegetable oil to keep the surface seasoned and to help develop that characteristic nonstick coating of well-used cast iron. For recipes and more details on choosing and caring for cast-iron cookware, check out *Cast-Iron Cooking For Dummies* by Tracy Barr (Wiley).

Saucepans

A saucepan can be stainless steel with a copper or aluminum core or a combination of metals. It is an all-around pan used for cooking vegetables, soups, rice, and sauces for pasta and other dishes (see Figure 2-3). You'll want to own two or maybe three saucepans in different sizes. A 1- to 1½-quart saucepan is perfect for melting small quantities of butter or chocolate or for warming milk. A medium 2- to 3-quart saucepan is essential for making sauces. And saucepans that are 4 quarts or larger are suitable for making soups, steaming vegetables, or boiling a moderate amount of pasta or rice.

Roasting pans

A well-equipped kitchen should have one oval roasting pan, about 12 inches long, and a large rectangular one, about 14 x 11 inches. An oval roasting pan is suitable for poultry and small roasts; a 14-inch rectangular one can handle two chickens, a large roast, or a load of vegetables from the farmer's market. The oval one should be enameled cast iron so that it can double as a gratin pan (which we describe later in this section); the rectangular pan can be heavy-gauge aluminum or stainless steel. If you can afford only one roasting pan right now, the covered oval pan is probably the most versatile.

9-x-13-inch baking dish or casserole with lid

Another classic you want to own is the versatile 9-x-13-inch baking dish or covered casserole. Whether made of aluminum, glass, or ceramic, it's great for making casseroles; roasting winter vegetables; or baking brownies, other bar cookies, and cakes.

Enameled cast-iron stew pot (Dutch oven)

This attractive, all-around stew pot, also called a *Dutch oven,* is ideal for slow-cooking stews, soups, and all sorts of hearty winter meals (see Figure 2-4). Enamel doesn't brown food as well as cast iron or plain stainless steel, however. You may want to brown or sear meat in a separate pan before adding it to the Dutch oven. A 4-quart version made by Le Creuset and a similar one from Copco are excellent.

Stockpot

A stockpot is indispensable in any kitchen (see Figure 2-5). It can serve many functions: soup making, braising, steaming, and poaching, to name a few. Look for a tall, narrow, 10- to 14-quart heavy-gauge pot with a tight-fitting lid that can hold a steamer basket. (Inexpensive circular steamers open and close like a fan to fit different sizes of pots and pans.) Heavy aluminum is fine for a stockpot; stainless steel costs twice as much.

Figure 2-5:
You make soups and much more in a stockpot.

stockpot

Getting fancy

If you really want to go to town with this pots-and-pans thing, you could probably buy a hundred different ones, each with its own specialized function. But is your kitchen really that big? You can do just about any cooking chore with the pots and pans we've listed so far. However, if you want to take it to the next level, you might consider acquiring some of these additional handy pans. They aren't essential, but they are pretty cool — and some of them even give you the opportunity to spout French to your guests. Who's not impressed by that?

Rondeau (shallow, straight-sided pot)

A rondeau (pronounced *ron-DOE*) is great to have on hand when you entertain — and of course you will! A straight-sided pot with two handles and a lid, as shown in Figure 2-6, a 12-inch rondeau (the size we recommend) can hold enough food to serve eight people or more. If you just got a raise (a whopper, that is), consider heavy-gauge copper. It's so beautiful you may want to set it out on the front lawn when guests are coming for dinner.

Figure 2-6:
A rondeau can go from oven to table.

rondeau

A rondeau has many uses, among them braising, stewing, and browning large quantities of meat, poultry, or fish. Look for brands like All-Clad, Calphalon, Cuisinart, Magnalite, Paderno, and Sitram.

Sauteuse evasée (slope-sided saucepan)

This Gallic mouthful refers to a little pan that is the workhorse of the French kitchen. If you ever splurge on a piece of copper cookware, we recommend a sauteuse evasée (pronounced saw-TOOZ eh-va-SAY), which is 8 to 9 inches in diameter with a volume of about 3 quarts (see Figure 2-7). A sauteuse evasée may be referred to as simply a saucepan, which is its major role. Its sloped sides (*evasée* refers to the sloped sides) make for easy whisking.

Figure 2-7:
You use a sauteuse evasée mainly as a saucepan.

sauteuse evasée

Wok or stir-fry pan

A wok is a large, bowl-shaped pan with a rounded bottom that sits inside a disk that fits over your heat source. Woks work best over a gas flame, but you can still use them if you have an electric stove. In a wok, the very bottom gets super hot, while the sides are cooler, so woks cook meat and vegetables very quickly, leaving vegetables bright and crispy and meats crisp on the outside and tender on the inside. You can cook meat and vegetables in a stir-fry–like technique by using a sauté pan, but for authentically cooked Chinese food, use a wok (or go to a Chinese restaurant).

Pasta pot

A large, 8-quart stainless steel pot fitted with a lid is the perfect size for cooking ½ to 2 pounds of pasta (or you can use your stockpot instead).

Pancake griddle

This flat, nonstick griddle is well suited for pancakes, grilled cheese sandwiches, bacon, and the like. Of course, you can always use the sauté pan for these chores.

Omelet pan or skillet

An 8- or 10-inch omelet pan, like the one shown in Figure 2-8, is handy to have around if you love your eggs. It's also handy for sautéing potatoes and other vegetables (see Chapter 6 for more information about sautéing), but of course you can do any of these tasks in your go-to skillet, too.

Figure 2-8:
Omelet pans are great for more than just omelets.

Gratin pan

Novice cooks tend to make many one-pot dishes. To give these entrees a delicious finishing touch, often by broiling to crisp the top, you should have a gratin dish, shown in Figure 2-9. Unlike Dutch ovens, gratin dishes are shallow, measure from 10 inches long and up, and do not have a lid. A 12-inch dish can feed six or more people. These pans are ideal for macaroni and cheese, turkey casserole, gratin of potatoes, and many other simple dishes. Some are attractive enough to go from oven to table.

Figure 2-9:
A gratin pan is handy for finishing one-pot dishes.

Selecting Tools for Mixing and Baking

Baking requires a wide assortment of pots, pans, bowls, spoons, whisks, and spatulas. While there is some crossover — for instance, you may make lasagna in your 9-x-13-inch baking pan— you'll probably reserve many of your baking pans, mixing bowls, and stirring equipment for baking because baking tools and equipment are designed specifically for that purpose.

Whether you're making bread, birthday cake, muffins, or your mother's killer recipe for homemade brownies, the right baking equipment makes these jobs easier. Here's what you need.

A kitchen scale: For the home baker, most name-brand scales will do the trick. Get one that can hold 3 or 4 cups of flour. It should be sturdy and feature bright, easy-to-read numbers.

Stainless steel, glass, or ceramic mixing bowls: Mixing bowls are among the most frequently used items in every kitchen. Buy bowls with flat bottoms for good balance in these sizes: 8 quarts, 5 quarts, 3 quarts, and 1½ quarts. Buy them in sets that stack and store easily. You can use these bowls to mix batters for cakes, cookies, or muffins; whip egg whites or whipped cream; let bread dough rise; or even toss salads, whip up sauces and dressings, or store leftovers (if you buy bowls that come with handy plastic lids).

Whisks: Whisks may be made of stainless steel or heat-proof plastic (for use with nonstick cookware). There are several types. A stiffer *sauce whisk* is about 8 to 10 inches long and perfect for blending sauces, such as béchamel and some cream sauces (see Chapter 14). The larger, rounder *balloon whisk* is generally 12 to 14 inches long and is better shaped for whipping and incorporating air into egg whites and heavy cream.

Spoons, spatulas, long-handled forks, and tongs: A few wooden spoons of various sizes work best for hand-mixing batters, scraping food bits off the bottom of a simmering casserole, or stirring anything cooking in nonstick cookware. You might also like to have a solid, one-piece stainless steel spoon, about 12 to 15 inches long, for stirring food in larger pots such as stockpots or pasta pots. A slotted, stainless steel spoon removes solid foods from hot liquid — use it to scoop pasta or vegetables from boiling water.

Use a long-handled, stainless steel ladle for doling out soups, sauces, stews, or chili, or for putting pancake batter onto a griddle or into a waffle iron. A heatproof rubber spatula will scrape batter and sauce from bowls or measuring cups. A square-tipped hard plastic turner can flip burgers and other foods cooking on nonstick pans. Metal tongs can turn over tender pieces of meat or fish, and can double as serving items at the table (for salad or spaghetti).

Baking (or cookie) sheet: For baking cookies, biscuits, and breads, a heavy-duty steel or nonstick baking sheet is essential. Some are flat, and some have raised or flared edges to keep butter and juice from spilling into your oven. Baking sheets come in different sizes. Buy two large ones that fit in your oven, leaving a 2-inch margin on all sides to allow an even flow of heat during baking.

Round cake pans: Standard layer cake recipes call for two 8-x-2-inch or 9-x-2-inch pans. Choose anodized or nonstick aluminum.

Square cake pan: For making brownies or gingerbread, you need an 8- or 9-inch square, 2-quart capacity pan. Anodized aluminum and other nonstick materials make removing the brownies easier.

Muffin tins: For baking muffins and cupcakes, most recipes call for a 12-cup or two 6-cup tins of nonstick or heavy-gauge aluminum (or try stoneware or even nonstick silicone). It's handy to have paper muffin liners on hand too, for recipes (like chocolate cupcakes) that tend to stick. No oil necessary!

Pie pan: A glass or aluminum pan that is 9 inches in diameter suits most standard recipes.

Rolling pin: You don't need an arsenal of rolling pins like professional pastry chefs have. For home baking, get a two-handled, hardwood or marble rolling pin that is about 15 inches long.

Cooling racks: Cookies and cakes removed from the oven need to cool. Racks allow air to circulate around them. Buy one or two 12- to 14-inch racks.

Silicone pastry mats: These thin mats go on top of your cookie sheet to prevent baked goods from sticking without oil. You can also use them to roll out piecrust and transfer it to your pie plate.

Loaf pan: For baking breads, terrines, and meat loaf, you want a sturdy, 6-cup loaf pan (see Figure 2-10). Look for heavy-duty aluminum or stonewear.

Figure 2-10:
You can bake all sorts of foods in a loaf pan.

loaf pan

Springform pan: With its hinge-release and detachable bottom, a springform pan easily unmolds cheesecakes, delicate tarts, and cakes with crumb crusts. Get a 9- to 10-inch pan of heavy-gauge aluminum (see Figure 2-11).

Figure 2-11:
Use a
springform
pan to make
delicious
desserts.

springform pan

Flour sifter: Not all baking recipes call for sifted flour, but when they do, you need a sifter to aerate the flour and eliminate lumps. A 3-cup sifter is handy, or just use a fine-mesh strainer (see Figure 2-12).

How to Sift Flour If You Don't Have a Sifter

1. Pour flour into a strainer.

2. Use your hand to lightly tap the strainer

– OR –
tap the strainer on the inside of the bowl.

Figure 2-12:
You can
sift flour
by using a
strainer.

Pastry brush: To apply glazes and coatings to breads and cakes, use an all-purpose, 1½-inch pastry brush with natural bristles. Pastry brushes are also essential for basting food with pan drippings or sauces. Buy several brushes at a time because they wear out quickly. Clean the brushes with mild dish soap, rinsing thoroughly.

Metal or plastic dry measuring cups: To follow precise recipes, you need a set of dry measuring cups — ¼ cup, ⅓ cup, ½ cup, and 1 cup.

Glass or plastic liquid measuring cup: Get one with a 1-cup and one with a 2-cup capacity, each with a spout for pouring liquids. Four-cup and 8-cup liquid measuring cups come in handy, too.

Metal or plastic measuring spoons: These items are essential for baking. Make sure that the set you purchase comes with ¼ teaspoon, ½ teaspoon, 1 teaspoon, and 1 tablespoon capacities.

Considering Small Appliances

You don't need to own every small appliance on the market, but some are essential and others can be useful and time-saving. Here is your guide to the basic small appliances.

Toasters and toaster ovens: Everybody needs either a toaster or toaster oven; you probably don't need both. A toaster oven is more versatile but takes up more counter space. If you use your toaster for, well, toast (or bagels, English muffins, or toaster pastries), just pick one that matches your kitchen décor. If you also want to be able to broil little meals for yourself, the toaster oven is nifty.

Mixers, beaters, and blenders: Mixers, beaters, and blenders are necessary for the home cook. You'll use these all the time, to mix up cake and cookie batters, blend homemade smoothies or milkshakes, or whip up a fluffy meringue. Here are your choices:

- *Stand-alone mixers:* Strong and durable, these workhorses come with a deep mixing bowl and attachments for whisking, beating, and bread making. Use the beater for batters, the whisk for egg whites and whipped cream, and the dough hook to knead bread dough while you kick back and read a magazine.

- *Beaters, or hand mixers:* These are great for mixing batters, beating egg whites, and making whipped cream. Most hand mixers aren't sturdy enough to handle bread dough or thick cookie dough.

- *Blender:* The blender is definitely a must-have. Even if you don't enjoy protein shakes for breakfast or daiquiris on the weekends, you'll certainly use your blender for many kitchen chores, from chopping a cup of walnuts to making homemade salsa. Blenders and food processors can do many of the same chores, but for beverages and really smooth purées, you can't beat a blender. Go for the high-quality, heavy-duty blender because it will last for years. A cheap plastic blender can burn out in a few months.

- *Immersion blender:* This appliance, a cross between a hand mixer and a blender, is very popular in professional kitchens. You immerse it in a saucepan of soup or anything else you want to purée in the pan without having to transfer it to a blender.

Slow cookers: Slow cookers (people often refer to any slow cooker as the brand name Crock-Pot) consist of stoneware crocks that sit in heated metal containers. They cook your chicken, roast, rice, veggies, soup, chili, beans, and so on for a long period at a low temperature. Incredibly handy for the time-pressed cook, slow cookers allow you to pop the food in before work in the morning and come home eight to ten hours later to a piping hot meal. Turn to Chapter 16 for more about how to use the slow cooker.

Food processor: A food processor (see Figure 2-13) is a versatile kitchen machine that used to be a luxury but has become a necessity for anybody who cooks a lot. Food processors have steel blades that can whip up pie crust dough in seconds, not to mention sauces, soups, and finely chopped nuts, herbs, or vegetables. Other attachments on the same machine can grate cheese or carrots; slice tomatoes; and chop celery, onions, garlic, or just about anything else. While your blender can do some of these things, it isn't as versatile. We recommend owning both so you can make great smoothies *and* flaky pie crust.

Figure 2-13:
Food processors can do a wide variety of tasks.

food processor

Getting Your Fill of Gizmos and Gadgets

Just when you thought you had everything you need, we're giving you more! These miscellaneous tools can be useful for all kinds of reasons.

Bulb baster: Using this tool is the most convenient way to coat a roast or chicken with pan juices. A large spoon also works as a basting tool, but a bulb baster is quicker and safer for removing hot grease from the bottom of a roasting pan.

Colander: Buy one made of stainless steel or plastic for draining pasta and rinsing salad greens, vegetables, and berries.

Cutting boards: Use cutting boards to save your counters from sharp knives and hot pots and pans. Plastic or composite boards are easier to clean than wooden ones and can be washed in the dishwasher. Chefs clean their wooden boards with a solution of water and bleach or rub them with lemon juice. Excessive soaking or placing wooden boards in the dishwasher causes them to splinter, warp, and crack.

Kitchen timer: Don't stand in front of the oven staring at the clock. Set a timer and go watch *American Idol.* Many ovens and microwaves have built-in kitchen timers, so you may not even need to buy a separate one.

Meat thermometer: Most people can't tell that a roast has finished cooking by pressing its surface. You can use two types of meat thermometers to check:

✔ An *instant-read thermometer,* our favorite, has a thin rod that lets you pierce into the roast periodically to test for doneness.

✔ An *ovenproof thermometer* remains inside the meat or poultry from beginning to end of cooking.

See Figure 2-14 for an illustration of both kinds of meat thermometers.

Figure 2-14:
Meat thermometers are essential for determining whether a roast is done.

meat thermometers

Steamer pots or basket: The conventional steamer model is a pair of pots, the top one having a perforated bottom and a lid. You can also buy bamboo steamers or little metal steamer baskets that fit inside saucepans.

Following are more handy utensils to have around your kitchen:

✔ Citrus juicer

✔ Lemon and cheese grater

✔ Multipurpose kitchen shears

✔ Oven thermometer

✔ Pepper mill

✔ Pie server

- ✔ Potato masher
- ✔ Salad spinner
- ✔ Shrimp deveiner
- ✔ Vegetable peeler

Chapter 3

The Bare Necessities: Stocking Your Pantry and Fridge

In This Chapter

▶ Getting the essential dried goods, herbs, spices, and canned and bottled goods

▶ Adding condiments and baking ingredients to your cupboard

▶ Finding out what you need in your refrigerator and freezer

▶ Selecting and storing vegetables, fruits, meats, and fish

*Y*ou could probably survive for quite some time on a diet of peanut butter, canned tuna, and saltines, but eventually you'd get bored (and you might get scurvy). When you've got interesting ingredients in your pantry, you can always whip up an interesting meal. Shopping thoughtfully not only cuts down on trips to the market but also saves you money — those 8 p.m. dashes to 7-Eleven for grated cheese add up. When you don't have time to make it to the market, what's for dinner often depends on the ingredients you have in the fridge and cupboard.

The payoff for keeping a well-stocked kitchen is that you can whip up satisfying meals on short notice. Add some vegetables and meat to a can of chicken broth for soup or to pasta or rice for a quick and delicious dinner. Add a salad, some bread, and a glass of good wine, followed by cheese and fruit for dessert, and you'll see how wonderful it is to have your pantry at your service.

Following are a series of checklists of pantry and fridge basics. Foods such as milk, cheese, eggs, and bread are obvious items to keep stocked. Less common staples such as sun-dried tomatoes, fruit chutney, dry sherry, anchovies, and artichoke hearts are important, too, because they can instantly impart flavor and dress up everyday dishes like tossed salads, omelets, and pasta. You won't need all of these, but if you always have a few exotic ingredients on hand, you'll feel ready for just about anything.

Dry Goods: The Pantry's Backbone

Every pantry should be well stocked with dry goods. You probably consume these foods at least once a week, so buy them in bulk to save on packaging costs. When possible, keep pantry items in airtight containers for freshness and to prevent *weevils* (those little bugs that like to feed on dry goods):

- ✓ **Bread, English muffins, bagels, tortillas, pita breads, and so on:** Keep what you will eat that week in the pantry. If you buy more (when bread is on sale), keep the extra loaves in the freezer and defrost as needed.

- ✓ **Coffee:** Buy ground or whole-bean coffee in small batches for freshness, or keep it in the freezer.

- ✓ **Cold and hot cereals:** Always tightly reseal cereal boxes after opening to keep them fresh.

- ✓ **Dry beans and grains:** See Chapter 17 for more information about the various types of dried beans and Chapter 13 for more information about the various types of grains, such as rice, oats, polenta, barley, and quinoa.

- ✓ **Herbal and regular teas:** After you open a box or other container of tea, store it in a sealed canister or enclose it in an airtight plastic bag.

- ✓ **Macaroni and other pasta:** Spaghetti and a short, stubby pasta like penne should meet most of your needs, but see Chapter 13 for more pasta possibilities.

Stocking Up on Baking Supplies

No one expects you to bake a cake when you get home from work at 7:30 p.m. But if you like to bake — if you even find it relaxing — you will want the supplies to jump in and bake at a moment's notice. Keep all baking supplies in a cool, dry place, tightly sealed for freshness. Here's what to keep in stock:

- ✓ **Baking powder:** This leavening agent is used in some cake, cookie, and quick bread recipes to lighten texture and increase volume. Check the sell-by date to ensure that the powder is fresh before buying. (Baking powder eventually expires, losing its effectiveness.)

✔ **Baking soda:** It's used as a leavening agent in baked goods and batters that contain an acidic ingredient such as molasses, vinegar, or buttermilk. Baking soda is also good for putting out grease fires and flare-ups in the oven or on the grill and for keeping your refrigerator and freezer deodorized.

✔ **Chocolate:** You may want unsweetened and bittersweet squares, semisweet chips, and cocoa powder for chocolate sauces, chocolate chip cookies, and hot chocolate.

When the temperature climbs above 78 degrees, chocolate begins to melt, causing the cocoa butter to separate and rise to the surface. When this happens, the chocolate takes on a whitish color called *bloom*. Bloomed chocolate is perfectly safe to eat, but to prevent bloom, store the chocolate in a cool, dry place (not the refrigerator), tightly wrapped.

✔ **Cornmeal:** Choose either yellow or white cornmeal for corn muffins, corn bread, polenta, and for use as a thickener.

✔ **Cornstarch:** You'll use it for thickening.

✔ **Cream of tartar:** This staple can stabilize egg whites and add tang to sugar cookies.

✔ **Flour:** All-purpose flour will do for most jobs, but it's nice to have bread flour and cake or pastry flour on hand, too. You could also try other flours for new flavors, such as oat flour, whole wheat flour, whole wheat pastry flour, brown rice flour, and nut flour. Flour is a must-have for dredging meats, fish, and poultry, and for pancakes, biscuits, and waffles, as well as baking.

Gluten-free flours, such as brown rice flour, soy flour, and nut flour, don't act exactly like wheat flour because they don't contain protein-rich gluten that gives baked goods their classic texture and ability to rise. When baking with gluten-free flours, be sure to follow a gluten-free recipe.

✔ **Gelatin:** Stock unflavored and powdered gelatin for molded salads and cold dessert mousses.

✔ **Sugar:** White granulated sugar, light and dark brown sugar, and powdered sugar should fulfill most of your sweetening needs.

✔ **Vanilla and almond extracts:** Both are used for flavoring whipped cream, desserts, and baked goods. (You can buy hundreds of extract flavors, so experiment if you feel daring. Some we like: orange, lemon, rum, hazelnut, and maple.) Avoid inferior imitation vanilla extract.

Spicing Up Your Life with Herbs, Spices, and Seasonings

Herbs and spices are essential flavoring ingredients. *Herbs* are produced from the leaves and stems of a variety of plants; *spices* can come from a plant's roots, seeds, bark, buds, or berries. If you stock the following, you will have the basics for most recipes:

- **Dry herbs:** Basil, bay leaves, dill, marjoram, oregano, parsley, rosemary, sage, tarragon, and thyme

- **Salt and pepper:** Table salt, kosher salt, sea salt, or other gourmet or flavored salts, as your taste dictates; whole or ground black pepper; whole or ground white pepper; cayenne pepper; and red pepper flakes

- **Spices:** Allspice, chili powder, cinnamon, whole and ground cloves, ground cumin, curry powder, ginger, dry mustard, nutmeg, and paprika

Purchase dried herbs and spices in small quantities. After a year or so of storage, their potency diminishes. Keep all dried herbs and spices tightly sealed and away from direct sunlight and heat (don't store them directly over the stove).

Working with herbs

While you want to always keep the essential dry herbs on hand, some herbs (such as cilantro) are best purchased fresh, kept in the refrigerator, and used within a few days. Others can be purchased in either dry or fresh varieties. Fresh herbs have a brighter, lighter, fresher taste than dried herbs, which have a more intense, concentrated flavor. Try both to see which you prefer in your favorite dishes.

Table 3-1 can help you decide which herbs go best with which kinds of dishes. (Also see Figure 3-1.) After you become familiar with the properties of these flavor enhancers, you can toss the chart and navigate on your own.

Figure 3-1:
Types of
herbs.

Table 3-1	Some Herbs You Should Know
Herb	*Description*
Basil	Essential to Mediterranean cooking, especially Italian and French cuisine. Excellent with tomatoes, eggs, pasta, poultry, fish, and in vinaigrette.
Bay leaf	Add the dried leaves to long-cooking dishes like soups, stews, poaching liquid, marinades, and pot roasts. (Remove the leaf before serving the dish.)
Chervil	Use with fish and shellfish, eggs, chicken, tomatoes, asparagus, summer squash, eggplant, and herb butter.
Chives	Try them in cream sauces or soups; with chicken, eggs, shellfish, or marinated salads; or sprinkled over cottage cheese.
Cilantro	Dried versions pale in comparison to fresh. Good with Mexican and Asian dishes, especially on rice, fish, and pork or in salsa and guacamole.
Dill	Use seeds in pickling recipes; use leaves on fish and shellfish, chicken, and omelets, and in salad dressing.
Marjoram	Add to almost any vegetable dish.
Mint	The most common varieties are standard peppermint and spearmint. Terrific with fresh fruit, in cold fruit soups and sauces, and in cold drinks like iced tea or mojitos.
Oregano	An essential ingredient in Italian and Greek cooking. A little goes far with poultry, tomato sauce, eggs, and vegetable stew.
Parsley	Better fresh than dried. An all-purpose herb, as well as a pretty plate garnish.
Rosemary	Excellent with grilled meat, especially lamb, and in herb bread, or to flavor oils and marinade.
Sage	Try it in poultry stuffing, in pâté, with fish and chicken, and in herb butter.
Savory	Comes in two types: winter and summer. Try it in fresh or dried bean salads, fish and shellfish dishes, omelets, rice dishes, and on tomatoes, potatoes, and artichokes.
Tarragon	This herb turns a Hollandaise sauce into a Béarnaise sauce. Also try it on chicken, pork, lamb, veal, fish, and shellfish, and as flavoring for white vinegar and hot or cold potato dishes.
Thyme	Add to vegetables, meat, poultry, fish, soups, stews, and cream sauces.

To get the most flavor from dried herbs, crush them between your fingers before adding them to a dish.

Studying spices

Spices, which are almost always sold dried, have been a vital element in international cooking since Byzantine times. Most spices come from the East, where they were introduced to Europe during the Crusades.

Store spices in a cool, dry place and try to use them within six to ten months. Whole spices, such as peppercorns, nutmeg, cinnamon sticks, cumin seeds, and coriander seeds, are more aromatic and flavorful than their pre-ground counterparts, so grind them yourself as needed. A coffee grinder reserved for spices works well for this purpose. Whole spices also can be wrapped and tied in a piece of cheesecloth, added to soup, stew, braises, and marinades, and then removed before serving.

Table 3-2 lists the more common spices.

Table 3-2	A Few Spices You Should Know
Spice	*Description*
Allspice	Spice berries with tastes of cinnamon, nutmeg, and cloves — hence the name. Excellent in both sweet and savory dishes, from pâtés and meatballs to fruit pie fillings, chutneys, and gingerbread.
Caraway	Common in German cuisine. Essential for rye bread and also in some cheeses.
Cardamom	Excellent in baked goods and pumpkin pie. One of the main ingredients in *garam masala,* an essential spice mixture in Indian cooking.
Cayenne or red pepper	A hot, powdered mixture of several chile peppers. Use sparingly for extra spice in any cooked dish.
Chili powder	A spicy mixture of dried chiles, cumin, oregano, garlic, coriander, and cloves. Use to flavor meat, bean dip, barbecue sauce, and, of course, chili.
Cinnamon	Sweet and aromatic spice from the bark of a tropical tree. Common as a baking spice and in Mexican chocolate, molé sauce, and Grecian cuisine.
Clove	Adds intense spice flavor to sweet or savory dishes — use sparingly!
Coriander	Seeds used for pickling; powder used for curries, sausage, and baked goods.
Cumin	Essential to Middle Eastern, Asian, and southwestern U.S. cuisine.

(continued)

Table 3-2	A Few Spices You Should Know
Spice	**Description**
Curry powder	A blend that can include more than a dozen different herbs and spices. Use to season lamb, chicken, rice, and sautéed vegetables, and in Indian curries.
Ginger	Essential in Asian cooking and in spice cakes and gingerbread. Use ground or grate the fresh root.
Nutmeg	Delicious in white sauces, sweet sauces, and glazes, over eggnog, in fruit and pumpkin pies and spice cakes. Best freshly grated.
Paprika	Varieties range from sweet to hot or smoked. Adds flavor and red color to dip, creamy salad, dressing, stew (like goulash), sautéed meat, chicken, and fish.
Peppercorns	Black pepper is perhaps the world's most popular spice, used to accent nearly every savory dish. Use white pepper to enrich cream sauces and white dishes for an unadulterated white color. Also try other colored peppercorns for a variety of flavor.
Saffron	The world's most expensive spice, made from dried stigmas hand-picked from a special variety of purple crocus flowers. Available as powder or whole threads. A little goes a long way. Essential to classic Mediterranean dishes like bouillabaisse and paella. Imparts a rich yellow color to cream sauces and rice dishes.
Turmeric	Yellow-orange powder that is intensely aromatic and has a bitter, pungent flavor; gives American-style mustard its color. Sold as a powder. Essential ingredient in Middle Eastern cuisine.

Peanut Butter and Beyond: Bottled and Canned Goods

With a well-stocked pantry full of useful bottled and canned food, you can jazz up a salad, spice up a soup, or make an entire dinner in a pinch. Stock your larder with these ready-to-heat-or-eat items:

✔ **Broth:** Chicken, beef, and vegetable broth, stock, or bouillon cubes add flavor and form the base for delicious homemade soup or sauce. Always have at least one can or carton at the ready.

✔ **Canned beans:** Pinto, white, black, kidney, garbanzo, and baked beans add quick and easy protein to soups, salads, and quick side dishes. Refried beans for tacos, burritos, and nachos come in handy, too.

- ✔ **Canned clams and clam juice:** Use them for quick pasta sauce or as a substitute for homemade fish stock.

- ✔ **Canned fish:** Tuna, crab, salmon, sardines, anchovies, and kippers make good snacks, quick sandwiches, or fancy salads.

- ✔ **Chutney, fruit relish, and cranberry sauce:** Serve with grilled meats and poultry or use as a basting sauce.

- ✔ **Condiments:** Ketchup, mustard, mayonnaise, barbeque sauce, and soy sauce are the basics, but there are lots of other possibilities: Tabasco, chipotle sauce, tamari, hoisin sauce, Asian chili sauce, brown mustard, hot mustard, and more.

- ✔ **Jam, jelly, or preserves:** Jars of preserved fruit spread make peanut butter and jelly sandwiches possible, but can also be used on breakfast breads and in many desserts and sauces.

- ✔ **Marinated vegetables:** Artichoke hearts, olives, red peppers, asparagus, pickles, olives, and capers all add jazz to salads and platters of vegetables, or put them on sandwiches or into pasta for a gourmet flair.

- ✔ **Nut butters:** Peanut butter is always great to have around, but also try almond, cashew, and sesame butters.

- ✔ **Oils:** Extra virgin olive oil, canola oil, grapeseed oil, and peanut oil work for cooking, frying, and dressing salads. For extra dashes of flavor, try toasted sesame oil, chili oil, walnut oil, or other gourmet oils that look interesting to you.

- ✔ **Syrup:** For sweetening desserts and drizzling over pancakes and waffles, keep real maple syrup and honey on hand. Also try brown rice syrup, agave nectar, and fruit-flavored syrups.

- ✔ **Tomato paste, sauce, and canned tomatoes:** You'll be glad to have canned Italian plum tomatoes and crushed tomatoes for making pasta sauces when fresh tomatoes are pale and tasteless. Tomato paste and sauce add flavor and texture to your Italian dishes and form the base of a good spaghetti sauce.

- ✔ **Vinegar:** Apple cider, white, and red wine vinegar are three basics to have on hand, but you can also try Balsamic, champagne, white wine, and other flavored vinegars for making your own salad dressings and marinades.

- ✔ **Wines:** Keep a dry white and a dry red wine for adding to sauces, stews, and long-simmering casseroles and soups. Dry sherry, Port, and Madeira are nice to have, too.

Condiments such as relishes, jellies, pickles, mayonnaise, mustard, and salsa keep for months in the refrigerator after you open them. Steak sauce, peanut butter, oil, vinegar, honey, and syrup do not require refrigeration after you open them and can be stored on a shelf or in a cool cabinet for months, away from heat and sunlight. When in doubt, always follow the storage instructions on the product's label.

Wining and dining: Knowing what to serve

Many a gracious host has at least a rudimentary wine cellar, whether this consists of built-in shelves in a damp basement or a simple metal wine rack on the kitchen counter. But what wines should you stock, and how do you know which wines to serve with what foods?

The best wine for a meal is the one you think tastes good with that food. In fact, a French saying confirms this: *A châque son gout,* or "personal taste rules." That being said, a few tried and tested concepts apply when pairing wine with food: walnuts and Port, lamb and red Bordeaux, salmon and pinot noir, dark chocolate and California Cabernet Sauvignon, to name just a few. More generally, you may have heard that white wines go with fish and poultry and other light dishes, like soup and salad, while red wines go with beef, pork, and other heavier foods such as rich casseroles and heavily sauced pasta.

Don't get too hung up on these guidelines. Keep in mind that in many cases, it's not the ingredient that dictates the wine choice, but the way in which it is prepared. A simple grilled chicken breast, for example, would go nicely with medium-bodied to light-bodied whites: pinot grigio, sauvignon blanc, fumé blanc, a light Chardonnay (not aged in oak), or chenin blanc. If that same chicken is jazzed up with a spicy Southwestern chili rub, it's a whole different game. You can go two ways. Try something fresh and fruity (served cool) to soften those smoky chilies, such as Beaujolais or dolcetto. Or go with Merlot or a "spicy" white wine high in acid so it doesn't get pushed around by that Southwestern sizzle. Don't let the food overwhelm the wine, but also don't let the wine overwhelm the food. Look for both balance and complementary flavors. The more you taste

and compare, the more you'll start to see these connections yourself, so why not start practicing? Some ideas to get you started:

- ✔ Easy-to-drink, lighter red wines go well with meat, poultry, and oily fish like salmon. Examples include Merlot, pinot noir, syrah (called shiraz in Australia), Beaujolais, and those small-winery offerings labeled simply "red table wine."

- ✔ Richer, more fully-flavored red wine can accompany rich meats and sauces, heavy casseroles, and other strongly-flavored foods. Examples include Cabernet Sauvignon, red zinfandel, and red Bordeaux.

- ✔ Easy-to-drink, light white wines match light dishes such as delicate fish, salads, and broth-based soups that aren't too highly spiced. Examples are dry Riesling, sauvignon blanc, Chablis, and pinot grigio.

- ✔ Rich, oaky, buttery California Chardonnay pairs with more strongly flavored fish, poultry, salads, and soups. A gutsy Chardonnay can also taste good with the leaner cuts of pork and beef.

- ✔ Sweet wines are suitable for serving with dessert (or *as* dessert). Try Riesling, gewürztraminer, white zinfandel, Vouvray, Sauternes, and fortified dessert wines like sherry and Port.

- ✔ Champagne or other sparkling wines are good to keep on hand because you never know when you may have cause for celebration! We think Champagne goes with just about any food.

For more detailed information about wines, see *Wine For Dummies* by Ed McCarthy and Mary Ewing-Mulligan (Wiley).

Cooling It with Refrigerated and Frozen Staples

Following are a few essential items to stock in the refrigerator or freezer:

- **Eggs:** Never be without them, for omelets, breakfast foods, and quick dinners. (See Chapter 11 for handy egg recipes and other egg tips.) Refrigerate eggs in the shipping carton to keep them from picking up odors and flavors from other refrigerated foods, and use them before the expiration or "use by" date stamped on the carton.

- **Fresh pasta:** Stock various stuffed pastas, such as ravioli, in the freezer for quick dinners. You can wrap fresh pasta in freezer bags and store it for six to eight months. Do not defrost before cooking; simply drop frozen pasta into boiling water and cook until *al dente* (tender but still pleasingly firm to the bite).

- **Milk:** We make our recipes with whole milk, which has about 3.5 percent butterfat. If you prefer, use 1 percent (lowfat), 2 percent (reduced fat), or skim (nonfat) milk, with the understanding that the recipe may not have as creamy a consistency. If you don't like milk or avoid dairy products, you can substitute soy, rice, coconut, or nut milk for regular milk in most recipes.

- **Sweet (unsalted) butter:** Use unsalted sweet butter in all recipes so that you can control the amount of salt. Butter has a refrigerator shelf life of about 2 to 3 weeks and can be frozen for 8 to 12 months in the original unopened carton or, if opened, in plastic freezer bags.

These items are nice to have, too:

- **Cottage cheese, ricotta, and cream cheese:** Keep them on hand for adding to dressings and dips, snacking, spreading on bagels or toast, and for cheesecakes. Store in the original, covered container or foil wrapping and consume within 1 to 2 weeks.

- **Hard and semihard cheeses:** Cheese has enjoyed somewhat of a renaissance in the United States, with a proliferation of artisanal cheese producers and cheese shops offering hundreds of types, so it's easy to become a connoisseur if you so desire (and don't mind asking questions at your local cheese counter). For starters, stock mozzarella, Parmesan, cheddar, and blue cheeses for salads, casseroles, omelets, white sauces, and sandwiches; to grate into pasta; and just to snack on! Then, we strongly suggest expanding your cheese horizons by tasting different cheeses whenever you can to determine what you like.

Wrap all cheese in foil, a resealable plastic bag, or plastic wrap after opening. Trim off any mold that grows on the outside edges of hard cheeses. Depending on its variety, cheese keeps in the refrigerator for several weeks to months.

Pre-grated Parmesan or Romano cheese quickly loses its potency and absorbs the odors of other refrigerated foods. Instead of buying pre-grated, keep a tightly wrapped wedge in the fridge and grate as needed. Or, if you'll use it all right away, save time with a high-quality Parmesan or Romano that has been freshly grated at the deli.

- ✔ **Heavy cream, light cream, or half-and-half:** They're great for making quick pan sauces for fish, poultry, and pasta. Use within a week of purchase or freeze for longer storage. Heavy cream (not half-and-half or light cream) is used for making whipped cream.

- ✔ **Ice cream or frozen yogurt:** Instant dessert (and great for eating guiltily in bed at midnight)! After you open it, you should eat ice cream and frozen yogurt within 2 weeks. You can freeze unopened containers for up to 2 months.

- ✔ **Plain yogurt:** This is a good ingredient for quick dips and low-fat sauces. It also makes pancake batters lighter. Follow the expiration date on the package.

- ✔ **Sour cream:** You can use standard (18 percent fat), low-fat, and nonfat sour cream interchangeably in recipes. As with all dairy products, heed the expiration date.

Squeezing the Melon: Buying and Storing Fruits and Vegetables

Fruits and vegetables add color, flavor, vitamins, minerals, and fiber to your diet, and the quality of the produce you buy directly impacts the quality of the dishes you cook with that produce. Who wants to eat a wilted salad or a dingy bowl of fruit? Always seek out the best sources for produce. If you have a local farmers' market featuring seasonal produce, browse the stalls and choose what looks best. You can plan a whole meal — or at least a memorable side dish — around a really ripe carton of tomatoes and a dewy bin of fresh lettuce, or what about those blushing peaches bursting with juice for dessert?

When choosing and storing fruits and vegetables, whether from a farm stand or the supermarket, a few rules apply across the board. Avoid fresh produce with brown spots or wrinkled skin or produce that doesn't look . . . well . . . fresh! Here are a few other produce rules to live by:

- **Apples:** Should be crisp and firm. Refrigerate or store in a cool, dark place. Keep for several weeks. Some varieties keep for several months.

  Apples release a gas that makes other fruits ripen more quickly, so if you don't want your fruit to ripen too fast, keep it away from the apple bowl and don't store it with apples in the refrigerator.

- **Artichokes and asparagus:** Refrigerate and use within 2 to 3 days of purchase.

- **Avocados:** These tropical delights should yield just slightly to pressure when ripe. Keep at room temperature until fully ripened. If you won't eat them right away, refrigerate them to keep for several more days.

- **Bananas:** Eat them before they turn completely brown. You can refrigerate them to slow down their ripening. Their peel continues to darken in the refrigerator, but not their flesh.

- **Bell peppers:** Store in the refrigerator for up to 2 weeks.

- **Broccoli and cauliflower:** Refrigerate and consume within a week.

- **Cabbage:** Keeps for 1 to 2 weeks in the refrigerator.

- **Carrots:** Best when firm, not rubbery, without a lot of little roots growing all over them. They keep in the refrigerator for several weeks.

- **Celery:** Fresh celery is crisp and firm. Old celery flops around like a rubber pencil. Keeps for 1 to 2 weeks in the refrigerator.

- **Cherries and berries:** Keep refrigerated. For best flavor, consume them the same day you purchase them. Cherries and berries get soft and moldy quickly.

- **Citrus fruits (such as lemons, grapefruits, and oranges):** When refrigerated, citrus fruits (which don't ripen further after they're picked and are relatively long-storage fruits) keep for up to 3 weeks.

- **Corn:** Refrigerate and use the same day of purchase. After corn is picked, its sugar immediately begins converting to starch, diminishing its sweetness.

- **Cucumbers and eggplant:** The skin should be firm, shiny, and smooth, without soft brown spots. Keep for up to 1 week in the cold crisper drawer of the refrigerator.

- **Garlic:** Garlic should feel firm, not soft, and should be without any green sprouts. Once it sprouts, it turns bitter. Keep garlic at room temperature, in a small bowl within reach of your food preparation area, to encourage you to use the fresh stuff. Garlic will last longer in the refrigerator, however, so if you don't use it often, keep it chilled to inhibit sprouting.

- ✔ **Grapes:** Fresh, ripe grapes are full and juicy looking with a powdery bloom on the skin. Keep in the refrigerator for up to a week.

- ✔ **Green beans:** Refrigerate and use within 3 to 4 days of purchase.

- ✔ **Leafy greens (beet tops, collards, kale, mustard greens, and so on):** Very perishable. Refrigerate and consume within 1 to 2 days.

- ✔ **Mushrooms:** Store in a paper bag in the refrigerator. Use within a week.

- ✔ **Onions, potatoes, shallots, and hard-shelled winter squash (like acorn and butternut):** Keep at room temperature for several weeks to a month. Store onions, potatoes, and winter squash in a cool, dry, dark drawer or bin. Onions, shallots, and potatoes should be firm. If they are soft or rubbery, they are past their prime.

- ✔ **Pineapple:** It doesn't ripen after it's picked and is best if eaten within a few days of purchase. Keep at room temperature, away from heat and sun, or refrigerate whole or cut up.

- ✔ **Salad greens:** Rinse thoroughly, trim, and dry completely before storing wrapped in paper towel or in plastic bags in the refrigerator crisper drawer. They keep for 3 to 4 days. (See Chapter 12 for more information.) Do we have to tell you not to buy slimy lettuce?

- ✔ **Spinach:** Trim, rinse, and dry thoroughly before storing in the refrigerator for 2 to 3 days.

- ✔ **Summer squash (zucchini and yellow squash):** Store in the refrigerator for up to a week.

- ✔ **Tomatoes:** Store at room temperature for more flavor. Keep in a cool, dark place or in a paper bag to ripen fully. Once ripe, eat them right away. If you can't, refrigerate them for two or three more days, although this can compromise the texture, making them mealier. Return them to room temperature before eating.

- ✔ **Tropical fruits:** Mangoes, papaya, and kiwi should be firm but yield slightly to pressure and should smell fruity. Store at room temperature for more flavor, but refrigerate when they are ripe and then return to room temperature before eating.

- ✔ **Unripe melons and tree fruits (such as pears, peaches, and nectarines):** Keep at room temperature so that they can ripen and grow sweeter. After they're fully ripe, you can store them in the refrigerator for several more days. Melons are ripe when they smell melon-y at the stem end.

And if we haven't mentioned a fruit or vegetable you want to try . . . try it anyway! There are many interesting produce options out there in the world. The more you taste, the more you know.

Selecting, Buying, and Storing Meat, Poultry, and Fish

Meat, poultry, and fish are highly perishable foods that need to be stored in the coldest part of your refrigerator. Keep them tightly wrapped, preferably in their own drawer, to prevent their juices from dripping onto other foods.

Always check expiration dates (avoid items that are older than your car's last oil change), and never allow meat, poultry, or fish to thaw at room temperature, where bacteria can have a field day. Always thaw them in the refrigerator, which takes more time (and planning) but is by far the safest method.

Beef

Beef is rated according to the animal's age and the amount of fat (or *marbling*) in the cut (the more marbling, the more moist and tender the meat), as well as its color and texture. *Prime* meat is the highest grade and the most expensive. In general, the most tender and flavorful meat falls under this category. Aging has an effect, too. If possible, buy from butchers who still age their own beef. You pay a little more, but the increased tenderness and superior flavor are worth the price.

Choice is the second tier of meat grading, leaner (and therefore a little tougher) than prime. *Select* meats are best for stewing and braising for long periods, which dissolves the tough connective tissue in these cuts.

The more tender cuts of meat include steaks such as porterhouse, sirloin, shell, New York strip, Delmonico, and filet mignon, as well as roasts like rib, rib eye, and tenderloin. Tender meats are usually cooked by the dry heat methods of roasting, broiling, grilling, and sautéing. (See Chapter 8 for roasting, Chapter 9 for broiling and grilling recipes, and Chapter 6 for sautéing recipes.)

Less tender cuts, such as brisket, chuck, shoulder, rump, and bottom round that have more muscle tissue and less fat are usually cooked by braising and stewing. (See Chapter 7 for braising and stewing recipes.) Figure 3-2 illustrates where the various cuts come from.

Figure 3-2:
Various cuts of beef come from different parts of a steer.

When choosing meat, look for cuts that are bright red, never dull or gray. Excess juice in the package may indicate that the meat has been previously frozen and thawed — do not purchase it. Boneless, well-trimmed cuts are slightly more expensive per pound but have more edible meat than untrimmed cuts, so in the long run they generally cost about the same.

Use raw meat within two days or by the "use by" date on the package, or freeze it. To freeze, rewrap in aluminum foil, heavy-duty plastic wrap, or freezer bags, pressing out as much air as possible and dating all packages. Freeze ground meat for a maximum of 3 months; freeze other cuts for up to 6 months. Defrost in the refrigerator or microwave.

Chicken

The tenderness and flavor of fresh poultry vary somewhat from one commercial producer to the next, so you should buy and taste a few different brands to determine which you like. Grade A poultry is the most economical because it has the most meat in proportion to bone. Skin color is not an indication of quality or fat content. A chicken's skin ranges from white to deep yellow, depending on its diet.

Here are five kinds of chicken to know:

- **Broiler/fryer:** A 7- to 9-week-old bird weighing between 2 and 4 pounds. Flavorful meat that is best for broiling, frying, sautéing, or roasting. A whole broiler/fryer is always less expensive than a precut one.

- **Capon:** A 6- to 9-pound castrated male chicken. Excellent as a roasting chicken because of its abundance of fat. Just to be sure, pour off or scoop out excess melted fat as the chicken roasts — especially if you do not have an exhaust fan — or your kitchen could resemble the Towering Inferno. Not widely available in supermarkets (it usually needs to be special-ordered).

- **Roaster or pullet:** From 3 to 7 months old and between 3 and 7 pounds. Very meaty, with high fat content under the skin, which makes for excellent roasting.

- **Rock Cornish game hen:** A smaller breed of chicken weighing 1 to 2 pounds. Meaty, moist, and flavorful for roasting.

- **Stewing chicken:** From 3 to 7 pounds and at least 1 year old. Needs slow, moist cooking to tenderize. Makes the best soups and stews.

Remove the package of giblets (the neck, heart, gizzard, and liver) in the cavity of a whole bird and then rinse under running cold water and dry before cooking it. Also trim away excess fat. After preparing poultry, wash your hands and work surfaces (counters and cutting boards) with soap and water to prevent cross-contamination from bacteria.

How free is free range?

Compared to cooped-up, antibiotic-blasted, sunshine-deprived regular chickens, free-range chickens have a pretty cozy life . . . theoretically. In many cases, *free range* is a bit of an exaggeration. These supposedly privileged chickens do not pack lunches and take daily outings across the vast countryside, stopping for a couple of pecks in fields of clover on the way home. Most free-range chickens are enclosed in fenced areas with very limited room to maneuver, or inside buildings with the door open. That doesn't mean they go actually outside. Because it costs more to produce free-range chickens, the chicken usually costs more — sometimes just a little more, sometimes a lot more, depending on the store, the brand, the source. If you can taste the difference and you think it's worth the price, go for it. Or, go a step further if it matters to you, and purchase organic free-range chickens, which must be fed organic food and must be treated according to certain humane standards that don't apply to conventional chickens. Many people claim organic chickens are the tastiest.

Consume whole or cut-up poultry within 1 to 2 days of purchase. A whole, raw chicken may be wrapped and frozen for up to 12 months; parts can be frozen for up to 9 months. Defrost in the refrigerator, never at room temperature. Be sure to place the thawing package in a pan or on a plate to catch any dripping juices. A 4-pound chicken takes 24 hours to thaw in the refrigerator; cut-up parts between 3 and 6 hours. If you use your microwave to defrost poultry, do so on a very low setting and be sure to cook the poultry immediately after thawing it.

Fish

Fish falls into two broad categories: lean and oily. Lean fish include mild-tasting sole, flounder, snapper, cod, halibut, and haddock. Oily fish have more intense flavor, higher levels of heart-healthy essential fatty acids, and generally darker flesh. These include bluefish, mackerel, salmon, swordfish, and tuna. As a general rule, purchase fillets of oily fish with the skin intact so the fish holds together better during cooking. Lean fish are usually packaged without the skin.

When buying fish, always ask your fish dealer what is the freshest that day. To break out of the salmon-or-tuna rut, try some of these other types of delicious fish:

- **Bluefish:** Rich flavor, especially when fresh and under 2 pounds. Bake or broil.

- **Catfish:** Dense, relatively mild fish. Usually cooked in a strong sauce or deep-fried.

- **Cod:** Mild-flavored, white, firm flesh. Can be broiled, baked, fried, or braised.

Right now, we are loving black cod, sometimes called *sablefish* or *butterfish*. This rich fish is high in heart-healthy fat and is a treat not to be missed, if you can find it. It costs more than regular cod, but oh how delicious it is!

- **Haddock:** Meaty, white flesh, mild flavor. Good pan-fried or braised.

- **Porgy:** Firm, low-fat, white-fleshed fish with delicate flavor. Excellent grilled or broiled.

- **Tilapia:** An increasingly popular and affordable farm-raised fish with a mild flavor. Tilapia holds together well and can therefore be cooked in many different ways, making it a favorite of restaurant chefs.

- **Whiting (silver hake):** Fine, semifirm white flesh. Subtle and delicious when broiled or pan-fried.

Freshness is the most important factor in purchasing fish. Learn to recognize it. In a whole fish, the eyes should be bright and clear, not cloudy. The gills of fresh fish are deep red, not brownish. The skin should be clear and bright with no trace of slime. Really fresh fish shouldn't smell like fish, either. Fish may smell briny but should not smell fishy.

If possible, have your fishmonger cut fresh fillets from whole fish while you wait. Purchase precut fillets only if they're displayed on a bed of ice, not sealed under plastic, which can trap bacteria and foul odors. Fillets should look moist and lie flat, with no curling at the edges. Consume fresh fish and seafood as soon as possible, ideally on the day of purchase. You can freeze freshly caught and cleaned fish for 2 to 3 months if they're wrapped well in two layers of freezer wrap. Although some fish merchants will tell you that you can refreeze shrimp, salmon, and other types of seafood, refreezing compromises the flavor and texture of many kinds of fish. We recommend never refreezing fish after thawing it.

Shellfish should be firmly closed and odorless when purchased. If clams or mussels don't close when tapped on the counter, toss them. Eat fresh clams, oysters, and mussels as soon as possible. Store for no more than 24 hours in the refrigerator in a plastic bag poked with small holes, allowing air to circulate. It's best to purchase shrimp in the shell. Eat shrimp the same day you purchase it. Most of all, never overcook shellfish because it gets rubbery.

Wild fish, sustainable fish

A recent trend in supermarkets and restaurants is to advertise that a fish is *wild-caught* or *sustainably fished.*

Wild-caught fish are not farmed, but caught in their natural habitats. Proponents of wild-caught fish claim that farmed fish contains fewer beneficial omega-3 fatty acids than wild-caught fish and that because of crowded conditions in "factory fish farms," farmed fish are dosed with antibiotics and other drugs and even dyed to look more appetizing. Fish farming also poses some environmental concerns. However, wild-caught fish can be a problem, too, if they are caught in a way that puts other fish at risk or if they are overfished and in danger of becoming endangered or extinct. *Sustainably caught* fish are carefully fished with an eye for sustaining populations and not putting other species in harm's way.

If these issues matter to you, download a Seafood Watch Pocket Guide from www.montereybayaquarium.org/cr/cr_seafoodwatch/download.aspx, or check out the Natural Resources Defense Council Sustainable Seafood Guide at www.nrdc.org/oceans/seafoodguide.

Part II
Know Your Techniques

The 5th Wave   By Rich Tennant

SOLAR GRILLING

"Burgers ready in 6 hours!"

In this part . . .

The focus of this part is *technique* — we're talking chopping, slicing, mincing, and other knife skills, as well as the techniques you need to know to actually apply heat to food: boiling, poaching, steaming, sautéing, braising, stewing, roasting, grilling, broiling, and baking. The goal is to give you the basic tools you need to cook from a recipe. We explain each technique from the ground up, giving you a variety of recipes to practice with. As you gain experience, you'll learn to improvise and maybe even invent some recipes yourself. Yes, you have a lot to absorb, but you already exhibited superior intelligence by buying this book, so the rest should be a cakewalk. (And when you learn about baking, cakes will be a cakewalk, too!)

Chapter 4

The Cutting Edge: Working with Knives

*T*his chapter is all about understanding and using the most important pieces of kitchen equipment you'll ever own: knives. Professional chefs revere their knives the way jockeys respect horses, and those knives can last for decades. A really high quality, super sharp knife that feels well-balanced and comfortable in your hand can practically give you kitchen superpowers. Seriously! A really great knife is one of the secrets of a really great cook.

In this chapter, we explain everything you need to know about kitchen knives, from buying and maintaining them to holding them and cutting with care. Whether you want to chop an onion, cube a potato, or carve a turkey, you find the how-to's in this chapter.

To supplement our instructions for mincing, julienning, carving, and so on, be sure to check out www.dummies.com/go/cooking. Search for the knife skill you're wondering about (such as "julienne" or "dice") and watch a video that brings it to life. And check out www.dummies.com/go/knives for a primer on the knives you need to have in your kitchen.

Buying Knives for All Occasions

Investing in quality knives yields dividends for years. A good chef's knife will be your constant companion in the kitchen, although as you progress you'll likely need several others.

Investing in the three essentials

Most home cooks can get along with three versatile knives: a 10- to 12-inch chef's knife, an 8- to 10-inch serrated (bread) knife, and a small paring knife.

Chef's knife

A *chef's knife* (shown in Figure 4-1) can be used for all sorts of chopping, slicing, dicing, and mincing. This knife is really the workhorse of the kitchen, so investing in a quality chef's knife always pays off.

A 10-inch chef's knife is the best choice for a home cook. It should feel comfortable in your hand and be *balanced*, which means the handle should not be significantly heavier than the blade or vice versa. You'll know a suitable one when you hold it.

Figure 4-1:
A chef's knife is handy for all sorts of chopping chores.

chef's knife

Serrated knife

Have you ever tried to slice a baguette with a regular knife? It's not only frustrating but also dangerous. For this reason (and many others), we include a serrated knife on our list of essentials.

A *serrated knife* (shown in Figure 4-2) generally has an 8- to 10-inch blade, and you want to find one that has *wide teeth* (meaning the pointy edges along the blade aren't too close together). This type of knife is essential for cutting bread; a chef's knife can do the job if you're in a pinch, but a hard-crusted bread dulls a chef's knife quickly. A serrated knife is also handy when slicing tomatoes and other foods that have thin but resistant skins.

Figure 4-2:
A serrated knife is great for cutting crusty breads, as well as tomatoes.

serrated knife

Paring knife

A *paring knife* (shown in Figure 4-3) has a blade from 2 to 4 inches long. You use it for delicate jobs like peeling apples and other fruits, trimming shallots and garlic, removing stems from strawberries, coring tomatoes, and making vegetable or fruit decorations.

Figure 4-3:
Use a paring knife for delicate cutting tasks.

paring knife

Adding to your knife block

As your cooking skills develop, you may want to consider buying one or more of these knives as well:

- ✔ **Boning knife:** This one, used to separate raw meat from the bone, is generally 8 to 10 inches long and has a pointed, narrow blade.

- ✔ **Fish filleting knife:** With a 6- to 11-inch blade, this knife resembles a boning knife, but its blade is thin and flexible to perform delicate tasks.

- ✔ **Slicer:** This type of knife is mostly used to slice cooked meat. It has a long, smooth blade — 8 to 12 inches — with either a round or pointed tip.

- ✔ **Cleavers:** These knives feature rectangular blades and look almost like hatchets. They come in many sizes, with some cleavers heavy enough to chop through bone and others intended for chopping vegetables.

Stores often sell knives in sets of four or six, which means the set includes one or more of the nonessentials in this list. You can usually save money if you buy a quality knife set instead of individual knives. The catch is that you need to be confident that you're actually going to *use* all the knives in the set. If you're a vegetarian and quite certain that you're never going to separate raw meat from any critter's bone, you most likely don't need a boning knife. If you don't like seafood, don't bother buying a set that features a filleting knife.

Shopping wisely

When you're ready to go knife shopping, you need to know a thing or two about what knives are made of, as well as how to compare those on the shelf.

Knowing the knife composition

Knives come in several types of materials, each of which has its advantages and disadvantages:

- **High-carbon stainless steel:** This material is the most popular choice for both home cooks and professionals because it combines the durability of stainless steel with the sharpening capability of carbon steel. It's also easy to clean and does not rust.

- **Carbon steel:** Used primarily by chefs who want an extremely sharp edge, carbon steel has the disadvantage of getting dull quickly. It also gets discolored from contact with acidic food.

- **Ceramic:** Made from superheated zirconium oxide, newly popular ceramic knives are denser, lighter, and sharper than steel. In fact, ceramic knives stay razor sharp for years. The main drawback is that the blades can shatter when dropped. They are comparable in price to other knives.

Homing in on what you want

Every department store carries kitchen knives these days, and many of them look quite impressive. But not all knives are the same. Some look great but are lightweights with thin, insubstantial blades that just won't last. How do you find knives that will still be part of your life years from now? When you're shopping for knives, keep the following tips in mind:

- **Before you buy a knife, hold it in your hand.** If the knife is well constructed, it should feel substantial and balanced for you.

- **Assess the knife handles.** When shopping for large knives, like chef's knives and cleavers, look for those with riveted handles featuring three circular bolts that provide stability.

- **Consider only knives whose blades are *forged*.** This means that the blades taper from the tip to the base of the handle.

✔ **Look for reputable brands.** Here are some to consider:

- Chef'sChoice
- Global
- Henckels
- Hoffritz
- International Cutlery
- Kyocera (ceramic knives)
- Sabatier
- Wüsthof

Caring for Your Knives

After you invest in quality knives, you want to make sure they give you peak performances for many years. The advice in this section can help.

Storing and washing

Here's rule number one: Don't store your good knives in the same drawer with other cutlery where they can be damaged. You don't want your good chef's knife getting into a wrestling match with a pizza cutter! Instead, keep your knives in a wooden knife holder or on a magnetic strip mounted on the wall (out of the reach of children).

Wash your knives with warm soap and water, using a sponge or plastic scrubber. Don't put them in the dishwasher, and don't scrub them with steel wool.

Also, because you want your knives to look shiny and nice, never leave acid such as lemon juice or vinegar on a knife blade; it can discolor the surface.

Sharpening twice a year

Quality knives are only as good as their sharpened cutting edges. To keep your knives in peak condition, you may want to have them professionally sharpened a couple times a year. Don't have them sharpened more often than that because over-sharpening wears down the blade. Your local butcher or a gourmet retailer may sharpen your knives for free, but if not, how do you find a professional knife sharpener? It may not be easy; they're becoming a rare breed. Ask the retailer who sold you the knives, or ask a chef.

If the nearest professional sharpener is a state or two away, you may want to consider investing in a home sharpening machine. These devices, which start at about $40, can be found at knife retailers and do a fairly decent job. But they definitely don't match the quality of a professional sharpening.

Honing before each use

To help maintain a knife's sharp edge, you should *hone* its blade — move it across a sharpening steel — before every use. A *sharpening steel* is a long (up to 12-inch) rod of steel or ceramic with a handle. The rod has ridges on it, and when you run a knife blade across at a 20-degree angle, it removes tiny fragments that dull the edge.

Keep in mind that despite its name, a sharpening steel doesn't actually sharpen a knife. To sharpen requires removing a certain amount of steel from the knife. Honing simply removes any rag-tag bits of steel that may be hanging on the knife's edge because of everyday wear and tear. Honing regularly can definitely help you extend the sharpness of your blade.

Honing a knife before you use it takes less than a minute. Here's how (and see Figure 4-4):

How to Use a Honing Steel

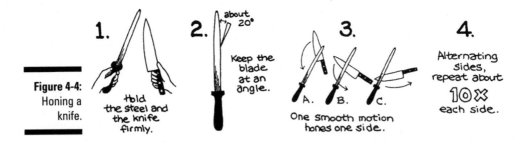

Figure 4-4: Honing a knife.

1. **Grab a sharpening steel firmly and hold it slightly away from your body and at a slight upward angle. Hold the knife firmly with the other hand.** The sharpening steel doesn't move during this process; only the knife does.

2. **Run the knife blade down the steel rod, toward the handle (don't worry, it has a protective lip on the top of the handle) at about a 20-degree angle.**

3. **Repeat step 2, alternating sides of the blade.** This may be nerve-racking at first because the technique has the knife coming at you, but with practice you'll get the hang of it.

4. **Keep alternating for at least 10 times until the blade is sharp.** Tip: To test for sharpness, run the blade lightly across the skin of a tomato. It should slice through effortlessly. Whatever you do, don't test it by running your finger along the blade!

Using Knives Correctly (and Safely)

Many knife injuries are the result of rushed, hungry people doing dumb stuff, like trying to separate frozen hamburgers or slicing through hard bagels. So rule number one is: Don't do dumb stuff! (Or maybe it should be "Don't use knives when you're starving!")

Seriously, you can avoid any knife-related accidents by following some simple rules:

- ✔ **Always slice away from your hand.** Notice the word *slice* here. If you're using a paring knife to peel an apple, the blade is going to be facing the hand holding the apple; you can't get away from that. But when you slice or chop or mince (all of which we explain in the next section of this chapter), the blade should never be turned toward the hand holding the food.

- ✔ **Keep your fingers clear of the blades.** Before you say "well, duh!" consider how often we take unnecessary chances. If you're slicing a tomato and get down to a half-inch piece remaining, what do you do? That half-inch piece is too thick to put on your sandwich, and you don't want to waste it, so don't you go ahead and slice it in two? Well, exactly how far away can your fingers get in this situation? Until you're really skilled at using a knife, let the tomato go — and find some other way to use it that doesn't require that final slice. And if you insist on making that final cut, at least use a serrated knife (which slices through tomato skins effortlessly).

- ✔ **Always use a cutting board, and don't let it slide around on the counter.** Either use a cutting board with rubber feet that help the board grip the counter, or put your cutting board on a moist dish towel so it won't slip.

- ✔ **Keep your fingertips curled under when slicing.** The knife should not move toward or away from the food; rather, you nudge the food toward the blade. This way, if you do misfire, you're more likely to hit a hard knuckle than a soft fingertip.

So, how exactly do you hold and move the knife? That depends on what you're cutting and how you want the finished product to look. Keep reading to find out more.

Chopping, Mincing, Julienning, and More

In this section, we define the terms you're most likely to see in a recipe that calls for you to prepare vegetables, fruits, herbs, and meats. We explain how to chop, mince, cube (or dice), julienne, and slice.

Chopping and mincing

Chopping food means to use your chef's knife to cut it into pieces. Those pieces don't have to be exactly uniform, but the recipe will often tell you whether you need to chop something finely, coarsely, or somewhere in between. Another word for chopping something very finely is *mincing*. You're most often asked to chop or mince veggies or herbs.

To chop or mince, hold the knife handle in a comfortable manner and cut the food into thin strips. Then cut the strips crosswise (as thickly as desired), rocking the blade with your hand and applying pressure on top. Your best bet is to grip the handle with one hand and place your other hand on top of the blade.

Practicing on an onion

Want to practice chopping? Many recipes call for chopped onions, so these are a good place to start. Follow these steps, which are shown in Figure 4-5:

Figure 4-5:
Chopping an onion.

1. **Chop off the stem, and then cut the onion in half lengthwise through the bulbous center and peel back the papery skin.**

   Leave the root end intact. As you slice through the onion, the intact root end holds together the onion half while you slice and chop.

2. **Place each half cut-side down and, with your knife tip just in front of the root end, slice the onion lengthwise in parallel cuts, leaving ⅛ to ¼ inch between the slices.**

3. **Make several horizontal cuts of desired thickness, parallel to the board.**

4. **Cut through the onion crosswise making pieces as thick as desired.**

5. **Finally, cut through the root end and discard.**

At www.dummies.com/go/choppingonion, you can find a video that shows you what we've just described.

No matter how you slice it, an onion releases intense flavor and juice, which is why so many recipes call for chopped or minced onion. The fumes they emit when sliced raw, however, can be irritating to the eyes. To minimize chopped onion tears, use a sharp knife that reduces cutting time, and frequently rinse off the onion in cold water as you go. Better yet, have someone else cut it.

Mincing garlic

Mincing garlic simply means chopping it very finely. In this section, we explain how.

First, a quick explanation of terms: In your grocery store, you find garlic bulbs. (Buy garlic that feels firm and hard, not soft.) A bulb is covered by papery skin. When you peel it off, you discover that the bulb contains multiple cloves with thin skins. If you have difficulty removing individual cloves, take a butter knife and pry them out. Then, here's what you do:

1. **Peel the cloves.**

   To help you get the skin off easily, set the cloves on your cutting board, and lay your chef's knife across them with the blade facing away from you. Hold the knife handle with one hand, and use your other hand to whack the side of the blade above the cloves. Doing so should break the skins and let you slip them off easily.

2. **Hold the garlic clove on the cutting board, with the knuckles of your index finger and middle finger leaning against the side of the knife blade.**

   Keep your fingertips folded inward to prevent cutting yourself.

3. **Keeping the tip of your knife on the cutting board, pump the handle up and down while you move the clove under the blade.**

   You've probably seen this technique used by the pros on cooking shows.

4. **Slowly move your knuckles toward the other end of the garlic as you mince.**

If this all sounds like too much work, use a *garlic press.* This handy gadget squeezes the clove of garlic through tiny holes, doing the mincing for you.

Using fresh garlic really is worth a couple extra minutes of prep time because the flavor is so superior to the stuff that comes prechopped in a jar. That ingredient works in a pinch, however, so it doesn't hurt to keep a jar in the refrigerator.

Julienning

Don't let the French accent scare you: Julienned vegetables are as simple as they are attractive. Just trim a vegetable, like a radish or carrot, so that it is flat on all sides. Slice it lengthwise into ⅛-inch thick pieces. Stack the pieces, and slice them into strips of the same width. See Figure 4-6 for an illustration of this technique and visit www.dummies.com/go/juliennecarrots to watch a chef in action.

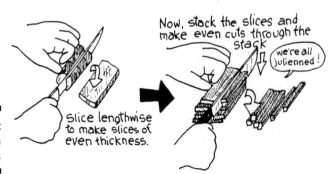

Figure 4-6: Julienning a carrot.

Cubing (or dicing)

If you can julienne vegetables, cubing is a breeze. Think of a potato. Trim all the sides until it is flat all around. Cutting lengthwise, slice off ½-inch-thick pieces (or whatever thickness you desire). Stack all or some of the flat pieces and cut them vertically into even strips. Cut them crosswise into even cubes.

Dicing is the same as cubing, except that your pieces are smaller: ⅛ to ¼ inch, usually.

Slicing

Slicing is the most common — and most important — knife task. There are really only two things to keep in mind. If you are slicing a hard, round vegetable like an onion or a winter squash, trim one side flat first so it does not roll around on the cutting board. Another tip is to take your time to assure evenly thick pieces, whether it is an onion or a pineapple. Doing so makes the food look better and cook more evenly.

Figure 4-7 shows how to slice a scallion. As you can see, you can slice with the knife straight in front of you or at a slight angle with the blade moving away from you.

HOW TO SLICE A SCALLION

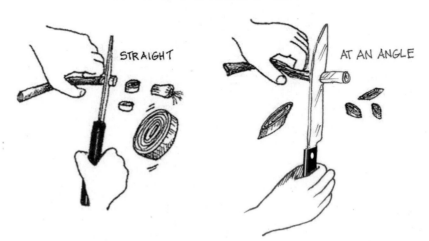

Figure 4-7:
Slicing a
scallion.

Paring

Paring is one of the only cutting tasks you perform while holding the ingredient in your hand. Don't worry — you don't need the first-aid kit nearby! Your hands are designed for this kind of work. *Paring* means to remove skin from fruits and vegetables, as well as to sculpt them into decorative shapes. They can be small items, like shallots and garlic, or larger ones, like apples and tomatoes. Above all, a paring knife must be razor sharp to perform well.

To pare an apple, for example, hold it in one hand, barely pressing it into your palm, with fingers bracing the surface (outside of where the cutting proceeds). Pierce the skin of the apple with the paring knife and carefully peel it toward you, slowly turning the apple with your thumb. Spiral all the way to the bottom (see Figure 4-8). While fruits and vegetables come in different shapes, this technique of holding food and slicing toward you is the same. Need a visual to help you figure out the best way to pare? Be sure to check out www.dummies.com/go/paring.

PARING AN APPLE

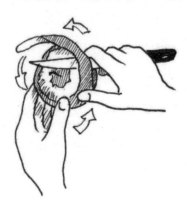

Figure 4-8:
Paring an apple.

Paper thin with a mandoline

A mandoline is one of those kitchen gizmos that many home cooks believe is too complicated to bother with. Think again. This little wonder tool can be so much fun that you may give away your toaster to make room for it on the counter. While it comes in various sizes, compositions, and price, it is fundamentally a tool that can slice vegetables more precisely even than any mere mortal could accomplish with a chef's knife. It can also make slicing soft vegetables like tomatoes easier and has attachments for paper thin slicing and other special effects, like slicing potatoes with ridges. The mandoline itself is a long, low-sided contraption made of plastic or steel with a blade in the center of a long flat plate. The food holder slides up and down over the blade, precisely slicing or otherwise perfectly processing its prey and dropping the pieces onto your cutting board. Always use the safety handle — trust us, you don't want to run your finger over that blade.

Place the mandoline on a cutting board. Choose a slicing blade and adjust it to a desired thickness...

..If your vegetable is too bulky to fit into the box under the handle, cut it down to size. Place the lid firmly down on the vegetable and run rapidly up and down over the slicing blade. The slices will fall onto the counter!

Carving Poultry and Meats

If you're daring enough to cook a whole chicken, turkey, roast, leg of lamb, or ham (all of which we show you how to do later in the book), you're definitely up to cutting your masterpiece in preparation for serving it. We offer illustrated instructions in this section, and you can find videos at www.dummies.com/go/cooking that put these steps into action.

While we don't include the steps here for cutting apart a whole raw chicken, that's a skill that can definitely save you some money. We have a step-by-step video available at www.dummies.com/go/cuttingchicken. Won't your mother be so proud!

Showing a turkey or chicken who's boss

If the thought of carving your Thanksgiving masterpiece or even your Sunday dinner staple gives you the chills, we're here to help. Because chickens and turkeys are anatomically similar, this technique works for both. Here are the steps to follow, which are illustrated in Figure 4-9:

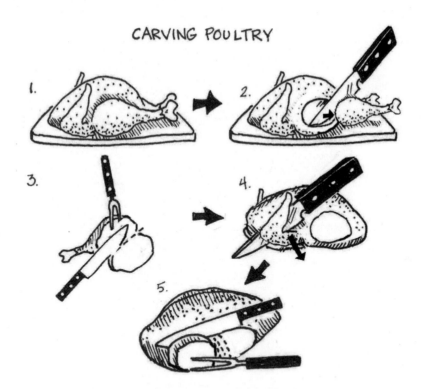

CARVING POULTRY

Figure 4-9:
Carving a chicken or turkey.

1. **Place the chicken or turkey, breast side up, on a carving board.**

2. **Remove one leg by slicing through it where it meets the breast.** Pull the leg away from the body, cut through the skin between the leg and body, and then cut through the joint.

3. **Separate the drumstick from the thigh.** On a cutting board, place the drumstick and thigh skin-side down. Look for a strip of yellow fat at the center. That is the joint. Cut through the joint.

4. **Remove the wing on the same side of the bird.** Cut as close to the breast as possible, through the joint that attaches the wing to the body.

5. **Carve the breast meat.** Hold your knife parallel to the center bone, and begin slicing halfway up the breast. Keep the slices as thin as possible. Continue slicing parallel to the center bone, starting a little higher with each slice.

6. **Repeat the whole process on the other side.**

Visit www.dummies.com/go/carvingturkey to see a video that shows you these steps.

Cutting a pot roast

When it comes to serving a pot roast, you need to follow one simple rule: Cut it against the grain so the meat holds together and doesn't shred. Figure 4-10 shows how to do it, as does www.dummies.com/go/carvingroast.

Cutting Pot Roast Across the Grain

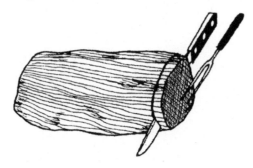

Figure 4-10:
Cut across the grain to avoid shredding the meat.

Slicing a leg of lamb

You may not make lamb as often as you do poultry, but won't your family or guests be impressed when you show off your expert carving skills! Figure 4-11 illustrates how to properly carve a leg of lamb. A chef's knife is best for this task, although you might use a boning knife for hard-to-get pieces.

Carving a Leg of Lamb

1.
Cut out a narrow wedge of meat.

2.
Carve the meat from either side of the wedge, down to the bone.

3.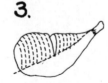
Slice through cuts to form pieces.

4.
Turn the leg over. Trim off the fat and carve off slices parallel to the bone.

Figure 4-11:
The proper technique for carving a leg of lamb.

Handling a ham

When you prepare a gorgeous ham (see Chapter 8 for a suggested recipe), you want to be sure to serve it thinly sliced rather than chopped into chunks. You can use a chef's knife or a serrated knife. Figure 4-12 offers a ham-carving primer, as does www.dummies.com/go/carvingham.

Carving a Ham

Place cooked ham on a cutting board. Steady it with a carving fork and cut off a few slices from the narrow side of the ham. Turn the ham onto the cut side to make carving easier.
Steady!

wedge cut from shank-end makes carving easier

Cut a small wedge of meat from the shank end; then cut evenly thick slices along the ham, down to the bone.

HAM IT UP!

Work the blade of the knife under the slices using a sawing motion to release them from the bone. Remove the slices to a serving platter.

Figure 4-12:
How to carve a ham.

Chapter 5

Boiling, Poaching, and Steaming

*W*ater can be your friend or your foe in the kitchen — but mostly, it's your friend. Too much water can dilute a soup or make some dishes soggy, but it can also boil, blanch, poach, or steam your favorite foods to tender and succulent perfection. Who knew such simple stuff could do so much . . . and it comes right out of your tap, practically for free!

In this chapter, we cover several basic cooking techniques that employ the almost magical powers of good ole' H_2O. From eggs and veggies to melt-in-your-mouth seafood, let water woo you. (For more recipes that involve boiling, flip to Chapter 13 to learn how to boil pasta, rice, and other great grains. And for visual aids to supplement this chapter, check out www.dummies.com/go/cookingwithliquid.)

Water, Water Everywhere . . . Now What?

Relax — even home ec dropouts can figure out the basic cooking techniques using water and other liquids. Cooking with liquid is simple, but it helps to understand the process in order to get the best results. Here are some terms to know:

  ✔ **Boiling:** Bringing water to 212 degrees Fahrenheit in a high-sided pot, like a saucepan or soup pot, or a tea kettle. Let the water come to a *full rolling boil* (when the bubbles are rapidly breaking the surface). Covering the pot speeds the process by trapping surface heat. And here is a tip based on our recent research: A watched pot *does* prevent water from boiling. We suggest you look out the window or start chopping veggies. (Just don't leave the kitchen because an unsupervised pot will definitely boil over!)

✔ **Parboiling** and **blanching:** Pre-cooking tough or salty foods to soften their textures and sometimes to remove harsh flavors or soften tough skin. Rice is sometimes parboiled (or "converted") and then packaged to shorten cooking time and retain nutrients. Tomatoes can be blanched to loosen their skins.

Blanch tougher vegetables like broccoli and cauliflower to make them more palatable and attractive than the raw versions in cold salads. You can even blanch bacon for use in recipes, to get rid of some of the salt.

✔ **Simmering:** Bringing liquid to a gentle pre-boil. In a simmer, tiny bubbles break the surface gently — like a soft summer shower on a still lake. (Are we going overboard? That really is what it looks like!) Simmering occurs at a lower temperature — just below a boil — and is used for long, slow cooking and braising. (Chapter 7 talks more about braising.)

By the way, *poaching* is cooking something like eggs or fish in simmering water or other liquid. *Simmering* is usually used to describe what the liquid itself is doing. You poach eggs, but you simmer soup.

✔ **Reducing:** Boiling down stock or other liquids to thicken and to intensify flavors. This technique is typically used for sauce making (see Chapter 14). Great care must be taken not to over-reduce and burn the reduction.

✔ **Steaming:** The gentlest way to cook. Steaming is better than boiling or poaching for retaining a food's color, flavor, texture, shape, and nutrients. Steaming often involves placing food over simmering water on a perforated rack in a covered pot.

When you steam foods set in a pan of water in the oven, it's called a *water bath.* Cheesecakes and custards are often baked this way. Sometimes this technique is also called a *bain marie,* or Marie's Bath. (You don't want to know where that term came from.)

Making Hard- and Soft-Cooked Eggs

Sometimes the dishes that look the easiest can really trip you up in the kitchen. If you've ever had trouble making boiled eggs, we're here to show you the light!

A quick language primer: Eggs really should never be hard-*boiled* or soft-*boiled* but rather hard-*cooked* or soft-*cooked.* That's because rigorous boiling causes eggs to jostle and crack, leaving the whites tough.

Here are the steps to follow to get the perfect hard-cooked egg, which are also available in video form at www.dummies.com/go/hardcookeggs:

1. **Place the eggs in a saucepan large enough to hold them in a single layer. Add cold water to cover by about 1 inch.**

2. **Cover the saucepan and bring the water to a boil over high heat as fast as possible.**

3. **Remove the pan from the heat and let eggs stand in the pan, still covered, for 15 minutes for large eggs, 18 minutes for jumbo, and 12 minutes for medium.**

4. **Drain the eggs in a colander and run cold water over them until completely cooled.**

For soft-cooked eggs, follow step 1 above to measure how much water to use, but remove the eggs before heating the water. After the water is boiling,

1. **Carefully lower the eggs into the boiling water with a slotted spoon and cook for 2 minutes with the pan covered.**

2. **Turn off the heat.** If your stove is electric, remove the pan from the burner.

3. **Let the eggs stand in the pan, still covered, for 5 minutes.**

4. **Remove the eggs from the water with a slotted spoon.** Put them in a bowl or colander and run cold water over them until they are cool enough to handle.

If you have one of those retro egg cups, you can try putting your soft-cooked egg in it and knocking the top off with a knife — in one fell swoop, like they do in the movies. (But don't blame us if the top of your egg ends up on the other side of the kitchen.) Or, for a more reliable result, cut the top one-third of the egg off with a scissors and eat the yummy yolk and white with a little egg spoon (with a 1950s-style glass and chrome salt shaker within reach and a cup of hot black coffee — *so* Donna Reed).

While you eat soft-cooked eggs right away, hard-cooked eggs have numerous uses. You can slice them into tossed green salads or potato salads, make deviled eggs, mash them for egg salad sandwiches (see our Easy Egg Salad recipe later in the chapter), or simply peel and eat them with a little salt. Always refrigerate hard-cooked eggs and eat them within a week to ten days.

Now, about peeling that egg. . . . The fresher the egg, the more difficult it is to peel, although running cold water over the eggs as you work can help separate the egg white from the shell slightly, making peeling easier. For perfect peeling, follow these steps:

1. **As soon as your hard-cooked egg is cool enough to handle, tap it gently on a table or countertop to crackle the shell all over.**

2. **Roll the egg between your hands to loosen the shell.**

3. **Peel off the shell, starting at the large end of the egg.**

Giving Your Veggies a Hot Bath

It's not that they are so very dirty. It's that a hot bath can make veggies melt-in-your-mouth tender. Water and veggies are a match made in veggie heaven, but forget boiling them to death in the manner you might remember from childhood (sorry, Mom, but it's what you did!). Instead, more sophisticated techniques for applying hot water to fresh veggies will yield superior results. You can even use some of these techniques on fruit.

Parboiling, blanching, and steaming veggies

Sometimes a recipe calls for parboiling vegetables. Certain dense vegetables, such as carrots, potatoes, and turnips, may be parboiled (cooked briefly in boiling water) to soften them slightly before another method finishes cooking them. This technique guarantees that all the ingredients in the dish finish cooking at the same time. You might, for example, parboil green peppers before you stuff and bake them. Or you might parboil pieces of broccoli, carrots, and cauliflower before tossing them into a stir-fry of egg noodles and shrimp. (See the Crispy Roasted Root Vegetables recipe in Chapter 8 for an example of this technique.)

Blanching, or plunging vegetables or fruits into boiling water for a few seconds and then into cold water to stop the cooking process, helps cooks remove the skins from tomatoes, nectarines, and peaches. (See Chapter 12 for instructions on removing the skins of tomatoes.) Some vegetables, like green beans, are blanched before they're frozen or canned to help retain their color and flavor.

Steaming is the gentlest way to cook vegetables (as well as seafood). It's also one of the most healthful because nutrients aren't lost in the cooking liquids. You can steam in two ways: in a perforated steamer set over simmering water (and covered) or in a deep, covered pot or saucepan holding about 1 to 2 inches of water. The latter method works especially well for vegetables like broccoli and asparagus.

If you steam foods often, you may want to invest in some sort of steamer. The conventional steamer model is a pair of pots, the top one having a perforated bottom and a lid. You can also buy bamboo steamers or little metal steamer baskets that fit inside saucepans you already own.

When you're ready to try cooking vegetables in water, check out two recipes that appear later in the chapter: Homemade Mashed Potatoes and Steamed Broccoli with Lemon Butter (which is shown in the color section of this book).

Something to keep in mind whenever you make mashed potatoes: Baking potatoes (like Russets, sometimes called Idaho potatoes) make fluffier, smoother
mashed potatoes than "boiling" potatoes like red or yellow potatoes. Boiled
potatoes contain a lot of moisture so they get gluey when mashed, but they're
great for recipes that call for firm cubes or slices, like potato salad and gratins.

Simple tips for boiling and steaming a dozen fresh vegetables

Following are specific instructions for boiling and steaming common
vegetables:

- ✔ **Artichokes:** Lay the artichokes on their side on a wooden cutting board.
  Using a sharp chef's knife (see Chapter 4), trim about ½ inch off the top.
  Use scissors to trim the prickly tips off each leaf. Pull off any very thick
  or tough leaves (but no more than 3 or 4) at the bottom of the artichoke.
  Place the artichokes in a deep pot with cold water to cover. (They
  should fit snugly to keep them from bobbing in the water.) Add about
  a teaspoon of salt per quart of water, plus some freshly ground black
  pepper and the juice of one lemon, and bring to a boil. Boil gently for
  30 to 40 minutes, depending on size. When the artichokes are done, you
  should be able to pierce the bottom with a fork or easily pull off a leaf.
  Use tongs to remove the artichokes and drain upside down on a plate or
  in a colander. Serve hot with a sauce of lemon juice and melted butter.
  Or marinate for several hours in a vinaigrette dressing (see Chapter 12)
  and serve at room temperature.

- ✔ **Asparagus:** Snap off the thick, woody stems at the natural breaking
  point. (If very coarse, use a vegetable peeler to remove some of the
  outer green layer at the thick end of each spear.) Rinse the stalks under
  cold water or soak them for about 5 minutes if they seem especially
  sandy. Place the spears in a covered skillet in one layer, if possible (and
  never more than two). Add boiling water to cover and salt to taste.
  Cover and boil gently until crisp-tender, about 8 minutes for medium
  spears. Cooking time varies with the thickness of the stalks. Drain and
  serve immediately with butter, lemon juice, salt and pepper, and, if
  desired, grated Parmesan cheese.

- ✔ **Brussels sprouts:** With a sharp paring knife (see Chapter 4), trim the
  tough outer leaves and trim a very thin slice off the stem end. Then cut
  an X in the stem end to ensure even cooking of the stem and leaves.
  Cook them in a covered saucepan with about 1 inch of water for 8 to 10
  minutes or until crisp-tender. Test for doneness by tasting. Drain and
  serve with about ¼ cup melted butter mixed with the juice of ½ fresh
  lemon and a dash of salt.

To steam Brussels sprouts, place trimmed sprouts in a steaming basket over about 1 inch of boiling water. Cover the pot and steam for about 8 minutes, depending on size.

✔ **Cabbage:** Cut the head into quarters and cut out the hard core. Add the quarters to a large pot of lightly salted boiling water, cover, and boil gently for about 12 minutes. Cabbage should remain somewhat crisp.

To steam, place the quarters in a large deep skillet or saucepan with about ½ inch of water and cook, covered, over low heat until crisp-tender. Cabbage is also quite delicious when braised. (See Chapter 18 for a recipe for Braised Cabbage with Apple and Caraway.) Or, cook it in your slow cooker with a splash of chicken broth and some diced ham.

✔ **Carrots or parsnips:** Trim off the ends and peel with a vegetable peeler. Place them sliced into a pot with lightly salted water just to cover. Cover the pot and boil gently for about 12 to 15 minutes for sliced carrots, or about 20 minutes for whole ones. Or place in a steaming basket and steam in a covered pot over about 1 inch of boiling water. Sliced carrots or parsnips steam in 5 minutes; whole and large, 2- to 3-inch pieces need about 12 minutes. Serve with butter sauce flavored with lemon juice and grated lemon or orange zest, or a sauce of melted butter and minced fresh dill.

✔ **Cauliflower:** First, cut a whole head into *florets* using your chef's knife: Cut the whole head in half, and then separate the head into individual buds, or small clusters, keeping a little of their stems. Boil gently in enough lightly salted water to cover for about 8 to 10 minutes, or until crisp-tender. Adding the juice of half a lemon to the cooking water helps to retain cauliflower's whiteness.

To steam, place florets in a steaming basket over about 1 inch of boiling water. Cover pot and steam for about 5 minutes or until desired doneness. Toss in a sauce of melted butter, lemon juice, and chopped fresh parsley.

✔ **Corn:** Don't husk or remove the ears from the refrigerator until you're ready to boil them. (The sugar in corn rapidly turns to starch at room temperature. To retain sweetness, keep ears cold and cook the same day of purchase.) Heat a large pot filled with enough water just to cover the corn, add the husked corn, cover the pot, and boil for about 5 minutes. Remove with tongs and serve immediately with butter.

✔ **Green beans:** Trim by snapping off the stem ends. Add the beans to lightly salted boiling water to cover and cook for 8 to 10 minutes, or until crisp-tender. They should retain their bright green color.

To steam, place steaming basket over about 1 inch of boiling water. Add beans, cover the pot tightly, and check for doneness after 5 minutes. Serve hot beans with a simple butter sauce or toss in a vinaigrette dressing and chill before serving.

- ✔ **Pearl onions:** Peel and boil in a covered pot with lightly salted water to just cover for about 15 minutes or until tender but still firm. Don't overcook, or they'll fall apart. Serve smothered in a sauce or gravy, or mixed with other vegetables.

- ✔ **Snow peas:** Rinse the peas, snap off the stem ends, and lift the string across the top to remove it. Place in boiling water to cover and cook for 2 minutes. Drain in a colander and run cold water over them to stop the cooking and retain their green color.

- ✔ **Sweet potatoes or yams:** Scrub and peel the potatoes using a vegetable peeler, trim the tapered ends, and cut out any bruised spots. (Cut very large sweet potatoes in half crosswise, or quarter them.) Place in a large pot, add cold water to cover the potatoes, cover the pot, and simmer for about 35 to 40 minutes for whole potatoes or 20 to 25 minutes for halved or quartered potatoes. Potatoes are done when you can pierce them easily with a fork. Don't overcook, or they'll fall apart in the water. Drain and cool slightly before peeling. Mash or serve in large chunks with butter, salt, pepper, and ground ginger or nutmeg to taste, if desired.

- ✔ **Yellow squash and zucchini:** Scrub clean and trim the ends. Slice into ½-inch-thick rounds. Place in a steaming basket over about 1 inch of boiling water and steam in a covered pot for about 4 minutes or just until crisp-tender. These tender vegetables are also delicious sautéed.

Fresh vegetables have more flavor and retain their nutrients better if you cook them only until *crisp-tender,* or firm to the bite. The B vitamins and vitamin C are water soluble and leach into the cooking water as the vegetables cook, so save the vitamin-packed cooking liquid to add to other dishes you're cooking, such as soups and stews.

Making vegetable purées

Vegetable *purées* are simply cooked vegetables (usually boiled or steamed but sometimes roasted) that are mashed, blended, or processed to a thick consistency. Starchy root vegetables like potatoes, sweet potatoes, rutabagas, parsnips, and carrots generally make the best purées, but broccoli, cauliflower, and roasted red peppers are also wonderful, especially when mixed with a dense root vegetable.

Thick purees make a great side dish. When thinned with water, broth, or sauce, they make delicious toppings for meat, potatoes, pasta, or rice.

To make a purée, put any soft-cooked vegetable or combination of vegetables in a blender or food processor with a bit of water or broth, and purée it. Serve it warm (you can reheat the purée in a saucepan over low heat if it's cooled off too much). Or, use an immersion blender and purée the vegetables right in the pan where you steamed or boiled them. Season with salt and pepper and your favorite herbs or spices, or in the case of sweet potatoes or winter squash, a bit of honey, maple syrup, or cinnamon. Mmm, comfort food!

Poaching Seafood

Poaching seafood is a fabulous way to preserve its flavor and texture, especially with firm-textured fish like salmon, tuna, halibut, cod, and swordfish. The only drawback is that it takes on no flavors while cooking, as it does when seasoned and sautéed. Therefore, poached seafood usually calls for a sauce of some sort (see Chapter 14). But if you poach seafood in seasoned vegetable broth, fish broth, or water with a splash of clam juice, it will take on a subtle, herby flavor.

You have to watch the clock to prevent overcooking and keep the poaching liquid to a gentle simmer. Vigorous boiling breaks up the fish's tender flesh.

Later in the chapter, we show you how to make Poached Salmon Steaks in Béarnaise Sauce. Sound too fancy to be easy? It's not — we promise.

Is that fish done or just resting?

One traditional guideline for cooking fish is the so-called Canadian Fish Rule: Measure the whole fish steak or fillet at its thickest point and cook it (whether you're boiling, steaming, baking, broiling, or poaching) for 10 minutes per inch. Personally, we've found that 8 to 9 minutes per inch works a little bit better, so we recommend that after about 8 minutes, you check for doneness. Using this guideline, if the thickest part of the fish is ¾ inch thick, you cook it for 6 to 7 minutes.

Whole fish is easiest to check. If the dorsal fin comes out easily, it's done; if not, it needs more cooking. However, as a beginning cook, you probably won't be cooking a whole fish just

yet. A fish fillet or steak is done when it flakes easily with a fork. Scallops turn opaque when done, and shrimp, which takes only a couple of minutes to cook, turns pink. Salmon and tuna are darkish pink at the center when medium. White fish should be glistening and wet looking only at the innermost core. Unless the recipe instructs you to do otherwise, remove all cooked fish from the heat or the poaching liquid immediately.

Mussels, clams, and oysters give you a clear indication that they're cooked: Their shells open when they're done, no matter how you cook them.

Easy Egg Salad

Prep time: 5 min • **Cook time:** About 15 min • **Yield:** 2 servings

Ingredients	Directions
4 eggs	*1* Hard-cook the eggs, cool them, and peel them.
2 tablespoons mayonnaise (or more to taste)	*2* Mash the eggs in a medium mixing bowl with a fork.
Salt and pepper	*3* Add the mayonnaise and season to taste with salt and pepper. Cover and refrigerate until ready to use.

Per serving: Calories 254 (From Fat 194); Fat 22g (Saturated 5g); Cholesterol 432mg; Sodium 493mg; Carbohydrate 2g (Dietary Fiber 0g); Protein 13g.

Vary It! Try adding flavored mustard, chopped pickles, minced onion, diced celery, fresh or dried herbs (such as parsley, dill, or tarragon), sweet relish, or Tabasco sauce.

Homemade Mashed Potatoes

Prep time: About 15 min • **Cook time:** About 20 min • **Yield:** 4 servings

Ingredients	Directions
4 large Idaho potatoes, about 2 pounds total	**1** Peel the potatoes and cut them into quarters.
½ teaspoon salt	**2** Place them in a medium saucepan with cold water to barely cover and add the salt.
½ cup milk	
3 tablespoons butter	**3** Cover and bring to a boil over high heat. Reduce heat to medium and cook, covered, for about 15 minutes or until you can easily pierce the potatoes with a fork.
Salt and black pepper	
	4 Drain the potatoes in a colander and then return them to the saucepan. Shake the potatoes in the pan over low heat for 10 to 15 seconds to evaporate excess moisture, if necessary.
	5 Remove the pan from the heat. Mash the potatoes a few times with a potato masher, ricer, or fork.
	6 Add the milk, butter, and salt and pepper to taste and mash again until smooth and creamy.

Per serving: Calories 263 (From Fat 88); Fat 10g (Saturated 6g); Cholesterol 27mg; Sodium 315mg; Carbohydrate 41g (Dietary Fiber 4g); Protein 5g.

Tip: Mashed potatoes are best when mashed by hand with a potato masher or fork, or when pressed through a ricer (a round, metal device with small holes through which foods are pressed). Blenders and food processors can leave them pasty.

Go-With: Try these potatoes with Roasted Fillet of Beef or Smoked Ham with Apricot Glaze (both in Chapter 8), and don't forget to serve them with the Thanksgiving turkey!

Vary It! For garlic mashed potatoes, wrap a whole, medium head of garlic in aluminum foil and roast it in a 350-degree oven for 1 hour. Remove the foil, allow the garlic to cool slightly, and then press the soft cloves to release the pulp. Mash the pulp into the potatoes with the butter and milk; then season with salt and pepper to taste. You can mash other cooked vegetables, such as broccoli, carrots, turnips, or sweet potatoes, and blend them into the potato mix.

Steamed Broccoli with Lemon Butter

Prep time: About 15 min • **Cook time:** About 10 min • **Yield:** 4 servings

Ingredients	Directions
1 head broccoli Salt and black pepper 3 tablespoons butter Juice of ½ lemon	**1** Wash the broccoli thoroughly. Trim off only the thickest part of the stems and the large leaves. Divide the larger florets by slicing through the base of the flower and straight down through the length of the stem. **2** Place the broccoli in a 3- or 4-quart saucepan holding about 2 inches of water. (The stalks should stand on the bottom with the florets facing up.) Add salt and pepper to taste and cover the pan. **3** Bring to a boil over high heat and then reduce the heat to low and simmer, covered, for about 8 minutes or until the stalks are tender but not soft. **4** While the broccoli steams, melt the butter in a small saucepan and add the lemon juice. Stir to blend. **5** Using tongs, carefully remove the broccoli to a serving dish. Pour the lemon-butter sauce over the broccoli and serve.

Per serving: Calories 109 (From Fat 80); Fat 9g (Saturated 5g); Cholesterol 23mg; Sodium 176mg; Carbohydrate 6g (Dietary Fiber 3g); Protein 4g.

Tip: Trim and cut the vegetables into equal-sized pieces so that they cook evenly.

Vary It! You can substitute vegetables like cauliflower and asparagus for the broccoli in this recipe.

Go-With: Fresh broccoli adds color and flavor to innumerable meals, including Roasted Fillet of Beef and Glazed Leg of Lamb with Pan Gravy and Red Currant Glaze (both in Chapter 8).

Poached Salmon Steaks with Béarnaise Sauce

Prep time: About 25 min • **Cook time:** About 10 min • **Yield:** 4 servings

Ingredients	Directions
1½ quarts (6 cups) vegetable broth or water	**1** Bring the vegetable broth or water to a boil over high heat in a large skillet. Submerge the salmon steaks or fillets in the boiling liquid. Add more water if there is not enough stock to just cover the steaks.
4 salmon steaks or fillets, about 6 ounces each, with skin	
Water (if necessary)	**2** Return to a boil; then lower the heat to a simmer and cook, uncovered, for about 5 minutes.
Béarnaise sauce (see Chapter 14 for a recipe)	**3** Turn off the heat and let the steaks stand in the poaching liquid about 3 to 5 minutes. Cut into the center delicately to check for doneness.
	4 Remove the poached steaks to a platter. Drizzle some béarnaise sauce over each salmon steak and serve immediately.

Per serving: Calories 340 (From Fat 177); Fat 20g (Saturated 9g); Cholesterol 207mg; Sodium 201mg; Carbohydrate 0g (Dietary Fiber 0g); Protein 38g.

Chapter 6

Sautéing

Sautéing, also referred to as *pan frying,* is generally associated with French cuisine. But in fact, many other nationalities sauté routinely to sear steaks, cook fillets of fish, glaze vegetables, and quick-cook shellfish.

Sautéing is nothing more than cooking food in a hot pan, usually with a little fat (butter or oil, for example) to prevent sticking. Sautéing imparts a crispy texture to foods and brings out all sorts of flavors from herbs and spices.

If you drop a steak onto a roaring-hot pan (maybe with a little oil to prevent sticking), it develops a dark crust in a few minutes. This effect is desirable because it intensifies any seasonings on the surface of the meat and gives it a pleasant crunchy texture. (Contrary to popular belief, sautéing has nothing to do with locking in meat juices. Cookbooks say this all the time, but it's not the case.) Seafood and vegetables glazed with butter benefit from sautéing in the same way; sautéing gives them texture and flavor.

The French word *sauté* translates literally as "to jump." Chefs shake the sauté pan back and forth over the heat, tossing the food to expose it evenly to the heat. You can actually practice this technique in a cold skillet with small candies! (Just do it when no one's watching.)

Because sautéing is done at high or medium-high heat, you have to be careful to keep your eye on the ball because food can burn in two seconds flat.

In this chapter, we discuss sautéing and provide some helpful tips and delicious recipes. Also be sure to visit www.dummies.com/go/sauteing.

Knowing When to Use Oil or Butter

When you sauté something, even in a nonstick pan, you need to use some kind of fat. But which one — butter or oil? Each is best suited for different kinds of sautéing:

✔ When cooking over very high heat, use oil, which is less likely to burn.

✔ When sautéing with medium-high heat, you may opt for butter, which adds a nice flavor. However, the milk solids in the butter can burn, or brown, affecting the color and taste of your food.

Typically, meats are sautéed in oil because they need a higher heat, while vegetables are sautéed in butter to impart a pleasant buttery flavor. Seafood may be sautéed in either one. Many chefs opt to use half butter and half oil when sautéing seafood: They get the benefit of the buttery flavor, but the added oil helps to keep the butter from burning as easily.

If you decide to use oil in your sautéing, it's helpful to know that some oils have a higher *smoke point* than others, which means they start to smoke at a hotter temperature (and so are preferable for sautéing). Good oils for sautéing include canola, corn, and peanut oil. If the recipe doesn't specify what type of oil to use, go with one of these three neutral-flavored oils.

Just like the professionals do, you can prevent butter from burning in a sauté pan by adding a few drops of vegetable oil or any neutral-tasting oil.

Oil alone should be hot but not smoking in the pan before you add food. Butter alone should foam at its edges but not brown. Some chefs insist on using only *clarified butter* when sautéing because it won't burn as quickly but retains the buttery flavor. (Clarified butter, called *ghee* in Indian cuisine, has been heated to separate out the milk solids, which are skimmed off, making it more like cooking oil with a higher smoke point.) Clarified butter is easy to make and lasts several months or more in the refrigerator. Here's how to make it:

1. **Put one pound of unsalted butter in a saucepan over medium heat.** Do not stir. Allow the butter to melt. It will begin to foam. Let it continue to cook and foam *without stirring* until the foaming stops. The milk solids will fall to the bottom of the pan and turn golden brown.

2. **When the butter begins to smell nutty and turns deeper gold (after about 20 minutes), remove it from the heat.** Let it cool for 20 to 30 minutes.

3. **Pour the butter through a fine mesh strainer lined with cheesecloth into a glass container, and cover.** Discard the solids.

Clarified butter will keep for one year, in or out of the refrigerator.

Making Great Sauce from Bits in the Pan: Deglazing

A very hot sauté pan begins to cook meat, poultry, or fish right away, browning the juices that flow from it and leaving bits of food sticking to the bottom of the pan. These browned bits are loaded with flavor. If *deglazed* (moistened and scraped up) in the pan, they become transformed into a delicious sauce.

Just follow these easy steps, illustrated in Figure 6-1, if you want to deglaze:

Deglazing a Pan

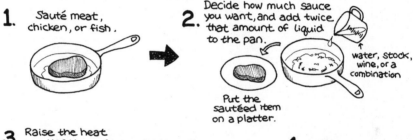

1. Sauté meat, chicken, or fish.

2. Decide how much sauce you want, and add twice that amount of liquid to the pan.
   water, stock, wine, or a combination
   Put the sautéed item on a platter.

3. Raise the heat to HIGH, scrape off all of the brown particles clinging to the bottom of the pan, and boil until sauce is reduced by half.

4. Spoon the sauce over the meat or fish.

Figure 6-1: Deglazing a pan enables you to intensify the flavor of your sauce.

Mise en place

The French term *mise en place* (meeze-on-plahs) translates as "everything in place" and means to have on hand all the ingredients that you need to prepare a dish. For example, onions and herbs are chopped, garlic is minced, vegetables are rinsed, ingredients are measured, and so on, all ahead of time. This preparation allows you to cook efficiently and without interruption, the way real restaurant chefs do it. Practice mise en place by having all your prep work completed right up to the point of cooking.

1. **Remove the meat, poultry, or fish from the pan onto a serving platter and immediately add liquid — you can use water, wine, stock, or a combination.**

   The liquid should be twice the amount of sauce you want to make. For example, if you want to make 1 cup of sauce, add 2 cups of wine.

   As a rule, the wine you use for deglazing depends on what you're sautéing: Use white wine for poultry and seafood, and red wine for meat.

2. **Raise the heat to high, bringing the liquid to a boil while you stir and scrape the browned bits off the bottom of the pan until they dissolve into the sauce.**

   This stirring and scraping is the key to deglazing — all those delicious little caramelized bits of cooked meat infuse the liquid, making it taste fantastic.

3. **Keep boiling and stirring until the sauce is reduced by half the volume or, in other words, until those 2 cups of wine (or water or broth) have boiled down to about 1 cup.**

   How can you tell? Just eyeball it. When it looks like you have half as much liquid as you did, it's time to take a taste.

And the verdict? Does your sauce taste delicious, or does it need more salt and/or pepper? Maybe a dash of fresh herbs? Add more seasoning if you think the sauce needs more flavor. You might also stir in a teaspoon or more of butter just before you drizzle it over your main course — this adds a smooth texture.

Getting Versatile with Your Sautéing

You can sauté just about any meat, fish, or vegetable, so experiment and enjoy some delicious meals. Later in the chapter, we offer several recipes for sautéed veggies, fish, chicken, and beef. Here, we offer just a quick overview of how to sauté each.

Vegetables

Vegetables are excellent when boiled or steamed until about 90 percent done and then transferred to a skillet to be finished in butter and maybe fresh herbs. Many classic recipes for potatoes call for sautéing; thinly sliced raw potatoes are delicious when cooked this way. In the Sautéed Skillet Potatoes recipe later in the chapter (and featured in this book's color section), you cut the potatoes into fine cubes and toss them in a hot pan until crispy.

Our Red Pepper Puree recipe later in the chapter (shown in the color section as well) also has you sautéing vegetables, but this time, you take an extra step after they've been cooked in the pan. As we note in Chapter 5, vegetable purees make wonderful side dishes or toppings for meat, poultry, or fish. After you've sautéed the red peppers, onions, and garlic called for in this recipe, you simply toss them in a blender with a few additional ingredients, let the blender work its magic, and enjoy a beautiful and tasty puree. To make this recipe, you first need to know how to seed and core a red pepper; Figure 6-2 can help.

How to Core and Seed a Pepper

Figure 6-2:
Removing
the seeds
and core
from a
pepper.

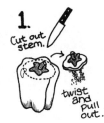

1. Cut out stem. twist and pull out.

2. Cut in ½... ...and remove membranes.

3. Cut into lengthwise strips.

4. For cubes, hold strips together and cut crosswise.

Be very careful when you put rinsed vegetables (or other foods) into a pan of hot fat. The water that clings to the vegetables makes the fat splatter, which can cause serious burns. Always dry vegetables before sautéing.

Firm, rich fish

Rich fish — those with a high fat content, such as salmon, tuna, and bluefish — are exceptionally good when sautéed. And you can enhance them with countless sauces that you can make in 15 minutes or less (see Chapter 14). Because these fish have relatively high fat contents, they also stand up to spicy sauces. The recipe for Tuna Steaks with Ginger-Chili Glaze later in the chapter (and shown in the color section) is a perfect example.

Keep in mind that a spicy sauce paired with a delicate fish, like sole or snapper, can be a flop. In general, firm-fleshed fish (or fatty fish) stands up best to spiciness.

Chicken and turkey

Sautéing is a great way to impart flavor to poultry. It stays juicy with a flavorful outside, especially with the addition of different herbs and spices. Sautéing is particularly good with the chicken or turkey's skin left on. You can also make a delicious sauce with the leftover oil (or butter) and herbs in the pan by adding wine, juice, or chicken broth to the pan after cooking the poultry and reducing the liquid to concentrate the flavor. Want to try some wonderful recipes to see what we mean? Check out the Sautéed Chicken Breasts with Tomatoes and Thyme later in the chapter (which is also featured in the book's color section), as well as the Lemon-Rubbed Chicken with Rosemary.

Beef

Beef is excellent for sautéing. Try the terrific Steak au Poivre recipe later in the chapter if you want proof! It's our version of one of the most popular beef dishes in restaurants in which beef is coated liberally with cracked black pepper before it's cooked in a hot pan. (You don't know how to make cracked black pepper? No problem! Check out Figure 6-3. Here's a tip: To prevent peppercorns from flying all over the place when you crush them, wrap them first in aluminum foil. And be sure to crush them shortly before cooking to get the most potency from the pepper.)

How to Crush Peppercorns

Figure 6-3:
Crushing pepper-corns with a heavy pan.

1. Gather whole peppercorns in the middle of a cutting board.

2. Use the heel of your hand to press the bottom edge of a pan.

3. Repeat steps 1 & 2 until peppercorns are crushed to desired size.

The doneness of steaks is defined by the meat's interior color. Rare meat is bright red and juicy. Medium meat has a light pink center with light brown edges. Well-done, which we don't recommend, is brown-gray and dry throughout.

Sautéed Skillet Potatoes

Prep time: About 15 min • **Cook time:** About 20 min • **Yield:** 4 servings

Ingredients	Directions
2 large baking potatoes, about 1½ pounds total	*1* Cut any eyes and bad spots out of the potatoes. Scrub them with a vegetable brush to remove dirt, but leave them unpeeled. Cut each into cubes of about ¼ inch.
¼ cup canola or corn oil	
2 tablespoons butter	*2* Place the cubes in a colander in the sink. Run very hot water over the potatoes for about 10 seconds to remove the starch. Drain well and dry on paper towels.
1 medium yellow onion, peeled and chopped	
½ green bell pepper, cored, seeded, and chopped	*3* Heat the oil in a large nonstick skillet over high heat. Add the potatoes and cook, stirring often, for about 10 minutes.
½ teaspoon dried oregano	
½ teaspoon or less of salt	*4* With a slotted spoon, remove the potatoes from the pan to a large bowl. Remove the oil from the skillet, and wipe the skillet with paper towels.
Few dashes black pepper	
⅛ teaspoon cayenne pepper or red pepper flakes (optional)	*5* Melt the butter in the skillet over medium-high heat.
	6 Sauté the onion, bell pepper, oregano, salt, black pepper, and cayenne pepper, if desired. Cook, stirring occasionally, for 4 to 5 minutes until the vegetables begin to get soft.
	7 Add the potatoes back into the skillet and sauté everything together until the potatoes are browned and crisp, about 5 more minutes. Serve immediately.

Per serving: *Calories 325 (From Fat 180); Fat 20g (Saturated 5g); Cholesterol 15mg; Sodium 307mg; Carbohydrate 35g (Dietary Fiber 4g); Protein 4g.*

Go-With: These potatoes are a delicious side dish to omelets (see Chapter 11), Roasted Fillet of Beef (see Chapter 8), or Roasted Loin of Pork (see Chapter 8).

Red Pepper Purée

Prep time: 10 min • **Cook time:** About 20 min • **Yield:** 6 servings

Ingredients	Directions
1 tablespoon olive oil	**1** Heat the olive oil in a skillet over medium-high heat until you begin to smell the oil, about 3 minutes.
3 medium red bell peppers, cored, seeded, and chopped	
¼ cup chopped red onion	**2** Add the peppers, onion, and garlic. Sauté until they are soft but not browned, about 15 minutes.
2 garlic cloves, peeled and minced or put through a garlic press	
1 teaspoon paprika	**3** Put the vegetables in a food processor with the paprika, cilantro, and lemon juice. Process until smooth, about 15 seconds.
1 tablespoon fresh chopped or 1 teaspoon dried cilantro	
Juice of ½ lemon	**4** Stir in the salt and pepper, and serve warm.
½ teaspoon salt	
Few dashes black pepper	

Per serving: Calories 42 (From Fat 22); Fat 2g (Saturated 0g); Cholesterol 0mg; Sodium 196mg; Carbohydrate 5g (Dietary Fiber 1g); Protein 1g.

Tip: If you make this dish in advance, you can warm it up for about 15 to 30 seconds in the microwave or for about 5 minutes in a saucepan over low heat on the stove.

Vary It! Try mixing this purée with a little cream or half-and-half and serve over pasta.

Go-With: This purée brightens up any mild meat or fish, or try it on baked potatoes or steamed asparagus.

Tuna Steaks with Ginger-Chili Glaze

Prep time: About 15 min • **Cook time:** About 15 min • **Yield:** 4 servings

Ingredients	Directions
4 tuna steaks, each about 6 to 7 ounces and ¾ inch thick **Few dashes of salt and pepper for each steak** **2 tablespoons butter** **1 cup white wine or white grape juice** **1 tablespoon red chili paste** **½ teaspoon dried ground ginger** **1 tablespoon brown sugar** **1 tablespoon dark sesame oil**	*1* Season both sides of the tuna steaks with salt and pepper. Melt the butter over medium-high heat in a nonstick skillet or sauté pan large enough to hold the steaks in one layer. *2* Add the tuna to the pan and cook until lightly browned on both sides, about 3 minutes per side. *3* Transfer the steaks to a warm platter and cover with foil. Leave the cooking butter in the skillet and scrape the bottom of the pan with a wooden spoon to loosen the browned bits clinging to the pan. *4* Add the wine or grape juice, turn up the heat to high, and cook until about half the liquid in the pan evaporates (less than a minute). *5* Lower the heat to medium. Add the chili paste, ginger, brown sugar, and sesame oil. Stir continuously until the ingredients are well combined. *6* Add the tuna steaks (and any of their juices on the platter) back into the pan, and bring to a simmer. Cook for about 1 minute or until warmed through, turning once to coat the steaks in the glaze. Do not overcook. *7* Using a flat metal spatula, remove each tuna steak to an individual plate. Spoon a little of the sauce over each serving and serve immediately.

Per serving: Calories 274 (From Fat 96); Fat 11g (Saturated 4g); Cholesterol 89mg; Sodium 305mg; Carbohydrate 4g (Dietary Fiber 0g); Protein 38g.

Tip: If you don't have a pan big enough to cook all the tuna steaks at once, use a smaller skillet and cook the tuna in batches. If you do so, be sure to save enough sauce for all the steaks.

Tip: Find red chili paste with the Asian food ingredients in your grocery store.

Sautéed Chicken Breasts with Tomatoes and Thyme

Prep time: About 20 min • **Cook time:** About 15 min • **Yield:** 4 servings

Ingredients	Directions
4 boneless, skinless chicken breast halves	**1** Place the chicken breasts on a cutting board, season generously on both sides with salt and pepper, cover with waxed paper, and pound them lightly so that they're of equal thickness. (Use the bottom of a heavy pan or a meat mallet.)
Salt and pepper	
2 tablespoons olive oil	
1 medium yellow onion, chopped	**2** Heat the olive oil in a large sauté pan or skillet over medium-high heat. Add the chicken and sauté for about 4 to 5 minutes per side or until done. Remove the pieces to a platter and cover with foil to keep warm.
1 large clove garlic, chopped	
2 medium tomatoes, peeled, seeded, and chopped	**3** Add the onion to the pan over medium heat. Stir for 1 minute, scraping the bottom of the pan. Add the garlic, stirring occasionally for another minute. Add the tomatoes, thyme, basil (if desired), and salt and pepper to taste. Stir for 1 minute.
1 teaspoon chopped fresh thyme, or ¼ teaspoon dried	
2 tablespoons chopped fresh or 2 teaspoons dried basil (optional)	**4** Add the wine or stock, increase the heat to high, and cook, stirring occasionally, for about 2 to 3 minutes until most of the liquid evaporates. (You want moist, not soupy.)
⅓ cup white wine or chicken stock	
	5 Place the chicken on four plates. Spoon equal portions of sauce over each piece.

Per serving: Calories 170 (From Fat 47); Fat 5g (Saturated 1g); Cholesterol 63mg; Sodium 203mg; Carbohydrate 6g (Dietary Fiber 1g); Protein 24g.

Vary It! You can modify this recipe in many ways. For example, use turkey breasts or slices of veal instead of chicken; add 1 cup fresh, frozen, or canned corn kernels with the chopped tomatoes; add 2 tablespoons heavy cream with the stock or wine; substitute tarragon, marjoram, or other herb of choice for the thyme; or grate some Parmesan cheese over the top of each serving.

Lemon-Rubbed Chicken with Rosemary

Prep time: 10 min • **Cook time:** 35–40 min • **Yield:** 4 servings

Ingredients	*Directions*
4 whole chicken legs, with drumsticks, trimmed of excess fat (about 1½ to 2 pounds)	*1* Rinse the chicken and pat dry with paper towels. With a large knife, separate the drumsticks from the thighs.
2 lemons, quartered **1½ tablespoons minced fresh rosemary leaves (or 3 teaspoons dried)**	*2* Rub the chicken pieces with four of the lemon wedges. Squeeze juice from those wedges over the pieces. Season with salt, pepper, and 1 tablespoon of the fresh rosemary (or 2 teaspoons dried rosemary).
2 tablespoons olive oil **2 cloves garlic, coarsely chopped**	*3* In a 10-inch fry pan over medium-high heat, cook the chicken pieces , skin side down, until golden brown, 7 to 10 minutes. Flip the chicken pieces and squeeze remaining lemon juice over them.
5 tablespoons chicken broth or water	*4* Reduce to medium-low heat and cook, covered, for 25 to 30 minutes or until the meat in the center along the bone is no longer pink. Transfer to serving plates.
	5 Return the skillet to medium-high heat. Add garlic and remaining rosemary. Cook for 45 seconds to a minute (the garlic should be barely golden — do not let it burn).
	6 Add the chicken broth or water. Scrape the dark bits clinging to the bottom of the pan and cook about 45 seconds, stirring. Drizzle over the chicken.

Per serving: Calories 551 (From Fat 339); Fat 38g (Saturated 9g); Cholesterol 161mg; Sodium 313mg; Carbohydrate 6g (Dietary Fiber 1g); Protein 46g.

Tip: To separate drumsticks from thighs, place the chicken pieces on a cutting board, fat side down; use your finger to locate the joint between the thigh and the drumstick and cut through.

Steak au Poivre

Prep time: About 5 min • **Cook time:** 10–15 min • **Yield:** 4 servings

Ingredients	Directions
4 tablespoons black peppercorns	*1* Crush peppercorns with a mortar and pestle, with a pepper grinder on very coarse setting, or with the bottom of a heavy skillet on a very hard surface.
2 trimmed boneless strip steaks, each about 1½ inches thick; about 1½ pounds total	*2* Lay the steaks over the peppercorns to coat on all sides. Pat in the pepper with your hand.
4 tablespoons minced shallots or white onions	*3* Lightly oil a heavy skillet (cast iron is best) and heat to nearly smoking. Lay the steaks in the pan and quickly sear both sides (1 minute per side).
4 tablespoons butter	
2 tablespoons brandy (optional)	*4* Reduce heat to medium high and cook for 5 to 7 minutes per side for medium rare. (Check doneness by making a small cut in the thickest part of the meat with a paring knife.) Transfer the steaks to a dish.
¾ cup dry red wine	
¼ cup fresh or canned beef stock	
1 teaspoon tomato paste	*5* Over medium heat add the shallots or onions and 1 tablespoon of butter. Cook for a minute and add the brandy (if desired) and red wine.
	6 Scrape the bottom of the pan with a wooden spoon to remove bits of meat clinging to the pan. Reduce liquid to half its volume.
	7 Add the stock and tomato paste, stirring. Reduce the liquid by roughly one-third.
	8 Add remaining butter and stir constantly until it melts. Season to taste. Serve immediately over the steaks.

Per serving: Calories 469 (From Fat 315); Fat 35g (Saturated 16g); Cholesterol 124mg; Sodium 145mg; Carbohydrate 6g (Dietary Fiber 2g); Protein 31g.

Tip: Four tablespoons of peppercorns make for a wonderfully hot and spicy sauce, but if you prefer a milder sauce, use only 2 to 3 tablespoons.

Go-With: Serve this dish with a side of Homemade Mashed Potatoes (see Chapter 5).

Chapter 7

Braising and Stewing: Slow and Seductive

*I*f you're like most people, you have precious little time, especially during the week, to stand at the stove or even the microwave. This chapter is for you. Braising and stewing are slow cooking methods that allow you to put all the ingredients in a pot, turn the heat to low, and do something else for an hour or two — maybe read last week's newspaper or shampoo the dog.

Braised and stewed foods have exceptional depth of flavor. Slow cooking allows seasonings to infuse the main ingredients, and it breaks down sinewy fibers. Also, over time vegetables release their natural sugars. The result? Sublime simplicity, or (to use an overworked cliché) comfort food.

Because braising and stewing take time, these dishes are best made in big batches so you can freeze individual portions. And, unquestionably, they are better the next day. We should point out that inexpensive braised and stewed dishes make great party vittles with a few condiments on the side (like beer).

Most meat dishes in this chapter use the less expensive front cuts of beef: the chuck, brisket, shank, and plate. (See Chapter 3 for an illustration of the various cuts of beef.) These more muscular cuts don't make much of a steak, but when you braise them for hours, their fibers break down and they become succulent. In some ways, these cuts are more flavorful than expensive tenderloin.

Slow cookers also use the concepts of braising and stewing, but they do it automatically. We talk about slow cooking in Chapter 16, and if you want even more information, check out *Slow Cookers For Dummies,* by Tom Lacalamita and Glenna Vance (Wiley).

Cooking in Liquid

Both braising and stewing involve long, slow cooking in liquid. The major difference is that in *braising,* foods lie in a few inches of liquid, not quite submerged, so that they stew and steam at the same time. *Stewing* involves submerging ingredients in a liquid and simmering the mixture for a long time.

Braising involves larger cuts of meat, whereas cut-up meat is stewed. For example, you braise a pot roast but stew cubed beef. Both methods make meat very, very tender.

Here, we further define braising versus stewing.

Browning before braising

Larger cuts of meat — and the very toughest — tend to be braised. The meat is usually browned in hot oil first, to give it a toothsome texture and appealing color. You can braise a beef roast, a pork roast, or any other large piece of meat, including a whole chicken, by browning it on all sides in hot oil to color it and add flavor, and then cooking it in a liquid.

Braising is so easy to do that you may as well jump right in and try it. Later in the chapter, we show you how to make delicious Beer-Braised Beef with Onions. One of the easiest and most basic things to braise is a good old classic pot roast, so we also offer a great recipe for Pot Roast with Vegetables. When you're shopping, keep in mind that the best cut of beef for a pot roast is the *first-cut* brisket. Sometimes referred to as the *flat cut,* the first-cut brisket has just the right amount of fat so it's not too dry after it's cooked. Ask your butcher for the first cut.

Taking time to stew

Dollar for dollar, meat goes a long way when you stew it. For instance, few dishes are more economical than beef stew, yet who would know it from the taste? More expensive ingredients such as seafood can make a stew seem luxurious, but you don't need nearly as much shrimp, crab, or fish per person as you would if you were serving these dishes on their own. You can also use cut-up boneless chicken or turkey breasts, cubed pork, or sliced sausage.

Lean, boneless chuck is one of the least expensive cuts of beef, and we show you a great way to prepare it with the Old-Fashioned Beef Stew recipe later in the chapter. The root vegetables (carrots and turnips) that surround it are also economical — and healthful. Other good cuts to ask for when stewing are the neck, brisket, and shank.

Where does a fricassee fit in?

A *fricassee* is a variation on stew. A traditional fricassee is made with poultry, usually chicken. Moreover, the poultry in a fricassee is not seared and browned first, as in a stew. The lack of browning makes the sauce paler than that of a stew, with a slightly milder flavor.

Keep in mind that many stew recipes — including the Old-Fashioned Beef Stew in this chapter — yield a hearty number of servings. For example, the recipe in this chapter serves 8, making it a perfect do-ahead meal for a small party. To reduce the yield to serve 4, simply use half the ingredients. But remember, stews are always better the next day after the seasonings have a chance to permeate the meat. If you make too much, you'll have delicious leftovers. And you also can store meat stews in the freezer in tightly covered containers for up to six months.

If beef isn't your thing, and you're wondering whether stew has any place on your menu at all, be sure to check out the Mediterranean Seafood Stew recipe later in the chapter (and shown in the book's color section). It just may change how you think about stew forever! Before you make it, you'll need to know how devein shrimp; Figure 7-1 shows you the easy steps to take using a tool called a *deveiner*.

Cleaning and Deveining Shrimp

1.

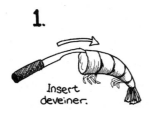

Insert deveiner.

2.

Push toward the tail.

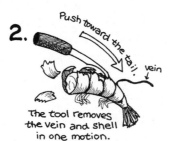

vein

The tool removes the vein and shell in one motion.

3.

Clean under cold water.

Figure 7-1: How to clean and devein shrimp.

Keeping Herbs and Spices in Check

Many braising and stewing recipes call for a blending of herbs and spices. Because the rainbow of herbs and spices available to home cooks is so exciting (see Chapter 3), you may be tempted to overdo it. The best way to get to know herbs and spices is to cook dishes that contain only one herb or spice — see how it interacts with different foods, watch how it intensifies with cooking, and find out whether you really like it.

For example, with rosemary, you can make a quick sauce for sautéed or grilled chicken breast by combining 3 parts chicken stock to 1 part white wine in a saucepan. Then add a teaspoon of minced fresh rosemary (or ½ teaspoon dry), some very thin slices of garlic, and salt and black pepper to taste. Cook down the liquid until it's reduced by three-quarters. Then strain the sauce and serve it over the chicken. This dish gives you a pure rosemary flavor. If you like it, you can refine it by adding more or less rosemary or even by adding a complementary herb, such as thyme, tarragon, or chives.

Here's a tip for recipes that call for using fresh herb sprigs: Tie them together with a little kitchen twine. Doing so makes removing the herb sprigs easier, and you get the benefit of the flavor without any stringy herb stems.

Got a recipe that calls for a dried herb? Before adding it to your stewing pot, crush the brittle leaves in a mortar and pestle or with your fingers into smaller, more palatable pieces. Doing so also releases more of the herb's flavor.

You may notice that some recipes, such as for Mediterranean Seafood Stew in this chapter, call for you to add an herb to a dish at the very last minute. (In the case of this stew, the herb is cilantro.) That's because fresh herbs are at their most fragrant that way. Cooking delicate chervil, cilantro, or parsley mutes their flavors. Moreover, herbs are more colorful when added at the last minute.

Solving cooking woes

What do you do if a stew or a braised dish is . . .

- **Flat-tasting?** Add salt and pepper. Or try a little sherry or Madeira.

- **Tough?** Cook it longer. Additional cooking breaks down the sinew in muscular cuts of meat. Make sure there is enough braising liquid; if not, add water. You may want to remove the vegetables in the dish with a slotted spoon to prevent them from overcooking.

- **Burned on the bottom?** It may be too late to salvage. Try carefully scooping out the unburned portion of the stew into a separate pot. Add water or stock to stretch it if necessary, and add sherry and a chopped onion. (The sweetness in an onion can mask many mistakes.)

- **Too thin?** Blend 1 tablespoon flour with 1 tablespoon water. Combine this mixture with 1 cup stew liquid and return to the pot with the rest of the stew. Stir well. Heat slowly until thickened.

Beer-Braised Beef with Onions

Prep time: About 10 min • **Cook time:** About 2 hrs 30 min • **Yield:** 8 servings

Ingredients	*Directions*
1 4-pound piece of beef chuck roast, cut into 1-inch squares	*1* Preheat oven to 350 degrees.
Salt and freshly ground pepper to taste	*2* Sprinkle meat with salt and pepper. Heat the oil in a Dutch oven over high heat and brown the meat on all sides. Remove the meat from the pot.
2 tablespoons vegetable oil	
1½ pounds onions, peeled and thickly sliced	*3* Add the onions and garlic to the pot and stir periodically until the onions brown, about 7 minutes. Season with salt and pepper.
1 tablespoon minced garlic	
2 tablespoons flour	*4* Stir in the flour, and then the beer. Add the cinnamon and cloves. Bring to a boil.
24 ounces dark beer	
⅛ teaspoon cinnamon	*5* Add tomato paste, bay leaf, thyme, and broth. Return meat to the pot, and bring to a boil.
4 whole cloves	
1 tablespoon tomato paste	*6* Cook, covered, in a 325-degree oven for about 2 hours and 15 minutes, or until the meat is tender (easily pierced with a carving fork). Slice it crosswise and serve in a deep dish with the cooking liquid.
1 bay leaf	
½ teaspoon dried thyme	
1 cup fresh or canned beef or chicken broth	

Per serving: Calories 336 (From Fat 121); Fat 14g (Saturated 4g); Cholesterol 119mg; Sodium 279mg; Carbohydrate 10g (Dietary Fiber 2g); Protein 41g.

Pot Roast with Vegetables

Prep time: 20 min • **Cook time:** About 3 hours • **Yield:** 8 servings

Ingredients	*Directions*
2 tablespoons vegetable oil 4 pounds first-cut beef brisket 2 large yellow onions, chopped	*1* Heat the oil in a large (preferably cast-iron) Dutch oven over high heat. Add the brisket and sear on both sides, about 7 to 8 minutes, until golden brown. Remove the brisket to a large plate.
3 large cloves garlic, chopped ½ cup dry white wine ½ cup water	*2* Reduce heat to medium-high. Add the onions and garlic, and sauté until the onions are lightly browned, stirring frequently. (Do not let the garlic brown.)
1 bay leaf ¼ teaspoon dried thyme	*3* Return the brisket to the pot. Add the wine, water, bay leaf, thyme, and salt and pepper to taste.
Salt and pepper 4 large Idaho potatoes, peeled and cut into bite-size chunks	*4* Cover, bring to a boil, lower heat, and simmer for 2¾ to 3 hours, turning the meat several times and adding ½ to 1 cup more water if the liquid evaporates.
3 large carrots, peeled and sliced crosswise into 2-inch pieces 3 tablespoons chopped fresh parsley	*5* About 10 minutes before the end of the cooking time, add the potatoes and carrots.

6 When the meat is tender (easily pierced with a fork), remove it to a carving board with a long-handled fork. Cover it with foil and let it rest for 10 to 15 minutes.

7 Continue cooking the potatoes and carrots in the covered pot until tender (about 10 to 15 minutes more).

8 Slice the brisket across the grain and arrange slices on a serving platter.

9 Remove the potatoes and carrots from the gravy and spoon them around the meat.

10 Skim the fat from the surface of the remaining juices, remove the bay leaf and discard, heat the juices through, and spoon over the meat and vegetables. Sprinkle with the chopped parsley. Serve the extra gravy in a gravy boat.

Per serving: Calories 546 (From Fat 199); Fat 22g (Saturated 7g); Cholesterol 133mg; Sodium 199mg; Carbohydrate 38g (Dietary Fiber 5g); Protein 47g.

Old-Fashioned Beef Stew

Prep time: About 25 min • **Cook time:** About 1 hr 40 min • **Yield:** 8 servings

Ingredients	*Directions*
¼ cup olive or vegetable oil	*1* Heat the oil in a large stew pot over medium-high heat, and add the beef cubes. Cook, stirring and turning the meat as necessary, for 5 to 10 minutes until evenly browned.
4 pounds lean, boneless chuck, cut into 2-inch cubes	
2 large yellow onions, coarsely chopped	*2* Add the onion and garlic and cook over medium heat, stirring occasionally, for about 8 minutes. Sprinkle the flour, salt, and pepper over everything. Stir.
6 large cloves garlic, chopped	
6 tablespoons flour	
Salt and pepper	*3* Add the wine, stock, and tomato paste, and stir over high heat until the cooking liquid thickens as it comes to a boil.
3 cups dry red wine	
3 cups homemade or canned beef or chicken stock	
2 tablespoons tomato paste	*4* Add the cloves, bay leaves, parsley, thyme, rosemary, and turnips. Cover and reduce the heat to low. Simmer for 1 hour, occasionally stirring and scraping the bottom of the pot.
4 whole cloves	
2 bay leaves	
4 sprigs parsley, tied together	*5* Add the carrots and cook until the meat and carrots are tender, about 20 minutes more. Remove the herb sprigs and bay leaves before serving.
4 sprigs fresh thyme, or 1 teaspoon dried thyme	
1 tablespoon minced fresh rosemary, leaves only, or 1 teaspoon dried and crumbled rosemary	
1 pound small turnips, trimmed and cut into 2-inch pieces	
6 large carrots, trimmed and cut into 1-inch lengths	

Per serving: Calories 409 (From Fat 155); Fat 17g (Saturated 5g); Cholesterol 119mg; Sodium 237mg; Carbohydrate 18g (Dietary Fiber 4g); Protein 43g.

Mediterranean Seafood Stew

Prep time: About 30 min • **Cook time:** About 25 min • **Yield:** 4 servings

Ingredients	*Directions*
3 tablespoons olive oil	*1* Heat the oil in a large, deep sauté pan or skillet over medium heat. Add the leeks and cook, stirring occasionally, about 4 minutes, or until they wilt.
2 large leeks, white and light green parts only, washed and cut into ½-inch pieces	
2 large cloves garlic, chopped	*2* Add the garlic and cook, stirring often, for another 1 to 2 minutes, until just golden.
1 red bell pepper, cored, seeded, and diced	*3* Add the red bell pepper, cumin, and red pepper flakes. Cook over low heat about 8 minutes, or until the peppers are tender, stirring occasionally.
¾ teaspoon ground cumin	
¼ to ½ teaspoon red pepper flakes, or to taste	
3 ripe plum tomatoes, cored and diced	*4* Add the tomatoes, wine, water, and salt and pepper to taste. Cover and bring the mixture to a boil. Reduce the heat to medium and cook, partially covered, for 6 to 8 minutes.
1 cup dry white wine	
1 cup water	
Salt and pepper	*5* Add the shrimp and scallops and cook, partially covered, about 5 minutes more, or just until the shrimp is evenly pink and the scallops are opaque.
1 pound medium shrimp, shelled and deveined	
¾ pound sea scallops, cut in half	*6* Remove from the heat, stir in the cilantro or parsley, and serve.
¼ cup coarsely chopped cilantro or parsley	

Per serving: Calories 318 (From Fat 111); Fat 12g (Saturated 2g); Cholesterol 210mg; Sodium 551mg; Carbohydrate 13g (Dietary Fiber 2g); Protein 36g.

Tip: You can prepare this stew several hours ahead of serving time. Complete the recipe through Step 4, and 5 minutes before you want to serve the stew, add the seafood and finish cooking.

Vary It! Can't find leeks? Substitute one medium white onion, chopped, for the leeks in this recipe.

Chapter 8

Roasting Poultry, Meats, and Veggies

A chicken, ham, or pot roast in your oven perfumes your home like nothing else can. Some people are intimidated by roasting, but we're here to show you that it's truly simple. Add in the facts that you don't have to stand over a stove for hours and the results taste fabulous, and you can see why we think roasting is the way to go, whether you're preparing a holiday feast or a small family meal.

Roasting Done Right

Roasting is easy, but knowing a few techniques can help you to make the most of your roasted dishes. How do you season meats, fish, and vegetables for roasting? Do you need to sear a meat roast before baking it? When and how do you baste? And why do some meat roasts need to take a rest before they're served? We answer all these questions in this section.

Seasoning your roasts

Have you ever eaten a superb beef roast or pork loin that lingers on the palate like an aged wine? Part of its appeal comes from being seasoned before cooking. You can season meat, poultry, fish, and vegetables with salt, pepper, herbs, and spices, but the trick is to know how much of which seasonings to use.

Salt is a flavor enhancer that brings out the best in many foods. However, it's easy to overdo it. We advise using no more than a teaspoon of salt per two pounds of meat roast, and many people would choose to use much less. Fresh herbs, dried herbs, and ground spices can all enhance a roast. It's all about balance and harmony, and this is something you can learn at home.

Until you are more accomplished, limit yourself to no more than two or three seasonings in any roasted dish. For instance, you might combine oregano, thyme, and parsley to season a pot roast. You might enhance a roasted chicken with tarragon and lemon pepper, or rosemary and white pepper. Cumin or chili powder can add punch to a roasted turkey. The possibilities are endless. (See Chapter 3 for more on seasonings.)

Searing meat before you roast

Searing refers to the technique of heating oil in a very hot pan and then browning meat or poultry on all sides. But why on earth would you cook your food twice: first in a hot pan and again in the oven?

The advantage of searing a meat roast or chicken before roasting it is this: Searing creates a nice texture and boosts the flavors of seasonings. Here's something searing does *not* do (contrary to what you've probably heard on many TV shows): Searing does ***not*** seal in meat juices. It merely creates a savory crust.

With all that said, just know that searing in an option; it isn't required prior to roasting. If you don't sear, your poultry or roast will likely be lighter in color and flavor, but you can always boost your seasonings if necessary.

Basting during cooking

Many recipes call for *basting* a roast or poultry, which means brushing or drizzling pan juices over it during cooking. Basting is a good way to add flavor to the surface of the meat or poultry, but contrary to popular belief, it doesn't create a crisp crust. In fact, just the opposite is true: Moistening poultry skin by basting prevents the skin from getting crispy.

To baste, use a large spoon, bulb baster, or basting brush to coat the roast's surface with the pan juices or oil. Baste the meat every 15 to 30 minutes throughout the roasting process.

Be careful when basting, however, because you will be reaching into a hot oven. You can pull out the oven rack to minimize the chances of burning your hands on the oven coils, but remember, you are still handling sizzling-hot juices, and a spill or a too-vigorous squeeze of the bulb baster could result in spattering juices and burns. Baste with care!

Taking a rest

If you're like us, by the time a pot roast emerges from the oven, the intoxicating aroma has you so hungry that you could tear at it like a dog. Instead, take a deep breath, have some brie and crackers, and let the roast sit out, covered with aluminum foil, for 15 to 20 minutes to allow internal juices to redistribute. Even a roast chicken or duck should sit for 10 minutes. Resting helps you keep more of the juice inside the meat or poultry when you cut into it. (It also makes carving easier because the food isn't quite so hot!)

Roasting Times and Temperatures for Poultry and Meat

Tables 8-1 through 8-4 give approximate cooking times and temperatures for roasting beef, poultry, pork, and lamb. You want to remove a meat roast when its internal temperature is 5 to 10 degrees *less* than final internal temperature, and then let it rest for about 15 minutes. During the resting time, the roast cooks 5 to 10 degrees more. None of this is an exact science, though; you have to use a meat thermometer to get the results you like. See Figure 8-1 for illustrated instructions for using a meat thermometer.

Where to put a Dial (or Oven-proof) Meat Thermometer

Boneless Roast

Poultry

Meat with bone

Figure 8-1:
How to insert a meat thermometer in various roasts.

 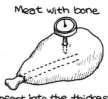

Insert to core

Insert inside of the thigh

Insert into the thickest part of the meat

＊ For an accurate reading, do NOT touch the bone, fat, or bottom of the pan with the thermometer.

When inserting a meat thermometer into a roast, do not let the metal touch the bone — the bone is hotter than the meat and registers a falsely higher temperature.

Keep in mind that every oven is different. Some ovens are off by as much as 50 degrees, which can be like trying to make gourmet coffee with hot tap water. Roasting can be a disaster without precision. Investing in an oven thermometer is worthwhile.

Table 8-1	Beef Roasting Chart			
Beef Roast	*Preheated Oven Temperature (°F)*	*Weight*	*Approximate Total Cooking Time*	*Remove from Oven at This Meat Temperature*
Boneless rib eye roast (small end)	350°	3 to 4 pounds	Medium rare: 1½ to 1¾ hours	135°
			Medium: 1¾ to 2 hours	150°
		4 to 6 pounds	Medium rare: 1¾ to 2 hours	135°
			Medium: 2 to 2½ hours	150°
		6 to 8 pounds	Medium rare: 2 to 2¼ hours	135°
			Medium: 2½ to 2¾ hours	150°
Bone-in rib roast (chine bone removed)	350°	4 to 6 pounds (2 ribs)	Medium rare: 1¾ to 2¼ hours	135°
			Medium: 2¼ to 2½ hours	150°
		6 to 8 pounds (2 to 4 ribs)	Medium rare: 2¼ to 2½ hours	135°
			Medium: 2¾ to 3 hours	150°
		8 to 10 pounds (4 to 5 ribs)	Medium rare: 2½ to 3 hours	135°
			Medium: 3 to 3½ hours	150°

Beef Roast	Preheated Oven Temperature (°F)	Weight	Approximate Total Cooking Time	Remove from Oven at This Meat Temperature
Round tip roast (sirloin tip)	325°	3 to 4 pounds	Medium rare: 1¾ to 2 hours	140°
			Medium: 2¼ to 2½ hours	155°
		4 to 6 pounds	Medium rare: 2 to 2½ hours	140°
			Medium: 2½ to 3 hours	155°
		6 to 8 pounds	Medium rare: 2½ to 3 hours	140°
			Medium: 3 to 3½ hours	155°
Tenderloin roast	425°	2 to 3 pounds	Medium rare: 35 to 40 minutes	135°
			Medium: 45 to 50 minutes	150°
		4 to 5 pounds	Medium rare: 50 to 60 minutes	135°
			Medium: 60 to 70 minutes	150°

Medium rare doneness: 140° to 145° final meat temperature after 10 to 15 minutes standing time
Medium doneness: 155° to 160° final meat temperature after 10 to 15 minutes standing time
Allow ¼ to ⅓ pound of uncooked boneless beef per serving and ½ to 1 pound of bone-in meat per serving, depending on the cut.
Source: National Cattlemen's Beef Association

Table 8-2	Poultry Roasting Chart		
Bird	**Weight**	**Preheated Oven Temperature**	**Cooking Time**
Chicken, broiler/fryer (unstuffed)	3 to 4 pounds	350°	1¼ to 1½ hours
Chicken, roaster (unstuffed)	5 to 7 pounds	350°	2 to 2¼ hours
Whole turkey (thawed and unstuffed)	8 to 12 pounds	325°	2¾ to 3 hours

(continued)

Table 8-2 *(continued)*

Bird	Weight	Preheated Oven Temperature	Cooking Time
Whole turkey (thawed and unstuffed)	12 to 14 pounds	325°	3 to 3¾ hours
	14 to 18 pounds	325°	3¾ to 4¼ hours
	18 to 20 pounds	325°	4¼ to 4½ hours
Duck (whole, unstuffed)	4 to 5½ pounds	325°	2½ to 3 hours

Depending on the size of the bird, allow 15 to 20 minutes additional cooking time if stuffed. Internal temperature for stuffing should be 165°. Internal temperature for meat should be minimum 180° in the thigh. Allow about ¾ to 1 pound of uncooked chicken or turkey on the bone per serving.
Source: National Chicken Council

The associations and companies that produce and market poultry use these roasting tables only as a rough guideline. For actual cooking times, they recommend always using a meat thermometer when cooking poultry of any kind.

Table 8-3   Pork Roasting Chart

Cut	Thickness/Weight	Final Internal Temperature	Cooking Time
Loin roast (bone-in)	3 to 5 pounds	155° to 160°	20 minutes per pound
Boneless pork roast	2 to 4 pounds	155° to 160°	20 minutes per pound
Tenderloin (roast at 425° to 450°)	½ to 1½ pounds	155° to 160°	20 to 30 minutes
Crown roast	6 to 10 pounds	155° to 160°	20 minutes per pound
Boneless loin chops	1 inch thick	155° to 160°	12 to 16 minutes
Ribs		Tender	1½ to 2 hours

Roast in a shallow pan, uncovered, at 350°.
Allow about ¼ to ⅓ pound of uncooked boneless meat per serving and about ½ to 1 pound of bone-in meat per serving, depending on the cut.
Source: National Pork Producers Council

Table 8-4		Lamb Roasting Chart	
Roast	**Weight**	**Final Internal Temperature**	**Approximate Cooking Time Per Pound**
Leg (bone-in)	5 to 7 pounds	Medium rare: 145° to 150°	15 minutes
		Medium: 155° to 160°	20 minutes
Boneless (rolled and tied)	4 to 7 pounds	Medium rare: 145° to 150°	20 minutes
		Medium: 155° to 160°	25 minutes
Sirloin roast (boneless)	about 2 pounds	Medium rare: 145° to 150°	25 minutes
		Medium: 155° to 160°	30 minutes
Top round roast	about 2 pounds	Medium rare: 145° to 150°	45 minutes
		Medium: 155° to 160°	55 minutes

Preheat oven to 325° and remove from oven about 10° below desired temperature.
Allow ¼ to ⅓ pound of boneless lamb per serving and ⅓ to ½ pound of bone-in lamb per serving.
Source: American Lamb Council

We understand that it can be irresistible , but don't keep opening the oven door to see whether your roasted dish is done. Your kitchen will get hot, you will get hotter, and the meat or vegetables will take longer to cook.

Putting Poultry in the Oven

Contrary to what some people think, roasting a chicken involves more than just tossing the bird into the oven and mixing a gin and tonic. Sometimes what seems to be the simplest of endeavors requires the most attention (like poker).

Let's start at the very beginning. Open the package. Congratulations. Now remove that mysterious paper packet inside the bird that contains the "giblets" (the neck, heart, gizzard, and liver). Set it aside while you are preparing the chicken, but don't throw it out — you can use it later to make delicious gravy. Rinse the bird thoroughly under cold running water, inside and out. Pat the skin dry with paper towels and season with salt and pepper.

If you want your bird to hold its shape perfectly while roasting, you can *truss* it (tie it with string). See Figure 8-2 for illustrated instructions, or visit www. dummies.com/go/trussingpoultry. You then place your poultry in a large metal roasting pan.

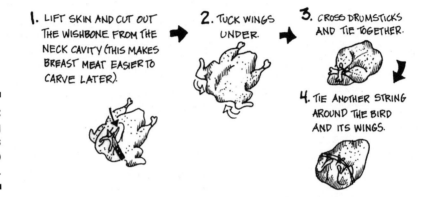

TRUSSING A CHICKEN

1. LIFT SKIN AND CUT OUT THE WISHBONE FROM THE NECK CAVITY (THIS MAKES BREAST MEAT EASIER TO CARVE LATER).

2. TUCK WINGS UNDER.

3. CROSS DRUMSTICKS AND TIE TOGETHER.

4. TIE ANOTHER STRING AROUND THE BIRD AND ITS WINGS.

Figure 8-2:
Trussing
helps
poultry keep
its shape.

The most common mistake home cooks make when roasting chicken is using an insufficiently hot oven. The Roasted Chicken recipe in this chapter calls for a 425-degree oven, which yields a crispy, golden-brown skin.

As you cook the bird, use a meat thermometer. As we explain in Chapter 2, you can choose between an *instant-read* type, which you stick in the meat when you suspect it's nearing doneness to get an immediate temperature reading, and an *ovenproof* version — the kind you insert in the meat when you first put it in the oven. Either way, insert your thermometer deep into the flesh between the bird's thigh and breast.

If you don't have a thermometer, insert a knife into the thick part of the thigh; if the juices run clear, the bird is thoroughly cooked. If they run pink, let the meat cook for another 15 minutes or so before testing for doneness. Then go buy a thermometer.

So what do you do with the packet of giblets? You can add them — all but the liver — to homemade soups and stocks, or to canned stocks to enrich their flavors. The Roasted Chicken recipe we provide later in this chapter uses the giblets to make a delicious pan gravy.

Here's a tip for using your roasted chicken leftovers: Roasted chicken, either hot or cold, goes well with a mildly spicy mustard mayonnaise. Blend Dijon mustard to taste into ½ cup of mayonnaise. (Start with about a teaspoon and work your way up if it isn't zippy enough for you.) Season with salt and pepper and freshly chopped herbs, such as tarragon, basil, chervil, parsley, or oregano. This spicy mayo is also good with cold pork, fish, and grilled meats.

Mastering Roasted Meats

Americans have two immutable love affairs: automobiles and meat. If you want proof of our carnivorous cravings, just look at the steakhouse explosion from coast to coast. Sure, people have become more health-conscious, and many seek leaner cuts of meat. The beef and pork industries have responded, making considerable strides in breeding leaner animals without sacrificing too much tenderness. Add to that America's continuing interest in low-carb protein diets, and (no offense to vegetarians), meat seems to be an integral part of American life.

Concerning pork and other meats, good butchers are frequently knowledgeable cooks. They can offer recipes, tips, and information on preparing your piece of meat so that it is "oven-ready." For example, an oven-ready roast is trimmed of excess fat and sometimes tied with butcher's string to make it as uniform as possible for cooking. A leg of lamb should have its fat and shank bone removed. The skin and rind of a smoked ham are trimmed away, leaving just a thin layer of fat that you can score to make a decorative diamond pattern. (Don't worry — we show you how!)

Beef

Roast beef is a traditional Anglo favorite. You simply *must* check out the Roasted Fillet of Beef recipe later in the chapter. This savory dish, although on the pricey side, is fast, simple, and always delicious — a real last-minute party saver. Serve it with simple dishes like garlic-flavored mashed potatoes and Steamed Broccoli with Lemon Butter (see Chapter 5).

The roast referred to as *fillet* is also called *tenderloin,* so you can use these terms interchangeably. But the fillet roast is different than the cut called *filet mignon,* which is defined as the extremely tender cut from the small end of the tenderloin.

Looking for a roast that's a bit more economical? A *round tip roast,* also referred to as a *sirloin tip roast,* is leaner and less tender than a more expensive roast such as prime rib. If cooked the right way, a round tip roast makes a great family dinner. To serve a round tip roast for six people, follow these steps:

1. **Purchase a 3- to 4-pound sirloin tip roast.**

2. **Rub it with fresh chopped garlic, a little olive oil, salt, pepper, and your favorite herbs.**

3. **Place it on a rack in a shallow roasting pan in a preheated 325-degree oven and cook until a meat thermometer inserted into the center of the roast registers 140 degrees for medium-rare, or 150 degrees for medium.**

   Remember that a resting roast continues cooking, adding about 5 degrees on a meat thermometer. A 3- to 4-pound roast will cook to medium-rare in 1¾ to 2 hours and to medium in 2¼ to 2½ hours.

4. **Remove the roast from the oven and let stand, loosely covered with foil, for 15 minutes before carving.**

What happens if you overcook a roast beef? Unfortunately, ovens do not have reverse gears. But you can salvage overcooked roast beef in many tasty ways. Make roast beef hash or beef pot pie, various soups such as the Vegetable Beef Soup in Chapter 12, or beef stroganoff. Any recipe that calls for liquid or a cream-based sauce is good, too, for making delicious use of overcooked beef.

Pork

Compared to some types of roasts, pork remains a relative bargain. Pork is lighter and leaner than ever before, and if you know how to cook it properly it will be moist and tender. Our recipe for Roast Loin of Pork later in the chapter is a perfect example.

People used to believe that if you ate pork that was cooked below 185 degrees, you could contract a disease called trichinosis. The average person didn't know what that was, but it sure sounded unpleasant. Thus, for years, everyone ate overcooked pork. About a decade ago, scientists discovered that harmful trichinae parasites are killed at 135 degrees. Cooking pork to 155 degrees is considered plenty safe and yields a much juicier result.

Ribs

Whether done over a grill or in an oven, ribs need long, slow cooking. Some recipes call for *parboiling* (partially boiling) ribs before roasting or grilling, but we have found that a lot of the flavor winds up in the cooking water. The best alternative we've found is roasting spareribs in a 300-degree oven for 2 hours, which leaves them succulent and flavorful.

Ribs are delicious when rubbed with spices before cooking. The recipe later in the chapter for Roasted Pork Ribs with Country Barbecue Sauce calls for brown sugar, salt, and pepper. A sweet element always gives the ribs a seductive flavor; the other ingredients can vary according to your taste. If you like them spicy, add a little cayenne pepper to the mix (about ¼ teaspoon or more if you like it extra hot). Other seasonings you could experiment with include sweet paprika, onion powder, garlic powder, ground cumin, ground coriander, cinnamon, dried thyme, and dried basil. However you choose to prepare ribs, they're great for casual entertaining. Just be sure to have lots of moist towels around. Ribs get messy! (But that's half the fun.)

Keep in mind that our Country Barbecue Sauce (featured in the color section) also works exceptionally well with barbecued chicken and beef. It may be prepared a day or two in advance, refrigerated, and reheated before using.

Ham

Hams have more identities than a secret agent. Sorting them out is not terribly complicated, however. Remember that all hams are *cured* (which means seasoned and aged), and some are also smoked. The two most common methods of preparing a ham are *dry curing* and *wet curing*. In the dry method, a ham is rubbed with salt and seasonings and hung in a cool, dry place to age, anywhere from a few weeks to a year or more. Wet cured hams are soaked in *brine* (salt water), or injected with brine, to give them more flavor.

Here is a primer on some other terms for hams:

- **Aged ham:** Heavily cured and smoked hams that have been dry-aged at least one year.

- **Bayonne ham:** A dry-cured ham from the Basque country of France, specifically the city of Bayonne.

- **Canned ham:** Cured but not always smoked, and ready to eat. A little cooking, though, improves the flavor.

- **Country ham:** A dry cured ham that is smoked, salted, and then aged for at least 6 months.

- **Half ham:** Comes from the shank bone, butt, or ham end. The shank portion is best and easiest to deal with.

- **Fully cooked ham:** The same as a "ready-to-eat" ham. You can eat it without cooking.

- **Prosciutto:** Strictly speaking, a ham from Parma, Italy, that is seasoned, salt cured, air dried, and pressed to make the meat very firm. It is usually eaten in very thin slices over bread.

- **Smithfield ham:** The pride of Smithfield, Virginia; a salty, wonderfully flavorful ham seasoned, smoked, and hung for at least a year.

- **Sugar-cured ham:** Rubbed with salt and brown sugar or molasses before aging.

- **Virginia ham:** Another salty, dry-cured ham. It's made from hogs that eat peanuts, acorns, and other high-protein foods.

- **Westphalian ham:** A rosy, sweetish, German ham made from hogs that are fed sugar beet mash. It is usually eaten like prosciutto.

Later in the chapter, we give you a recipe for Smoked Ham with Apricot Glaze. In this recipe, the ham is brushed with an apricot-and-mustard glaze and then served with a pan sauce made from the luscious drippings. Ham and fruit make a natural pairing, and you can use this combination to good effect not only in the glaze but in the garnish. Decorate your platter with pieces of fruit, such as pineapple slices, apricot halves nestled in pear halves, or slices of oranges. You can also brush the fruits with the glaze for a beautiful presentation.

If you're used to buying your ham precooked, you may wonder why some hams have a pretty little diamond pattern all over them. That pattern is created by *scoring* the ham with a sharp knife. To do so, you first remove the thick skin, or *rind,* of the ham by cutting it away to expose a thin layer of fat. Then you make small cuts in the fat all over the surface , as shown in Figure 8-3. Doing so helps a glaze penetrate the meat. (If you want to add a decorative effect, you can also insert a clove into the center of each diamond cut.)

Figure 8-3: How to score a ham.

Because ham is a fatty meat, if you want to use the juices that accumulate during roasting (to help create a glaze, for example), you likely need to skim the fat before using them. To do so, after roasting the ham, pour its juices into a bowl. Tilt the bowl, and with a spoon, skim the surface fat. Or you can use a fat skimmer such as the one shown in Figure 8-4.

Sweet little piggies

Baked hams — more accurately called "roasted hams" — are often brushed with a sweet marmalade or other glaze that counterbalances the saltiness of the meat. The glaze is applied during the last 30 minutes of baking, or when the ham has reached an internal temperature of 120 degrees; if applied sooner, the glaze could burn. Glazes can be mixtures of all sorts of flavors: jams, brown sugar, molasses, corn syrup, mustard, cinnamon, cloves, ginger, whiskey, rum, orange juice, Port, or white wine. Some producers douse the ham with Coca-Cola to produce a syrupy coating — no kidding.

In the recipe for smoked ham in this chapter, we show you how to use the ham's pan juices when serving the ham slices. You can flavor a ham's pan juices in many ways. Try adding 2 to 3 tablespoons of dark raisins, 2 tablespoons of dark rum, or some dry white wine or apple cider. Grated orange zest and freshly squeezed orange juice give the pan juices a clean, citric edge.

Figure 8-4: A fat skimmer.

Lamb

Hankering for some lamb instead? We offer a delicious, easy to make recipe for Glazed Leg of Lamb with Pan Gravy and Red Currant Glaze later in the chapter. This dish is excellent with some root vegetables like carrots and potatoes scattered around the roasting pan.

If you enjoy lamb cooked medium to well, roast it until the internal temperature reaches 155 to 160 degrees or more — and it will continue to cook for about 15 minutes after being removed from the oven. But keep in mind that a roasted leg of lamb yields meat of varying degrees of doneness. The meat at the thin, shank end, is browned and well done, and the meat at the thicker end ideally is quite pink and medium rare. The drier meat is great for hash.

A whole leg of lamb can leave you with delicious leftovers. Prepare cold lamb sandwiches or Shepherd's Pie (see Chapter 16), or substitute lamb for the beef in Vegetable Beef Soup (see Chapter 12). Or turn to Chapter 19 for a delicious Lamb Curry recipe using leftover cooked lamb.

Remember to Roast Your Veggies!

Virtually all kinds of vegetables can be roasted by using the simple techniques explained in the two great recipes later in this chapter: Crispy Roasted Root Vegetables (for winter root veggies) and Roasted Summer Vegetables (shown in the book's color section).

The Crispy Roasted Root Vegetables are a great companion for many entrees. If you're roasting a side of beef or a chicken, for instance, just scatter a variety of root vegetables (such as cut-up carrots, onions, and peeled potatoes) in the roasting pan. Turn them every so often in the pan drippings. This makes for a great presentation at the table — that is, if you don't eat them all in the kitchen.

Keep in mind that summer vegetables release quite a bit of water when roasted. To get them browned and crisp, place them on the lowest oven rack, close to the heating element. You may also sprinkle a little brown sugar over the vegetables to bring out their natural sweetness and counterbalance the tastes of fresh ginger, garlic, and hot pepper.

If you have leftover roasted vegetables, use them the next day in a salad, rolled in a tortilla with hot sauce, or even in an omelet. If you want to make them crisp again, place them in a 400-degree oven for about 5 minutes.

If you combine different vegetables on the same roasting pan, be sure to choose those that will cook in about the same amount of time. Tomatoes cook much faster than carrots, so you wouldn't combine those two, for example. Another way to achieve even cooking is to cut the hardest vegetables (carrots, parsnips, potatoes, and so on) into smaller pieces than the soft vegetables (celery, bell peppers, eggplant, and so on). Or *blanch* the hard vegetables before roasting: Plunge them into boiling water for a few seconds and then into cold water to stop the cooking process.

Roasted Fillet of Beef

Prep time: About 10 min • **Cook time:** About 45 min • **Yield:** 8 servings

Ingredients	Directions
1 beef fillet (tenderloin) roast, oven-ready, about 4 pounds	**1** Preheat the oven to 425 degrees.
Salt and pepper	**2** Sprinkle the fillet of beef with salt and pepper to taste.
2 tablespoons vegetable oil	
Herb butter (optional)	**3** Place the meat on a rack in a heavy roasting pan and brush or rub it with the oil. Roast for about 45 minutes for medium rare or until desired doneness. Halfway through the roasting time, invert the meat and baste once with the pan juices.
	4 Transfer the meat to a carving board, cover with aluminum foil, and let stand for 10 minutes.
	5 Carve the fillet into approximately ½-inch-thick slices and serve immediately, topped with a pat of butter and a sprinkle of herbs (such as fresh chopped or dried basil), if desired.

Per serving: Calories 528 (From Fat 356); Fat 40g (Saturated 15g); Cholesterol 135mg; Sodium 176mg; Carbohydrate 0g (Dietary Fiber 0g); Protein 40g.

Go-With: You can serve fillet of beef (tenderloin) with almost anything, from a simple avocado and tomato salad (see Chapter 17) to a fancy risotto (see Chapter 4).

Roasted Chicken

Prep time: About 15 min • **Cook time:** About 1 hr 15 min • **Yield:** 4 servings

Ingredients	Directions
1 chicken, 4 to 4½ pounds, with giblets	**1** Preheat the oven to 425 degrees. Remove the giblets from the chicken's cavity; rinse and reserve. Rinse the chicken under cold running water, inside and out, and pat dry with paper towels.
Salt and pepper	
1 lemon, pricked several times with a fork	**2** Sprinkle the chicken inside and out with salt and pepper to taste. Insert the lemon, thyme, and garlic into the cavity of the chicken. Rub the outside of the chicken all over with the olive oil.
2 sprigs fresh thyme, or ½ teaspoon dried thyme	
1 whole clove garlic, peeled	**3** Truss the chicken with string, if desired.
2 tablespoons olive oil	
1 medium yellow onion, quartered	**4** Place the chicken, breast side up, on a rack in a shallow metal roasting pan. Scatter the giblets and onions on the bottom of the pan. Roast for 45 minutes.
½ cup homemade or canned chicken stock	
½ cup water, or more as necessary	**5** Remove the roasting pan from the oven. Using a large spoon, skim fat from the pan juices. Add the chicken stock, water, and butter to the pan. Roast for another 20 to 30 minutes.
2 tablespoons butter	
Parsley, rosemary, tarragon, or other fresh herbs to taste (optional)	

6 Lift the chicken to let the cavity juices flow into the pan. Transfer chicken to a carving board or serving platter, cover with aluminum foil, and let rest for 10 to 15 minutes.

7 Place the roasting pan on top of the stove. Using a slotted spoon, remove and discard any pieces of giblets or onion. Add water or stock if necessary to make about 1 cup liquid.

8 Bring the liquid to a boil and reduce for 1 to 2 minutes to let the sauce condense while you stir and scrape the bottom of the pan. If desired, add fresh herbs to taste.

9 Turn off the heat when the sauce is reduced to about ¾ cup. Strain the sauce into a gravy boat or small bowl just before serving.

10 If you trussed the chicken, cut the string off. Remove and discard the lemon and thyme sprigs.

11 Carve the chicken into serving pieces and serve with the hot pan juices.

Per serving: *Calories 636 (From Fat 395); Fat 44g (Saturated 13g); Cholesterol 194mg; Sodium 395mg; Carbohydrate 0g (Dietary Fiber 0g); Protein 57g.*

Roast Loin of Pork

Prep time: About 25 min • **Cook time:** About 1 hr 5 min • **Yield:** 6 servings

Ingredients	*Directions*
Center-cut boneless loin of pork, about 3 pounds	**1** Preheat the oven to 400 degrees.
4 tablespoons olive oil	**2** Place the pork in a large roasting pan (without a rack) and brush or rub the meat all over with 3 tablespoons of the oil. Season with the thyme and salt and pepper to taste. Roast, fat side up, for 15 minutes.
2 tablespoons chopped fresh thyme, or 1 teaspoon dried thyme	
Salt and pepper	**3** Remove the pan from the oven and reduce the oven temperature to 350 degrees.
6 medium red potatoes, peeled and halved lengthwise	
3 medium yellow onions, peeled and quartered	**4** Scatter the potatoes, onions, carrots, and bay leaf around the roast and drizzle the remaining 1 tablespoon of oil over the vegetables. Using a large spoon, turn the vegetables in the cooking juices.
4 carrots, peeled and cut into 2-inch pieces	
1 bay leaf	**5** Sprinkle the garlic over the vegetables and season them with salt and pepper to taste. Add the water to the pan.
2 large cloves garlic, finely chopped	
½ cup water	**6** Roast for 45 to 50 minutes or until a meat thermometer registers 155 degrees in the thickest part of the roast.
¼ cup chopped fresh parsley	
2 cups applesauce (optional)	

7 Transfer the roast to a cutting board. Cover with aluminum foil and let rest for 15 minutes.

8 Reduce the oven temperature to 300 degrees and place the pan with the vegetables in the oven to keep warm.

9 Carve the meat and transfer it and the vegetables to a large platter. Pour any juices that have collected around the meat into the roasting pan. Remove the bay leaf from the pan, and place the pan over two burners on high.

10 Bring the juices to a boil, stirring and scraping the bottom and sides of the pan with a wooden spoon. Cook about 1 to 2 minutes or until the sauce is reduced and slightly thickened. Pour the juices over everything, sprinkle with the chopped parsley, and serve with applesauce (if desired).

Per serving: Calories 574 (From Fat 175); Fat 20g (Saturated 5g); Cholesterol 150mg; Sodium 244mg; Carbohydrate 43g (Dietary Fiber 5g); Protein 54g.

Go-With: This hearty dish is delicious with winter vegetables like Southern Greens (see Chapter 16) or Sautéed Spinach Leaves (see Chapter 5), or a simple salad of mixed greens (see Chapter 12).

Roasted Pork Ribs with Country Barbecue Sauce

Prep time: About 20 min (plus chill time) • **Cook time:** About 2 hr 30 min • **Yield:** 4 servings

Ingredients	Directions
1 tablespoon brown sugar, packed	*1* Preheat the oven to 300 degrees.
1½ teaspoons salt, or to taste	*2* Make a spice rub by combining the brown sugar, salt, and pepper in a small bowl. Stir well.
1 teaspoon pepper, or to taste	*3* Trim excess fat from the ribs. Place the ribs on a cutting board. Cut the slabs into pieces of one to two ribs each.
3 to 4 pounds pork spareribs	*4* Arrange the spareribs in one layer on a roasting pan. Sprinkle the ribs with the spice rub, pressing the seasonings firmly onto the meat all around. Cover loosely and refrigerate about 30 minutes.
	5 Roast in the oven for 1½ hours, turning them over after 45 minutes. While the ribs cook, make the barbecue sauce.
	6 Increase the oven temperature to 350 degrees. Remove the roasting pan from the oven; carefully pour off all the fat (or transfer ribs to a clean roasting pan).
	7 Brush the ribs generously on all sides with the barbecue sauce and roast another 25 to 30 minutes, or until the meat easily pulls away from the bone. Serve with extra sauce on the side.

Country Barbecue Sauce

2 tablespoons vegetable oil

1 small yellow onion, minced

2 cloves garlic, minced

¾ cup water

⅔ cup ketchup

½ cup dark brown sugar, packed

6 tablespoons cider vinegar

1 tablespoon Worcestershire sauce

1 tablespoon molasses

1 teaspoon ground cumin

Salt and pepper

1 Heat the oil in a saucepan over medium heat. Add the onion and cook, stirring often, until it starts to soften; add the garlic and continue cooking and stirring for about 1 minute.

2 Add the water, ketchup, brown sugar, vinegar, Worcestershire sauce, molasses, cumin, and salt and pepper to taste, and stir well. Increase the heat to high and bring to a boil.

3 Reduce the heat and simmer 25 to 30 minutes, or until thickened, stirring occasionally.

Per serving: Calories 875 (From Fat 495); Fat 55g (Saturated 19g); Cholesterol 191mg; Sodium 1,699mg; Carbohydrate 47g (Dietary Fiber 1g); Protein 47g.

Smoked Ham with Apricot Glaze

Prep time: 20 min • **Cook time:** About 2 hrs 15 min • **Yield:** 14 servings

Ingredients	Directions
½ of a smoked cooked ham, bone-in (7 to 9 pounds)	**1** Preheat the oven to 325 degrees.
About 30 whole cloves (optional)	**2** Remove the rind from the ham with a sharp knife and discard. With a sharp knife, score the thin layer of fat remaining.
About 1 cup water	**3** Place the ham in a heavy roasting pan; add ½ cup of water to the pan and put it in the oven. While the ham roasts, prepare the Apricot Glaze.
1 cup homemade or canned chicken stock	**4** If the roasting pan gets dry, add ½ cup more water to it. When a meat thermometer inserted into the center of the ham reads 120 degrees (after about 1½ to 2 hours), remove the ham from the oven and increase the oven temperature to 400 degrees.
	5 Brush or spoon the glaze all over the ham and return it to the oven. Bake for 20 to 25 minutes, or until a thermometer inserted in the center registers 140 degrees (be careful not to burn the glaze).
	6 Place the ham on a large carving board; cover with foil and let rest 15 minutes.

7 Pour the juices from the roasting pan into a small shallow bowl. Skim the fat that accumulates on the surface, and return the skimmed juices to the pan. Place it over a burner on high heat, and add the chicken stock.

8 Cook the juices, stirring and scraping up browned bits on the bottom of the pan, until the liquid is reduced and slightly thickened. Pass the sauce through a fine strainer.

9 Thinly slice the ham; serve with pan juices and, if desired, a good mustard.

Apricot Glaze

½ cup apricot preserves or orange marmalade

2 tablespoons Dijon-style mustard

1 tablespoon dark rum (optional)

Pepper

1 In a small pan, heat the preserves over low heat; mash any large pieces of fruit with a fork. Stir in the mustard and, if desired, the rum. Season with pepper to taste.

2 Boil, stirring occasionally, until the mixture thickens enough to coat a spoon, about 3 minutes.

Per serving: Calories 435 (From Fat 253); Fat 28g (Saturated 10g); Cholesterol 103mg; Sodium 2,076mg; Carbohydrate 8g (Dietary Fiber 0g); Protein 36g.

Glazed Leg of Lamb with Pan Gravy and Red Currant Glaze

Prep time: About 20 min • **Cook time:** About 1 hr 40 min • **Yield:** 10 servings

Ingredients	Directions
1 leg of lamb (6 to 7 pounds), well trimmed	**1** Preheat the oven to 425 degrees.
3 cloves garlic, thinly sliced	**2** With a paring knife, make small incisions along the leg. Insert the garlic slivers into the incisions.
1 tablespoon vegetable oil	
½ teaspoon ground ginger	**3** Rub the lamb with the oil and place it on a rack in a shallow roasting pan, fat side up. Sprinkle the meat with the ginger and salt and pepper to taste.
Salt and pepper	
	4 Roast for 20 minutes; reduce the heat to 350 degrees and roast for an additional 1 hour and 20 minutes (until a meat thermometer registers 145 degrees in the thickest part of the leg for medium rare or 155 degrees for medium).
	5 During the last 30 minutes of roasting (starting when the meat thermometer reads 115 degrees), brush the top and sides of the lamb every 10 minutes with Red Currant Glaze and pan juices.
	6 Remove from the oven, cover with foil, and let rest for 20 minutes. Carve and serve with some of the pan juices spooned over the slices.

Red Currant Glaze

¼ cup red currant jelly	Combine all the ingredients in a small saucepan and heat until the jelly is melted (about 1 minute). Use as a basting sauce for the leg of lamb.
Juice and grated peel of ½ lemon	
1½ teaspoons Dijon-style mustard	

Per serving: Calories 287 (From Fat 105); Fat 12g (Saturated 4g); Cholesterol 117mg; Sodium 168mg; Carbohydrate 6g (Dietary Fiber 0g); Protein 37g.

Crispy Roasted Root Vegetables

Prep time: About 10 min • **Cook time:** About 30 min • **Yield:** 4 servings

Ingredients	Directions
4 medium carrots, washed (skins on), halved, and chopped crosswise into about 4 pieces	*1* Preheat the oven to 400 degrees.
2 red or yellow bell peppers, cored, seeded, and sliced into ½-inch strips	*2* Place the vegetables, fennel, and rosemary in a large mixing bowl. Pour the olive oil over them and season generously with salt and pepper. Toss well to blend.
3 medium red potatoes, quartered	
3 small turnips, peeled and quartered	*3* Transfer vegetables to a roasting pan that can hold them in one layer. Place the pan in the oven and roast for 25 to 30 minutes, turning the vegetables several times.
2 medium yellow onions, quartered	
2 small bulbs fennel, trimmed and quartered	
1 tablespoon minced fresh rosemary, or ½ tablespoon dried rosemary	
¼ cup olive oil	
Salt and black pepper	

Per serving: Calories 334 (From Fat 127); Fat 14g (Saturated 2g); Cholesterol 0mg; Sodium 252mg; Carbohydrate 48g (Dietary Fiber 9g); Protein 6g.

Tip: If after 25 minutes the vegetables are tender but not browned, place them under the broiler for a minute or two — but don't let them burn.

Roasted Summer Vegetables

Prep time: About 15 min • **Cook time:** About 35 min • **Yield:** 4 servings

Ingredients	Directions
3 medium carrots, peeled and cut into ¼-inch slices	**1** Preheat the oven to 425 degrees.
2 to 3 tablespoons olive oil	**2** Scatter the carrots over a large roasting pan. Drizzle them with 1 tablespoon of the olive oil; toss to coat. Place the pan on the oven rack closest to the heating element, and roast for 10 minutes.
1 red or yellow bell pepper, cored, seeded, and cut into ½-inch cubes	
1 small zucchini, halved lengthwise and cut into ½-inch-thick slices	**3** Take the pan from the oven and add the bell pepper, zucchini, squash, asparagus, onion, garlic, and jalapeño. Sprinkle with the basil, ginger, brown sugar (if desired), and salt and pepper to taste.
1 small yellow squash, halved lengthwise and cut into ½-inch-thick semi-round slices	
½ pound asparagus, trimmed of thick stems and cut diagonally into 1-inch pieces	**4** Drizzle the remaining 1 to 2 tablespoons of olive oil over the vegetables, using only enough to lightly coat them. Toss well, spreading the vegetables out in a single layer.
1 small red onion, chopped into ⅛-inch cubes	
1 large clove garlic, chopped	**5** Return the roasting pan to the oven and roast about 20 to 25 minutes, or until tender, turning once with a spatula or wooden spoon after 15 minutes so the vegetables brown evenly.
½ to 1 jalapeño pepper or small red chile pepper (according to taste), seeded and minced	
1 tablespoon chopped fresh (or 1 teaspoon dried) basil, marjoram, or thyme	
2 teaspoons peeled and minced fresh ginger	
1 teaspoon brown sugar (optional)	
Salt and black pepper	

Per serving: Calories 123 (From Fat 63); Fat 7g (Saturated 1g); Cholesterol 0mg; Sodium 181mg; Carbohydrate 14g (Dietary Fiber 4g); Protein 3g.

Tip: If after 25 minutes the vegetables are tender but not browned, place them under the broiler for a minute or two — but don't let them burn.

Chapter 9

Coals and Coils: Grilling and Broiling

*L*oosely speaking, the terms *grilling* and *broiling* are almost interchangeable. In grilling, which is done on a barbecue grill, the heat source is below; in oven broiling, it's above. Because both methods involve intense heat, they're best reserved for relatively thin pieces of meat, poultry, and vegetables — thick cuts of meat can burn on the outside before cooking sufficiently in the middle. The advantage of grilling and broiling is that the surface of the food develops that characteristic browned, crispy, flavorful "grilled" quality.

Broiling is usually done 4 to 6 inches from the heating coil. It is always best to put the food on a broiler pan with sides and a grated top that allows juices to fall into the pan. And watch out for flare-ups, either in the oven or on the grill. Flare-ups not only pose a fire danger, but they also can burn meat and give it an acrid flavor. Use the oven door or grill's cover to extinguish flames, and keep a spray bottle of water on hand.

The grilled recipes in this chapter work for broiling as well. Because you can't see food that is broiling as readily as food on a grill, check it more often until you get used to the timing. Keep in mind that broilers are typically hotter than charcoal, so food usually cooks faster.

Watch the video at www.dummies.com/go/grilling for visual tips on grilling and broiling.

Mastering Your Grill

If you're in the market for a grill, your choices range from a small hibachi to a "grilling unit" that is roughly the size of a Fiat and sports everything from gas burners and cutting boards to rotisseries and satellite TV (just kidding . . . we think). High-end grills can run into the thousands of dollars. Are the pricey models worth it? Or are you good to go with the hibachi? Look more closely at your grill options before you shell out the big bucks.

Obviously, the grill you choose is a matter of personal preference. But after you make your decision, you need to know how to master your heat source. This section covers the fundamentals you need to know if you're using a charcoal, gas, or electric grill.

Charcoal grilling

Many hard-core barbecue experts prefer charcoal grilling over any other type because of the flavor it imparts to meat and vegetables. Charcoal grills can be short or tall, large or small, but they all have one thing in common: Instead of turning a switch or lighting a gas flame, you actually light briquettes or wood and cook your food over this sometimes temperamental heat source.

Charcoal grilling does produce a unique flavor you can't get from a gas or electric grill, and charcoal grills are usually much less expensive than gas or electric grills. Some double as smokers. Moreover, you don't have to worry about buying and/or refilling a propane tank; for charcoal grilling, you can use charcoal briquettes or real wood briquettes (which are dense chunks of wood). Some briquettes are pretreated with lighter fluid so they are easy to light; we prefer real wood briquettes and/or special woods like mesquite, hickory, apple and others.

 If you add wood chips to your grill to increase the smoke flavor of your meat, soak them first in water for about 15 minutes. Doing so makes them smolder and smoke rather than burn up in a flash.

The key to successful charcoal grilling is the same as for stovetop cooking: an even source of heat. Probably the most common failing of amateur cooks is cooking with a charcoal fire that is too hot. This could result from having too many briquettes, or positioning the grate too close to the fire. Here are more tips for having the perfect charcoal grilling experience:

- ✔ As a rule, 30 charcoal briquettes can cook about 1 pound of meat. If you're cooking 2 pounds of meat, you need around 45 briquettes. Don't overload your grill with charcoal — too hot a fire will char food before it is fully cooked.

✔ Spread the coals in a solid layer about 4 to 6 inches below the food grate.

✔ Never light cooking fires with kerosene, gasoline, or other chemicals unless you have a terrific home insurance plan.

How *do* you light the grill? Dry newspaper and a little patience work wonders. Or use the *plug* — an electric rod that you place in the center of a charcoal pile until it ignites. Using lighter fluid (or charcoal presoaked in lighter fluid) remains the most popular way of starting a fire.

Perhaps the best lighting technique is using a *stovepipe starter,* which looks like a piece of stovepipe with a handle. All you do is crumple some newspaper in the center of the empty grill and place the pipe over it. Then fill the top with briquettes. When you ignite the paper, the heat intensifies and shoots straight up, quickly lighting the coals. When the coals are mostly white, reverse the pipe and spread them over the bottom of the grill. (If you need extra briquettes just place them over the hot ones.)

✔ Allow 30 to 35 minutes for the coals to burn to medium (they should be about 75 percent white). To gauge the temperature, place the palm of your hand just above the grill's grid. If you can hold your hand in that position for 2 seconds, the coals are hot; a 3-second hold tells you the coals are medium-hot; 4 seconds is medium; and 5 indicates it's time to think about the microwave.

✔ If you're cooking a large quantity of food and the fire begins to fade before you finish, add a small amount of fresh charcoal.

Axioms of outdoor grilling

When it comes to grilling, you can count on the following:

✔ The fire is always at its peak 15 minutes after you finish cooking the food.

✔ If you overhear the cook say, "No problem, I'll just dust it off," it's time to visit the salad bowl.

✔ The chances of getting good food at a home barbecue are in inverse proportion to the silliness of the chef's apron. If the apron is plain and solid in color, you have reason for hope; if it says, "Who Needs Mom?" or "Kiss the Cook," hit the onion dip fast.

✔ Barbecues benefit from the "Hot dogs taste better at the ballpark" syndrome. That is, the very nature of having a barbecue somehow makes all the food taste better.

Gas grilling

Gas grills can get pretty fancy . . . and pretty expensive! But they look impressive on the patio. Thankfully gas-powered grills have become increasingly popular and more affordable in recent years. And they have several advantages over charcoal grills:

- They heat up quickly.
- The heat is adjustable and consistent.
- They are easy to clean and maintain.
- You won't throw your back out lugging 17-pound bags of charcoal.

Some gas grills use lava rocks to simulate charcoal, which works exceedingly well. The cooking technique is the same as for charcoal grills, but the flavor is not as pronounced.

One major difference between a gas and a charcoal grill is that gas grills run off a propane tank. That means you need to buy propane, attach it to your grill, and refill it when it runs out — usually when the steak is barely seared. Some people shy away from propane, but if you follow the directions for your grill, propane is safe.

Electric grilling

The electric grill is easy to operate. Some models are designed for indoor use, such as the George Foreman Grill, and others are made for either indoor or outdoor use. Electric grills are essentially like portable electric stoves, and some contain smokers. The main advantage of an electric grill is that you can use it indoors if you want but can simulate the effect of an outdoor grill.

Barbecuing doesn't equal grilling

The terms *barbecuing* and *grilling* are often incorrectly interchanged. Grilling, like broiling, is a quick technique that cooks relatively small, tender pieces of food (such as chicken breasts, pork kebabs, or skewered shrimp) directly over a heat source. Barbecuing is more like oven roasting. With barbecuing, larger cuts of meat (such as spare ribs, pork butts, or whole turkeys) are slowly roasted over an indirect fire, in a covered grill, sometimes for hours, until the food is very tender and succulent. To make an indirect fire, the coals are moved to one side of the grill in the fire box. (On a gas grill, only one side of the grill is heated.) The food is cooked opposite the fire and covered, to trap the heat and smoke. This chapter focuses on grilling only. For both grilling and barbecuing information, tips, and recipes, check out *Grilling For Dummies*, by Marie Rama and John Mariani (Wiley).

Marinating for Flavor

A common misperception is that marinades tenderize meat. They don't. A marinade barely penetrates the outer ⅛ inch of the surface of meat, poultry, or game. What a marinade can do is add flavor to the surface.

We could write a book about marinades. Suffice it to say that most marinades involve an acidic ingredient (vinegar, lemon, or some kinds of wine), oil, herbs, and perhaps a base flavor ingredient (beef or chicken stock, for example). You want to end up with a marinade that is well balanced and flavorful.

Consider this example: You have a chuck shoulder steak. Ask yourself whether you want to add a hot, medium, or sweet flavor. Your answer depends largely on the main ingredient. You may not want a sweet flavor on fish, for example. With pork, though, you may.

Say for now that you want a hot marinade for the steak; you want to give the steak some zip. Start with red chile flakes (carefully!). Then what? You need a liquid that goes with beef as well as chiles. You can use beef stock (homemade or canned beef broth) or red wine. Suppose that you choose red wine. So you have the foundation of your hot marinade, which you can now jazz up. What goes well with hot things? Minced garlic and black peppercorns maybe. Chopped cilantro adds flavor, too. (As you begin to cook, you'll discover more about ingredients in the supermarket and how to blend them.) Depending on your taste, you may want to add a little dried cumin or coriander seed. Then, at the end, add 2 to 3 tablespoons of good olive oil, salt, and black pepper.

So there you have your basic hot marinade for steak, which you can vary as you go along to make it hotter, milder, or whatever. Now you try!

Put your meat into a Ziploc bag or shallow pan and cover it with the marinade. Turn it once to coat the meat, and let it soak up the flavor for at least one hour — or even overnight in the refrigerator. Remove it from the marinade, pat it dry, and grill as you like.

Be sure to marinate meats, fish, poultry, and vegetables in the refrigerator. Bacteria forms on the surface of room-temperature food very quickly. And don't reuse marinade from pieces of raw chicken or fish.

Perfecting Your Grilling Technique

Before you fire up the grill, keep in mind the following tips:

- ✔ Clean the grill grate well with a wire brush between uses. A dirty grate can affect the taste of your food — and it looks gross.

✔ Before igniting the fire, brush some vegetable oil over the grates to prevent sticking.

✔ Get yourself organized. Set up a small table next to the grill with all your ingredients, utensils, serving platters, and so on. What utensils do you need? It depends on what you're making. Common examples include a long-handled metal spatula, fork, and tongs.

✔ Trim meat of excess fat to avoid grease flare-ups that blacken the meat and give it a burned flavor.

After you place your meat, chicken, or veggies on the grill, take these tips to heart:

✔ Cooking times for outdoor grill recipes are approximate, so don't throw the meat on and jump in the pool for 15 minutes. Many variables affect cooking time: wind, intensity of coals, thickness of meat, and your fondness for dancing every time a Supremes song comes on.

✔ Use the grill lid. Many barbecue grills come with lids, which, when secured, create an oven that can exceed 450 degrees. Certain foods that take a relatively long time to cook — chicken legs, thicker slices of steak, and so on — grill faster and better with the lid on. Essentially, you're grilling and roasting at the same time. A lid traps much of the heat, directing it into the food rather than allowing it to blow away. The lid also can create a smoky effect that infuses the food with delicious aromas and flavors (especially if you grill over woods like apple, hickory, and mesquite). But be sure to lift the lid frequently to check on the food.

✔ Do not apply sweet barbecue sauces to meat until the last 10 minutes of cooking or the sugar in them may burn.

Be sure to shut off the valve of your gas grill when finished. On a charcoal grill, close the lid to extinguish the hot coals.

Making Each Dish Delicious

In this section, we offer a few words of advice for how to create some outdoor masterpieces.

Burgers

If you want the perfect hamburger — juicy and meaty, moist and not fatty — you have to start with the right meat. The best all-around meat for hamburgers is ground chuck, which has about 15 to 20 percent fat, just enough to keep it moist. (Supermarkets usually list the percentage of fat on the label.) Also look for coarsely ground meat, which yields a looser patty. Many people think that if they buy the "best" meat, like ground sirloin or ground round, they'll have a superior burger. The flavor may be good, but those cuts are so lean that they tend to be dry.

Hamburgers for the grill should be plump and well seasoned. The ingredients and flavors you can add are limitless. Consider minced onions, minced garlic, minced basil, and chopped thyme or rosemary; soy sauce, seasoned breadcrumbs, and a beaten egg; Worcestershire sauce; minced bell peppers; or Tabasco sauce if you like it hot. And you don't even have to stick to beef: Lamb and turkey burgers, or blends of all three, are super, too.

You may enjoy getting your hands (washed, please!) into a mound of rosy ground meat and playing sculptor. But if you get too aggressive when forming your hamburger patties and mold them too firmly, they'll tighten up on the grill. And nobody wants a tight hamburger! To get the most tender burger, keep it loose and don't overwork the meat.

How long should you cook a burger? What constitutes "done" is a question of taste, but the U.S. Department of Agriculture suggests an internal temperature of 160 degrees for safety; the inside of the burger should not show any pink. When you're grilling, make a small incision in each patty to determine doneness — they should be just cooked through and still juicy in the center.

Keep all this advice in mind as you check out our recipe for The Perfect Hamburger later in the chapter.

Chicken

Barbecued chicken has a smoky, sweet, tangy flavor that can come from a broiler but that we think tastes even better off the grill. Just be sure the chicken is cooked all the way. Prick the chicken with a fork. If the juices run clear, the chicken is done, but to be really accurate, use a meat thermometer. The internal temperature of chicken parts on the bone should be 180 degrees. (Be sure the thermometer isn't touching a bone, which can give a false high reading.)

Remember, grill times in recipes are approximate, depending on the heat of your grill and the size of the chicken pieces. To shorten cooking time, you can microwave chicken pieces for about 3 minutes per pound before grilling.

If the mere thought of chicken hot off the grill makes you salivate, you'll love the Barbecued Chicken recipe we offer later in the chapter (and shown in the color section of this book). We suggest that you use our Chapter 8 recipe for Country Barbeque Sauce when making it, but you can take a shortcut and use store-bought sauce if you wish.

Vegetables

Charcoal imparts a pleasing texture and a smoky essence to vegetables. Moreover, preparation is easy and quick. Here are some examples:

- ✔ **Corn:** Pull back the husks to remove the silk, but leave the husks attached to the base of the ear. Wrap the husks back around the corn and tie at the top with string or a strip of husk. Grill 20 minutes or until tender, turning frequently. Serve with melted butter flavored with herbs and fresh lemon juice.

- ✔ **Eggplant and zucchini:** Cut them lengthwise into 1-inch-thick slices. Brush with oil, season to taste, and grill, turning occasionally, for 5 to 8 minutes or until golden brown and tender. For additional flavor, marinate in a 3-to-1 oil/vinegar mixture with salt and pepper and maybe Dijon-style mustard for about 15 minutes before grilling.

- ✔ **Potatoes, carrots, onion, and turnips:** Peel and slice into uniform pieces and precook in boiling water until almost tender. Rinse in cold water to stop the cooking and drain well. Wrap in aluminum foil with seasonings such as olive oil, lemon juice, fresh herbs, and salt and pepper to taste. Grill for 10 to 15 minutes or until tender. (You can also thread them onto skewers before grilling.)

- ✔ **Tomatoes:** Slice firm, ripe tomatoes into 1-inch-thick pieces. Brush with olive oil; sprinkle with dried basil or parsley and salt and pepper. Grill until heated through, about 5 minutes total, turning once.

Porous vegetables, such as mushrooms and sliced eggplant, need not be marinated before grilling. You simply brush them with a flavorful liquid, as in the recipe for Garlic-Grilled Portobello Mushrooms later in the chapter.

If you're going to grill mushrooms, you need to know how to clean, trim, and slice them. First, wipe them clean with a damp paper towel to gently brush off any dirt. Don't rinse them, as they become water-logged and quickly lose their flavor and meaty texture. For trimming and slicing instructions, see Figure 9-1.

Steak

Steak on the grill may be one of summer's nicest luxuries, as long as you cook the steak the right way! A dry, tough steak is disappointing, so don't overcook. Medium or medium-rare yields a more tender steak than well-done. You can also add flavor with a good marinade. Check out our recipe for The Perfect Steak later in the chapter.

How to Trim and Slice Mushrooms

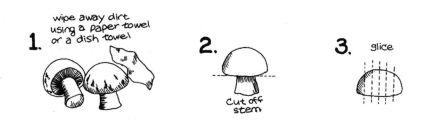

Pork

Grilling a pork tenderloin couldn't be easier, and the results are simply delicious. Our recipe for Grilled Pork Tenderloin later in the chapter shows you how to brine the pork prior to cooking it so it retains maximum moisture and flavor. As a bonus, we throw in a scrumptious recipe for Southern Fried Grits, which are the perfect accompaniment to the grilled pork. No, the grits aren't grilled, but we think you'll forgive us for straying from the topic when you taste them!

Seafood

Shrimp require minimal cooking time. It takes only a few minutes before they turn pink and succulent. Be sure not to overcook them, or they could become rubbery.

To prepare shrimp for grilling, you may want to remove the bitter black vein that runs along the outside. Some cooks do, some don't. In grilling, the vein likely burns off, but see the illustration in Chapter 7 if you want to devein. You can leave the tails on, or pull them off. You want to double-thread the shrimp onto skewers so that the skewer pierces both ends of the shrimp (which prevents them from sliding off). If you use wooden skewers, soak them for 30 minutes in cold water and cover the tips with foil to prevent burning. (***Note:*** Don't pack the shrimp too tightly on the skewers; allow a little space between each piece so the heat can circulate and to ensure even cooking.)

Get creative with our Grilled Shrimp Skewers recipe by alternating each shrimp with veggies, or even fruit. Try chunks of onion and cherry tomatoes, or cubes of pineapple. You can also serve shrimp skewers with a dipping sauce, such as melted butter with a squeeze of fresh lemon juice, barbecue sauce (store-bought or the Country Barbecue Sauce recipe in Chapter 8), or Asian chili sauce (available in the Asian food section of your grocery store).

Our Grilled Tuna with Niçoise Dressing recipe is a variation on the classic French dish and makes a delicious light lunch. If you don't want to fire up the grill, you can also make it under the broiler. (Keep in mind that some people prefer grilled tuna very rare, and others medium, so don't overcook it.) Other types of fish and shellfish work with this recipe as well. Choose those that can hold up to grilling, such as firm-fleshed salmon, halibut, swordfish, mako shark, and monkfish. Avoid delicate fish such as sole, which tends to flake and fall apart on the grill.

The Perfect Hamburger

Prep time: About 10 min • **Cook time:** 10–14 min • **Yield:** 4 servings

Ingredients	*Directions*
Oil for the grill rack **1½ pounds ground chuck** **¼ teaspoon salt, or to taste** **¼ teaspoon black pepper, or to taste** **4 hamburger buns**	*1* Oil the grill and prepare a medium fire in a charcoal or gas grill.
	2 While the grill is heating, combine in a bowl the ground chuck, salt, and pepper. Mix lightly but thoroughly, using your hands. Shape the mixture into 4 patties, each about ¾ inch thick.
	3 Place the patties on the grill grid. Grill directly over the heat for 5 to 7 minutes per side for medium, or less for rare or medium rare.
	4 Just before the burgers are finished, toast the buns on the edges of the grill. Serve.

Per serving: Calories 344 (From Fat 105); Fat 12g (Saturated 4g); Cholesterol 97mg; Sodium 450mg; Carbohydrate 22g (Dietary Fiber 1g); Protein 35g.

Go-With: In our opinion, nothing goes better with a great burger than French Potato Salad (see Chapter 12).

Tip: Quick and tasty burger toppings include thinly sliced red or yellow onions, tomato slices marinated in a basil vinaigrette dressing, flavored mustards, mango or tomato chutney, tomato-based salsa, grilled peppers, and garlic-grilled mushrooms.

Barbecued Chicken

Prep time: About 10 min • **Cook time:** About 50 min • **Yield:** 4 servings

Ingredients	Directions
Oil for the grill rack 1 chicken, cut into 4 pieces, or 4 chicken breasts with ribs (about 3 pounds total) Salt and pepper 1 cup Country Barbecue Sauce (see Ch. 8) or store-bought barbecue sauce	**1** Oil the grill grid and prepare a medium-hot fire in a charcoal or gas grill. **2** Rinse the chicken pieces in cold water and dry thoroughly with paper towels. Season each piece with salt and pepper on both sides. **3** Put the chicken pieces, bone side up, on the grill. Cook for 30 minutes. Flip chicken pieces with tongs. Cook for an additional 20 minutes or more, as needed. **4** During the last 10 minutes of cooking, brush the chicken pieces with barbecue sauce. The chicken is done when it's no longer pink inside.

Per serving: Calories 514 (From Fat 253); Fat 28g (Saturated 7g); Cholesterol 134mg; Sodium 452mg; Carbohydrate 21g (Dietary Fiber 0g); Protein 43g.

Go-With: The assertive flavor of the barbecue sauce marries well with side dishes like French Potato Salad or Bell Pepper Rice Salad (both in Chapter 12), or traditional Perfect Corn on the Cob and All-American Coleslaw (in Chapter 20).

Garlic-Grilled Portobello Mushrooms

Prep time: About 10 min • **Cook time:** About 6 min • **Yield:** 4 servings

Ingredients	Directions
Oil for the grill rack	*1* Oil the grill grid and prepare a medium-hot fire in a charcoal or gas grill.
1 pound portobello mushrooms	
⅓ cup extra-virgin olive oil	*2* Clean the mushrooms and remove the stems.
3 tablespoons lemon juice	
2 large cloves (about 2 teaspoons) garlic, minced	*3* In a small bowl, combine the oil, lemon juice, and garlic. Brush the caps with the flavored oil and season to taste with salt and pepper.
Salt and pepper	
2 tablespoons minced fresh parsley (optional)	*4* Place the caps on the grill, top side down, for about 3 minutes. (Do not let them burn.) Turn the caps over and grill for another 3 to 4 minutes, or until you can easily pierce the caps with a knife and the mushrooms are nicely browned.
	5 Remove the mushrooms to a platter, garnish with the parsley (if desired), and serve.

Per serving: Calories 213 (From Fat 171); Fat 19g (Saturated 3g); Cholesterol 0mg; Sodium 152mg; Carbohydrate 6g (Dietary Fiber 1g); Protein 2g.

Go-With: Steak — such as the Broiled Skirt Steak, Cajun Style (see Chapter 18) — is the natural accompaniment to these savory mushrooms.

The Perfect Steak

Prep time: 5 min plus marinate time • **Cook time:** 8–20 min • **Yield:** 4 servings

Ingredients	Directions
2 T-bone, porterhouse, or top loin steaks, about 1 inch thick	*1* Place the steaks in a large resealable plastic bag. Add the wine, Worcestershire sauce, garlic, cumin, and pepper to the bag, seal, and marinate in the refrigerator for about 30 minutes, turning once after about 15 minutes.
½ cup dry red wine (try Merlot or Shiraz)	
1 tablespoon Worcestershire sauce	*2* Oil the grill grid and prepare a medium fire in a charcoal or gas grill.
1 large clove garlic, minced (about 1 teaspoon)	
1 teaspoon ground cumin	*3* Remove the steaks from the bag and discard the marinade. Put the steaks on the grill.
¼ teaspoon pepper	
Oil for the grill rack	*4* Grill for about 8 minutes for rare, 15 minutes for medium, or 20 minutes for well-done, turning the meat once with the tongs halfway through cooking. Season with the salt and serve immediately.
1 teaspoon salt	

Per serving: Calories 273 (From Fat 137); Fat 15g (Saturated 5g); Cholesterol 77mg; Sodium 675mg; Carbohydrate 0g (Dietary Fiber 0g); Protein 30g.

Go-With: This steak tastes great with side dishes that are a step above standard picnic fare. Try Penne with Parmesan Cheese and Basil (see Chapter 13), Risotto (see Chapter 13), or a Grilled Vegetable Platter with Fresh Pesto (see Chapter 12).

Grilled Pork Tenderloin

Prep time: 5 min plus brine time • **Cook time:** About 1 hr • **Yield:** 6–8 servings

Ingredients	Directions
3 tablespoons kosher salt	*1* In a large container, dissolve the salt and sugar in the hot water, stirring. Add the cold water and stir again. Let the brine cool.
½ cup granulated sugar	
2 cups hot tap water	
2 cups cold water	*2* Add the tenderloin, cover, and refrigerate for one to three hours. The pork should be submerged in the brine; if necessary, add more cold tap water to cover.
1½ to 2 pounds pork tenderloin (either one or two pieces)	
Salt and freshly ground pepper to taste	*3* Remove pork from the brine, rinse well, and dry thoroughly with paper towels.
	4 Turn gas burners to high or let charcoals get white. Season the tenderloins generously with salt and pepper.
	5 Cook the pork with the grill lid closed. Turn it every few minutes so all sides get well browned. Cook for 8 to 10 minutes, until an instant-read thermometer inserted into the thickest part registers 145 degrees.
	6 Transfer pork to a cutting board, cover loosely with foil, and let rest 5 minutes. To serve, slice crosswise into 1-inch-thick pieces.

Per serving: Calories 173 (From Fat 60); Fat 7g (Saturated 2g); Cholesterol 78mg; Sodium 318mg; Carbohydrate 2g (Dietary Fiber 0g); Protein 25g.

Southern Fried Grits

Prep time: 10 min plus chill time • **Cook time:** About 20 min • **Yield:** 8 servings

Ingredients	*Directions*
2 cups water	*1* In a medium saucepan, combine the water, milk, and salt. Bring to a boil and immediately lower to simmer.
2 cups plus 2 tablespoons milk	
1 teaspoon salt, or to taste	*2* Gradually stir in the grits and continue simmering, stirring frequently, until finished according to package directions — about 4 minutes. (The grits should be very thick.) Remove from the heat.
1 cup quick cooking grits	
3 eggs	
1 cup fine fresh bread crumbs	*3* Lightly beat two of the eggs and stir them thoroughly into the grits. Pour the mixture into an 8-inch-square baking pan. Chill for an hour or more until very firm throughout.
2 tablespoon butter (or more as needed)	
½ teaspoon vegetable oil (or more if you cook in batches)	*4* Put bread crumbs in a shallow bowl. In another shallow bowl, lightly beat the remaining egg.
	5 Cut the grits into 1½-inch squares.
	6 Heat a large fry pan to medium high and add the butter and ½ teaspoon vegetable oil. (If the butter begins to burn, reduce heat to medium.)
	7 Dip grits squares into the beaten egg, let excess drain, coat with bread crumbs, and place them in the pan. Cook until golden on one side, then flip and cook until finished (about 5 minutes total).

Per serving: Calories 233 (From Fat 71); Fat 8g (Saturated 4g); Cholesterol 96mg; Sodium 463mg; Carbohydrate 30g (Dietary Fiber 1g); Protein 8g.

Grilled Shrimp Skewers

Prep time: About 10 min • **Cook time:** About 15 min • **Yield:** 4 servings

Ingredients	*Directions*
Oil for the grill rack	*1* Oil the grill grid and prepare a medium fire in a charcoal or gas grill.
¼ cup butter, melted	
2 teaspoons lemon juice	*2* Combine the butter, lemon juice, and garlic in a small bowl. Reserve half the lemon-butter mixture in a glass measuring cup.
1 clove garlic, minced	
1 pound medium shrimp (the size that equals about 20 per pound)	*3* Peel the shrimp, devein them, and double-thread them onto four skewers.
	4 Brush the shrimp on both sides with the lemon-butter mixture in the bowl.
	5 Place skewers on the grate and grill for about 8 minutes, or until golden, turning the skewers once halfway through the cooking time.
	6 Remove to a platter and drizzle with the remaining lemon-butter mixture from the glass measuring cup. Serve immediately.

Per serving: Calories 188 (From Fat 111); Fat 12g (Saturated 7g); Cholesterol 199mg; Sodium 195mg; Carbohydrate 1g (Dietary Fiber 0g); Protein 18g.

Go-With: Try this dish with a light accompaniment like Sautéed Spinach Leaves (see Chapter 5), or Roasted Summer Vegetables (in this chapter).

Grilled Tuna with Niçoise Dressing

Prep time: 10 min plus marinate time • **Cook time:** 6–7 min • **Yield:** 4 servings

Ingredients	Directions
1 green onion, trimmed and minced	**1** Make the dressing by combining in a bowl the green onion, olives, and capers. Stir in the vinegar and pepper. Beat in the anchovy fillets or paste (if desired) and parsley and then ½ cup of the oil. Set aside.
1 tablespoon finely chopped black olives	
1 tablespoon finely chopped capers	**2** Put the tuna on a roasting pan and season with the remaining 3 tablespoons of oil, thyme, and salt and pepper to taste. Turn the steaks to coat well. Let sit, refrigerated, for about 15 minutes.
2 tablespoons balsamic vinegar	
¼ teaspoon pepper	**3** Brush the grill grid with oil and heat a gas or charcoal grill to medium-high.
1 teaspoon finely chopped anchovy fillets or anchovy paste (optional)	**4** Place the tuna on the grill and cook for about 3 minutes. Using a spatula, turn the fillets and grill for 3 minutes on the other side. Remove one of the steaks and test for doneness by making a small incision in the center.
2 tablespoons chopped parsley	
½ cup plus 3 tablespoons olive oil	**5** When the steaks have cooked, transfer them to warm serving dishes. Spoon half of the dressing over the steaks. Serve the remaining dressing on the side.
4 tuna steaks, about 1 inch thick, 1½ pounds total	
1 teaspoon minced fresh thyme or ½ teaspoon dried thyme	
Salt and pepper	
Oil for the grill rack	

Per serving: Calories 454 (From Fat 288); Fat 32g (Saturated 4g); Cholesterol 74mg; Sodium 200mg; Carbohydrate 2g (Dietary Fiber 0g); Protein 38g.

Go-With: This entrée goes nicely with a soup such as the Carrot Soup with Dill or a salad such as Bell Pepper Rice Salad or Cucumber-Dill Salad (all in Chapter 12).

Chapter 10

Baking Basics

In This Chapter

▶ Measuring accurately

▶ Handling eggs

▶ Defining baking techniques

▶ Mastering pie crusts and bread dough

▶ Tossing the box and making a cake (or cupcakes) from scratch

For some reason, people find baking intimidating. But why? Sure, baking may seem a little mystical. Get flour wet and put it in a hot oven, and it turns into something entirely different: bread, cake, cookies, cupcakes, pie, pastry. What kind of magic could be more fun than that?

Baking *is* fun, if you know the basics. However, it also requires a more scientific approach than other kinds of cooking. You can't just throw in a little of this, a little of that, and hope for the best. Baking is more a science than an art. Throw off the proportion of dry ingredients (like flour, baking powder, and salt) to wet ingredients (like milk, eggs, and vanilla extract), for example, or fail to mix, whip, or knead the batter or dough as directed, and your results will not be the same as the recipe intended. In fact, the recipe may not turn out at all, with cookies running all over the tray, cakes falling in the center, or breads refusing to rise.

But that fact, viewed from a different perspective, should actually make baking *less* intimidating: All you have to do is follow the recipe — exactly — and your baked goods will fill the house with their heavenly scent. And you'll find that people will begin to do you little favors . . . *just in case* you make another one of those batches of cupcakes.

Don't Wing It: Measuring with Care

Baking's number one rule is to measure accurately. Recipes for baked goods, if they are good recipes, are carefully formulated so that all the elements result in the perfect texture and flavor. In baking, different kinds of ingredients must be measured in different ways for accuracy. Here's what you need to know.

Measuring dry ingredients

Baking generally begins with dry ingredients like flour and sugar, and these must be measured in a particular way. Use a dry measuring cup — not the kind with a spout, but the kind with a flat top.

Pick a flour

Will a flour by any other name bake the same? Absolutely not! Different kinds of flours are made from either high-protein hard wheat, low-protein soft wheat, or a combination, and each kind of flour has a different gluten content. (*Gluten* is a protein in wheat and some other grains that gets stretchy with beating or kneading and helps baked goods rise.) Choosing the right kind of flour for your recipe can have a big impact on the results, so choose wisely:

- *All-purpose flour* is made from a mixture of hard and soft wheat, with a mid-range gluten content, making it appropriate for many baked goods and adequate for most baked goods. Use it for cookies, biscuits, quick bread, and cake — unless you want a very light, delicate cake, in which case you should use cake flour.

- *Cake flour* is made mostly from soft wheat and has a finer texture, lower gluten content, and higher starch content than all-purpose flour. Similarly, *pastry flour* is made primarily from soft wheat, although it has a slightly higher protein content than cake flour, so it's better for pastries that need a flakier structure, such as puff pastry, pie crust, and biscuits.

- *Bread flour* is made primarily from hard wheat. Its high protein/gluten content makes it best for yeast breads that need to rise.

- *Gluten-free flour* (which could contain rice, garbanzo, amaranth, quinoa, corn, sorghum, tapioca, or any number of other flours) is more difficult to use in baking precisely because it lacks gluten, which is largely responsible for the characteristic texture of many baked goods. However, when other ingredients are added to compensate for the lack of gluten, gluten-free flour can stand in for regular flour. For best results, follow a recipe designed for gluten-free flour.

Flour and sugar are measured the same way, but let's focus on flour as our example. Stir up your flour (in the bag or canister) to fluff it up, then dip in your measuring cup — whatever size the recipe calls for (1 cup, ½ cup, and so on) — so that the flour is mounded higher than the rim of the measuring cup. Using the flat side of a knife, skim it over the top of the cup — this is called *leveling* — so you push the excess flour back into the bag or canister. When you're done, the flour should come *exactly* to the top of the measuring cup — no higher, no lower. Now you can add the flour to your recipe.

If the recipe calls for *sifted flour,* you must sift it *before measuring.* Sifting changes the volume of the flour, and because measuring is so important, sifting is too. Using a dry measuring cup, scoop out the approximate amount of flour called for in the recipe and place it in the top of the sifter. Sift the flour into a large mixing bowl or over a piece of wax paper. After sifting, so as not to lose the flour's new "lightness," gently spoon the flour into the appropriate measuring cup, fill to overflowing, and then level it off with the straight edge of a knife.

Some recipes call for dry ingredients in terms of weight, which is actually an even more accurate way to measure baking ingredients. If you decide to get serious about your baking (or if you just want to try a recipe that uses weights instead of cups), invest in a kitchen scale. When you weigh your flour, sugar, and other ingredients in pounds rather than measuring in cups, you can be even more confident in your accuracy.

Recipes often call for smaller amounts of other dry ingredients such as baking powder, baking soda, active dry yeast, and salt. You can also level dry ingredients in a tablespoon, teaspoon, or smaller measure. Don't use your table silverware to measure dry ingredients — use measuring spoons. As with a measuring cup, scoop the measuring spoon into your dry ingredient so you have a heaping spoonful, then run the flat side of a knife over the top to level the ingredients. Some baking ingredients, like baking powder cans and baking soda boxes, come with a built-in leveling surface so you can dip in your spoon and level as you pull it out of the can or box by running the top of the spoon along the flat surface.

Measuring wet ingredients

Wet or liquid ingredients, such as milk, water, and oil, require different kinds of measuring cups than dry ingredients — namely *liquid* measuring cups. These cups typically have spouts for easy pouring and rims that are higher than the highest measuring mark. For example, a 2-cup liquid measuring cup will hold more than 2 cups if you fill it to the brim. To measure liquid ingredients, pour them into the measuring cup exactly to the line indicated for the amount you need. Make sure the cup is sitting on a flat surface. Be exact for best results.

When you need to measure smaller quantities of liquid ingredients, such as vanilla or almond extract, use the same measuring spoons that you use for dry ingredients.

Don't measure liquid or dry ingredients over your working bowl, especially if it's filled with other ingredients. You may accidentally add too much of an ingredient.

Measuring other types of ingredients

Certain ingredients require other measuring techniques. When a recipe calls for brown sugar, for example, you don't measure it the same way you do regular sugar. Instead, you pack the brown sugar tightly into your measuring cup, pressing it down with the back of a spoon. The same is true when you're working with shortening or peanut butter.

To easily remove sticky foods like shortening, peanut butter, honey, or molasses from a measuring cup or spoon, coat the cup or spoon first with a small amount of vegetable oil or spray.

When a recipe calls for butter or margarine, your best bet is to use the kind that's packaged in stick form. Use the measure marks on the wrapper to slice off a specific amount.

Working with Eggs

Many baking recipes call for eggs, and you can probably surmise that they don't mean for you to include the shell. Eggs are technically a liquid ingredient, but you don't have to measure them the way you do water, milk, and oil. Instead, you have to be able to break them so you get all the good stuff into your bowl and the crunchy stuff into the garbage can or compost pile. In this section, we help you do just that — and we walk you through the process of separating the yolk from the egg white.

Breaking with care

To get the good stuff out of that mysterious ovoid, follow these instructions:

1. **Hold the egg in one hand.**

2. **Tap the egg on the side of a small bowl or glass measuring cup to gently break the shell.**

Don't tap too hard, or you'll shatter the egg and your egg will be full of shell pieces.

3. **Put your two thumbs inside the crack and gently open the egg so that the yolk and white fall into the bowl or measuring cup.**

   If a piece of shell falls in the egg, use the edge of one of the egg shell halves to nudge it up the side of the bowl and out. Egg shell pieces tend to stick to other egg shell pieces.

Always break eggs into a separate bowl or cup before adding them to a recipe. That way, you can remove any stray shell pieces before they get lost in, say, the birthday cake batter.

Separating an egg

Many recipes require separated egg whites and yolks. Separating eggs isn't difficult; it just takes a little practice. Follow these steps, as illustrated in Figure 10-1, to separate an egg without breaking the yolk. (If a recipe calls for just egg whites, you don't want any yolk in them or the recipe likely won't turn out as expected.)

How to Separate an Egg

1. Hold the egg in one hand over two small bowls.
2. Crack the shell on the side of one bowl.
3. Let the white fall into one of the bowls.
4. Pass the yolk back & forth, each time releasing more white.
5. When all the white is in the bowl, drop yolk in the other bowl.

Figure 10-1: Separating an egg.

1. **Hold the egg in one hand above two small bowls.**

2. **Crack the shell on the side of one bowl — just enough to break through the shell and the membrane without piercing the yolk or shattering the shell.**

   This step may take a little practice. Repeat on the other side if necessary.

3. **Pry open the eggshell with both thumbs and gently let the bulk of the white fall into one of the bowls.**

4. **Carefully pass the yolk back and forth from one shell cavity to the other, each time releasing more white.**

5. **When all the white is in the bowl, carefully transfer the yolk to the other bowl (it doesn't matter if the yolk breaks at this point). Cover and refrigerate the yolk if you're not using it right away.**

If you're more of a visual learner, be sure to check out the video at www. dummies.com/go/separatingegg.

Folding, Whipping, Kneading, and More: Getting the Techniques Right

You've got your flour, your baking powder, your milk, your eggs. It's all measured and ready to go. Now what? Next, you have to mix it all together, but not willy-nilly. Remember, *follow the directions,* which will include some techniques for mixing that you need to know if you want light cakes, chewy cookies, tender cupcakes, and bread that actually rises. When you work the batter or dough the right way, you get good results, so consider this your official guide to (literally) whipping that batter or dough into shape. Here's what the various baking techniques mean:

- ✔ **Stirring:** Moving ingredients around with a spoon until they are combined.

- ✔ **Beating:** Mixing ingredients together vigorously (more vigorously than stirring), in a circular motion, by hand or with an electric mixer, until they become smooth. If you are the sort who likes to keep track of such things, 100 brisk hand-beaten strokes generally equal one minute with an electric mixer.

- ✔ **Whipping:** Similar to beating, but whipping incorporates more air into ingredients such as egg whites or cream by using a whisk or electric beater with a whisk attachment instead of a spoon or standard beater attachment.

Many recipes call for egg whites whipped into soft or stiff peaks, to lighten batters or make meringues or soufflés. Before whipping egg whites, make sure that your mixing bowl and beaters are clean and dry. Even a speck of dirt, oil, or egg yolk can prevent the whites from beating stiff. To get your bowl really clean, wipe it with a cloth dipped in vinegar, which will remove any fat or grease. Then rinse and dry the bowl. Avoid using plastic bowls when beating whites; fat and grease adhere to plastic, which can diminish the volume of the beaten whites.

The copper connection

We won't go into the scientific details of why copper bowls are best for whipping egg whites — just believe us. As far back as the mid-eighteenth century, this was common knowledge. Just remember that if you are making a meringue or other dish that requires whipped whites, whipping the whites in a copper bowl with a balloon whisk yields a fluffier and more stable foam.

A 10-inch copper bowl for whisking costs about $60. If you don't have a copper bowl, a pinch of cream of tartar added to the egg white can also stabilize the foam.

If any of the yolk breaks and falls into the separated whites before you beat them stiff, remove the yolk by dabbing with a piece of paper towel. Beat the whites slowly until they're foamy; then increase the beating speed to incorporate as much air as possible until the whites form smooth, shiny peaks. If you overbeat the egg whites so that they lose their shine and start to look dry and grainy, add another egg white and beat briefly.

✔ **Whisking:** Whipping briefly and lightly by hand using a wire whisk, to combine ingredients (such as eggs and milk) and incorporate air.

✔ **Creaming:** Beating butter, margarine, or shortening with sugar by hand or with an electric mixer until it is completely combined and turns light and fluffy.

✔ **Kneading:** Working yeast bread dough by hand or with dough hook attachments on an electric mixer. The pushing, folding, and pressing action develops the gluten in the dough and gives it a smooth, elastic texture so it will rise.

✔ **Folding:** Combing a light mixture, such as beaten egg whites or whipped cream, into a heavier mixture, such as cake batter. For example, to fold egg whites into cake batter, begin by stirring about one-quarter of the beaten whites into the yolk mixture. (This step lightens the batter somewhat.) Then pile the remaining egg whites on top. Use a large rubber spatula to cut down through the center of the mixture, going all the way to the bottom of the bowl. Pull the spatula toward you to the edge of the bowl, turning it to bring some of the batter up over the whites. Give the bowl a quarter-turn and repeat this plunging, scooping motion about 10 to 15 times (depending on the amount of batter) until the whites and batter are combined. Be careful not to overblend, or the beaten whites will deflate. See Figure 10-2 for illustrated instructions of this technique.

How to Fold Egg Whites into a Cake Batter

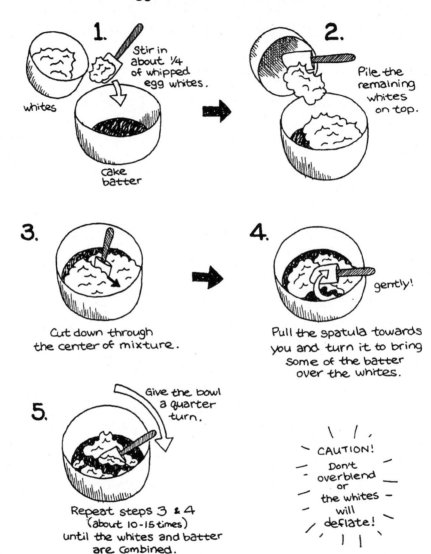

1. Stir in about ¼ of whipped egg whites.

whites

cake batter

2. Pile the remaining whites on top.

3. Cut down through the center of mixture.

4. gently! Pull the spatula towards you and turn it to bring some of the batter over the whites.

5. Give the bowl a quarter turn. Repeat steps 3 & 4 (about 10-15 times) until the whites and batter are combined.

CAUTION! Don't overblend or the whites will deflate!

Figure 10-2:
Folding egg whites into a cake batter involves a plunging, scooping motion.

Perfecting Your Pie Crust

Everybody loves pie, or so the saying goes. But everybody can love *your* pie the most if you master homemade pie dough (easier than it sounds) and the art of a thick, rich, fruity, creamy, or chocolaty pie filling. The two keys to pie are a light flaky crust and a proper filling that doesn't run all over the pie plate when you cut the pie.

Your food processor is a helpful ally in your quest for the perfect pie dough. Pie dough is a delicate blend of flour, butter, and shortening, and the less it is handled, the flakier it will be. The goal is to mix cold butter into flour and keep it from melting, which would make your pie crust tougher and greasier. A food processor blends the butter and flour *fast,* with no warm hands touching the delicate dough. However, you can make pie the old-fashioned way, too, with a pastry blender (see Figure 10-3).

You want to chill the dough at every stage, to keep those flaky butter layers intact. Roll out the chilled disks quickly, and transfer them to your pie plate. If your effort falls apart, try again. Practice makes perfect pie crust.

When your pie crust is nicely in the pan, let it rest for 30 minutes in the refrigerator before trimming off the edges. The crust shrinks a bit during this resting period, so this trick keeps your pie crust in the proper shape.

Not sure how to roll out the dough or get it safely tucked into the pie plate? Figure 10-4 shows the steps involved, including how to deal with dough when you're making a pie with both a top and bottom crust.

When you make a pie with a single crust, the recipe often calls for you to prebake the crust before adding the pie filling. In that case, you want to prevent the crust from bubbling up during baking. Figure 10-5 shows that by covering the pie shell with foil and pouring in dried beans, your crust will stay flat in the pan. To bake a single crust, put it in a 400-degree oven for 15 minutes; then lower the heat to 350 degrees and bake another 10 minutes. Check the crust during the final few minutes of baking to make sure it isn't getting too brown.

Making Pie Dough by Hand

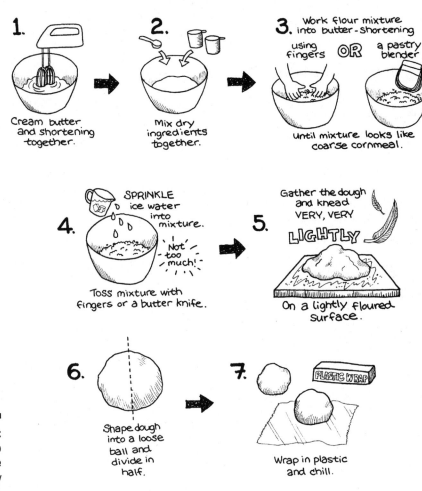

1. Cream butter and shortening together.

2. Mix dry ingredients together.

3. Work flour mixture into butter-shortening using fingers **OR** a pastry blender

   Until mixture looks like coarse cornmeal.

4. SPRINKLE ice water into mixture. Not too much!

   Toss mixture with fingers or a butter knife.

5. Gather the dough and knead VERY, VERY **LIGHTLY**

   On a lightly floured surface.

6. Shape dough into a loose ball and divide in half.

7. PLASTIC WRAP

   Wrap in plastic and chill.

Figure 10-3:
How to make pie dough by hand.

How to Roll Dough

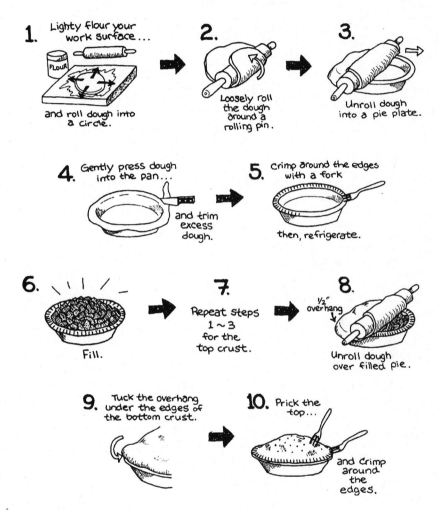

1. Lighty flour your work surface... and roll dough into a circle.

2. Loosely roll the dough around a rolling pin.

3. Unroll dough into a pie plate.

4. Gently press dough into the pan... and trim excess dough.

5. Crimp around the edges with a fork then, refrigerate.

6. Fill.

7. Repeat steps 1 ~ 3 for the top crust.

8. ½" overhang. Unroll dough over filled pie.

9. Tuck the overhang under the edges of the bottom crust.

10. Prick the top... and crimp around the edges.

Figure 10-4:
The technique for rolling pie pastry dough.

The toothpick test

Cake and quick bread recipes frequently call for the "toothpick test." To check that a cake or quick bread is done, pull it carefully out of the oven and insert a wooden toothpick most of the way into the bread or cake, and then pull it back out. If batter clings to the toothpick, your bread or cake isn't done yet. Try again every 5 minutes. If a few moist crumbs cling to the toothpick, the bread or cake is probably done or mostly done. If the toothpick comes out clean, your recipe has definitely cooked for long enough.

For a Single Crust

Figure 10-5: Preparing dough for a single crust.

1. Follow "How to Roll Dough," steps 1~5.

2. Prick the bottom & sides with a fork and/or line the pan with aluminum foil filled with dry beans as weight.

We recommend making pie as often as possible — you know, just so you can refine your technique. Of course, then your family and friends will just have to consume the happy byproducts of your homework assignment. Why not start practicing now? Look for our Basic Pastry Crust recipe later in the chapter, and then use it to make the Apple Pie recipe that follows.

For the Apple Pie recipe, you need to peel and core apples for the filling. Figure 10-6 shows you how.

Peeling and Coring an Apple

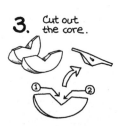

Figure 10-6: How to peel and core and apple.

1. Quarter the apples.

2. Peel the skin with a paring knife.

3. Cut out the core.

Making Cakes that Rise

Cake = heaven. At least, we think so. The fairy queen of baked goods, cake should be tender, moist, rich, light, and full of melt-in-your-mouth flavorful sweet goodness. And cupcakes? The fairy princesses! Shall we go on? Okay, we'll stop waxing poetic about cake if you promise to try baking one without the crutch that is a box of prepackaged cake mix. Those boxes may be easy to prepare, but actual from-scratch cake takes just a tiny bit more effort and isn't laden with artificial ingredients. Get used to home-baked cake, and the boxed stuff won't ever be quite as satisfying again. Top a home-baked cake with homemade frosting, and you've got the stuff of sweet dreams.

The secret to great cake is to follow directions precisely, mix ingredients thoroughly, have all ingredients at *room temperature* before you start mixing, and be sure your baking powder has not expired.

Try your hand at cake with two recipes at the end of this chapter. The first is a dense, fudgy Perfect Chocolate Cake, which is bliss for choco-holics. (When you're shopping for the bittersweet chocolate called for in the recipe, keep in mind that Lindt, Valrhona, and Callebaut are excellent brands.) The second may be a bit trendy, but we don't care. Rosy Red Velvet Cupcakes (shown in the book's color section) are simply a delight, and we find them delicious *and* charming.

Springform pans

If you love cake but hate turning the cake out onto a plate (because it breaks, it crumbles, it comes out in chunks, your birthday is ruined!), you may love a simple cake pan with a design that eliminates the hassle. Springform pans have sides that unbuckle, so you just run a sharp knife around the edge of your cake and take the sides off. The bottom stays put. You still need to remove a layer cake from its pans so you can stack it, but a springform pan is perfect for one-layer cakes, as well as cakes you couldn't remove from the pan, such as cheesecake. We like nonstick versions. Springform pans make baking easier, and isn't easier almost always better?

Bread Basics

Baking yeast bread isn't exactly a speedy affair, which is probably why most people don't do it. You can buy good bread in a bakery or even in a supermarket for just a few dollars. Even in France, where good bread is practically a religion, most home cooks buy their bread in a bakery. That being said, baking bread can be a relaxing, interesting, even addictive activity, if you enjoy it. When you have a few hours and you want to do something with your hands, give it a try.

Yeast bread is, essentially, flour and water mixed with yeast so it rises. It takes several steps, and most of the time involved is labor-free because the bread rises in several stages. Mix it, let it rise. Knead it, let it rise. Shape it, let it rise. Bake it. Some recipes have fewer steps than this.

Your bread will probably be most successful if you use bread flour, but many recipes use other kinds of flours, with or without bread flour mixed in. Because you are probably new to bread-making, we start you out with recipes that use bread flour just because it's easier and so rewarding when your very first handmade loaf of bread rises so nicely.

The other important key to good bread is good yeast. Yeast is full of live organisms that make bread rise, but if your yeast is dead, your bread will remain dense, flat, and uninspiring. Professional bakers often use *moist yeast,* sold in cakes, but this type isn't always easy to find. Instead, we recommend packets of *active dry yeast.* Active dry yeast is easy to use and has a longer shelf-life than moist yeast, but it does expire eventually. Packets should have an expiration date. Heed it. Although so-called *instant* or *quick-rising yeast* may sound tempting because it promises faster results, we don't recommend it. When bread rises faster, it doesn't develop the same attractive texture and tasty flavor.

Quick bread is fast and easy to make, and it's tough to find a good reason *not* to make it if you crave sweet banana bread, zucchini bread, pumpkin bread, cranberry bread, or any other favorite. Quick breads are called "quick" because they don't use yeast. Instead, they rise via the action of baking powder. Mix them up as you would a cake, pour into a loaf pan, bake, and enjoy the sweet results. (Some quick breads, such as Irish soda bread or Boston brown bread, are not sweet, but they are quick nevertheless.)

So we say, *embrace bread!* Try our recipes later in the chapter for a long, skinny, oh-so-European French Baguette and a hearty and healthful Multigrain Loaf that rises like a charm. And be sure to make the practically effortless and delectable Chocolate Chip Banana Bread that you really can't pass up if you don't want to waste those three over-ripe bananas that we just know are sitting on your countertop right now.

Basic Pastry Crust

Prep time: About 30 min (plus chill time) • **Yield:** Enough for a 9-inch double-crust pie

Ingredients	Directions
⅓ cup plus 1 tablespoon cold butter, cut into small pieces ⅓ cup plus 1 tablespoon vegetable shortening 2 cups all-purpose flour ¾ teaspoon salt 4 to 5 tablespoons ice water	**1** In the bowl of a food processor fitted with a steel blade, add the butter, shortening, flour, and salt. Process in pulses until the mixture resembles coarse cornmeal, stopping as necessary to push the mixture with a rubber spatula toward the blade.
	2 Add the cold water a little at a time, pulsing after each addition, just enough to hold together the dry ingredients. Do not overblend.
	3 Divide the dough into two halves. Shape each half into a flat disk, handling as little as possible, and wrap each disk in plastic wrap. Refrigerate the disks for at least 1 hour.
	4 When ready to make your pie, lightly flour a large cutting board, pastry board, or counter and roll out one dough ball into a circle that is a few inches larger than a 9-inch pie plate.
	5 Transfer the dough to the pie plate and gently press it against the sides and rim. Trim off any excess dough with a knife.
	6 Follow the pie recipe instructions regarding whether to bake the shell before filling it or to put the filling in the unbaked shell.
	7 If you need a top crust, roll out the second ball of dough and lay it over the filled bottom crust, leaving an overhang of about ½ inch. Tuck the overhang under the lower crust; crimp firmly by pressing the tines of a fork around the edge or by pinching the dough together at 1-inch intervals. Prick the top crust a few times with a fork before baking.

Per serving: Calories 281 (From Fat 173); Fat 19g (Saturated 8g); Cholesterol 24mg; Sodium 220mg; Carbohydrate 24g (Dietary Fiber 1g); Protein 3g based on eight servings.

Apple Pie

Prep time: About 30 min • **Cook time:** About 1 hr • **Yield:** 8 servings

Ingredients	*Directions*
6 medium tart-style apples, peeled, cored, and sliced about ½-inch thick	*1* Preheat the oven to 450 degrees.
¾ cup sugar	*2* Combine the apples, sugar, flour, lemon juice, cinnamon, lemon zest, and nutmeg in a large bowl. Toss gently to evenly coat the apples with sugar and seasonings.
2 tablespoons all-purpose flour	
1 tablespoon fresh lemon juice	*3* Fill the uncooked 9-inch pie shell with the apple mixture. Dot with the butter. Fit the top crust over the apples, trim off excess, and crimp the edges firmly.
¾ teaspoon cinnamon	
½ teaspoon grated lemon zest	
⅛ teaspoon nutmeg	*4* Prick the top crust several times with a fork. For an attractive crust, use a pastry brush to brush the crust lightly with milk or water and then sprinkle sugar over it.
Prepared pastry for double-crust pie (see the preceding recipe)	
1 tablespoon butter	*5* Bake for 15 minutes. Reduce the heat to 350 degrees and bake another 45 minutes, or until the pie crust is golden brown. Cool the pie on a wire rack for at least 20 minutes before serving.
About 2 tablespoons milk or water (optional)	
About 1 teaspoon sugar (optional)	

Per serving: Calories 430 (From Fat 189); Fat 21g (Saturated 9g); Cholesterol 28mg; Sodium 220mg; Carbohydrate 59g (Dietary Fiber 3g); Protein 4g.

Vary It! You can substitute fruits such as peaches, strawberries, apricots, and berries, varying the spices as desired. For example, toss peaches with sugar, cinnamon, and rum extract. For pears, try sugar, nutmeg, and vanilla extract. A tablespoon of rum or brandy adds sophistication. Substituting brown or raw sugar for white gives the filling a slightly caramelized flavor. Also, try this classic taste pairing: Melt slices of cheddar cheese on top of apple pie servings.

Tip: You also can use the basic pie crust for individual ramekins (single-serving, porcelain baking dishes) and fill them with fruits. Reduce the baking time by half.

Perfect Chocolate Cake

Prep time: About 15 min • **Cook time:** About 30 min • **Yield:** 8–10 servings

Ingredients	*Directions*
6 ounces bittersweet chocolate, chopped into small pieces	*1* Preheat the oven to 350 degrees. Line the bottom of a 9-inch springform cake pan with a circular piece of greased parchment paper. Grease the sides of the pan.
½ cup butter (1 stick)	
5 eggs, separated	*2* Fill the bottom of a double boiler halfway with water and bring to a boil. Place the chocolate and butter in the top of the double boiler. Turn off the heat, leaving the double boiler on the stove. Stir until the chocolate and butter are melted and combined.
½ cup sugar	
½ teaspoon cream of tartar	
¼ cup sifted cake flour	*3* Using an electric mixer on high with beater or whisk attachment, beat the egg whites, 1 teaspoon of the sugar, and the cream of tartar until the mixture gets fluffy. Drizzle in the remaining sugar as you continue to beat the mixture until it forms stiff peaks.
½ cup chopped walnuts (optional)	
1 teaspoon ground cinnamon (optional)	
2 tablespoons unsweetened cocoa powder or confectioner's sugar (optional)	*4* Beat the egg yolks in a medium bowl, and whisk them into the cooled chocolate mixture. Add the flour, and the walnuts and/or cinnamon (if desired). Stir to combine.
	5 Gently fold the egg white mixture into the chocolate with a rubber spatula. Immediately pour the mixture into the prepared cake pan. Smooth the top with the spatula.
	6 Bake for 25 minutes, or until a knife or toothpick inserted into the middle comes out clean. Let the cake cool in its pan.
	7 When the cake is cool enough to handle, run a sharp knife along the edge and remove the side of the pan. If desired, decorate the cake with the cocoa powder or confectioner's sugar. Shake either topping through a sieve, dusting the surface of the cake evenly.

Per serving: Calories 254 (From Fat 170); Fat 19g (Saturated 10g); Cholesterol 131mg; Sodium 33mg; Carbohydrate 22g (Dietary Fiber 1g); Protein 5g based on 10 servings.

Rosy Red Velvet Cupcakes

Prep time: About 20 min • **Cook time:** About 20 min • **Yield:** 24 servings

Ingredients	Directions
3 cups sifted cake flour	**1** Preheat the oven to 350 degrees. Line two 12-cup muffin pans with cupcake liners.
1 teaspoon baking powder	
1 tablespoon unsweetened cocoa powder	**2** In a mixing bowl, combine flour, baking powder, cocoa powder, and salt. Stir to mix everything together.
¾ teaspoon salt	
1½ cups sugar	**3** In a separate bowl, use an electric mixer to cream the sugar and butter until light and fluffy (about 2 minutes). Add buttermilk, eggs, food coloring, vinegar, and vanilla extract and beat until well combined, about 2 minutes.
1 cup butter (2 sticks), softened	
1 cup buttermilk	
2 eggs	**4** Add the dry ingredients to the wet ingredients and beat until smooth and combined, about 1 minute.
2 tablespoons red food coloring	
1 tablespoon white vinegar	**5** Divide the batter among the cupcake tins, filling each well about ⅔ full. Bake for 15 minutes or until a toothpick inserted into a cupcake comes out clean. Cool completely, and then frost with a small spatula or butter knife.
1 teaspoon vanilla extract	
Cream Cheese Frosting (see the following recipe)	

Many dishes that look restaurant-fancy are surprisingly simple to make. Need proof? Try our recipes for savory Mediterranean Seafood Stew (Chapter 7) and creamy Carrot Soup with Dill (Chapter 12).

When you cook at home, you can feed your family healthy, great-tasting food even on a tight budget.
Make a meal of our Barbecued Chicken (Chapter 9) with Country Barbecue Sauce (Chapter 8)
and a side of Roasted Summer Vegetables (Chapter 8).

Add a spicy kick to your meal to turn up the flavor. Pair some simple Steamed Broccoli with
Lemon Butter (Chapter 5) and Basic Rice Pilaf (Chapter 13) with our Tuna Steaks with
Ginger-Chili Glaze (Chapter 6) for a healthy meal with just a touch of heat.

You don't always need to splurge on the most expensive ingredients to create a meal that wins raves. Our Broiled Skirt Steak, Cajun Style (Chapter 18) uses a very affordable cut of meat that pairs nicely with Red Pepper Purée (Chapter 6) and Sautéed Skillet Potatoes (Chapter 6).

Sautéing is a great way to impart flavor to poultry, especially when herbs and spices are in the mix. Try our recipe for Sautéed Chicken Breasts with Tomato and Thyme (Chapter 6), and match it with a quick and easy side of Polenta with Fresh Herbs (Chapter 13).

Need to feed a lot of mouths in very little time? One-pot meals are the way to go. Taco Casserole (Chapter 16) is an easy, filling, and delicious crowd pleaser. Add some Avocado and Tomato Salad (Chapter 18), and you've got yourself a meal!

Sensational sauces can be a snap to make. In Chapter 14, we show you how to create
(clockwise from top) Fresh Strawberry Sauce, Blender Dill Sauce, Mint Mango Sauce, and
Blender Salsa Verde with just a few ingredients and a blender. What could be easier?

You can brighten your dessert table and indulge your sweet tooth at the same time.

Cream Cheese Frosting

1 pound (two 8-ounce packages) cream cheese, softened

1 cup butter (2 sticks), softened

1 teaspoon vanilla extract

4 cups sifted confectioner's sugar

1 In a mixing bowl, combine cream cheese, butter, and vanilla extract. Beat with an electric mixer until smooth.

2 Add the confectioner's sugar, ½ cup at a time, beating after each addition until smooth. If the frosting is too stiff, add milk, 1 teaspoon at a time, until it's spreadable.

Per serving: Calories 383 (From Fat 201); Fat 22g (Saturated 14g); Cholesterol 79mg; Sodium 152mg; Carbohydrate 44g (Dietary Fiber 0g); Protein 3g.

Tip: All the ingredients in this recipe should be brought to room temperature before beginning. If you're out of buttermilk, add 1 tablespoon of white vinegar to a liquid measuring cup. Fill the cup to the 1-cup mark with milk. Let it sit for 10 minutes, and use it in place of 1 cup buttermilk.

French Baguette

Prep time: About 25 min (plus rising time) • **Cook time:** About 20 min • **Yield:** 12 servings

Ingredients	Directions
8 ounces warm water (not hot)	*1* In a large mixing bowl, combine the water, yeast, and honey. Stir until the yeast and honey are dissolved. Set aside until foamy, about 5 minutes.
1 packet (2¼ teaspoons) active dry yeast	
2 teaspoons honey	
2¼ cups bread flour, plus additional for dusting surfaces	*2* Add the bread flour and whole wheat flour to the yeast mixture and stir until well combined, or mix with the dough hook attachment on your stand mixer on low for one minute. Cover the bowl with plastic and set aside for 30 minutes.
¼ cup whole wheat flour	
¾ teaspoon salt	*3* Sprinkle salt over the dough. Turn it out onto a lightly floured surface (such as a cutting board or your countertop) and knead by hand for 10 minutes. Or knead with the dough hook on your mixer at low speed for 5 minutes and at medium speed for 1 minute. (If the dough sticks to the sides of the bowl, sprinkle in up to 2 tablespoons more flour.)
Cooking spray	
1 tablespoon cornmeal	
	4 Spray a second large bowl and a rubber spatula with cooking spray. Using the spatula, ease the dough ball into the greased bowl and spray it lightly with cooking spray. Cover with plastic and let it rise for 2 hours, or until doubled in size.

5 Press down on the dough ball, deflating it. Take it out of the bowl. Knead it a few more times, reshape it, and return it to the bowl for another 30 minutes to an hour of rising, or until doubled in size again.

6 Preheat the oven to 450 degrees. Dust your counter or cutting board with flour. Turn out the dough and cut it in half with a sharp knife.

7 Working with one half at a time, press the dough into a long rectangle, about as long as a baking sheet or baguette loaf pan. Roll up the dough to form a long thin loaf (not longer than your baking sheet), tucking the ends under so they look smooth.

8 Sprinkle the baking sheet or loaf pan with the cornmeal and place the loaves on it. Using your knife, make diagonal slashes about every two inches on the top of each loaf. Spray the loaves with water.

9 Put the sheet or pan in the oven and quickly spray the oven walls (not the heating coils) with water to make steam, and close the oven door. Bake for 10 minutes.

10 Turn the oven temperature down to 400 degrees and bake for 10 more minutes, or until crusts are a deep golden brown. Remove from the oven and cool the loaves on wire racks for one hour.

Per serving: Calories 109 (From Fat 5); Fat 1g (Saturated 0g); Cholesterol 0mg; Sodium 146mg; Carbohydrate 22g (Dietary Fiber 1g); Protein 4g.

Multigrain Loaf

Prep time: About 30 min (plus cooling and rising time) • **Cook time:** About 40 min • **Yield:** 12 servings

Ingredients	*Directions*
2 cups boiling water 1 cup multigrain hot cereal ¼ cup molasses or honey ¼ cup melted butter 1 packet (about 2¼ teaspoons) active dry yeast 2 cups whole wheat flour 2 cups bread flour 1 tablespoon salt ½ cup old-fashioned oatmeal (not instant, quick, or steel-cut)	*1* In a large mixing bowl, combine boiling water and hot cereal. Stir and set aside to cool to about 100 degrees (about 1 hour — use an instant-read thermometer to check). *2* Add the molasses or honey, melted butter, and yeast packet to the warm cereal. Stir to combine thoroughly. *3* Beat the cereal with an electric stand mixer on low speed. Add the whole wheat and bread flour, alternating flours, ½ cup at a time, beating each addition in completely before adding the next. *4* Cover the bowl with plastic wrap and set aside for 20 minutes. *5* Sprinkle salt over the dough. Turn it out onto a lightly floured surface and knead by hand for 10 minutes, or knead with the dough hook on your mixer at low speed for 5 minutes and at medium speed for 1 minute. (If dough sticks to the sides of the bowl, sprinkle in up to 2 tablespoons more flour.) *6* Spray a second large bowl and a rubber spatula with cooking spray. Using the spatula, ease the dough ball into the greased bowl and spray it lightly with cooking spray. Cover with plastic and let it rise for 1 to 2 hours until doubled in size.

7 Press down on the dough to deflate it and remove it from the bowl. Return it to the floured surface and knead it a few times. Reshape into a ball, cover with plastic sprayed with cooking spray, and let it rise for another 30 to 45 minutes.

8 Preheat the oven to 375 degrees. Dust the counter or cutting board with flour. Turn out the dough and cut it in half with a sharp knife.

9 Working with one half at a time, press the dough into a rectangle, about 8 inches by 12 inches. Roll up the dough along the short side to form an 8-inch loaf. Tuck in the ends.

10 Spread the oats onto your floured surface. Spray the loaves with water, and roll the top of each loaf over the oats. Place each loaf into a standard-sized loaf pan (about 8x4 inches).

11 Put the loaves in the oven and quickly spray the oven walls (not the heating coils) with water to make steam, and close the oven door. Bake for 20 minutes.

12 Turn the loaf pans in the opposite direction and bake for 20 more minutes, or until the crusts are a deep golden brown. Remove from the oven and cool the loaves on wire racks for one hour.

Per serving: Calories 251 (From Fat 47); Fat 5g (Saturated 3g); Cholesterol 10mg; Sodium 587mg; Carbohydrate 45g (Dietary Fiber 4g); Protein 7g.

Vary It! You can substitute oatmeal for the multigrain cereal and call it Oat Bread. Or you can replace the oatmeal in the recipe with sunflower seeds, sesame seeds, poppyseeds, or flax seeds. Make this hearty bread even heartier by adding up to ½ cup seeds, chopped nuts, or dried fruit to the dough while kneading in step 4.

Chocolate Chip Banana Bread

Prep time: About 15 min • **Cook time:** 45–50 min • **Yield:** 12 servings

Ingredients	Directions
2 cups all-purpose flour	**1** Preheat the oven to 350 degrees. Spray two loaf pans (8x5 or 9x5) with cooking spray.
1 cup granulated sugar	
½ teaspoon baking powder	**2** Into a sifter set over a mixing bowl, add flour, granulated sugar, baking powder, baking soda, and salt. Sift into the bowl.
1 teaspoon baking soda	
¾ teaspoon salt	
1½ cups mashed bananas	**3** In a separate bowl, combine mashed bananas, brown sugar, eggs, yogurt, oil, and vanilla extract.
1 cup brown sugar	
2 eggs, lightly whisked together	**4** Pour liquid ingredients into flour mixture and stir with a wooden spoon until just combined.
½ cup plain or vanilla yogurt	
⅓ cup canola oil	**5** Add chocolate chips and nuts (if using) and stir to distribute them evenly through the batter.
1 teaspoon vanilla extract	
1 cup chocolate chips	**6** Pour the batter evenly in the two loaf pans. Bake for 50 minutes or until the top is deep golden brown and a toothpick inserted near the center comes out mostly clean. Cool completely (about an hour) before slicing.
½ cup chopped nuts (optional)	

Per serving: Calories 376 (From Fat 105); Fat 12g (Saturated 3g); Cholesterol 36mg; Sodium 293mg; Carbohydrate 67g (Dietary Fiber 2g); Protein 5g.

Part III
Expand Your Repertoire

The 5th Wave   By Rich Tennant

"Oh for gosh sake—you've got to figure out what
you're doing wrong when making upside-down
cake, or you're gonna kill yourself."

In this part . . .

Here's where the music starts. You grab your culinary baton and start off slowly, executing the basics. From there, we tell you how to jazz things up — always in a harmonious way.

This part covers various categories of food — classic breakfast foods; soups and salads for lunch; grains and pastas; and sauces to augment the meat, poultry, and fish you learned to prepare in various ways in Part II. And don't forget dessert — we certainly won't! We explain the foundations of each category and also give you some ideas for improvising. Now you're cooking!

Chapter 11

Mastering Breakfast

We love breakfast. What a perfect way to start the day! We think few things are more fun than rolling out of bed and grabbing the nearest skillet, but even if you feel more bleary-eyed than bright-eyed in the morning, you can still cook breakfast without too much effort, as long as you have some basic know-how under your bathrobe sash and a little inspiration to give you a spring in your fuzzy bunny slippers. This chapter is your secret weapon.

Of course you can eat cereal or toast or a boring old energy bar with your cup of coffee, but we think a motivating morning meal should consist of eggs, with or without some breakfast meat, and some kind of bread (whether it's muffins, pancakes, waffles, coffee cake, or scones).

In this chapter, we walk you through the basics of a good breakfast and then set you free to go further. You've mastered muffins? Try popovers. You've perfected pancakes? Try coffeecake. You've aced the omelet? Try Eggs Benedict. After this chapter, you'll be ready for anything.

All about Eggs

They just may be the quintessential breakfast food, and they're one of nature's most perfect protein sources. We're talking about eggs, a great way to start the morning, especially if you're one of those savory breakfast people more tempted by a bacon omelet than a gooey cinnamon roll. But you can't just put a raw egg on your plate and dig in. (Well, you could, but we're guessing that's not the way you prefer your eggs.) So let's talk about egg cookery. You'll be frying, poaching, boiling, and folding faster than you can hit the snooze button.

Julian who?

Egg consumers rely on the expiration date on the carton, as well as on the *Julian date,* a number stamped near the expiration date that indicates the day of the year on which the eggs were actually packed in the carton. For example, a Julian date of 002 indicates that the eggs were packed on January 2, the second day of the year. A Julian date of 105 means the eggs were packed on April 15, the 105th day of the year (in a non-leap year). Generally, you should use eggs within 4 to 5 weeks of their Julian date.

Grade, size, and color

So what's up with eggs — aren't they all the same? Actually, they aren't. Eggs are distinguished by grade, size, and color.

In the supermarket, you generally see two grades of eggs: AA and A. Grade AA is the highest quality, but A is also a high quality egg, and the differences between the grades are hardly noticeable to the average home cook. Purchase either grade; it doesn't matter one bit to us. Grade B eggs wouldn't normally be available in the supermarket — they're used mostly for making commercial products that contain eggs.

Egg size is based on a minimum weight per dozen: 30 ounces per dozen for jumbo eggs, 27 ounces for extra large, 24 ounces for large, and 21 ounces for medium. Most recipes (and all of them in this book) call for large eggs, and this is important for baking, when slight changes in ingredient amounts can actually alter the finished product. If you're making breakfast, however, we can honestly say that size doesn't matter.

Shell color is not related to quality and is simply a function of the breed of hen. Cooking beside a stoneware crock filled with brown eggs may help you feel like you are channeling Martha Stewart or invoking your grandma's farm kitchen, but we would bet money that you couldn't tell the difference between white and brown eggs in a blind taste test.

What's that spot?

Contrary to what most people believe, blood spots inside a raw egg are not a sign that the egg was fertilized. They are usually the result of a blood vessel rupturing on the surface of the yolk. The spot does not affect flavor, and the egg is perfectly safe to eat. You can remove the blood spot with the tip of a knife, but you don't need to do so. It's not going to hurt you.

Specialty eggs: Worth the extra bacon?

You may have noticed some additional choices in your supermarket beyond the standard range of size and color. What's with those specialty eggs available today? You know, the ones that say "free-range" or "organic" or "added omega-3s for better health." They may imply a promise of improved nutrition or environmental responsibility, but look at that price tag! If you shell out all that extra money for these so-called superior eggs, are you going to end up with egg on your face? The following info may help you decide whether that highfalutin carton is worth the highfalutin price:

✔ **Free-range eggs:** These eggs come from hens that have the opportunity to leave the dark shelter of the hen house for sunnier spots, but that doesn't mean they will do so. Often, they just stay inside and are not out pecking in dirt, as you may have imagined. Similarly, cage-free eggs mean the hens are likely confined inside a dark, windowless building, milling around in a sort of poultry mosh pit (but less fun). On the other hand, hens in tiny cages are probably not particularly enjoying life, either. "Free range" versus conventional eggs may be six of one, half-a-dozen of the other. If you really want to know how the hens who produced your eggs live, buy from a small local farm and pay it a visit, to see for yourself.

✔ **Organic eggs:** These eggs come from chickens that weren't fed any drugs, hormones, antibiotics, or animal by-products (something chickens really aren't meant to eat). Proponents believe this type of diet makes the eggs safer, more pure, and (some say) more nutritious, although there is little if any evidence of this. There are also standards for humane treatment of animals whose products are labeled "organic," so if cruelty is your issue, consider organic eggs.

✔ **Eggs with added omega-3s:** These eggs have more of those fatty acids purported to benefit heart health, and they typically have a higher vitamin E content than regular eggs. These benefits result when hens are fed a diet high in omega-3s, typically including flax seed. They are probably a good source of these healthy fats. Only you can decide if you want to pay for your omega 3s that way, or just eat more fish or take a supplement.

Some brands of eggs have all the above qualities: free-range hens on organic diets producing eggs with extra essential fatty acids. Many people buy these eggs not only because they want the extra dose of nutrition and they want to support farmers who treat their hens more humanely but also because they think (and we generally concur) the eggs taste better.

 Eggs from local farmers tend to be fresher because they are likely to be recently collected. Keep in mind that some locally produced eggs will be organic, even if the farmer can't afford to pay for official certification. If you get the chance to visit the farm or meet the farmer at the market, just ask.

Cooking Perfect Eggs

Eggs can become so many delectable dishes. From simple scrambled eggs to complex meringues and soufflés, eggs have it all, but in our opinion, the incredible edible egg reigns supreme at breakfast. Here's the scoop on the breakfasty egg dishes we all know and love (and please feel free to have them for *any* meal).

Simply scrambled

Scrambled eggs are one of the easiest things in the world to cook, which is why we include a recipe for them in Chapter 1. Mix eggs in a bowl, add a splash of water or milk (or not), and cook in a hot buttered skillet for just a few minutes, stirring all the while. You can whip up scrambled eggs in minutes, and they will keep you satisfied for hours.

Frankly fried

A fried egg is like a scrambled egg but without the beating and mixing. For the classic sunny-side-up fried egg, break an egg into a hot buttered skillet and wait until it looks done: The whites turn white rather than clear, and the yolk is cooked to your preferred consistency. It takes just a few minutes for a soft yolk and a few more minutes if you like the yolk firm, not runny.

To make fried eggs "over," begin the same way as with a sunny-side up egg. When the whites are set (they're not runny), carefully coax a spatula under the egg and gently flip it over. Sometimes the yolk will break; sometimes it won't. The more you practice, the better you'll get at flipping the egg without breaking the yolk. Plenty of butter (or cooking spray) will make flipping easier. Cook for just a minute on the flip side, and then serve. Practice with a few eggs to see how long it takes to cook one to your desired degree of doneness.

If you like your eggs sunny-side up but you prefer a firmer yolk, get your skillet lid ready. Pour a tablespoon of water into the skillet and quickly cover it. Steam the egg for one or two minutes.

Perfectly poached

A poached egg is cooked in boiling water—not a drop of butter. While you can poach eggs in an egg poacher, isn't that so, well . . . 1950s? We think so. Who has an egg poacher anymore? (No offense to those who do.) All you need is a saucepan and a slotted spoon. Fill the saucepan a little over half full of water, cover it, and bring the water to a heavy simmer: The water should have frequent gentle bubbles but not be boiling vigorously, as this will break up the egg white too much. When the water is simmering, remove the cover and add a tablespoon of white vinegar to the water.

Break an egg carefully into a small cup or bowl. Using your slotted spoon, stir the boiling water in a circle until you get a little whirlpool of water (be careful not to splash). Then with your other hand, gently and slowly pour the egg from the cup into the middle of your whirlpool. Let it cook for 3 minutes (or up to 5 minutes if you like a firmer yolk). Remove the egg with your slotted spoon and enjoy it immediately.

Poached eggs aren't usually symmetrical or even very smooth. Some of the egg white will break away from the egg and form long thin strands as it's cooking. That's fine; everything is just the way it is supposed to be. Just leave those parts in the water. Even if your poached egg isn't going to win any beauty contests, it will still taste delicious on toast or an English muffin.

The key to losing as little egg white as possible is 1) to use the vinegar and 2) to ease the egg *very gently* into the center of the whirlpool you create with your spoon.

Beautifully boiled

Hard-cooked eggs make great snacks and a much more nutritious grab-and-go breakfast than a doughnut. Soft-cooked eggs are nice in a cup or a bowl while still warm, with a good thick slab of crispy toast to mop up the runny yolk. Boiling eggs is even easier than scrambling, although it takes a little bit longer.

Because boiled eggs are great for any meal — not just breakfast — we include the cooking instructions in Chapter 5. With our step-by-step guidance, you'll never over- or undercook a boiled egg again.

Ode to omelets

> Oh, omelet, lovely as a cloud,
>
> We taste you and we cheer out loud . . .

Okay, okay, we'll spare you from actually writing an ode to omelets. Instead, let's talk about how to cook them.

A classic French omelet (or omelette, depending on your preference) is a simple dish of beaten eggs cooked until set and folded over themselves, with or without a filling. Omelets are quick and easy in their basic form. Some people prefer to make a fancier version called a *soufflé omelet,* which is thicker and puffier, lightened with whipped egg whites and beaten yolks and finished in the oven, or in a special soufflé omelet pan. We don't usually go to those lengths because the basic French-style omelet literally takes about 1 minute to make.

If you cook an omelet properly, the outside will be smooth and the center a little moist. Omelets can be simplicity itself or a party in your mouth — try adding any kind of cheese, cooked vegetables, chopped meat, pesto, salsa, or whatever else you have in your refrigerator. (See the sidebar "Omelet variations" for suggestions.)

The only potentially intimidating aspect to cooking an omelet is that it all happens very fast. You have to have all your senses firing so your omelet doesn't end up brown or rubbery or burned. But although making an omelet is a bit of a "ready, set, go!" proposition, once you know how to do it, you can whip them out one after the other. Beat your eggs, melt your butter, pour the eggs in the pan, shake the pan, and voila! *Your omelet is served, monsieur or madam.*

Afraid that you won't be able to properly fold an omelet? It does take a bit of practice, but it isn't too tough. Figure 11-1 can help.

Are you ready to practice making an omelet? *Of course you are!* Try the recipe for Omelet with Herbs that appears later in this chapter.

Folding an Omelet

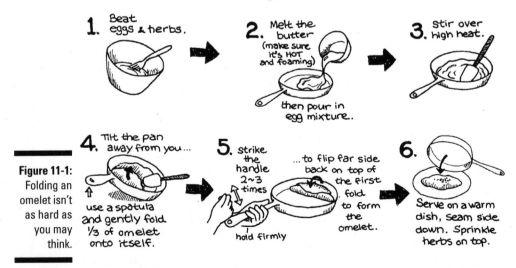

Figure 11-1: Folding an omelet isn't as hard as you may think.

1. Beat eggs & herbs.

2. Melt the butter (make sure it's HOT and foaming) then pour in egg mixture.

3. Stir over high heat.

4. Tilt the pan away from you... use a spatula and gently fold ⅓ of omelet onto itself.

5. strike the handle 2~3 times. hold firmly ...to flip far side back on top of the first fold to form the omelet.

6. Serve on a warm dish, seam side down. Sprinkle herbs on top.

Omelet variations

The great thing about omelets is that they can contain just about any savory filling. To alter the Omelet with Herbs recipe in this chapter, omit the herbs and chives and use ½ cup of any of the following ingredients. Have your filling all ready to go before you start cooking the eggs. For a cheese omelet, add grated hard cheese, such as cheddar, Swiss, or Gruyère, or soft and semisoft cheese, such as mozzarella, goat, or Brie, to the egg mixture before pouring it in the pan.

To make the following types of omelets, place the fillings on the omelet just before folding:

- **Spanish:** Fried onions, fried potatoes, and olive oil instead of butter.

- **Vegetarian:** Any combination or cooked, chopped vegetables, such as asparagus, artichoke hearts, mushrooms, spinach, broccoli, or cauliflower — a great way to use leftover cooked vegetables.

- **Western, also known as Denver:** Chopped ham, onions, and green bell peppers.

- **Mediterranean:** Feta cheese, tomatoes, chopped olives, onions, and spinach.

- **Seafood:** Smoked salmon or trout, crab meat, or cooked shrimp.

- **Meat:** Cooked, crumbled bacon or sausage; diced cooked ham; or salami.

- **Mixed greens:** Watercress, arugula, or spinach, with a dollop of sour cream.

- **Mushrooms:** Sautéed button, portobello, cremini, or oyster mushrooms, with or without a sprinkling of cheese.

Oven-worthy eggs: Frittatas and stratas

Your poor, neglected oven. Doesn't it get to have any fun with eggs? That's all up to you! When you've had enough of the skillet and want to try something new, why not go for the decidedly impressive but secretly simple frittata or strata?

Frittata rhymes with strata, but the two dishes are completely different. They have only the oven, and eggs, in common. Frittatas are basically omelets made in the oven without the folding and flipping part (read: *easier!*). And they feel *so* Italian.

Stratas are casseroles made with torn-up bread, omelet-style fillings, and eggs as a custard poured over the whole thing and baked until puffy. You can have your eggs, bacon, cheese, and toast, all in one handy dish. You can prepare a strata the night before and then pop it in the oven whenever you desire. We think of stratas as a bit "Junior League," so you may want to serve yours with crustless cucumber sandwiches or a Waldorf salad for lunch in the garden (don't forget your floppy hat). But we also think they are just dandy with orange juice or fruit and coffee, particularly when you've invited company for brunch.

Both dishes are delicious and can get time-pressed cooks out of a jam. Either dish is great for breakfast, but it can also make a wonderful lunch main course or light supper, accompanied by a salad.

To give frittatas and stratas a try, see the recipes later in this chapter for Mushroom-Swiss Frittata and Bacon and Cheese Strata.

A Carnivore's Breakfast

Meat eaters, rejoice — breakfast is your meal! Many delicious and savory meats star at the breakfast table, flirting with the eggs, ravishing the waffles, and pushing the pancakes straight over the edge of ecstasy. Hot, crispy, salty bacon dripping with real maple syrup? Still, our beating hearts!

Breakfast meats are also relatively easy to cook, making them practically irresistible. While you may not want to start every single day with bacon, sausage, ham, or a nice breakfast steak, after this section, you'll know just what to do come Sunday morning when you've got a little extra time and a hankering for something above and beyond your usual bowl of cereal.

Everything's better with bacon

What is it about bacon? Luscious, luscious bacon? We aren't naming any names, but we know a few fellows who would do just about anything for the crispy, smoky stuff.

Bacon is cured side pork meat. (*Curing* is a process of preserving meat, typically involving salting and smoking.) It is usually sold sliced and packaged, but you may also be able to find slab bacon, which you slice yourself. You can buy it in the supermarket cut thick or thin, peppered or sugared, maple-flavored or spicy. If you live in farm country, you can probably also buy bacon from local farmers. Some enterprising souls even buy side pork or pork belly and cure it and smoke it themselves.

For starters, however, a regular old package of good quality bacon from the supermarket is all you need to practice makin' the bacon. Fortunately, bacon is easy to cook, if you can remember two things: 1) Keep the heat low to prevent grease spatters, and 2) Watch it carefully so it doesn't burn.

Unwrap the package and lay out the desired number of bacon strips neatly in a cold skillet or on a griddle. Do not overlap the strips. Turn the heat to medium-low. (You can also cook bacon on medium heat, but if the fat gets too hot, it can spatter and pop, so be careful.) When the bacon begins to sizzle, lift up the edge of a slice with a pair of tongs. When the underside looks like it is beginning to get crispy, flip the slice over and cook the other side.

Watch your bacon like a hawk! One trip to the computer to check e-mail, and all could be lost, so don't allow yourself to get distracted.

Cook the strips just until they are golden and crisp. You can flip them over several times if you like. When they are done, use your tongs to transfer them to a double layer of paper towels (to drain off some of the fat), and then serve. If you like, pour the flavorful bacon fat remaining in the pan into a jar and use it in place of butter in other savory recipes (just keep in mind that bacon grease tends to be salty). When it cools, the fat will turn white and look like lard. It will keep in the refrigerator for a couple weeks.

Savory sausage

Links, patties, crumbles — sausage can make the difference between an oh-hum and an oh-yum breakfast. Sausage is meat ground up with fat and mixed with salt and spices. Typically made with pork in its breakfast incarnation, it can also be made with other meats, from lamb to chicken to venison.

Fry links and patties in a skillet over medium heat, turning every few minutes until the surface is golden brown and the center is hot and no longer pink. (Some sausage links and patties available in the supermarket are pre-cooked, and while these heat up more quickly and can even be cooked in the microwave, we think they don't taste quite as fresh and delicious.) If you're cooking crumbled sausage, fry it in a skillet while stirring and breaking chunks apart with your spatula until it is no longer pink.

Ham (or Canadian bacon) it up

Lighter, leaner, and (to some folks) tastier than breakfast meats with a higher fat content, ham and Canadian bacon pair well with eggs and add a meaty component to a breakfast sandwich of egg and cheese (as in that classic fast-food favorite, the Egg McMuffin). Ham is the cured meat from the pig's hind leg. Canadian bacon is the smoked meat from the eye of the loin, in the pig's mid-back. Both are lean and tasty, and they're pre-cooked so you don't have to cook them (although you can heat them up and even brown them a bit in the skillet if you prefer them hot and a bit crispy). Just chop some up and add to scrambled eggs, or make your own "fast food" by adding a slice of ham or Canadian bacon to a buttered English muffin with a fried or poached egg and a slice of good cheese. (You may never visit the drive-thru again.)

About veggie breakfast "meats"

How does a vegetarian still enjoy her savory sausage and eggs? How does a fat-conscious cook keep breakfast in line with his dietary goals? So-called "veggie meats" have the flavor and texture of sausage patties, links, or crumbles but are made with vegetable protein, from sources like soy and wheat. (Some brands also contain egg and/or milk ingredients.) You can also buy veggie "bacon" and other veggie "meats," from chicken nuggets to burgers to barbecued ribs.

We're not saying these lower-fat options are going to fool anybody. Some are better than others and the bacon, in particular, is obviously not really bacon. You may need to sample a few brands to find the one you think tastes best. However, if you are trying to decrease your fat intake or you choose not to eat meat, these veggie options can give you the impression of eating those good old-fashioned breakfast meats. Find them refrigerated or frozen in the health food section of your supermarket, and cook according to package directions (which usually call for pan frying or microwaving).

Steak your claim (to breakfast!)

If you are a rancher and you've been up since sunrise wrangling your wayward herds (can you tell that we're not ranchers?), you are going to need a heartier breakfast than most folks. Or, maybe you just love a good hunka beef for breakfast. Breakfast steaks are small steaks, pan fried and served with eggs. For directions on how to pan fry a steak, see Chapter 6.

Breakfast Breads

You poor sweet-toothed people — all this talk of meat and eggs, and you've been so patient, waiting to find out how the heck a person can get a short stack of pancakes or a nice muffin for breakfast. At last, your patience will be rewarded.

Some people can imagine no sweeter breakfast than a crispy piece of toast and a cup of hot coffee or tea, but breakfast bread doesn't have to be quite so literal. Bread can come in many forms; English muffins, bagels, biscuits, and croissants come to mind. So do French toast, pancakes, and muffins — all of which we feature in this section.

French toast

French toast takes toast to the next level. Stale bread, dipped in an egg-and-milk mixture, is fried in a skillet and then topped with butter and syrup — *ooh la la*. French toast is an easy and satisfying dish to make and a great way to use up bread that has gone slightly stale. To give it a try in your own kitchen, look for the recipe for Fabulous French Toast later in this chapter.

Pancakes and waffles

Cake, without all the baking? With syrup? What's not to like? Pancakes are an essential part of a classic American breakfast. They also make a perfect canvas for fanciful additions: blueberries, chocolate chips, walnuts, sliced almonds, peanut butter, bananas, coconut — pancake adornment need know no limits! Try the recipe for Perfect Pancakes later in this chapter.

Muffins, scones, and quick breads

Something about a muffin says "comfort," and muffins have become one of the most popular breakfast offerings in coffee shops and cafés, maybe because they go so well with an espresso or a latte, or maybe because they are so cute and tidy. But you don't have to pay $3 for a muffin. You can bake them at home for a fraction of the price, and yours will be even better because you can put anything you like in your own muffins. Try the recipe for Berry Good Muffins later in this chapter to get started.

Other muffin-like breakfast options include *scones,* which are like a cross between a muffin and a biscuit, and quick breads, which are essentially muffins baked in a loaf pan and sliced. All are sweet, tender, delicious breakfast options that are simple to bake and just might turn your grumpy family members into morning people.

Omelet with Herbs

Prep time: About 10 min • **Cook time:** About 1 min • **Yield:** 1 serving

Ingredients	Directions
1 teaspoon chopped fresh (or ¼ teaspoon dried) tarragon	*1* Combine the tarragon, parsley, and chives in a medium mixing bowl. Remove and set aside 1 teaspoon of the fresh herb mixture for garnish. (If you're using dried herbs, chop extra chives for garnish.)
2 teaspoons chopped fresh (or ½ teaspoon dried) parsley	
1 tablespoon chopped chives (fresh or dried)	*2* Add the eggs and a few dashes each of salt and pepper to a mixing bowl and beat with a fork for about 20 seconds, combining the whites and yolks without over-beating.
3 eggs	
Salt and pepper	*3* Heat an 8- or 10-inch omelet pan or skillet over medium-low heat. Let it heat up for at least 5 minutes, then add the butter and melt it, turning the pan to coat evenly. The butter should be hot and foaming, but not browned, before you add the eggs.
2 teaspoons butter	
	4 Pour in the egg mixture. It should begin to set at the edges immediately.

5 Using a spatula, stir the eggs just a few times to fluff them up, then gently pull the cooked edges up a bit so the runny mixture in the middle can flow around the edge.

6 When the mixture solidifies but the center is still a bit moist, shake the pan sharply a few times to loosen the omelet from the bottom. Remove the pan from the heat and let it rest for a few seconds. (Add any fillings at this point.)

7 Fold the omelet and use a spatula to press the omelet closed at the seam.

8 Roll the omelet onto a warm dish, seam side down. Sprinkle the remaining herbs on top.

Per serving: Calories 294 (From Fat 204); Fat 22g (Saturated 9g); Cholesterol 658mg; Sodium 773mg; Carbohydrate 2g (Dietary Fiber 0g); Protein 19g.

Go-With: For lunch or a light dinner, serve this omelet with a tossed green salad and Sautéed Skillet Potatoes (see Chapter 6) or the French Potato Salad in Chapter 12.

Tip: Another way to fold an omelet is to slide half the omelet onto a serving plate and turn the pan over to flip the omelet into a half-moon shape. This technique helps if the omelet gets stuck in the pan.

Mushroom-Swiss Frittata

Prep time: About 20 min • **Cook time:** About 25 min • **Yield:** 4 servings

Ingredients	Directions
8 eggs	*1* Preheat the oven to 400 degrees. Beat the eggs and water in a medium mixing bowl with the basil or parsley and the salt and pepper to taste. Add the cheese and set aside.
2 tablespoons water	
2 tablespoons finely chopped basil or parsley (or 2 teaspoons dried basil or parsley)	
Salt and pepper	*2* Heat the butter in an omelet pan or 10-inch cast-iron skillet over medium-high heat. Add the mushrooms and onions and sauté for about 7 minutes, until the onions get soft and translucent (but not brown) and the mushrooms begin to shrink.
¼ pound Swiss cheese, cut into small cubes	
2 tablespoons butter	*3* Scoop out the mushrooms and onions with a slotted spoon and put them on a plate.
2 cups sliced white mushrooms	
1 small yellow onion, chopped	*4* Add the olive oil and the egg-cheese mixture to the skillet and cook for about 1 minute. Don't stir, but run a rubber spatula around the edges to make sure it doesn't stick.
1 tablespoon olive oil	

5 Spread the mushroom-onion mixture over the top of the eggs. Cover and reduce the heat to medium. Cook for about 4 to 5 minutes, or until the bottom is set and golden brown. The top should still be wet.

6 Uncover the skillet and place it in the oven on a middle rack. Bake for an additional 10 minutes, or until the top is cooked solid and golden.

7 Run a rubber spatula around the outside of the frittata to loosen it. Coaxing with your spatula, slide the frittata onto a plate and cut into wedges (like a pizza) to serve.

Per serving: Calories 349 (From Fat 243); Fat 27g (Saturated 12g); Cholesterol 466mg; Sodium 348mg; Carbohydrate 5g (Dietary Fiber 1g); Protein 22g.

Tip: For this recipe, you need a skillet that can go into the oven. That means no plastic handle (unless it's oven-proof). An all-metal skillet is oven-proof.

Bacon and Cheese Strata

Prep time: About 25 min (plus standing time) • **Cook time:** About 40 min • **Yield:** 6 servings

Ingredients	*Directions*
Butter to grease the baking dish	*1* Butter the bottom and sides of a 2½- to 3-quart shallow baking dish. (Use a rectangular dish that allows bread slices to fit snugly in one layer.)
8-ounce loaf seedless Italian bread (or about 8 ounces of any slightly stale bread)	*2* Trim and discard about 1 inch off each end of the loaf of bread and cut it into about 16 slices. If the bread is fresh, dry the slices in a 175-degree oven for about 15 minutes. Arrange the slices in the baking dish, overlapping the edges so they fit.
5 slices bacon	
1½ cups grated Gouda, Gruyère, Italian fontina, or other favorite cheese	*3* Sauté the bacon in a large skillet over medium-high heat, about 5 minutes or until crisp. Drain on paper towels. When it's cool enough to handle, crumble it into small pieces.
½ cup rinsed, chopped, packed fresh spinach or sorrel leaves	
5 eggs	*4* Sprinkle the crumbled bacon over the bread slices and top with cheese and spinach or sorrel.
2 cups milk	
2 tablespoons tomato-based salsa (optional)	*5* In a medium bowl, beat together the eggs, milk, salsa (if using), and a few dashes each of salt and pepper. Pour the mixture evenly over the bread, bacon, cheese, and spinach.
Salt and pepper	
	6 Using a fork, press the bread slices down to soak them in the egg mixture. Let it set for about 15 minutes.
	7 Preheat the oven to 350 degrees.
	8 Bake the strata about 35 minutes, or just until the custard mixture is firm and lightly browned. Remove from the oven and serve immediately, cutting into squares.

Per serving: Calories 363 (From Fat 185); Fat 21g (Saturated 10g); Cholesterol 230mg; Sodium 729mg; Carbohydrate 24g (Dietary Fiber 1g); Protein 20g.

Tip: You can prepare this strata through step 6 and let it sit overnight, covered, in the refrigerator.

Fabulous French Toast

Prep time: About 5 min • **Cook time:** About 5 min • **Yield:** 4 servings

Ingredients	*Directions*
8 slices French or 4 slices (larger) Italian or sourdough bread, preferably stale	*1* Heat a skillet or griddle over medium heat.
4 eggs ¼ cup milk or cream ½ teaspoon vanilla extract ¼ teaspoon cinnamon ¼ teaspoon salt	*2* Break the eggs into a shallow pan and beat them with a fork or whisk until yolks and whites are combined, about 20 seconds. Add milk or cream, vanilla extract, cinnamon, and salt. Whisk a few more seconds.
	3 Place bread slices into egg mixture. Turn them over to coat both sides and let them sit for about1 minute.
1 tablespoon butter, or cooking spray Syrup, butter, or fresh fruit for serving	*4* Put butter into the skillet or griddle, or spray with cooking spray.
	5 Pick up each bread slice, dip both sides again in egg mixture, and place it on the skillet or griddle. Slices can be touching but should not overlap. (Cook in batches if needed.)
	6 Cook for 2 minutes, then use a hard spatula to lift up one slice to see if it is done. If it's golden brown, flip it over and repeat on the other side.
	7 Remove the French toast to individual plates with the spatula and serve immediately with butter and syrup or fresh fruit.

Per serving: Calories 462 (From Fat 110); Fat 12g (Saturated 5g); Cholesterol 222mg; Sodium 996mg; Carbohydrate 68g (Dietary Fiber 4g); Protein 18g.

Perfect Pancakes

Prep time: About 5 min • **Cook time:** About 10 min • **Yield:** 6–12 pancakes

Ingredients	*Directions*
1½ cups all-purpose flour	*1* In a large bowl, sift together flour, baking powder, cinnamon, and salt.
1 tablespoon baking powder	
½ teaspoon cinnamon	*2* In a separate bowl, combine milk, egg, butter, maple syrup, and vanilla extract. Whisk together until completely combined.
½ teaspoon salt	
1¼ cups milk	
1 egg	*3* Add the wet ingredients to the dry and mix together gently, just until combined. Don't over-mix or your pancakes will be tough. Let the mixture stand for 5 minutes.
3 tablespoons butter, melted and cooled, or vegetable oil	
1 tablespoon maple syrup	
1 teaspoon vanilla extract	*4* Heat a skillet or griddle to medium heat.
	5 Using a ¼-cup measure or ladle, scoop the batter and pour onto the hot skillet or griddle, making as many pancakes as you have room for without letting them touch.
	6 In about 2 minutes, when bubbles start to form around the edges and the edges look slightly dry, carefully flip the pancakes over with a spatula. Cook on the second side for no longer than 1 minute.

Per serving: Calories 218 (From Fat 77); Fat 9g (Saturated 5g); Cholesterol 58mg; Sodium 421mg; Carbohydrate 29g (Dietary Fiber 1g); Protein 6g.

Tip: For best results whenever making any pancakes or waffles, let all ingredients come to room temperature before mixing the batter.

Tip: Wrap leftover pancakes individually in plastic and freeze. To reheat, unwrap and microwave for about 30 seconds, or pop them in the toaster.

Vary It! Jazz up these pancakes by sprinkling each one with a few berries, chocolate chips, chopped nuts, banana slices, shredded coconut, or dried fruit just after putting the batter on the griddle. For chocolate pancakes, add 1 tablespoon cocoa powder to the flour mixture before adding the wet ingredients.

Berry Good Muffins

Prep time: About 5 min • **Cook time:** About 20 min • **Yield:** 12 muffins

Ingredients	Directions
2 cups all-purpose flour	**1** Preheat the oven to 350 degrees. Spray a 12-cup muffin tin with cooking spray.
1 tablespoon baking powder	
½ cup firmly packed brown sugar	**2** In a mixing bowl, stir to combine flour, baking powder, brown sugar, and salt. In another bowl, stir to combine yogurt, oil, beaten egg, and vanilla extract.
½ teaspoon salt	
1 cup plain or vanilla yogurt	
½ cup canola oil	**3** Pour the wet ingredients into the dry ingredients and mix gently with the spatula just until combined. (A few lumps are fine.) Add berries and gently fold them into the batter.
1 egg, lightly beaten	
1 teaspoon vanilla extract	
2 cups fresh or frozen defrosted berries (blueberries, blackberries, raspberries, sliced strawberries)	**4** Using a spoon or ladle, fill each muffin cup about ⅔ full. Sprinkle each muffin with one teaspoon chopped nuts (optional).
¼ cup chopped pecans or almonds (optional)	**5** Bake the muffins for 20 minutes, or until the tops are golden brown and a toothpick inserted into the center of a muffin comes out clean.
	6 Cool on a wire rack for 10 minutes. Serve warm or at room temperature with butter.

Per serving: Calories 226 (From Fat 93); Fat 10g (Saturated 1g); Cholesterol 19mg; Sodium 217mg; Carbohydrate 30g (Dietary Fiber 1g); Protein 4g.

Vary It! Replace the berries with 1 cup chocolate chips, or use 1 cup each berries and chocolate chips. Add up to ½ cup chopped nuts, grated coconut, or dried fruit to the batter with the fresh berries. Chopped peaches, nectarines, apricots, or plums could also stand in for the berries.

Chapter 12

Super Soups and Savory Salads

No offense to the gastronomic wizards at major commercial soup companies, but most 7-year-olds with a recipe and a stepladder can make soup that is superior to the canned version. For one, canned soups are always overcooked. You can't keep vegetables bright and crisp in the sterilization process necessary for canning. What's more, canned soup seasonings typically consist of two things: salt (a *lot* of salt) and parsley. Not very interesting, but designed so as to offend the smallest number of people — sort of like your run-of-the-mill American beer.

Salads aren't exactly rocket science, either. Chop up some fresh raw veggies, sprinkle with specialty items like nuts, fruit, cheese, or meat, drizzle it all with a little bit of dressing (oil, acid, salt), and you've got a great salad.

Homemade soups and salads are easy to make, impressive to serve, and create a soul-satisfying meal. They're also nutritious and taste so good that you'll wonder why you ever ate any other kind. Whether you serve them as the centerpieces of a meal or as the first two courses on the road to something even greater, soups and salads are a home cook's best friends.

Mastering Essential Soup Skills

Making soup is a great way to clean out your vegetable crisper. No, it doesn't have magical powers and can't transform moldy ingredients into something edible. But if you aren't sure how to use up that bag of carrots or that whole bunch of celery, soup is the answer! Carrots, celery, an onion, a clove of garlic, some pepper . . . sounds like a tasty vegetable soup to us. Strain out the vegetables after boiling them for an hour, and you have vegetable stock for use in your next super soup. Or, purée the whole business, stir in a splash of that half-and-half you use in your coffee, and call it a bisque.

Soup can get pretty fancy and complicated, but here we stick to the basics: simple pureed soups and easy chunky soups in classic flavors you'll want to make again and again. (For even more soup recipes, check out Wiley's *Cooking Soups For Dummies,* by Jenna Holst.)

How do you make soup? You *could* just throw all your leftover vegetables and last night's pot roast into a pot, cover it with water, heat it up, and call it soup. But we don't think you should. If you have a few tricks up your sleeve, your soup will taste delectable. Follow these soup trade tricks, and your family or guests will marvel at the sparkling flavor and irresistible texture of your homemade soups.

Sautéing meat and vegetables first

First off, let's talk about sautéing. Chapter 6 shows you how to sauté both meat and vegetables, but essentially, sautéing means cooking something quickly in fat, such as butter or olive oil, until it gets golden brown and extra tasty.

When you sauté your soup ingredients before adding them to the pot, you add an extra level of complexity to the flavor. Just about any soup can benefit from the addition of sautéed onions and garlic, as well as other ingredients like meat, poultry, fish, and vegetables from tomatoes to turnips.

We like to use our soup pot as a sauté pan. Heat up the soup pot (a high-sided pot such as a Dutch oven), add a little oil or butter, throw your soup ingredients in, toss them around for a few minutes, and then add your broth. If you are making up your own soup recipes, give this a try. Many soup recipes you'll see (including the ones at the end of this chapter) have some similar process involving cooking the soup ingredients in oil before adding the broth or water.

What am I eating? Soups defined

Soups come in several different categories. Here are some types of soup you've probably heard about:

Bisque: A thick, rich, puréed soup with added cream, traditionally made from shellfish (such as crab or lobster) but now often made from other ingredients, such as tomatoes.

Broth: A clear, flavored liquid made from simmering vegetables, herbs, meats, poultry, or fish bones in water. Strain the solids and refrigerate or freeze to use as a base for your next great soup.

Chili: A thick, stew-like concoction of beef or other meat in a tomato base with chili powder and typically onions, peppers, and kidney or pinto beans.

Chowder: A typically thick and chunky fish soup, usually with vegetables such as potatoes.

Consommé: The "consummate" broth, made by simmering egg whites, and sometimes finely chopped meat and vegetables, in stock. As the egg whites solidify, they trap any impurities. After simmering an hour or more, the stock is strained through layers of cheesecloth, resulting in a very clear, pure soup.

Court bouillon: A broth, usually strained, that simmers for only a short time — no more than 30 minutes — but long enough to draw out the flavor of the vegetables added to the broth. It's used as a poaching liquid for fish, seafood, and vegetables.

Fumet: A strained stock of fish bones, water, vegetables, and herbs. Fumet (French for "fish stock") cooks for about 30 minutes and is used as a flavoring base for soups and sauces.

Gumbo: A soup that typically combines assorted shellfish, poultry, vegetables, a long-cooked dark brown roux of flour and oil, okra, and *filé powder* (a seasoning made from ground sassafras leaves), which thicken and flavor the soup as it cooks. Gumbo is the African word for okra.

Puréed soup: A creamy textured soup in which solid ingredients are whirled in a blender or food processor or forced through a food mill until smooth.

Stew: Thicker than your basic soup but thinner than, say, a casserole, stew consists of meat and vegetables simmered in a small amount of broth, or in their own juices.

Stock: The foundation of countless soups and sauces, stock is essentially a richly flavored broth. White stock involves poultry or veal bones or carcasses boiled with vegetables and strained. Brown stock requires that bones be browned first by roasting, then added to the water, boiled, and strained. Vegetable stock is essentially the same as vegetable broth.

Thickening your soup

It's easy to thin a soup: Just add water or more broth. However, sometimes you want to thicken your soup so that it looks more luxurious and tastes richer. Try this classic thickening technique:

1. **Work 1 tablespoon of slightly softened butter together with 1 tablespoon of all-purpose flour.** Mash them together in a small bowl with the back of a spoon or a fork until they form a smooth buttery paste.

   The French call this mixture a _beurre manié,_ but don't worry about that — they have a different word for everything.

2. **Scoop a cup or so of soup liquid into a small bowl and mix in the flour-butter mixture until it has fully melted and been incorporated into the soup liquid.**

3. **Stir this mixture back into the soup pot and cook over medium heat for about 5 minutes, until you notice the soup has slightly thickened.**

Here's another thickening method that's even easier:

1. **Using a fork or a small wire whisk, blend 1 tablespoon all-purpose flour, corn starch, potato starch, arrowroot powder, or other starch with 2 tablespoons soup broth.**

2. **Stir, add about 1 cup more broth, stir again, and add to the soup.**

3. **Cook over medium heat for 5 to 10 more minutes, or until the soup has slightly thickened.**

Dare we admit it? Instant potato flakes make a great and almost instantaneous thickener! Add a tablespoonful and stir until the soup thickens. You can also add leftover mashed potatoes, cooked rice, stale corn tortilla pieces, or vegetable purée to any soup to make it thicker.

You can always simmer or even boil down a soup to get it to thicken because the longer a soup cooks, the more moisture evaporates (and flavors concentrate). However, don't boil soups containing milk or cream unless the recipe calls for it. Cream soups burn easily, which ruins the taste. Typically, milk or cream is stirred in toward the very end of cooking so it gets only gently warmed.

Skimming soups and stocks

Some soups, like some people we know, attract scum. When making soup, especially one that contains dried beans or lentils, meat, or poultry, you may need to skim the scum from the surface as the soup cooks. To do so, use a spoon with a long handle. Throw the scum out. You don't want it to spoil your soup's good reputation.

Sometimes, fat also rises to the surface, especially if your soup contains high-fat meat, such as sausage. As the soup cooks, skim off any fat floating on the surface with a large spoon. Or, to make the job even easier, if you're making the soup the day before, refrigerate it and, when the fat congeals on the top, just scoop it off and throw it away before reheating the soup.

Peeling and seeding a tomato

For many soup recipes, tomatoes are a staple, but you don't want their peels or seeds — just the meat. To peel and seed a fresh tomato, bring a covered pot of water to a rolling boil over high heat, and then follow these steps (shown in Figure 12-1):

How to Peel, Seed, and Chop Tomatoes

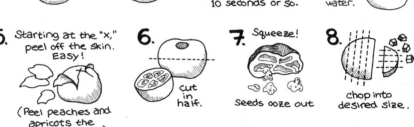

Figure 12-1: Dropping tomatoes in boiling water makes peeling them much easier.

1. **Cut the core out of the tomato at the stem end with a paring knife.**

   Run your knife around the stem at an angle pointing inward, and then lift out the core.

2. **Cut a shallow X in the bottom of the tomato, just slicing through the skin.**

3. **Put the tomato in a sieve with a handle, remove the lid from the pot, and lower the tomato into the boiling water for 10 to 30 seconds.**

   If you don't have a sieve, you can use a slotted spoon or even a pair of kitchen tongs for this step.

4. **Remove the tomato from the pot and immerse it in cold water until it's cool enough to handle.**

5. **Peel off the skin, starting from the X you cut in the bottom.**

   The skin should come off easily, but if it doesn't, return the tomato to the boiling water for another 30 seconds.

6. **Cut the peeled tomato in half.**

7. **Squeeze out the seeds and discard them.**

8. **Chop the remaining tomato flesh.**

Showing garlic, onions, and herbs some respect

In Chapter 4, we show you exactly how to chop an onion and mince cloves of garlic. You may want to flip back to that chapter because so many soup recipes call for one or both of these ingredients.

Herbs are another soup mainstay, and here's a crucial how-to: Always add fresh herbs to soups (or sauces) at the last minute before serving. That way, the herbs remain vibrant and alive with flavor. If you use dried herbs, add them earlier in the cooking process, to help release their flavors. Flip back to Chapter 3 for lots of info about herbs and spices.

Trying Your Hand at Puréed or Chunky Soups

Puréed soups use a blender or food processor to whirl the ingredients into a smooth texture. After you understand the puréeing technique, the variations you can make on this cooking theme are limitless. Asparagus, broccoli, corn, cucumbers, mushrooms, parsnips, spinach, rutabaga, tomatoes, winter squash, pumpkin, turnips, and watercress are among the vegetables that purée to a rich and smooth consistency.

In this chapter, we present recipes for three puréed soups:

✔ Carrot Soup with Dill (shown in the cook's color section) uses lowfat ricotta cheese instead of cream, making this a delicious and health-conscious recipe. Dill is a natural sidekick to carrots. *Port* (a Portuguese dessert wine) adds a touch of sweetness, but it's optional.

✔ Cream of Potato Soup is simple, quick, and easy. It isn't particularly low in calories or fat, but it sure tastes good! It's also good if you don't purée it and instead prefer a soup with chunks of potato. Your call.

✔ What child (or adult!) doesn't love tomato soup with a grilled cheese sandwich? It's comfort food supreme. Our Tomato Soup recipe is almost as easy as opening a can, and it tastes fantastic. It's a great way to use up overflow from a tomato garden in the summer, but canned tomatoes work, too.

If you're going to purée a soup in a blender, let it cool slightly first. Otherwise, the trapped steam could explode and redecorate your ceiling (not to mention burn you!).

We also like chunky soups and think they should be hearty, meaty, and thick with tender morsels of meat, poultry, or fish, and plenty of vegetables. We have two recipes to get you started:

- ✔ Chicken Noodle Soup is a classic — and guaranteed to help cure your winter sniffles.
- ✔ French Onion Soup is a restaurant staple that's easy to make and elegant enough for parties but simple enough for a quiet dinner at home.

Salad Days

We love salad; it's the yin to soup's yang. We think salads are the very best way to feature the freshest seasonal vegetables, or even fruits. A salad can be many things to a meal: a stimulating first course, a fresh and crisp accompaniment to a main dish, or the centerpiece of the meal itself.

The key to really great salads is twofold: Use only the freshest ingredients, and chop everything into bite-sized portions for easy eating. Who wants to try to fold unwieldy pieces of lettuce dripping with oily vinaigrette onto a fork? If everything is neatly chopped into small pieces, lightly dressed with a delicious creamy dressing or tangy vinaigrette, and arranged to present a colorful and attractive plate, you have a truly spectacular dish without ever turning on the stove.

In this section, we show you how to select your greens and whip up your own salad dressings. (Sorry, salad dressing companies, but we're tired of all the high fructose corn syrup.) Plus, we offer ten quick salad ideas that show you how simple it is to jazz up some greens with yummy ingredients to make your salads seem truly gourmet.

The soul of the salad: Crisp, fresh greens

A salad demands the freshest greens and herbs and the tastiest vegetables you can find. If at all possible, buy produce in season the day (hour?) you plan to eat it, and then speed home with your lights flashing. Better yet, grow some in your yard, if you can.

Getting your greens squeaky-clean

Did you ever fall asleep at the beach with your mouth open and the wind blowing sand in your direction? That's just what unwashed salad can taste like. To make sure that you get all the grit out of lettuce, remove the leaves from the stem and soak them briefly in cold water, shaking occasionally. Then run them under the tap, being careful to rinse the root ends thoroughly.

Drying lettuce completely is critical, or else the dressing slides right off. Layering greens between paper towels works, but it's a nuisance — and not "green" in the environmentally friendly sense. The easiest method is to use a salad spinner that dries with centrifugal force.

Buying and storing greens

When buying greens, avoid those that are wilted or limp. A fresh head of romaine should look like a bouquet of green leaves, clumped tightly together without any rust-colored edges or signs of decay. Pass up the watercress if its leaves are yellowing. Brown spots on iceberg lettuce indicate rot. Greens sold in bunches, such as arugula and dandelion, are especially delicate and prone to quick decay; consume them within a day or two of purchase. And don't believe (just because you watched your mother do it) that wilted greens revive when plunged into cold water.

Store rinsed and dried greens in the extra-cold crisper drawer of the refrigerator, wrapped in damp paper towels. You can place bunches of watercress, arugula, parsley, and other fresh herbs in a full glass of water, stem ends down, like fresh-cut flowers. These are all heroic measures to keep greens fresh, but just remember that the gold standard is to buy greens in the afternoon for dinner that evening.

Now that prebuttered rolls and pregrilled chicken are commonly available at supermarkets, you shouldn't be surprised to find prepackaged salad greens complete with dressings, croutons, and other "instant" salad ingredients. Bagged salads are convenient, and some are organic. You may be able to find greens you couldn't find otherwise in your supermarket. However, the bagged salad greens are more expensive and frankly, they aren't always that fresh. If you want to spend the extra cash for the convenience of dumping your greens, preplucked and washed, from bag to salad bowl, that's your call. If you already know that's the only way you're going to eat your greens, then we say go for it.

A glossary of greens

Greens range in taste from mild to pungent and even bitter. Don't limit yourself to bland iceberg lettuce, which lacks the higher flavor and nutritional content of more deeply colored greens. The more variety of greens in the bowl, the better. Our favorite salad greens, some of which are pictured in Figure 12-2, include those listed in the following sections.

Figure 12-2: Our favorite salad greens.

Mild greens

Typically crunchy and slightly sweet, these greens are easy to eat and go well with a highly flavored vinaigrette:

- ✔ **Bibb (or limestone) lettuce:** Tender, rippled leaves form a small, compact head. Bibb has the mildness of Boston lettuce, but more crunch. It tends to be expensive, but a little makes a big impression.

- ✔ **Boston lettuce:** Buttery textured, this lettuce looks like a green rose. It mixes well with all varieties and stands well alone topped with sliced, ripe summer tomatoes.

- ✔ **Iceberg lettuce:** The white bread of the salad world, iceberg is common to salad bars and political banquets. Iceberg has more texture than flavor, and, if wrapped, can be used for foul-shot practice.

  To remove the core of iceberg lettuce, smash the head (core side down) on a cutting board or countertop. The hard core should then twist out easily.

- ✔ **Loose-leaf lettuce:** This green is also called *red leaf* or *green leaf* lettuce, depending on its color. Its long, curly leaves are buttery and almost sweet. Add the red leaf variety to green salad for an elegant contrast, or mix red and green leaf together in one bowl.

- ✔ **Red oak leaf lettuce:** Named for the oak tree leaves it resembles, this green is sweet and colorful. It's good mixed with Boston or Bibb lettuce and makes a pretty plate garnish.

- ✔ **Romaine lettuce:** The emperor green of Caesar salad, romaine has dark green exterior leaves with a pale yellow core. It mixes well with other greens. One advantage of romaine is that it keeps well for up to a week in the refrigerator. Like other dark, leafy greens, romaine is a good source of vitamin A.

Pungent greens

Composing a salad of tart radicchio with a sharp vinaigrette is like catching baseballs without a glove — ouch! These more pungent greens have a bite. Use them to add interest to milder greens, or serve them with a mild creamy dressing, such as the Homemade Ranch Dressing in this chapter.

- ✔ **Arugula:** You can practically taste the iron in arugula's dark green leaves. The peppery flavor mixes well with any mild lettuce, or you can toss it with grilled portobello mushrooms, red onions, and a lemon vinaigrette.

- ✔ **Belgian endive:** Its pale yellow and white leaves are packed tightly together in a cigar-like shape. This green has lots of crunch and a slightly bitter taste. Pull the leaves away from the base and tear them into pieces in green salads, or use an entire leaf as a serving base for various cheese and vegetable spreads and fillings.

- ✔ **Cabbage:** Red or green, cabbage is a great salad addition and amazingly inexpensive. Tear or shred leaves with a knife and toss with other greens to add color and texture. Cabbage is a long-storage vegetable and a good source of vitamin C.

- ✔ **Curly endive (sometimes called chicory):** Similar to escarole in flavor, this green has very curly leaves.

- ✔ **Dandelion:** A green that you can probably harvest off your front lawn (if you don't have dogs and don't spray your yard with chemicals), dandelion leaves arrive on the market in the spring. Italians cherish its bitter, crunchy qualities. Choose young, tender leaves; the older ones are too bitter and tough. Toss in a mixed green salad with chopped, hard-cooked eggs and a vinaigrette dressing. Dandelion greens are a good source of vitamin A, vitamin C, and calcium.

- ✔ **Escarole:** You can consume this green raw in salad or sauté it in olive oil and garlic. A member of the endive family, escarole is rather tart and stands up to strong-flavored dressings.

- ✔ **Frisée:** Mildly bitter, this pale yellow green has lacy leaves. Mix it sparingly with other greens for contrasting texture and taste. It's similar to curly endive in appearance, but with a more delicate taste.

- ✔ **Mesclun (pronounced *mess-clan*):** This type of green is a salad mix that usually contains frisée, arugula, radicchio, red leaf lettuces, mustard, and other delicate greens. Mesclun is very expensive, so purchase it only if it appears very fresh, or the greens will wilt before you get home. It's best to buy a small amount to mix with other less expensive salad greens.

- ✔ **Radicchio:** A small, tightly wound head with deep magenta leaves that can add brilliant splashes of color to a bowl of greens, radicchio is extremely pungent and comparatively expensive. Use it sparingly. It keeps well in the refrigerator (up to two weeks), especially if wrapped in moist paper towels. Like cabbage, radicchio also may be grilled, baked, or sautéed.

- ✔ **Spinach:** These deep green, slightly crumpled leaves are full of iron. Discard the thick stems. The leaves of baby spinach are smaller, oval shaped, smooth, and buttery. Rinse all spinach thoroughly to rid the leaves of sand. Dry well. Mix with milder greens like Boston, Bibb, or loose-leaf.

- ✔ **Watercress:** Its clover-shaped leaves lend peppery crunch to any salad. Snap off and discard the tough stems and be sure to rinse well. Watercress makes a pretty soup or plate garnish.

Don't overdress

A common mistake with salads is overdressing them, which is like overdressing for dinner — *so* tacky, just when you were trying to be *so* cool. Drizzle just enough dressing over the greens to lightly coat them when tossed well. And when you toss, really toss. Using salad tongs or a large fork and spoon, mix those leaves up really well. The dressing should be evenly distributed on every piece of greenery. Now that's class.

Later in the chapter, we show you how to assemble an Easy Mixed Green Salad. Try it with different kinds of greens, whatever looks freshest, and a variety of chopped vegetables, such as halved cherry tomatoes, cucumber slices, endive leaves, radish slices, bell pepper strips, or even apple wedges. In the winter, try adding preserved vegetables, such as olives, marinated artichoke hearts, and hearts of palm.

Skipping the greens but keeping the salad

Sometimes, a great salad doesn't require any greens at all. Other vegetables such as green beans, peas, tomatoes, and cauliflower may serve as the salad's centerpiece, not to mention beans, potatoes, and pasta. If you're curious to try a green-less salad, be sure to check out our recipes for Broccoli Salad with Warm Bacon Dressing and French Potato Salad later in the chapter. Also look at our upcoming section "Ten salad ideas — so easy you don't need a recipe!" You'll discover that several of them don't involve greens at all.

So many dressings, so little time

A good dressing is a lot like a good outfit. It decorates in a pleasing way, adding style to the basic substance. If you go to the supermarket and look at the dressing section, you find many kinds and brands of dressing. You probably tend to reach for the same thing every time: the Italian dressing perhaps, or the creamy ranch dressing. Store-bought dressing can be quite good if you choose a quality brand with quality ingredients, but a store-bought dressing can't possibly be fresh. A homemade dressing is something extra special — it has fresh ingredients and a personal touch. Why not try making yours at home?

When you break them down, dressings are essentially of two kinds: those based on oil and vinegar (vinaigrette) and those based on a creamy mayonnaise (like ranch or Thousand Island). Both types are simple to prepare.

Puckering up for tangy vinaigrettes

Vinaigrette is among the most versatile of dressings. It goes with all sorts of salad greens and grilled vegetables, but it can also work with meat, poultry, and fish, as a marinade or as a light and tasty sauce. The advantage of vinaigrette-based dressing is that you can make a large quantity and store it, sealed, in an old wine bottle or Mason jar. It lasts for weeks in the refrigerator. Homemade vinaigrette in a fancy bottle makes a great gift, too.

Vinaigrette has two essential ingredients: vinegar (or another acid, like lemon juice or lime juice) and oil. Add herbs, spices, and other flavorings, and you can give your vinaigrette its unique character.

The skinny on olive and other salad oils

Some people say that a salad dressing is only as good as the oil it contains, and few oils make a more delicious, complex, and interesting salad dressing than olive oil. But buying olive oil in the supermarket has become as confusing as ordering coffee, what with all the nationalities and fancy labels and terminology in baffling languages. Do you get Italian or Spanish or a blend, or maybe something artisanal from California? What color and what brand do you buy? Should it be green or yellow or as light as possible?

Don't worry about all that. The most important thing to look for in olive oil is its *grade,* which is usually printed right on the front of the bottle. In ascending order of quality, you'll find *pure, virgin,* and *extra-virgin.*

The grade has to do with the oleic acid content of the oil, with the finest oils having the least acidity. All three varieties of olive oil come from the olive's first *pressing* (the crushing process that releases the oil from the olives), but extra-virgin is the highest quality. Extra-virgin olive oil usually has the richest aroma and strongest flavor. Pure olive oil can come from both the first and second pressing of the tree-ripened olives and may be blended with 5 to 10 percent virgin olive oil to enrich its flavor.

Don't be misled by olive oil sold as "light." The "light" has nothing to do with its fat content; instead, it refers to its pale color and extremely bland flavor, a result of the way it's processed. One tablespoon of any olive oil contains the same 120 calories.

Other salad oils include base oils like canola, corn, safflower, and other neutral-tasting vegetable oils; more intensely flavored oils such as walnut, hazelnut, and sesame; and oils flavored with garlic, herbs, citrus, or hot chilis. Each has its place. The neutral oils can be mixed with equal amounts of olive to lighten the taste (and the cost), or you can add smaller dashes of nut oils or flavored oils for drama.

The shelf life of oil depends on its variety. Olive oils should keep for up to a year if tightly capped and stored out of the sun in a cool, dark place. Nut oils last only a few months, so purchase them in small quantities.

What puts the vinegar in vinaigrette?

Oil in a salad dressing needs an acidic counterpoint — a tart ingredient that stimulates the palate and cuts through the oil's richness. In most cases, vinegar is the choice, but fresh citrus juice can also add a pleasing tartness.

Vinegar comes in many different forms. Red or white wine is the most common liquid base, but anything that ferments can be used to make vinegar:

- **Cider vinegar:** Made from apples, this strong, clear, brownish vinegar holds up well with pungent greens and is especially good sprinkled on meat, fish, or fruit salads. It's also excellent with ginger or curry dressings.

- ✔ **Red or white wine vinegar:** Made from any number of red or white wines, this vinegar is full bodied and perfect for dressing pungent, dark greens.

- ✔ **Rice vinegar:** Common to Japan and China, rice vinegars are less tart than white vinegars and combine well with sesame oil for an Asian-inspired flavor. They're also good in seafood salads.

- ✔ **White vinegar:** Colorless and sharp, white vinegar is distilled from assorted grains, and it's terrific in cold rice or pasta salads.

Experiment with different vinegars to find ones with flavors you enjoy. Your unique choices will make your homemade vinaigrette dressing all yours.

Making your own vinaigrette

We offer a basic recipe for Vinaigrette Dressing later in the chapter, but the proportions in the recipe are only approximations. You must taste it as you go along to balance the vinegar and olive oil flavors.

Keep in mind that vinaigrette is a basic formula to which you can add many different ingredients for color, flavor, texture, and taste. Following are some variations on the basic Vinaigrette Dressing recipe in this chapter:

- ✔ Replace 2 tablespoons of the olive oil with 2 tablespoons of walnut or hazelnut oil to give the vinaigrette a distinctive, nutty flavor. Serve with mixed green salads or salads with grilled poultry.

- ✔ Add 1 teaspoon drained capers and 1 tablespoon chopped fresh chervil, tarragon, basil, or lemon thyme. This herby vinaigrette really enlivens a cold pasta salad.

- ✔ Place one small ripe tomato in a blender or food processor container with the rest of the dressing and blend well.

- ✔ To thicken the vinaigrette, combine it in a blender with 1 to 2 tablespoons of ricotta cheese. Lowfat ricotta enriches just like cream, with far fewer calories.

After you create your perfect vinaigrette, be sure to check out our recipe for French Potato Salad later in the chapter. A delicious European-style potato salad hinges on a good vinaigrette. It's not your grandmother's potato salad (unless your grandmother is French).

Concocting creamy dressings

A creamy dressing can enhance various greens, complementing bitter or pungent flavors with the mellow flavor of mayonnaise. Creamy dressings also go well with cold shellfish, meat, and poultry. One downside to creamy dressings is that they spoil more quickly than vinaigrettes, so be sure to keep them refrigerated and use them within a week or so.

Balsamic: The world's most expensive vinegar

Traditional balsamic vinegar is a dark, sweet, syrupy, aged liquid that is worth its weight in gold. The real thing is made in the area around Modena, Italy, and nowhere else (the word "Modena" should be on the label). Virtually all those large bottles of balsamic vinegar you see in supermarkets are imitations — some aged, some not — made to look like the real thing. This "fake" balsamic vinegar is not necessarily bad, just different. And way less expensive.

Recognizing real balsamic vinegar is easy: You start to hyperventilate upon seeing the price. Real balsamic vinegar is sold only in little bulb-shaped bottles — they look like perfume. It is usually more than 25 years old and costs $100 and up for a tiny portion. Such rarefied vinegar is not to be tossed around in salads. Italians use it for sauces or just drizzle some on fresh fruit (strawberries are best).

Later in the chapter, we provide a recipe for Homemade Ranch Dressing. We suggest using both sour cream and mayonnaise in this dressing because the combination adds a nice, sharp edge, but you can use all mayo if you prefer. You can drizzle this dressing on your salad, or add 1 teaspoon horseradish (or to taste) and use it as a sandwich spread.

Ten salad ideas — so easy you don't need a recipe!

Salads are easy to improvise. Simply follow the advice of your taste buds to create your own salads. Need some inspiration to get you started? Try a few of these simple combinations, but don't be afraid to substitute, experiment, or add different vegetables or dressings according to your taste:

- **Tomato, Red Onion, and Basil Salad:** Slice ripe, red tomatoes ¼ inch thick and layer on a platter with diced red onion and 4 or 5 large chopped fresh basil leaves. Drizzle with oil and vinegar and season with salt and pepper. This salad tastes great with fresh mozzarella cheese, too.

- **Bell Pepper–Rice Salad:** Combine about 3 cups cooked white rice with 1 cup cooked green peas and 2 cups seeded, cored, and chopped red, green, or yellow bell peppers (or any combination of colors). Toss with enough herb vinaigrette dressing to moisten the ingredients sufficiently, add salt and black pepper to taste, and chill before serving.

- **Cucumber-Dill Salad:** Toss peeled, sliced, and seeded cucumbers in a dill-flavored vinaigrette.

- **Cherry Tomato and Feta Cheese Salad:** Toss 1 pint cherry tomatoes, rinsed and sliced in half, with 4 ounces crumbled feta cheese and ½ cup sliced, pitted black olives. Season with vinaigrette dressing to taste.

✔ **Pasta Medley Salad:** Combine about 2 cups of your favorite pasta, cooked, with ½ cup chopped, sun-dried tomatoes. Season lightly with oil, vinegar, and black pepper to taste.

✔ **Garbanzo Bean Toss:** Combine 1 can (15½ or 16 ounces) drained garbanzo beans, ½ cup chopped red onion, 1 or 2 cloves crushed garlic, and the grated zest of 1 lemon. Toss with lemon vinaigrette dressing.

✔ **Layered Cheese and Vegetable Salad:** Arrange alternating thin slices of ripe tomatoes and mozzarella cheese on a round platter. Fill the center with slices of avocado sprinkled with fresh lemon juice to prevent discoloration. Drizzle with olive oil and lemon juice; garnish with fresh basil.

✔ **Grilled Vegetable Platter with Fresh Pesto:** Arrange any assortment of grilled vegetables (see Chapter 9) on a platter. Serve with spoonfuls of fresh pesto (see Chapter 14).

✔ **Fruit Salsa:** Combine 1 ripe, peeled, pitted, and chopped avocado; 2 ripe, peeled, seeded, and chopped mangoes; ½ cup chopped red onion; and 1 teaspoon seeded, chopped jalapeño pepper with a dressing of 1 tablespoon honey and the grated zest and juice of 1 lemon. Serve as a side salad with broiled hamburgers, chicken, or fish.

✔ **Three-Berry Dessert Salad:** Combine 2 pints rinsed and hulled strawberries, 1 pint rinsed blueberries, and 1 pint rinsed raspberries in a bowl. Toss with a dressing of ½ cup heavy cream sweetened with confectioner's sugar to taste.

Carrot Soup with Dill

Prep time: About 15 min • **Cook time:** About 1 hr • **Yield:** 6 servings

Ingredients	Directions
2 tablespoons butter	*1* In a large, deep saucepan or soup pot over medium heat, melt the butter. Add the onion and cook, stirring often, until it softens, about 5 minutes.
1 medium yellow onion, finely chopped	
1½ pounds carrots, peeled and cut into 1-inch-thick pieces	*2* Add the carrots, stock, water, and salt and pepper to taste. Cover and bring to a boil.
4 cups homemade or canned chicken or vegetable stock	*3* Reduce the heat and simmer, uncovered, for 30 minutes, skimming off any foam that rises to the surface. Cool for 15 minutes.
2 cups water	
Salt and pepper	
½ cup lowfat ricotta cheese	*4* Set a colander over a big bowl or another pot. Carefully pour the soup into the colander. Save the liquid.
2 to 3 tablespoons Port (optional)	
2 tablespoons chopped fresh dill, or 2 teaspoons dried dill	*5* Put the drained carrot-onion mixture into a blender or food processor. Add the ricotta cheese and about a cup of the saved liquid. Purée until smooth.
	6 Add the purée to the pot holding the remaining cooking liquid and turn the heat to medium-high. Stir well with a wooden spoon until the soup just comes to a boil, about 10 minutes.
	7 Remove from the heat, stir in the Port (if desired), garnish with the dill, and serve.

Per serving: Calories 120 (From Fat 42); Fat 5g (Saturated 3g); Cholesterol 15mg; Sodium 588mg; Carbohydrate 15g (Dietary Fiber 3g); Protein 5g.

Vary It! If you prefer, omit the dill and add ½ to ¾ teaspoon ground ginger.

Cream of Potato Soup

Prep time: About 15 min plus cooling time • **Cook time:** About 50 min • **Yield:** 6 servings

Ingredients	Directions
4 tablespoons butter	*1* In a large saucepan or pot, melt the butter.
6 medium red potatoes, peeled and quartered	*2* Add the potatoes and garlic cloves and stir to coat. Cook for about 5 minutes.
4 garlic cloves, peeled	
4 cups chicken broth	*3* Add the chicken broth and bring the soup to a simmer. Cook until the potatoes are tender and easy to mash against the side of the pan, about 30 minutes.
1 cup heavy cream	
1½ teaspoons salt (optional)	
½ teaspoon pepper	*4* Remove the soup from the heat and cool for 15 minutes. Spoon the mixture into a blender and purée well.
6 slices bacon, cooked until crispy and crumbled	
1 tablespoon chopped chives, fresh or dried	*5* Return the soup to the pot and turn the heat to medium-low. Add the cream and stir constantly until the soup is hot and just barely simmering (showing tiny bubbles), about 10 minutes.
	6 Add the salt, if desired, and pepper and garnish each soup bowl with the bacon and chives.

Per serving: Calories 425 (From Fat 255); Fat 28g (Saturated 16g); Cholesterol 84mg; Sodium 798mg; Carbohydrate 36g (Dietary Fiber 3g); Protein 8g.

Tip: If you don't want to purée this soup, cut the potatoes into bite-sized pieces, mince the garlic, and skip step 4.

Tomato Soup

Prep time: About 15 min • **Cook time:** About 15 min • **Yield:** 6 servings

Ingredients	*Directions*
2 tablespoons butter	*1* In a medium saucepan, melt the butter over medium-high heat. Add the onions and garlic and sauté until soft, about 10 minutes.
1 small yellow onion, peeled and chopped	
1 clove garlic, minced	
3 cups canned chicken or vegetable stock	*2* Add the stock and tomatoes to the onion-garlic mixture. Bring to a boil.
6 large ripe tomatoes, peeled, seeded, and coarsely chopped, or 2 cans (14 ounces each) tomatoes, undrained and coarsely chopped	*3* Remove from the heat and allow to cool 5 minutes.
	4 Pour carefully into a blender or food processor. Purée until smooth.
2 tablespoons fresh lemon juice	*5* Return the mixture to the saucepan; add the lemon juice, sugar, and salt and pepper to taste; and heat over medium until hot again, about 5 minutes, stirring with a wooden spoon. Garnish with the cilantro, basil, or tarragon, if desired.
2 teaspoons sugar	
Salt and pepper	
1 tablespoon chopped fresh cilantro, basil, or tarragon (optional)	

Per serving: Calories 102 (From Fat 58); Fat 6g (Saturated 3g); Cholesterol 13mg; Sodium 614mg; Carbohydrate 11g (Dietary Fiber 2g); Protein 2g.

Chicken Noodle Soup

Prep time: About 25 min • **Cook time:** About 55 min • **Yield:** 6 servings

Ingredients	Directions
2 tablespoons butter	*1* In a large saucepan or pot over medium heat, melt the butter.
1 large yellow onion, chopped	
2 cloves garlic, peeled and minced	*2* Add the onion, garlic, carrots, celery, oregano, and basil. Stir to coat with the butter and cook, stirring occasionally, until the onions are transparent but not browned, about 5 minutes.
3 carrots, peeled and cut into ¼-inch rounds	
3 ribs celery, washed, ends trimmed, and cut into ½-inch pieces	*3* Add the chicken broth and chicken breasts. Cover and bring to a boil. Reduce the heat and simmer, uncovered, for about 30 minutes, or until the chicken is cooked all the way through.
1 teaspoon dried oregano	
1 teaspoon dried basil	
8 cups canned chicken broth	*4* Increase the heat again and bring to a boil. Add the egg noodles and reduce the heat again, simmering uncovered until the noodles are tender, about 20 minutes.
1 pound boneless, skinless chicken breasts	
1½ cups dried egg noodles	
1½ teaspoons salt (optional)	*5* Remove the chicken breasts to a cutting board and chop or shred them into bite-sized pieces. Return the chicken and any juice to the pot
Dash of cayenne pepper (optional)	
Few dashes of black pepper	*6* Season with the salt and cayenne pepper, if desired, and the pepper. Garnish each serving with the parsley or cilantro.
3 tablespoons chopped fresh parsley or cilantro, or 1½ tablespoons dried parsley or cilantro	

Per serving: Calories 235 (From Fat 102); Fat 11g (Saturated 4g); Cholesterol 66mg; Sodium 1,417mg; Carbohydrate 14g (Dietary Fiber 3g); Protein 19g.

French Onion Soup

Prep time: About 20 min • **Cook time:** About 1 hr • **Yield:** 6 servings

Ingredients	*Directions*
4 tablespoons butter **4 large sweet onions, like Vidalia, peeled and thinly sliced**	*1* Melt the butter over medium heat in a large soup pot. Add the onions. Toss to coat the onions with the butter and cook until they become transparent, about 10 minutes.
7 cups beef broth **1 bay leaf** **6 slices French bread, toasted**	*2* Add 1 cup of the beef broth and continue stirring until the broth almost completely cooks away, scraping the pan to keep the caramelized parts moving, about 35 minutes.
1 cup grated Swiss cheese	*3* Add the remaining 6 cups broth and the bay leaf. Cover and bring to a boil. Reduce the heat and simmer for 15 minutes, stirring occasionally.
	4 Remove the bay leaf from the soup and discard. Ladle the soup into 6 ovenproof crocks or bowls. Put a slice of French bread in each bowl and sprinkle each with one-sixth of the cheese. Put the crocks on a sturdy baking sheet.
	5 Turn on the broiler of your oven and carefully put the baking sheet under the broiler on the top rack, about 4 inches from the heat source. When the cheese turns golden brown (in 1 or 2 minutes), carefully remove the baking sheet and serve.

Per serving: Calories 364 (From Fat 131); Fat 15g (Saturated 8g); Cholesterol 37mg; Sodium 1,606mg; Carbohydrate 41g (Dietary Fiber 3g); Protein 16g.

Tip: When simmering thick soups like this one, occasionally stir and scrape the bottom of the pot with a wooden spoon to prevent the mixture from sticking and burning. Add more broth (or water) if necessary.

Easy Mixed Green Salad

Prep time: About 20 min • **Yield:** 6 servings

Ingredients	Directions
6 cups mixed lettuces, such as romaine, red leaf, Boston, or mixed spring greens	*1* Rinse the lettuce leaves in cold water. Remove tough stems, and spin the greens in a salad spinner to dry.
⅓ cup coarsely chopped red onion	*2* Tear the greens into bite-sized pieces and put them in a salad bowl. Add the onion, carrots, celery, and, if desired, the cabbage.
2 carrots, grated	
1 rib celery, minced	
½ cup grated red or green cabbage (optional)	*3* Put the vinegar in a small bowl and add the basil or oregano and the salt and pepper to taste. Start beating while gradually adding the oil.
1½ tablespoons red or white wine vinegar	
½ teaspoon dried basil or oregano	*4* Pour the dressing over the salad and toss to evenly coat.
Salt and pepper	
¼ cup olive oil	

Per serving: Calories 107 (From Fat 82); Fat 9g (Saturated 1g); Cholesterol 0mg; Sodium 133mg; Carbohydrate 6g (Dietary Fiber 2g); Protein 1g.

Vary It! For variety, substitute freshly squeezed lemon juice for the vinegar; add 2 teaspoons mayonnaise, yogurt, or sour cream for a creamy vinaigrette; or whisk 2 teaspoons Dijon-style mustard into the vinaigrette. Add minced herbs, such as tarragon, thyme, chervil, sage, or savory, to taste. Crumble goat cheese or blue cheese over the greens.

Broccoli Salad with Warm Bacon Dressing

Prep time: About 25 min • **Cook time:** About 10 min • **Yield:** 4 servings

Ingredients	*Directions*
1 large head broccoli, cut into bite-sized pieces (include part of the stalk)	*1* In a mixing bowl, toss together broccoli, onion, celery, raisins, and walnuts. Set aside.
1 medium red onion, cut in quarters and thinly sliced	*2* In a skillet over medium heat, fry the bacon pieces until crispy. Drain off bacon fat, reserving 2 tablespoons.
2 stalks celery, minced	
½ cup raisins	*3* In a small mixing bowl, combine reserved bacon fat, vinegar, mayonnaise, and mustard. Whisk to combine. Stir in bacon pieces.
¼ cup chopped walnuts	
1 pound bacon, cut into small pieces	
½ cup red wine vinegar	*4* Drizzle the bacon mixture over the broccoli mixture and stir to coat all the vegetables with the dressing. Serve immediately.
¼ cup mayonnaise	
2 teaspoons Dijon mustard	

Per serving: *Calories 460 (From Fat 314); Fat 35g (Saturated 9g); Cholesterol 40mg; Sodium 790mg; Carbohydrate 25g (Dietary Fiber 5g); Protein 16g.*

Vinaigrette Dressing

Prep time: 5 min • **Yield:** 6 servings

Ingredients	Directions
2 tablespoons red or white wine vinegar	**1** Place the vinegar and mustard in a bowl. Whisk to blend well.
1 teaspoon Dijon-style mustard	**2** Add the olive oil in a stream while whisking. Season with salt and pepper to taste.
⅓ cup olive oil	
Salt and pepper	

Per serving: Calories 107 (From Fat 106); Fat 12g (Saturated 2g); Cholesterol 0mg; Sodium 119mg; Carbohydrate 0g (Dietary Fiber 0g); Protein 0g.

Vary It: Try a flavored vinegar or substitute fresh lemon juice for the vinegar.

French Potato Salad

Prep time: About 15 min plus standing time • **Cook time:** About 30 min • **Yield:** 4 servings

Ingredients	Directions
2 pounds red potatoes, well scrubbed	*1* In a medium saucepan, cover the potatoes with lightly salted cold water and bring to a boil.
6 tablespoons olive oil	
1 tablespoon white vinegar	*2* Boil for 20 minutes or until the potatoes are tender when pierced with a knife. Drain and let stand until cool enough to handle.
½ cup red onion, chopped	
¼ cup finely chopped parsley	*3* As the potatoes cook, make the dressing. Whisk together the oil and vinegar in a small bowl. Whisk in the red onion, parsley, garlic, and salt and pepper to taste.
1 large clove garlic, finely chopped	
Salt and pepper	
¼ cup dry white wine at room temperature	*4* Peel the cooked potatoes and cut them into ¼-inch slices. Layer the slices in a shallow serving bowl, sprinkling the wine between the layers.
	5 Pour the dressing over the potatoes and gently toss to blend well.
	6 Let the salad stand about 30 minutes to blend the flavors. Stir from the bottom before serving, either chilled or at room temperature.

Per serving: Calories 401 (From Fat 186); Fat 21g (Saturated 3g); Cholesterol 0mg; Sodium 167mg; Carbohydrate 47g (Dietary Fiber 5g); Protein 6g.

Vary It! Instead of white wine, use ¼ cup white grape juice or 2 tablespoons cider vinegar.

Vary It! Add ¼ cup minced green onions; 2 tablespoons chopped herbs like rosemary, chervil, or basil; or 1 cup diced, roasted bell peppers.

Homemade Ranch Dressing

Prep time: 5 min • **Yield:** 6 servings

Ingredients	*Directions*
½ **cup mayonnaise**	Combine all ingredients in a bowl and whisk well. Adjust seasonings to taste.
⅓ **cup sour cream**	
¼ **cup buttermilk or regular milk**	
¼ **cup minced yellow onion**	
1 teaspoon garlic powder	
2 tablespoons minced fresh or dried parsley	
2 teaspoons dried dill	
1 teaspoon salt	
¼ **teaspoon pepper**	

Per serving: Calories 169 (From Fat 157); Fat 17g (Saturated 4g); Cholesterol 17mg; Sodium 221mg; Carbohydrate 3g (Dietary Fiber 0g); Protein 1g.

Vary It! For a seafood salad, add 1 tablespoon drained capers and 1 tablespoon minced tarragon or 1 teaspoon dried tarragon. For a cold meat dish or for a chicken or shrimp salad, make a curry dressing by adding 1 teaspoon curry powder (or to taste) to this dressing. For cold vegetable salad, crumble ½ cup or more blue cheese or Roquefort and mix it into the dressing.

Chapter 13

From Sides to Mains: Great Grains

Throughout history, many people all over the planet have survived almost solely on grains and grain-like foods: rice, wheat, barley, oats, cornmeal, wheat berries, quinoa, amaranth, buckwheat, and more. Grains make bread, pasta, even beer. They are the staff of life, and despite what the low-carb lovers say, we love them. Chewy, tender, moist — they make a meal filling.

Most grains are prepared by boiling or steaming, which you can learn about in Chapter 5. In this chapter, we celebrate the great diversity of grains with recipes for rice and other grains, as well as all the fantastical things you can do with pasta.

Rice is Nice

Rice is one of the most versatile foods on the planet. Quite literally, it feeds most of the world. It's not all that glamorous on its own, but because of its mild taste, pleasing texture, and affinity with about a billion and seven other flavors, rice is one of the best things a home cook can have in the cupboard.

So many different cultures use rice, and preparing a variety of rice dishes can feel like taking a trip around the globe. India alone has more than 1,100 rice varieties. To give your rice international flair, you don't even really need a recipe. Channel your inner traveler by picking a country and then adding the listed components to plain white rice:

- **France:** Garlic, tomatoes, fresh herbs (thyme, tarragon, basil)

- **India:** Curry and spices like cumin, coriander, cardamom, and fennel

- **Mexico:** Garlic, hot peppers, onions, pinto or black beans

- **Middle East:** Onions, raisins, cinnamon, allspice, turmeric, cardamom

- **Spain:** Saffron, nuts, bell peppers and other vegetables, garlic

- **United States (Louisiana):** Spicy sausage, onions, garlic, cayenne, okra, bell peppers

Here are the most common types of rice used in the United States:

- **Converted or parboiled rice:** No, your rice hasn't suddenly found religion. The term *converted* refers to a process by which whole grains of rice are soaked in water, steamed, and then dried. This precooking, also called *parboiling,* makes milling easier and also conserves nutrients that are otherwise lost. Steaming also removes some of the rice's sticky starch, leaving each grain smoother in texture, and it shortens cooking time.

  If you can't wait to try your hand at rice, see the simple recipe for Converted Rice that appears later in this chapter.

- **Long-grain rice:** This basic form of white or brown rice has (obviously) a longer grain. This category includes the fragrant Indian basmati rice essential for Indian cuisine.

  The term *pilaf* refers to a dish in which the grain (rice or another whole grain) is browned slightly in butter or oil and then cooked in a flavored liquid, like chicken or beef stock. After you get the technique down, you can add any flavors you like. We offer a recipe for Basic Rice Pilaf later in the chapter (and a photo of it in the book's color section).

- **Short-grain rice:** This rice also comes in white or brown and has a shorter, stubbier shape. It is used to make *risotto* (the creamy, long-stirred specialty of northern Italy), as well as sushi.

  The technique for cooking long-grain rice and short-grain rice is essentially the same, except when making risotto, which frequently uses the short-grained rice called *Arborio rice* (available in gourmet markets).

When making risotto (as you can do with the help of our recipe later in this chapter), you want the rice to slowly absorb enough of the hot broth to form a creamy blend of tender yet still firm grains. It's difficult to give exact proportions for making risotto because absorption rates can vary. The key is to keep stirring the rice over low heat, adding only enough liquid (a little at a time) so that the rice is surrounded by, but never swimming in, broth.

✔ **Instant rice:** Precooked and dehydrated, it's fast, we must admit — but it's not nearly as good as rice you cook for the *first* time. It doesn't have the same texture and toothsomeness as other forms of rice.

✔ **Brown rice:** This healthful, unrefined rice has not been "polished"; that is, nothing but the tough, outer husk has been removed. With its bran layer intact, brown rice is superior in nutrition to polished (white) rice and is also a little more expensive. Brown rice has a faintly nutty flavor and a shorter shelf life than white rice. You can store white rice almost indefinitely, but brown rice should be consumed within 6 months of purchase.

✔ **Wild rice:** Not really rice at all, *wild rice* is a remote relative of white rice — it's actually a long-grain, aquatic grass. The wild version (it is now cultivated) grows almost exclusively in the Great Lakes region of the United States and has become quite expensive because of its scarcity. You can save money by combining it with brown rice.

Wild rice is especially good with robust meat dishes, game, and smoked foods because of its more intense flavor. We include a recipe for Basic Wild Rice later in the chapter.

Grain-o-Rama

Rice is nice, but other grains are great, too. Most grains cook quickly in boiling water or flavored boiling liquid, like beef stock or chicken stock. They usually don't need to be soaked before cooking, but they should be rinsed to remove any surface grit. Here are some of the more common whole grains, other than rice:

✔ **Barley:** A great substitute for rice in soups and side dishes, barley is commonly sold as "pearl" barley, with its outer hull and bran removed. It cooks relatively quickly — about 25 minutes in boiling water or stock. You season it with butter, salt, and pepper.

✔ **Buckwheat:** Although buckwheat isn't really a grain, we treat it like one. Buckwheat is really a grass and a cousin of the rhubarb plant. It has an earthy, almost nutlike flavor and tastes more like brown rice than other grains. Kasha, also called *buckwheat groats,* is simply buckwheat that has been roasted.

✔ **Wheat berries and bulgur:** *Wheat berries* are unprocessed grains of wheat. *Bulgur wheat,* used to make tabbouleh, is a wheat berry that has been steamed and then hulled, dried, and cracked. Bulgur cooks very quickly. (Note that a much more processed form of wheat berries is *cream of wheat* hot cereal, a breakfast porridge.)

In the Tabbouleh Salad recipe toward the end of this chapter, you use bulgur wheat that is rehydrated with boiling water and mixed with some simple ingredients. The result is a fresh grain salad with a Middle Eastern flair.

✔ **Cornmeal:** Basic cornmeal is often called by its Italian name, *polenta.* While it is a less common grain-based side dish in this country than rice and pasta, it tastes delicious. *Grits,* that southern specialty often served with breakfast, is also made of cornmeal. (See Chapter 9 for a terrific Southern Fried Grits recipe.)

Cornmeal comes finely or coarsely ground. The finely ground type cooks much faster than the coarsely ground meal. The latter has a nuttier texture and takes longer to cook. Try both to see which you prefer.

For a change of pace, try polenta with your meal. If you don't have time to make polenta from scratch, you can buy it ready-made, wrapped in a tube of plastic that looks like a fat sausage; it's available in most supermarkets. Ready-made polenta is good sliced, brushed with a little butter or olive oil, and grilled on both sides until lightly browned. Use polenta in any form — homemade or store-bought — as a base for grilled chops, chicken, sausages, and vegetables.

Making polenta from scratch doesn't actually take much time at all. To prove it, we've included a Polenta with Herbs recipe later in the chapter for you to try. (Look for a photo of it in the book's color section.) It makes a great side dish that is a delightful change from pasta or rice, or it's a quick and tasty light meal in itself when covered with a good tomato-meat sauce.

✔ **Oats:** Most popular as a breakfast cereal, oats boiled with water make a creamy porridge that tastes great with milk or cream and a little sugar, maple syrup, or honey.

✔ **Quinoa:** A small grain that is power-packed with nutrients, quinoa (pronounced *keen-wah*) is available in most health food stores, Middle Eastern shops, and quality supermarkets. You must rinse quinoa a few times before cooking. It takes about two parts liquid to one part quinoa and cooks in about 15 minutes.

You can make a protein-rich pilaf out of quinoa, for a change of pace from rice. Try the Quinoa Pilaf recipe later in this chapter.

Pasta-Mania

Ah, the unassuming noodle — so simple, yet so delectable. Pasta can be transformed into so many different kinds of meals, from side dish to main course, from modest macaroni and cheese to multi-layered lasagna to exotic Thai-spiced rice noodles in coconut milk.

Americans learned to love pasta when Italian immigrants brought classic dishes from Italy to the United States, and Italian-American cuisine is among the most beloved cuisines in this country today, but you don't have to know Italian cooking to make great pasta. All you really have to do is follow the simple preparation instructions on any package of dried or fresh pasta.

You can eat pasta hot or cold or anywhere in between, dressed in a little butter and freshly grated Parmesan cheese, tossed with a handful of chopped fresh tomatoes and garlic, or drenched in a long-simmered meaty meatball marinara. Try rice noodles with a drizzle of sesame oil, soy sauce, a pinch of ginger, and some chopped scallions for an Asian-inspired side dish or, with the addition of sautéed meat or tofu, a main course.

Most pasta is made out of *semolina,* a coarsely ground grain (usually durum wheat). However, most grocery stores now stock a variety of gluten-free pastas (such as rice, quinoa, and buckwheat) for those who avoid wheat. If you stick to moderate portions, pasta is low in calories and fat. (One big ladleful of Alfredo sauce can easily destroy all that, but don't blame us!) No matter how you love your pasta, learn how to cook it perfectly at home and the next time you crave noodles in any shape, you won't have to go out to a restaurant to get them.

When you start cooking your own pasta, you'll be hooked. To get you going, we provide two great recipes later in the chapter: Spaghetti with Quick Fresh Tomato Sauce, and Penne with Parmesan Cheese and Basil.

Don't sweat the fresh stuff: Dried versus fresh pasta

America's attics and closets must be jammed with pasta-making machines. In the late 1970s and early 1980s, anyone who knew how to boil water wanted to make fresh pasta. Somehow — maybe through a conspiracy of glossy food magazines — people started believing that if you didn't roll your own pasta, you were unpatriotic. Young couples spent weeknights in the kitchen with flour flying, eggs cracking, and bits of dough falling onto the floor. They cranked and cranked and cranked some more. Then they hung the pasta overnight to dry on chairs, books, tables, and lampshades.

This trend didn't last long. But you can always spot the lapsed pastamaniacs — they're the ones who always remark in Italian restaurants, "Oooh, fresh pasta. We love making fresh pasta! Say, we haven't done that in a while."

The truth is that fresh pasta is not inherently better than dried; it's just different. Many fine dried pastas are available, and the choice between fresh and dried is really a matter of personal taste. Homemade pasta — that is, well-made homemade pasta — is definitely lighter and more delicate, in part because it is usually made from all-purpose flour rather than semolina.

Specialty food markets and many supermarkets sell fresh pasta in the refrigerator section, so if you want to try fresh pasta, you really don't need to make your own. Fresh pasta is good, but you pay a premium. For purposes of this chapter, we concentrate on dried pasta because it is widely available, lasts longer in the pantry, and is more economical. In any case, the sauce is what really elevates pasta from ordinary to sublime.

Pasta tips and tricks

Cooking pasta isn't difficult, but a few pieces of select pasta knowledge make the job easier and ensure perfectly cooked pasta every time:

- ✔ *Al dente* **is not the name of an Italian orthodontist.** It is a sacred term in Italy that means "to the tooth" or "to the bite." In cooking, *al dente* means "slightly firm to the bite." Cook pasta to this point — not until it is soft all the way through. When pasta cooks too long, it absorbs more water and becomes mushy. Here are three ways to test for doneness:

    - The time-tested method for checking pasta for doneness is still the best: Scoop out a strand or two with a fork, take the pasta in hand, jump around and toss the scorching pasta in the air, and then taste it. (You don't really have to toss it in the air, but it makes the process more fun.)

    - Some people swear by the old method of throwing a piece of pasta against the wall. If it sticks, it's done. If it slides down onto the floor and the dog eats it, it isn't ready yet.

    - Pull the ends of a piece of cooked pasta until it snaps. You can actually hear the snap. Look at the broken end and, if it's cooked correctly, it will have a very small dot of uncooked pasta running through the center.

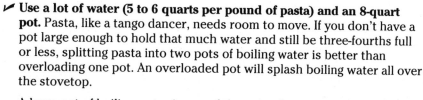

✔ **Use a lot of water (5 to 6 quarts per pound of pasta) and an 8-quart pot.** Pasta, like a tango dancer, needs room to move. If you don't have a pot large enough to hold that much water and still be three-fourths full or less, splitting pasta into two pots of boiling water is better than overloading one pot. An overloaded pot will splash boiling water all over the stovetop.

A large pot of boiling water is one of the most dangerous elements in any kitchen. Use a pot with short handles that cannot be tipped easily and set it to boil on a back burner, away from small and curious hands or clumsy kitchen helpers.

✔ **Salt the water to add flavor and to help the pasta absorb the sauce.** As a general guideline, 5 quarts of water take about 2 teaspoons of salt, and 6 quarts of water call for 1 tablespoon of salt.

✔ **Oil is for salads, not pasta water.** You don't need to add oil to the water if you use enough water and stir occasionally to prevent sticking.

Stir the pasta immediately and thoroughly after adding it to the water, to prevent it from sticking together.

✔ **Cover the pot to hasten heat recovery.** After you add pasta to the water, the water ceases to boil. When the water begins boiling again, remove the lid and finish cooking. Stay with the pot and pay attention so you catch it before it boils over.

✔ **Save a cup of the cooking liquid when the pasta is done.** You can use some of the liquid to add moisture to the sauce. The starch in the water binds the sauce, helping it adhere to the pasta.

✔ **Do not rinse pasta.** When the pasta is al dente (tender but firm), pour it gradually into a colander. *Do not rinse!* You want starch on the pasta to help the sauce adhere to it. The only exceptions are if you're making a cold pasta salad or a casserole such as lasagna where the ingredients are layered.

✔ **After draining it, you may want to place the pasta in the pan in which the sauce is cooking and stir well.** This method coats the pasta better than spooning the sauce on top. Serve from the saucepan.

✔ **Never combine two types or sizes of pasta in the same pot of water.** Fishing out the type that is done first is a real nuisance.

✔ **Always have the sauce ready and waiting before the pasta is cooked.** Cooked pasta needs to be sauced immediately after it's drained, or it becomes stiff and gluey. In many recipes, you work on the sauce as the water for the pasta boils or the pasta cooks. This way, you can ensure that your pasta and sauce will be ready at about the same time.

✓ **In general, figure about 2 ounces of dried pasta per person.** If the pasta is the main course, or you have a lot of big eaters at the table, you may need to figure up to 4 ounces person. In other words, on average, when served as a side dish, a pound of pasta will feed about eight people (or one teenaged boy). The pasta box or bag tells you how many servings it includes.

✓ **Don't try to speak broken Italian when you serve your pasta.** "Bonissimo! Perfect-amente mia amigas, Mangia, Mangia!" You will sound silly and irritate your guests.

Name that pasta: Pasta types and cooking times

Pasta comes in several basic forms:

✓ *Macaroni* has distinctive shapes, hollows, and curves. Also known as *tubular pasta,* macaroni is served with thick, rich sauces.

✓ *Spaghetti,* which means "little strings," is pasta cut into delicate strands. Strand pasta is best served with thin, flavorful sauces that are rich in oil, which keeps the very thin pasta from sticking together.

✓ Sometimes linguine and fettuccine noodles are identified apart from spaghetti because their strands are flattened. *Flat ribbon pasta* is excellent with rich, creamy sauces such as Alfredo or with simple butter sauces with fresh sautéed vegetables.

✓ Filled with meat, cheese, fish, or vegetables, *stuffed pastas* are best coated with simple tomato or light, cream-based sauces. The dough is often flavored and tinted with spinach, tomato, mushrooms, or *saffron,* a fragrant spice. Typically, stuffed pastas are fresh or frozen. Frozen stuffed pasta takes longer to cook than fresh. If buying fresh, just follow the directions on the package.

✓ *Asian pasta* is usually in spaghetti-like form. The most common types are soba noodles made from buckwheat flour, udon noodles made from wheat flour, and rice noodles.

Figure 13-1 depicts some common Italian pasta shapes.

Figure 13-1:
Various
shapes of
pasta.

Sauce: Pasta's Best Friend

Pasta sauce comes in many forms and flavors, from light to rich, creamy to tangy, and everything in between.

Before you serve up a sauce, check out these tips for making foolproof sauces:

- Figure about ½ cup of sauce per person.

- Stir sauces often to prevent sticking.

- A tablespoon of olive oil adds flavor and a rich texture to tomato-based sauces.

- Sauces are a great place to hide puréed vegetables. The kids will never know!

- For added sweetness, try a grated carrot instead of sugar.

- To jazz up a canned pasta sauce, add one or two of the following: sliced green or black olives, sautéed chopped shallots, a drained can of tuna, 1 cup of white beans, 4 slices of crumbled bacon, sliced smoked sausage, ½ pound of small cooked shrimp, or ¼ cup freshly grated Parmesan cheese.

Italian pasta sauces are as inventive and varied as pasta shapes. We briefly describe a few of the classic ones, so the next time you dine at an expensive trattoria where the puttanesca is $24 a plate, you'll know what you're paying for.

- **Alfredo:** A rich sauce of cream, butter, Parmesan cheese, and freshly ground black pepper (which is usually tossed over fettuccine).

- **Carbonara:** Crisply cooked bacon (usually Italian pancetta) combined with a sauce of eggs, cream, garlic, and Parmesan cheese, served over strand pasta.

- **Marinara:** The basic Italian tomato sauce, slow cooked and infused with garlic and Italian herbs like oregano and basil. Marinara is easy to adapt to different recipes by adding mushrooms, ground meat, meatballs, and vegetables like onions and sweet peppers.

- **Pesto:** Fresh basil leaves, pine nuts, garlic, Parmesan cheese, and olive oil blended to a fine paste and tossed with any hot pasta.

- **Primavera:** A mixture of sautéed spring vegetables (such as sweet red pepper, tomatoes, asparagus, and snow peas) and fresh herbs, which is tossed into pasta.

- **Puttanesca:** A pungent sauce of anchovies, garlic, tomatoes, capers, and black olives, typically served with strand pasta.

- **Ragù alla Bolognese:** A long-simmered sauce of meat (usually ground beef, veal, pork, or a combination) and tomatoes, named for the city of Bologna, where it was invented. For a true Bolognese, you brown the meat lightly and then cook it in a small amount of milk and wine before adding tomatoes.

Converted Rice

Prep time: 5 min • **Cook time:** About 25 min • **Yield:** 4 servings

Ingredients	Directions
2¼ cups water	**1** Bring the water to a boil in a medium saucepan. Add the rice, butter, and salt. Stir and cover.
1 cup converted rice	
1 tablespoon butter	**2** Reduce the heat to low and simmer for 20 minutes.
½ teaspoon salt, or to taste	
	3 Remove from the heat and let stand, covered, until all the water is absorbed, about 5 minutes. (If you have excess water, strain it off. If the rice is too dry, add a little boiling water and stir; let sit for 3 to 5 minutes.)
	4 Fluff the rice with a fork and check the seasoning, adding more salt (or pepper) to taste.

Per serving: Calories 195 (From Fat 26); Fat 3g (Saturated 2g); Cholesterol 8mg; Sodium 291mg; Carbohydrate 38g (Dietary Fiber 0g); Protein 4g.

Vary It! To boost the flavor of your rice, cook it in chicken, beef, or vegetable broth. You can also add seasoned herbs, a dash of saffron, lemon zest or juice, or any combination of herbs and spices you like to flavor the cooking liquid. If adding fresh herbs, do so in the last 10 minutes of cooking.

Basic Rice Pilaf

Prep time: 5 min • **Cook time:** About 25 min • **Yield:** 4 servings

Ingredients	Directions
1 tablespoon olive oil	**1** In a medium saucepan, heat the olive oil over medium-high heat. Add the onion, bell pepper, cumin powder, and salt. Sauté until the onion begins to soften, about 5 minutes.
½ medium yellow onion, minced	
½ red bell pepper, minced	
1 teaspoon cumin powder	**2** Add the rice and cook, stirring until the rice is coated, about 3 minutes.
½ teaspoon salt, or to taste	
1 cup converted rice	**3** Pour the chicken broth into the sauté pan and bring to a boil. Stir and cover.
2¼ cups chicken broth	
½ cup chopped almonds (optional)	**4** Reduce the heat to low and simmer for 20 minutes.
¼ cup currants or raisins (optional)	**5** Remove from the heat and let stand, covered, until all the chicken broth is absorbed, about 5 minutes. (If the rice is too dry, add a little boiling water and stir; let sit for 3 to 5 minutes.)
Black pepper	
	6 Fluff the rice with a fork. Stir in the almonds, currants, or raisins, if desired. Add black pepper to taste.

Per serving: Calories 311 (From Fat 114); Fat 13g (Saturated 2g); Cholesterol 3mg; Sodium 854mg; Carbohydrate 43g (Dietary Fiber 2g); Protein 8g.

Go-With: This slightly sweet, starchy side dish is delicious with Osso Buco (see Chapter 18) or Roasted Pork Ribs with Country Barbecue Sauce (see Chapter 8).

Risotto

Prep time: About 15 min • **Cook time:** About 35 min • **Yield:** 4 servings

Ingredients	Directions
1 teaspoon olive oil	**1** Place the olive oil and bacon in a large skillet or sauté pan and cook over medium heat, stirring occasionally until the bacon is brown, about 2 to 3 minutes.
3 strips lean bacon, cut into 1-inch pieces	
½ cup chopped shallots or yellow onions	**2** Add the chopped shallots (or onions) and lower the heat to medium-low. Cook the shallots until golden but not browned, stirring occasionally.
About 5 cups chicken or vegetable stock	**3** While the shallots are cooking, bring the stock to a boil in a small, covered saucepan. Reduce the heat to a simmer.
1½ cups Arborio rice	
Salt and black pepper	**4** When the shallots are golden, add the rice to the skillet. Raise the heat to medium and cook 1 to 2 minutes, stirring constantly, until the rice is well coated with the oil.
	5 Add ½ cup hot stock to the rice and stir it in with a wooden spoon. When most of the liquid is absorbed, add another ½ cup stock to the rice, stirring constantly. Loosen the rice from the bottom and sides of the pan to keep it from sticking.
	6 Continue cooking for 25 to 30 minutes, stirring and adding the remaining stock in increments after most of the broth is absorbed.
	7 Remove from the heat. Taste for seasoning and add salt and pepper, if desired. Serve immediately.

Per serving: Calories 406 (From Fat 92); Fat 10g (Saturated 3g); Cholesterol 10mg; Sodium 1,477mg; Carbohydrate 68g (Dietary Fiber 1g); Protein 12g.

Tip: When you add the liquid in this recipe, the rice should be surrounded by liquid but never swim in the stock.

Vary It! A few minutes before the risotto is done, try stirring in l cup fresh or frozen peas or ½ cup chopped parsley. Or add chopped fresh kale, spinach leaves, sliced mushrooms, or broccoli rabe to the pan after browning the shallots. Small shrimp or bits of crab can make risotto into a special main course.

Basic Wild Rice

Prep time: About 15 min • **Cook time:** About 50 min • **Yield:** 4 servings

Ingredients	Directions
1 cup wild rice	**1** Wash the rice thoroughly: Place the rice in a pot filled with cold water and let stand for a few minutes. Pour off the water and drain well in a colander.
2½ cups water	
2 tablespoons butter	**2** Fill a medium saucepan with the 2½ cups of water, cover, and bring to a boil over high heat.
Salt and black pepper	
	3 Add the rinsed rice, butter, and salt and pepper to taste. Stir once. Reduce the heat to low and simmer, covered, for 45 to 55 minutes until the rice is tender.
	4 Fluff the rice and add more salt and pepper, if desired, before serving.

Per serving: Calories 211 (From Fat 56); Fat 6g (Saturated 4g); Cholesterol 15mg; Sodium 151mg; Carbohydrate 34g (Dietary Fiber 3g); Protein 6g.

Go-With: Basic Wild Rice tastes great with highly flavored meats. Try it with The Perfect Steak (see Chapter 9) or Glazed Leg of Lamb with Pan Gravy and Red Currant Glaze (see Chapter 8).

Tabbouleh Salad

Prep time: 5 min plus absorption and chill time • **Yield:** 4 servings

Ingredients	Directions
½ cup bulgur wheat	*1* Put the bulgur wheat in a large bowl. Add the boiling water. Let sit until all the water is absorbed, about 25 minutes.
1 cup boiling water	
2 tomatoes, coarsely chopped	
3 scallions, chopped, including green parts	*2* Fluff the bulgur with a fork. Stir in the tomatoes, scallions, cucumber, parsley, mint, lemon juice, olive oil, garlic, salt, and pepper.
½ medium cucumber, peeled and chopped	
1 cup fresh parsley or cilantro leaves, or a combination of both, minced	*3* Cover and chill for at least 30 minutes. Serve cold or at room temperature.
½ teaspoon dried mint leaves or 1 tablespoon minced fresh mint leaves	
¼ cup lemon juice (fresh or bottled)	
¼ cup extra-virgin olive oil	
2 cloves garlic, minced	
½ teaspoon salt	
Few dashes black pepper	

Per serving: Calories 213 (From Fat 128); Fat 14g (Saturated 2g); Cholesterol 0mg; Sodium 312mg; Carbohydrate 21g (Dietary Fiber 5g); Protein 4g.

Tip: If possible, make this salad the night before you eat it so the flavors have time to meld.

Polenta with Herbs

Prep time: 5 min • **Cook time:** 3–5 min • **Yield:** 4 servings

Ingredients	Directions
3¼ cups chicken stock or water	*1* In a heavy, deep pot, bring the stock or water to a boil.
1 cup precooked polenta	*2* Slowly stir in the polenta. Reduce the heat to low and continue stirring until the mixture thickens to a porridge consistency, about 3 to 5 minutes.
⅓ cup freshly grated Parmesan cheese (optional)	
1 tablespoon butter	*3* Stir in the cheese, if desired, and then the butter, tarragon (or marjoram or thyme), and salt and pepper to taste. Serve hot.
1 tablespoon fresh, chopped tarragon, marjoram, or thyme, or 1 teaspoon dried	
Salt and black pepper	

Per serving: Calories 219 (From Fat 55); Fat 6g (Saturated 3g); Cholesterol 12mg; Sodium 958mg; Carbohydrate 36g (Dietary Fiber 4g); Protein 5g.

Tip: Continuous stirring helps prevent polenta from getting lumpy. If lumps form, stir with a wire whisk to break them up. Also, polenta hardens very quickly after it's cooked, so be sure to bring it to the table steaming.

Vary It! Add sautéed onion and garlic along with the butter and herbs. You can also blend in cooked carrots, celery, turnips, broccoli rabe, or even hot Italian sausages. After the polenta is cooked, spread it over a greased baking pan, brush it with melted butter or olive oil (flavored, if you like), and place it under a broiler to brown. Then cut it into squares and serve like bread.

Quinoa Pilaf

Prep time: About 5 min • **Cook time:** About 30 min • **Yield:** 4 servings

Ingredients	Directions
1 cup quinoa	*1* Rinse the quinoa with cold water in a fine-mesh strainer.
1 tablespoon olive oil	
½ medium yellow onion, minced	*2* In a medium saucepan, heat the olive oil over medium-high heat. Add the onion. Sauté until the onion begins to soften, about 5 minutes. Add the garlic and sauté for 1 minute longer.
1 clove garlic, minced	
2 cups vegetable broth	
1 bay leaf	*3* Add the quinoa, stir until it's coated with the oil mixture, and cook about 2 minutes.
Juice and grated rind from one fresh lemon	
Salt and pepper	*4* Pour the vegetable broth into the saucepan. Add the bay leaf, lemon juice, and grated lemon rind. Bring to a boil. Stir once and cover the pan.
	5 Reduce the heat to low and simmer for 15 to 20 minutes, or until all the liquid is absorbed.
	6 Remove from the heat and let stand, covered, until all the vegetable broth is absorbed, about 5 minutes. Remove and discard bay leaf. Season with salt and pepper. Serve warm.

Per serving: Calories 208 (From Fat 57); Fat 6g (Saturated 1g); Cholesterol 0mg; Sodium 656mg; Carbohydrate 33g (Dietary Fiber 3g); Protein 7g.

Spaghetti with Quick Fresh Tomato Sauce

Prep time: About 15 min • **Cook time:** About 10 min • **Yield:** 4 servings

Ingredients	Directions
5 to 6 ripe plum tomatoes, about 1½ pounds	**1** Core, peel, and chop the tomatoes.
Salt and pepper	**2** Bring 4 to 5 quarts lightly salted water to a boil over high heat in a large, covered pot. Add the spaghetti, stir thoroughly with a long fork to separate the strands, and cook, uncovered, for about 8 minutes (just until al dente).
¾ pound spaghetti (or other pasta)	
3 tablespoons olive oil	
2 teaspoons peeled and minced garlic (about 2 large cloves), or 1 teaspoon garlic powder	**3** While the spaghetti cooks, heat the oil in a saucepan or skillet over medium heat. Add the garlic. Cook and stir about 30 seconds with a wooden spoon.
2 tablespoons coarsely chopped fresh basil leaves, or 2 teaspoons dried basil	**4** Add the cubed tomatoes to the saucepan or skillet, and add salt and pepper to taste. Cook, crushing the tomatoes with a fork and stirring often, for about 3 minutes.
3 tablespoons grated Parmesan cheese	**5** When the pasta is ready, drain it and put the pasta in a serving bowl or on individual plates. Ladle the sauce over it. Garnish with basil and Parmesan. Serve immediately.

Per serving: *Calories 418 (From Fat 116); Fat 13g (Saturated 2g); Cholesterol 3mg; Sodium 430mg; Carbohydrate 63g (Dietary Fiber 5g); Protein 12g.*

Vary It! You can omit the Parmesan cheese and add a small can of drained, flaked tuna. Or keep the cheese and toss in some sliced black olives and cooked artichoke hearts. A few sautéed shrimp and asparagus spears, or even sautéed chicken livers, also work with this classic sauce.

Penne with Parmesan Cheese and Basil

Prep time: About 5 min • **Cook time:** About 12 min • **Yield:** 4 servings

Ingredients	*Directions*
Salt	*1* Bring 3 to 4 quarts lightly salted water to a boil in a large, covered pot over high heat. Add the penne, stir thoroughly to separate the macaroni, and return to a boil. Cook, uncovered, for about 10 minutes or until the pasta is al dente.
½ pound penne pasta	
2 tablespoons olive oil	
1 tablespoon butter	
¼ cup grated Parmesan or Romano cheese	*2* Just before the penne is done, carefully scoop out ¼ cup of the cooking liquid.
¼ cup chopped fresh basil or Italian parsley	*3* When the penne is ready, drain it and return it to the pot. Add the olive oil and butter and toss to coat. Add the cheese, basil, nutmeg, pepper to taste, and the reserved cooking liquid.
⅛ teaspoon freshly grated or ground nutmeg	
Pepper	*4* Toss together over medium-high heat for 30 seconds. If necessary, add salt to taste. Serve immediately.

Per serving: Calories 315 (From Fat 107); Fat 12g (Saturated 4g); Cholesterol 12mg; Sodium 156mg; Carbohydrate 43g (Dietary Fiber 2g); Protein 10g.

Vary It! To transform this recipe into Pasta Primavera, add 1 to 2 cups of fresh, lightly steamed summer vegetables to the pasta in step 3, before adding the olive oil and butter. Some good choices are broccoli and/or cauliflower florets, sliced carrots, sliced summer squash, and sliced zucchini. One-half cup each marinated artichoke hearts and pitted olives would also be good.

Chapter 14

Making Sensational Sauces: Fear No More

*P*robably no aspect of cooking sends a kitchen novice running for a restaurant like sauce making. All this reducing and whisking and straining can seem as abstruse as DNA testing. In fact, sauce making is within the reach of the cooking rookie. Some sauces require nothing more than cooking several ingredients in a pan (or not cooking them at all) and tossing them in the blender.

The image of sauces as loaded with cream and butter is somewhat outdated. Many sauces served in restaurants today are Mediterranean, Californian, and Asian inspired. They are made with olive oil, sesame oil, flavored vinegars, vegetable purées, aromatic herbs, wine, yogurt, and other healthy ingredients.

We show you how to master a variety of savory sauces in this chapter, as well as dessert sauces, which can be a sweet fruit purée spiked with a flavored liqueur, a simple custard, or a luscious chocolate creation.

What Is a Sauce Anyway?

Think of a sauce as a primary liquid (chicken stock, beef stock, fish stock, vegetable stock, or wine) flavored with ingredients (sautéed shallots, garlic, tomatoes, and so on) and seasoned with salt and pepper and herbs of choice.

Before it's served, a sauce is often reduced. *Reduced* simply means that the sauce is cooked and evaporated on the stove so that it thickens and intensifies in flavor. Sometimes you strain a sauce through a sieve to eliminate all the solids, such as parsley sprigs or chunks of onion. Other times, you purée everything in a blender.

The best way to understand sauces is to become familiar with their foundations:

- ✔ *White sauces* usually contain milk or cream.

- ✔ *White butter sauces* are based on a reduction of butter, vinegar, and shallots.

- ✔ *Brown sauces* are based on dark stocks like lamb or beef.

- ✔ *Vegetable sauces* are made from cooked puréed vegetables, such as tomatoes.

- ✔ *Vinaigrettes* are made up of oil, vinegar, mustard, and seasonings.

- ✔ *Hollandaise* and its variations, like béarnaise sauce, are based on cooked egg yolks and butter.

- ✔ *Mayonnaise* is based on uncooked or slightly cooked egg yolks and oil.

- ✔ *Dessert sauces* are typically made with fruits or chocolate with sugar; they may also have a caramel, butterscotch, or nut base.

Classic White Sauce from ze French

For centuries, *béchamel* sauce (pronounced besh-ah-mel) has been the mortar that supports the house of French cuisine. With its buttery, faintly nutty flavor, béchamel is also the base of hot soufflés and such homey dishes as macaroni and cheese and pot pies.

Béchamel and its variations go with all kinds of foods, including grilled fish, chicken, veal, and vegetables like pearl onions, Brussels sprouts, broccoli, and cauliflower. (See Chapter 5 for information about steaming and boiling these vegetables before coating them with béchamel.) The thickness of béchamel varies from dish to dish.

Like most white sauces, béchamel, in all its incarnations, is based on a *roux*, which is nothing more than butter melted in a pan and then sprinkled with flour (equal quantities of each) and stirred into a paste over low heat. Knowing how to make a roux is the first and most important step in knowing how to make a good French-inspired sauce. Note how, in our Béchamel recipe later in the chapter, we begin with a roux.

Variations on béchamel

Béchamel is so basic that it makes the perfect starting point for many different sauces. Here are some classic variations:

✔ **Mornay sauce:** Add grated cheese, like Gruyère or Parmesan, to the simmering béchamel, along with fish stock or chicken stock and butter.

✔ **Horseradish sauce:** Add freshly grated horseradish to taste. Serve with game, fish such as trout, or long-braised sinewy cuts of beef from the shoulder and neck.

✔ **Soubise:** Boil or steam yellow onions until they're soft; purée them in the blender and add to the sauce, seasoning to taste with salt and pepper. Slightly sweet from the onions, soubise sauce is suitable for many types of game, poultry, and meat.

But don't feel limited by this list. You can use dozens of other ingredients commonly found in a well-stocked pantry or refrigerator to easily alter the flavor of béchamel. A short list of possibilities includes fresh tomatoes (skinned and finely chopped); sautéed mushrooms, shallots, onions, garlic, or leeks; ground ginger or curry powder; chopped fresh tarragon, dill, parsley, or marjoram; paprika; grated lemon zest; white pepper; and Tabasco sauce. Add them to taste when the béchamel has almost finished cooking.

You can modify béchamel to suit whatever dish it garnishes. For example, if you're cooking fish, you can add fish stock to the sauce. If you're cooking poultry, you can add chicken stock. A *velouté* (pronounced ve-lou-tay) is essentially a béchamel made with a stock (fish or chicken) in place of the milk, which gives it extra flavor.

Sometimes you enhance a velouté before serving by adding a little cream (for a smoother texture) or some fresh lemon juice (for a little tartness). Our Velouté recipe later in the chapter calls for cream.

Velouté is wonderful with poached fish, poultry, veal, vegetables, and eggs. Our recipe is a simplified version of a classic velouté; variations are endless after you get the technique down.

Delicious Deglazing

Basic brown sauce (made from dark stock) has been the culinary keystone of Western restaurant cooking for decades. However, it's becoming far less common today as diners seek lighter, less complex fare. Brown sauces are also tremendously time consuming and easy to botch. For these reasons, we bypass brown sauces in this book and focus on more contemporary recipes.

Dried versus fresh herbs

Unless you live in the southern or western regions of the United States — areas where fresh herbs are available year-round — you may need to substitute dry herbs in the off season. Keep in mind that dried herbs are three times as concentrated as fresh. So if a recipe calls for 1 tablespoon of fresh thyme, use just one-third of that amount for dried herbs. See Chapter 3 for much more information about using herbs and spices.

Today's "dark" sauces are typically made using the deglazing technique. Not sure what deglazing is? Do you ever have a casserole of macaroni and cheese and, when dinner is over, go over and pick at the little semiburned nuggets of cheese and pasta that cling to the dish? Aren't they the best part?

Well, think of deglazing as more or less the same thing. When you sauté a steak or chicken in a hot pan, it leaves behind little particles that stick to the surface. These bits are packed with flavor, and you want to incorporate them into any sauce you make.

For example, when you remove a steak from the pan, you might deglaze with red wine (you generally deglaze with wine or stock of some sort). As the wine (or stock) sizzles in the pan, you scrape the pan's bottom (preferably with a wooden spatula or spoon) to release those tasty little particles. That process is called *deglazing*. After you do that, you finish the sauce with seasonings of choice and serve. We talk more about deglazing in Chapter 6, which focuses on sautéing. In that chapter, you find a recipe for Steak au Poivre that walks you through the deglazing process.

Food does not cling to nonstick cookware (or at least not much); for this reason, it's handy to have a stainless steel sauté pan when you want to deglaze. Cast iron also works well.

Here's Egg in Your Sauce

Egg-based sauces in general are emulsified with egg yolks. Hollandaise is the most common of all egg-based sauces. Your first introduction to hollandaise probably came when you went with your parents to a fancy restaurant brunch where eggs Benedict was served — hopefully not from the buffet steam table, because egg-based sauces don't hold up for long.

Hollandaise is a good exercise for beginners, which is why we include a recipe for it later in the chapter. Why is it good for beginners? Because if you blow the recipe, you can repair it. The most common foul-up that people make when preparing hollandaise is leaving the heat on until the sauce curdles. If that happens, or if the sauce becomes too thick, you simply beat in 1 to 2 tablespoons of boiling water and stir vigorously until the sauce becomes smooth again. To avoid lumpy hollandaise, you reduce the heat to simmer.

The rich, lemon-tinged hollandaise has chameleon-like qualities: Add tomato, and you have Choron (good with steak); fold in lightly whipped heavy cream and you have Chantilly, also called *mousseline* (decadently delicious on chicken); add dried mustard, and you have a fine accompaniment to boiled vegetables.

If you add tarragon and chervil to hollandaise, you have béarnaise. We offer a recipe for Béarnaise Sauce later in the chapter, and we recommend serving it with salmon, fillet of beef, or any other rich meat.

Light Blender Sauces in Minutes

For cooks in a hurry, the blender is an invaluable tool. You can make blender sauces literally in minutes. And they can be healthful, too, especially if bound with vegetables, lowfat cheeses (like ricotta), yogurt, and the like.

Although food processors are unsurpassed for chopping, slicing, and grating, blenders have an edge when it comes to liquefying and sauce making. Their blades rotate faster, *binding* (or pulling together) liquids better. The two-level slicing blade on a food processor cuts through liquids instead of blending them, and its wide, flat work bowl is too large for mixing small quantities of sauce. If you don't have a food processor, you can also use the blender for chunkier sauces. Just use the pulse function, which lets you more closely monitor the sauce's consistency.

You can transform simple poached fish into something special by combining some of the poaching liquid with wine, fresh watercress, seasonings, and just a dab of cream or ricotta cheese. All kinds of great vinaigrette-based sauces can be created using fresh herbs of your choice.

Certain fruit sauces for desserts also work better in a blender, whether it's a purée of raspberries spiked with framboise (French raspberry brandy) or of mango with lime and rum.

Here are some ideas for everyday blender sauces:

- ✔ **Blender Dill Sauce:** Place about ½ cup of chopped dill and an equal amount of finely chopped scallions in a blender. Add ½ cup vegetable oil and blend thoroughly. In a mixing bowl, combine ½ cup sour cream and 1 tablespoon Dijon mustard. Whisk. Add 2 teaspoons red wine vinegar. Mix the blender ingredients into the bowl and season to taste. The recipe makes about 1½ cups and is good with just about any cold summer entrée. See the color section for a photo.

  Variations: Use basil or fresh coriander in place of the dill.

✔ **Blender Salsa Verde:** Combine in a blender a finely chopped medium bunch of scallions, a clove of garlic, ½ small white onion coarsely chopped, 2 stalks celery coarsely chopped, and a medium peeled and chopped cucumber (seeded). Add 3 tablespoons olive oil, 3 tablespoons Dijon mustard, and 2 tablespoons red wine vinegar. Blend until smooth. Taste for seasonings. The recipe, shown in the color section, yields 1½ cups and is superb with grilled or broiled meat and fish.

Variation: For a thicker sauce, add one boiled potato.

✔ **Sour Cream and Watercress Sauce:** Place 1 cup of sour cream and 4 tablespoons of watercress in a blender and mix at slow speed until the sour cream liquefies and begins to incorporate the watercress. Turn the blender to high for several seconds. Add just enough salt to bring out the flavor of the watercress. The recipe makes about 1 cup. This sauce is terrific with smoked fish, cold poultry and meats, and cold shellfish.

Variations: Add grated fresh horseradish or well drained store-bought horseradish; add fresh dill, basil, or thyme.

✔ **Mint Mango Sauce:** Scoop about 3 cups of flesh from one or two ripe mangoes and combine in a blender with 6 tablespoons water and 4 tablespoons sugar (more if the mango is not very sweet). Blend until slightly smooth. Stir in 2 to 3 tablespoons chopped mint. The recipe yields about 2 cups and is wonderful with desserts. See the color section for a photo.

Variation: Substitute papaya for mango.

Delectable Dessert Sauces

Dessert sauces come in two basic types: cream based and fruit based. Cream-based recipes usually require cooking, but you can often make the fruit sauces in a blender.

Later in the chapter, you find recipes for some popular dessert sauces and ways to modify them:

✔ Our smooth and creamy Vanilla Custard Sauce dresses up ice cream, fresh strawberries, pound cake, poached pears, soufflés, cold mousses, and more. Keep in mind that when you're making this sauce, as well as custards, you scald milk primarily to shorten the cooking time. To scald milk, heat it in a saucepan over a medium-low setting until it foams. Don't bring it to a boil.

Also, be careful not to cook the vanilla sauce too long, to prevent scorching it. Maintain a low to medium-low heat setting to prevent the sauce from *curdling*: separating into coagulated solids (curds) and liquids (whey). A curdled sauce is not a pretty sight. If the sauce curdles, whisk it quickly or whirl it in a blender container to cool it rapidly.

Many recipes for ice cream, custards, puddings, cakes, cookies, and chocolate desserts are flavored with vanilla. You can use either the whole vanilla bean or pure vanilla extract. Although the whole beans are somewhat preferable because they have much more of an intense flavor than the extract, they're also more expensive and less convenient. *Never* purchase "artificial" or "imitation" extracts.

✔ Our Cracklin' Hot Fudge Sauce is a twist on regular chocolate sauce and is ideal for ice cream. Because it has butter in it, the sauce turns hard when poured over ice cream and forms a thin, cracklin' crust. You can buy this kind of sauce in the grocery store, but it is laden with hydrogenated fat. Our version, while hardly diet food, is free from trans fats.

One great thing about this recipe is that you can prepare it up to a week ahead of time and keep it covered and refrigerated. Rewarm it in a double boiler or in the microwave.

✔ You have no excuse for serving chemical-tasting, aerosol whipped cream. The real thing is so easy and so good that everyone should know how to make it. We show you how in our Whipped Cream recipe. Spoon sweetened, flavored whipped cream over pies, pudding, cakes, mousses, poached fruit, your cat's nose — anything!

When making a recipe that requires homemade whipped cream, be careful not to overbeat it or it can turn to butter. Be sure to start with very cold cream, cold beaters, and a cold bowl (cold hands can't hurt, either). Whether using a hand-held beater or a stand-up kitchen mixer, start beating slowly, and gradually increase the speed. Don't strive for stiff cream but rather soft, floppy peaks. Always refrigerate whipped cream, covered, unless you're serving it right away.

✔ Caramel forms when the moisture is cooked out of sugar and the sugar turns a deep golden brown. Our Caramel Sauce recipe shows you how to make caramel thinned out with a little water or lemon juice, and a bit of cream, so that it pours easily. It's delicious as a coating on meringue, or with vanilla cake and ice cream.

✔ Quick sauces made with fresh, seasonal fruit could not be easier. The technique we illustrate in our Fresh Strawberry Sauce recipe also works for blueberries and raspberries. (When making raspberry sauces, strain the sauce through a fine sieve before serving to remove the seeds.) Fresh strawberry sauce, shown in the book's color section, is wonderful as a topping for ice cream, custards, and puddings.

Béchamel

Prep time: About 5 min • **Cook time:** About 8 min • **Yield:** 8 servings

Ingredients	*Directions*
1¼ cups milk	*1* Heat the milk over medium setting in a small saucepan until almost boiling. Remove from the heat.
2 tablespoons butter	
2 tablespoons flour	*2* Meanwhile, in a medium saucepan, melt the butter over medium heat (don't let it darken or burn). Add the flour and whisk constantly for 2 minutes. The mixture should reach a thick paste consistency.
¼ teaspoon ground nutmeg, or to taste	
Salt and pepper	
	3 Gradually add the hot milk while continuing to whisk the mixture vigorously. When the sauce is blended smooth, reduce heat and simmer for 3 to 4 minutes, whisking frequently. The sauce should be very thick.
	4 Remove from heat, add the nutmeg and the salt and pepper to taste, and whisk well.

Per serving: Calories 56 (From Fat 37); Fat 4g (Saturated 3g); Cholesterol 13mg; Sodium 92mg; Carbohydrate 3g (Dietary Fiber 0g); Protein 2g.

Tip: If the butter burns or even gets brown, you should probably start over, or your white sauce will have a brown tint.

Vary It! Whip up some creamed spinach by adding béchamel to cooked spinach. Or do the same thing with other cooked vegetables, such as corn, peas, or sliced carrots.

Velouté

Prep time: About 10 min • **Cook time:** About 8 min • **Yield:** 6 servings

Ingredients	*Directions*
1½ **cups homemade or canned chicken or vegetable stock**	*1* Heat the stock almost to boiling in a small saucepan over medium heat.
2 **tablespoons butter**	*2* Melt the butter over medium heat in a medium saucepan (don't let it brown or burn). Add the flour and whisk until blended smooth. Reduce heat to low and cook for about 2 minutes, whisking constantly.
3 **tablespoons flour**	
⅓ **cup heavy cream or half-and-half**	*3* Raise the heat setting to medium and gradually add the hot chicken broth, whisking for about 1 minute or until the sauce thickens.
Salt and white pepper	
	4 Raise the heat and bring to a boil. Immediately lower the heat to simmer and cook for about 2 minutes, whisking often.
	5 Add the cream and salt and pepper to taste. Raise the heat and whisk constantly while bringing the mixture back to a boil.
	6 When it boils, immediately remove the saucepan from the heat and cover with waxed paper (to prevent a thin film from forming on the surface) until served.

Per serving: Calories 97 (From Fat 78); Fat 9g (Saturated 5g); Cholesterol 28mg; Sodium 257mg; Carbohydrate 4g (Dietary Fiber 0g); Protein 2g.

Tip: If you forget to cover the velouté with waxed paper and a thin film or skin forms on the sauce's surface, simply whisk it back into the sauce. If the sauce cooks too long and gets too thick, add a little more stock or cream.

Hollandaise

Prep time: About 10 min • **Cook time:** About 10 min • **Yield:** 6 servings

Ingredients	*Directions*
4 egg yolks	*1* In the top of a double boiler, whisk the egg yolks for about 2 minutes or until they're thick and pale yellow.
1 tablespoon cold water	
½ cup (1 stick) room-temperature butter, cut into 8 pieces	*2* Add the water and whisk for another minute until the mixture easily coats a spoon.
2 tablespoons fresh lemon juice	*3* Set the top of the double boiler with the egg mixture into the bottom of the double boiler over, but not touching, water that is almost boiling. Heat until just warm, about 3 minutes, stirring constantly with a rubber spatula or whisk.
Salt and white pepper	
	4 Add the butter 2 tablespoons at a time, whisking vigorously until each batch is incorporated completely.
	5 Continue cooking, stirring and scraping the sides of the pot, until the sauce thickens enough to coat the back of a metal spoon.
	6 Add the lemon juice and salt and pepper to taste and cook about 1 minute more, or until the sauce is smooth and heated through.

Per serving: Calories 175 (From Fat 167); Fat 19g (Saturated 11g); Cholesterol 183mg; Sodium 104mg; Carbohydrate 1g (Dietary Fiber 0g); Protein 2g.

Tip: See Chapter 10 for instructions on separating egg yolks from whites.

Tip: You can make a double boiler by setting any heat-resistant bowl snugly into one of your saucepans. Be sure to allow 2 to 3 inches between the bottom of the bowl and the bottom of the pan, for the boiling water.

Béarnaise Sauce

Prep time: About 5 min • **Cook time:** About 15 min • **Yield:** 8 servings

Ingredients	*Directions*
½ **cup (1 stick) butter**	*1* Put the butter in a glass measuring cup and melt it in the microwave. Set aside.
3 tablespoons dry white wine (such as Chardonnay or sauvignon blanc)	*2* In a saucepan over medium heat, cook the white wine, vinegar, onion, half the tarragon leaves, and pepper, stirring occasionally, until the amount of liquid is reduced by about half. Remove from heat and set aside.
3 tablespoons white wine vinegar or tarragon vinegar	
1 tablespoon minced white onion	
1 teaspoon dried tarragon leaves, or 1 tablespoon fresh chopped tarragon leaves	*3* Put about an inch of water in a medium saucepan over medium heat.
⅛ **teaspoon black pepper**	*4* Meanwhile, in the top of a double boiler, combine the egg yolks and water. Whip vigorously with a whisk for about 2 minutes, or until the egg yolks begin to look lighter.
3 large egg yolks	
1 teaspoon water	
¼ teaspoon salt	*5* When the water in the saucepan is just beginning to simmer, set the double boiler with the egg yolks over the pan. (The water shouldn't touch the bottom of the double boiler.)
	6 Continue to beat the yolks. In a slow stream, add the warm melted butter to the yolks. Add the butter very slowly and keep whisking so you don't scramble the eggs. When the butter is completely incorporated, remove sauce from the heat.
	7 Stir in the wine mixture, the remaining half of the tarragon leaves, and the salt. Serve immediately.

Per serving: Calories 124 (From Fat 120); Fat 13g (Saturated 8g); Cholesterol 110mg; Sodium 77mg; Carbohydrate 0g (Dietary Fiber 0g); Protein 1g.

Fresh Summer Pesto Sauce

Prep time: About 15 min • **Yield:** 8 servings

Ingredients	*Directions*
2 cups lightly-packed fresh basil leaves, stems removed, about 2 ounces	*1* Rinse and pat dry the trimmed basil leaves.
½ cup extra-virgin olive oil	*2* Put the basil leaves in the container of a food processor or blender. Add the oil, pine nuts or walnuts, garlic, and salt and pepper to taste.
3 tablespoons pine nuts or walnuts	
3 large cloves garlic, coarsely chopped	*3* Blend mixture to a fine texture but not a smooth purée, stopping the motor once to scrape down the sides of the container and force the ingredients down to the blades.
Salt and pepper	
½ cup grated Parmesan cheese	*4* Add the Parmesan cheese and water and blend just a few seconds more. Chill until served.
1 tablespoon hot water	

Per serving: Calories 158 (From Fat 146); Fat 16g (Saturated 3g); Cholesterol 3mg; Sodium 139mg; Carbohydrate 1g (Dietary Fiber 1g); Protein 3g.

Vanilla Custard Sauce

Prep time: About 15 min plus cooling time • **Cook time:** About 25 min • **Yield:** 8 servings

Ingredients	Directions
1 cup heavy cream 1 cup milk 2 vanilla beans, split lengthwise 4 egg yolks ¼ cup sugar	*1* Place the cream, milk, and vanilla beans in a heavy medium saucepan. *Scald* (bring to a foam but do not boil) the milk-cream mixture over medium-low heat. Remove from the heat and let sit for 15 to 20 minutes. *2* Using a handheld or stand mixer, beat the egg yolks and sugar in a bowl for several minutes. The mixture should be pale yellow and thick. *3* Return the cream mixture to the heat and scald it again. *4* Pour about one-quarter of the hot cream mixture into the egg yolks and whisk vigorously. *5* Pour the egg mixture into the saucepan that is holding the rest of the cream mixture. Cook over low heat, stirring with a wooden spoon, about 4 to 5 minutes or until it thickens enough to coat the back of the spoon. *6* Strain sauce through a sieve into a bowl, discard the vanilla beans, cover, and chill.

Per serving: Calories 175 (From Fat 131); Fat 15g (Saturated 8g); Cholesterol 151mg; Sodium 30mg; Carbohydrate 9g (Dietary Fiber 0g); Protein 3g.

Tip: To split open a vanilla bean, take a sharp knife and make an incision lengthwise to expose the tiny black seeds; scrape the seeds out with a knife and add them to the recipe. Look for vanilla beans in the spice section of your supermarket.

Vary It! Add 3 or 4 tablespoons of Grand Marnier, kirsch, or brandy to the sauce.

Cracklin' Hot Fudge Sauce

Prep time: About 15 min • **Cook time:** About 5 min • **Yield:** 8 servings

Ingredients	Directions
1 cup confectioner's sugar, sifted	*1* In a heavy medium saucepan over medium-low heat, combine the confectioner's sugar, butter, and cream. Stir with a wooden spoon until the butter is melted and the mixture is smooth.
½ cup (1 stick) butter	
½ cup heavy cream	
8 ounces (8 squares) bittersweet chocolate, finely chopped	*2* Remove the pan from the heat and add the chocolate, stirring until smooth. Add the vanilla and stir to blend.
2 teaspoons vanilla extract	

Per serving: Calories 354 (From Fat 261); Fat 29g (Saturated 17g); Cholesterol 51mg; Sodium 7mg; Carbohydrate 30g (Dietary Fiber 2g); Protein 2g.

Vary It! If you can't find bittersweet chocolate, substitute semisweet chocolate and reduce the powdered sugar by 2 tablespoons.

Tip: Chop chocolate into pieces on a cutting board with a sharp knife or whirl the chocolate in the container of a blender or food processor for a few seconds.

Whipped Cream

Prep time: About 5 min • **Yield:** 8 servings

Ingredients	Directions
1 cup well-chilled heavy cream	In a chilled bowl, combine the cream, sugar, and vanilla. Beat with a whisk or electric mixer on medium speed until the cream thickens and forms peaks. (Do not overbeat, or the cream will become lumpy.)
1 tablespoon sugar, or to taste	
1 teaspoon vanilla extract, or to taste	

Per serving: Calories 110 (From Fat 99); Fat 11g (Saturated 7g); Cholesterol 41mg; Sodium 11mg; Carbohydrate 2g (Dietary Fiber 0g); Protein 1g.

Vary It! Before mixing, add 1 tablespoon unsweetened cocoa powder; 1 tablespoon instant coffee; or 1 or 2 tablespoons Grand Marnier, Kahlúa, Cointreau, crème de menthe, or other liqueur.

Caramel Sauce

Prep time: About 5 min • **Cook time:** About 10 min • **Yield:** 8 servings

Ingredients	Directions
1 cup sugar **⅓ cup water** **½ teaspoon fresh lemon juice** **⅔ cup heavy cream**	**1** Combine the sugar, water, and lemon juice in a medium saucepan over medium-low heat. Stir with a wooden spoon, about 3 minutes, until the sugar dissolves.
	2 Increase the heat to medium-high and cook until the mixture reaches an amber color, about 3 to 4 minutes. (The mixture comes to a boil rather rapidly.)
	3 For a medium-colored caramel, remove the mixture from the heat when it is still light golden. For darker, more flavorful caramel, remove when medium golden-brown.
	4 After removing the pan from the heat, gradually pour in the heavy cream, stirring with a wire whisk. (Be careful: The cream bubbles wildly as you do so.)
	5 When all the cream is incorporated, return the saucepan to medium-low heat and stir for 2 to 3 minutes or until the mixture is velvety. Serve warm.

Per serving: Calories 166 (From Fat 66); Fat 7g (Saturated 5g); Cholesterol 27mg; Sodium 8mg; Carbohydrate 26g (Dietary Fiber 0g); Protein 0g.

Tip: To rewarm this sauce after it cools, place it in a microwave or over medium heat on the stove.

Fresh Strawberry Sauce

Prep time: About 10 min • **Yield:** 8 servings

Ingredients	Directions
1 quart fresh strawberries, hulled (stems removed) and washed	Place all the ingredients in the bowl of a blender or food processor; purée until smooth. Taste for sweetness and add more sugar, if desired.
2 tablespoons confectioner's sugar, or to taste	
1 tablespoon fresh lemon juice	

Per serving: Calories 29 (From Fat 0); Fat 0g (Saturated 0g); Cholesterol 0mg; Sodium 1mg; Carbohydrate 7g (Dietary Fiber 2g); Protein 0g.

Vary It! For extra flavor, add rum, kirsch, flavored vodka, or other liquor of choice. You also can make this sauce with frozen strawberries; just thaw them first.

Chapter 15

Sweet Dreams

For most of us, desserts are hard to resist. Even if you're counting calories, a sweet indulgence every now and then lifts the spirit, and it can serve as a reward for your hard-earned efforts. That's what this chapter is all about. Here you find everything from cinnamon-scented wobbly puddings and old-fashioned cobblers to luscious baked fruits and ever-popular chocolate creations.

Many home cooks — and even some professionals — shy away from making desserts and pastries because they are so precise and unforgiving. That may be true, but the recipes in this chapter are as doable as they are delicious.

Cozy Puddings and Elegant Ices

Puddings, ice creams, and refreshing granité make satisfying yet light finishes to any meal. We offer these recipes later in the chapter:

✔ **Homey Rice Pudding:** Rice pudding is one of those all-American desserts that you find in roadside diners across the country. It has many incarnations. Sometimes it's firm and custardy, and other times it's creamy and rich. Our recipe falls on the rich and creamy side, with a nice sharp bite from cinnamon.

✔ **Double Chocolate Pudding:** Put away your packaged pudding mixes forever. This pudding is so rich and delicious that it will be everyone's favorite, and it's a snap to make, too! You can dress it up by spooning it into a tall wine or parfait glass and topping it with sweetened whipped cream and chocolate shavings.

✔ **Chocolate Mousse:** You can assemble this popular dessert in just minutes, and it doesn't require the skills of a pastry chef. Mousse is lighter, airier, and less rich than pudding. Because it has less sugar than some other desserts, chocolate mousse is a good lower-carb option for weight watchers. And you can make this simple yet festive dessert days in advance.

✔ **Lime Ice Cream:** What's special about this ice cream, aside from its wonderful citrus flavor, is the ease of preparation. You don't need an ice cream maker to prepare it. You simply combine all the ingredients and freeze them until solid. It's creamy, refreshing, and so rich that a small serving is all that you and your guests need.

✔ **Lemon Granité:** *Granité* is the French word for flavored ices, and they are perfect for summer. They require no fancy equipment beyond a fork and a little elbow grease. Essentially, granités are flavored and sweetened water that is frozen. You can use all kinds of fruits to flavor them. Every once in a while during the freezing process you scrape the ice with a fork to create little crystals. That's it! Granités also make great palate cleansers between courses in a meal — and they're much tastier than mouth wash.

Several of our recipes in this chapter are wonderful if served with homemade whipped cream. We provide the recipe in Chapter 14.

Fruit from the Oven

Later in this chapter, we serve up three fruit-based recipes: Peach-Blueberry Cobbler, Free-Form Fresh Fruit Tart, and Apple-Pear Crisp. Here's how they differ:

✔ *Cobblers* are deep-dish fruit desserts in which sweetened fruits (fresh berries or apples are the traditional choices) are topped with biscuit dough before baking. Almost any type or combination of fruits can be used, and just about any kind of baking dish — round, square, oval, or rectangular.

✔ A *tart* features a pastry crust topped with artfully arranged slices of fruit. The crust in our recipe combines the richness of an egg yolk with the sweetness of a little sugar to make a rich cookie-like dough that's easy to roll out. The open-faced tart is baked until the fruit is soft (but not mushy) and the pastry golden brown.

- In a *crisp,* the fruit is baked under a crumbly topping, usually made with flour, butter, and sugar, and sometimes oats, nuts, and spices.

Baked fruit recipes aren't difficult, but a few simple tips will help you to make them great:

- Baked fruit recipes often contain spices like cinnamon, ginger, nutmeg, and cloves. Before cooking, smell the spices that have been sitting on your shelf for months or years. If they've lost their potency, replace them. (See Chapter 3 for the scoop on spices and their shelf life.)

- Throughout this book, we often call for unsalted butter, and with good reason: Margarine doesn't taste as good as butter, and if you use salted butter, the salt can affect the delicate sweetness of many baked goods. Sometimes, however, margarine or shortening is used in combination with butter to add a light and flaky quality to pastry crusts. (Our pastry crust recipe in Chapter 10 calls for both butter and shortening.)

- Baked fruit recipes often include lemon juice to keep the fruit from turning brown. The acid in lemon juice slows the oxidation of fruit when it is exposed to air. When a recipe calls for fresh lemon juice, never use the bottled reconstituted kind; it tastes more like furniture polish than lemon juice.

For the best results with our Peach-Blueberry Cobbler recipe, be sure the fruit is ripe. Taste the sweetened fruit mixture before covering it with the biscuit dough. If the fruit isn't quite ripe (or if it's tart), you may need to sprinkle on a little more sugar. Some recipes call for removing the skins of the peaches by blanching them in boiling water for 1 minute and then peeling them off. However, we don't think it's necessary. And note that nectarine skins, which are thinner than peach skins, do not need to be removed.

When you try the Free-Form Fresh Fruit Tart, have Figure 15-1 on hand to help you roll out the pastry, place it on the baking sheet, and arrange the fruit beautifully on the pastry crust.

Free-Form Fresh Fruit Tart

On a lightly floured counter, use a floured rolling pin to roll out the dough into a free-form rectangle (about 9×12 inches).

Carefully drape dough over the rolling pin and transfer to a buttered baking sheet. Fold up and crimp edges of dough all around to form a neat rim.

Halve and pit the fruit. Slice each half into 4 or 5 thin wedges. Start at one corner, arrange slices side by side on dough, overlapping + fitting them snugly, until the surface is completely covered. (cozy...)

Figure 15-1:
Making a gorgeous fruit tart.

Cookie Collection: All You Need Is a Glass of Milk

Cookies make a delicious, fun, informal dessert for kids and adults alike. Cookie dough can be "dropped" by the spoonful onto a greased cookie sheet and patted into cookie shapes, or rolled into a log and sliced. You can also shape the dough with cookie cutters or roll it by hand into balls and dust with sugar and cinnamon. From there, you may want to add chocolate chips, nuts, or slivers of raw garlic (kidding).

Here are a few important cookie-baking tips:

- ✔ **Timing:** Every oven is different, and some can be alarmingly imprecise (especially gas ovens; electric ovens are more consistent). Always check the cookies a few minutes before they're supposed to be done. Buy an oven thermometer to determine whether your oven temperature setting is accurate; if it's not, adjust the temperature dial as necessary each time you bake. Or better yet, call your range service person or gas company to have your oven properly calibrated.

  The same rule about timing applies to bar cookies, which should be moist (but not raw) in the center.

- ✔ **Baking sheets:** Traditional aluminum sheets can produce cookies with burnt bottoms and pale tops. We prefer these two options:

  - *Insulated baking sheets,* which have two layers of aluminum with air space between them. They're less likely to burn the cookies.

  - *Stone cookie sheets,* which are similar to pizza stones but are rectangular. They produce an evenly baked cookie.

  For bar cookies, glass or aluminum baking pans both work, but dark aluminum cooks faster than lighter, silver-colored aluminum, and both cook faster than glass, so keep an eye on those cookies!

  Nonstick baking equipment makes removing things like cookies, breads, cakes, and other baked desserts much easier.

- ✔ **Greasing the sheets:** For recipes that call for a greased cookie sheet, you don't need to degrease baking sheets after you've removed one batch of baked cookies. If you use a nonstick sheet, you don't need to grease the cookie sheet at all — doing so can make your cookies spread out too much and turn out too thin.

  For recipes containing butter, just use the wrapper from the stick of butter to rub on the cookie sheet. Or use cooking spray for a lower-fat nonstick option (as long as your type of bakeware doesn't specifically warn against using cooking spray).

If you never want your cookie jar to be empty, you can find lots of recipes in *Cookies For Dummies* by Carole Bloom (Wiley). Or try some of ours that we provide later in the chapter:

- ✔ **Old-Fashioned Chocolate Chip Cookies:** A chocolate chip cookie manufacturer once told us that the secret to his famous cookie dough was a little bit of grated lemon peel. It makes sense. Lemon zest, loaded with rich, lemony oil and without a trace of sourness, is frequently used by bakers to heighten the flavors of cookies and other sweet desserts. When grating citrus peel, be sure to remove only the colored portion of the skin. The white portion underneath, called the *pith,* is bitter.

  In our recipe, the grated lemon zest punches up the flavor of the chocolate chips, and a little heavy cream in the dough gives the cookie a pleasant, melt-in-your-mouth softness. These cookies freeze very well in covered, plastic containers; they also keep for a week at room temperature in an airtight tin, provided you place it where the kids can't reach it.

- ✔ **Divine Brownies:** Many cooks, even good ones, don't consider making brownies from scratch, because so many great commercial mixes are available. But we believe that homemade is almost always better than the mix. So we give you this classic brownie recipe that's easy, rich, moist, and better (we guarantee it!) than any boxed mix you can buy. Plus, the brownies freeze well, so you can bake them ahead of time and save them for an upcoming event.

- ✔ **Lemon Bars:** This recipe is a Sunkist Growers classic that we've altered just a bit by decreasing the sugar and adding flaked coconut. The results are perfectly chewy bars with intense lemon flavor. You can serve these bars as is or sift powdered sugar over the top for a prettier finish.

For our Lemon Bars recipe, you need to line a 13-x-9-inch pan with foil. Figure 15-2 shows you how.

Figure 15-2: Lining a baking pan with aluminum foil.

Line Your Pan with Foil!

Line a 13×9 inch baking pan with foil so the ends extend over the two 9 inch sides of the pan.

Butter the foil lining pan. Set the pan aside. (Lining the pan with foil allows you to lift the baked dessert easily from the pan before cutting squares.)

The foil should cover all 4 sides of the pan, but hang longer, over the 9 inch sides.

ready to cut! easy!

Taking on Tiramisù

In Chapter 10, we feature a recipe for the Perfect Chocolate Cake — a surefire favorite. When you're feeling more adventurous in the cake department, try our recipe for the oh-so-trendy Tiramisù, which you find later in this chapter. This coffee-flavored confection is arguably one of the most beloved desserts in U.S. restaurants. Over the years what originally was a simple little treat has been altered, so that the one often served in the United States is more like a cream-drenched, coffee-flavored chocolate cake.

Tiramisù comes from Italy where, as the story goes, older ladies used to play cards in the afternoon, and, after their card games were finished, they made a sweet treat called tiramisù, which means "pick me up." They would take out some biscuits or cookies, drench them with espresso, and then slather some mascarpone cheese on top. And tiramisù was born.

This terrific recipe comes from our friend Bill Yosses, the wizard pastry chef at The White House (yes, that one!). It calls for a combination of sweetened whipped cream, sour cream, and mascarpone cheese. (If you can't find mascarpone, use softened cream cheese or increase the amount of whipped cream and sour cream.) The hallmark of a good tiramisù is a strong coffee flavor. You don't need to make espresso; instant coffee does the trick just fine.

Homey Rice Pudding

Prep time: About 10 min • **Cook time:** 1 hr • **Yield:** 8 servings

Ingredients	*Directions*
5 cups milk	*1* Pour the milk and cream into a heavy-bottomed saucepan and add the vanilla bean or extract. Bring the mixture to a boil and stir in the rice and sugar; stir from the bottom to keep the rice from sticking.
1 cup heavy cream	
1 vanilla bean, split lengthwise so the inner seeds are exposed (or 1 teaspoon vanilla extract)	*2* Reduce the heat to low and simmer, stirring occasionally, until the rice is tender and most of the milk is absorbed, about 30 minutes.
1 cup converted rice	
1¼ cups sugar	*3* Meanwhile, put the raisins in a bowl and pour boiling water over them. Let them stand until the rice is cooked.
¾ cup raisins	
3 egg yolks	*4* In another bowl, whisk the egg yolks and then blend in the lemon zest.
1 tablespoon grated lemon zest	
1 tablespoon butter for greasing the dish	*5* When the rice is cooked, remove it from the heat and slowly whisk it into the egg mixture.
1 teaspoon cinnamon	
	6 Preheat the oven to 400 degrees.
	7 Drain the raisins and fold them into the cooked rice.
	8 Butter an oval baking dish measuring 14 x 8 x 2 inches (approximately). Pour the rice mixture into the dish, sprinkle with the cinnamon, and place in a larger ovenproof dish with sides (like a casserole dish). Pour boiling water into the exterior dish about 2 inches up the sides.
	9 Bake for about 30 minutes, or until the custard is set (a toothpick inserted into the center comes out clean).

Per serving: Calories 484 (From Fat 176); Fat 20g (Saturated 12g); Cholesterol 145mg; Sodium 94mg; Carbohydrate 71g (Dietary Fiber 1g); Protein 9g.

Double Chocolate Pudding

Prep time: 10 min • **Cook time:** About 8 min • **Yield:** 4 servings

Ingredients	Directions

Ingredients

¼ cup water

2½ tablespoons cornstarch

½ cup sugar

⅓ cup unsweetened cocoa powder

Pinch of salt

⅓ cup milk, heated just to warm

2 ounces (2 squares) semisweet chocolate, coarsely chopped

2 cups heavy cream

1¼ teaspoons vanilla extract

Sweetened whipped cream (optional)

Chopped pecans or almonds, lightly toasted (optional)

Directions

1 In a small bowl, stir together the water and the cornstarch thoroughly until the cornstarch is dissolved and the mixture is smooth. Set the mixture aside.

2 In a heavy, medium saucepan, mix together the sugar, cocoa, and salt. Using a wooden spoon, stir in the warm milk to make a smooth paste.

3 Place the saucepan over medium heat and bring the mixture to a boil while stirring constantly, about 2 to 3 minutes. Add the chopped chocolate and stir until it completely melts.

4 Gradually stir in the heavy cream. Add the cornstarch mixture and stir it thoroughly into the chocolate mixture.

5 Continue stirring over medium heat for about 5 minutes, or until the pudding begins to thicken and boil. (Sweep the spoon along the bottom and sides of the pan to prevent the pudding from getting lumpy or burning.)

6 Reduce the heat to low and cook for about 1 minute more while stirring constantly.

7 Remove the saucepan from the heat and stir in the vanilla.

8 Pour the pudding into a serving bowl or individual serving cups. To prevent a skin from forming, lay a piece of plastic wrap or wax paper directly on the surface of the pudding.

9 Refrigerate for several hours or until chilled before serving. If desired, garnish with sweetened whipped cream and/or chopped nuts.

Per serving: Calories 626 (From Fat 462); Fat 51g (Saturated 32g); Cholesterol 166mg; Sodium 93mg; Carbohydrate 44g (Dietary Fiber 3g); Protein 6g.

Chocolate Mousse

Prep time: About 10 min plus chill time • **Cook time:** About 10 min • **Yield:** 12 servings

Ingredients	Directions
8 ounces bittersweet chocolate	*1* Chop the chocolate coarsely with the chef's knife. Place the chocolate pieces in a saucepan or pot and set the pot over a larger pot holding barely simmering water. Cover the pot containing the chocolate.
6 eggs, separated	
3 tablespoons water	*2* Meanwhile, put the egg yolks in a saucepan and add the water. Place the saucepan over very low heat while whisking vigorously. When the yolks thicken slightly, remove the saucepan from the heat.
2 cups heavy cream, well chilled	
6 tablespoons sugar	
Whipped cream or grated bittersweet chocolate for garnish	*3* Check the chocolate. When it is melted, stir well with a whisk. Add the melted chocolate to the egg mixture and blend thoroughly. Scrape the mixture into a large mixing bowl.
	4 With a hand-held electric mixer, beat the cream in a chilled bowl until it forms soft peaks, adding 2 tablespoons of the sugar toward the end. Fold this into the chocolate mixture.
	5 Wash and dry both the bowl and the mixer thoroughly to remove the cream before proceeding.
	6 Using the mixer, beat the egg whites in the clean bowl until they form soft peaks. Beat in the remaining 4 tablespoons sugar and continue beating until the egg whites form stiff peaks. Fold this into the chocolate mixture.
	7 Spoon the mousse into a serving bowl and chill thoroughly before serving. Garnish with whipped cream or grated bittersweet chocolate.

Per serving: *Calories 293 (From Fat 228); Fat 25g (Saturated 14g); Cholesterol 161mg; Sodium 47mg; Carbohydrate 17g (Dietary Fiber 1g); Protein 5g.*

Vary It! To make this mousse extra elegant, pour about ¼ cup of amaretto or Grand Marnier into the egg yolk and chocolate mixture just before it thickens.

Warning: Some raw egg whites may contain salmonella bacteria, which could compromise the health of certain individuals. If you're worried about this risk, use commercially prepared pasteurized egg white product or egg white powder.

Lime Ice Cream

Prep time: 5–10 min plus freeze time • **Yield:** 4 servings

Ingredients	*Directions*
2 cups heavy cream 1 cup sugar 2 teaspoons grated lime zest ⅓ cup fresh lime juice	*1* In a large bowl, combine the cream and sugar; stir the mixture until the sugar is dissolved. Stir in the lime zest and juice. The mixture will start to thicken slightly.
	2 Pour the mixture into an 8- or 9-inch square cake pan. Cover with foil and freeze until firm, about 4 hours.
	3 Scoop or spoon into individual serving bowls with sliced fruit, such as mango, blueberries, kiwi, or strawberries.

Per serving: Calories 610 (From Fat 397); Fat 44g (Saturated 27g); Cholesterol 163mg; Sodium 46mg; Carbohydrate 55g (Dietary Fiber 0g); Protein 3g.

Tip: Grated citrus peel, also referred to as zest, has the unpleasant tendency of clinging to the holes of the grater. To loosen these pieces, brush the holes with a pastry brush so the grated peel falls onto a cutting board or right into the dish you're preparing.

Lemon Granité

Prep time: 10 min plus freeze time • **Yield:** 6 servings

Ingredients	*Directions*
¾ cup freshly squeezed lemon juice	**1** In a saucepan, combine the lemon juice, water, and sugar. Stir well. Bring to a boil and remove from the heat.
1 cup water	
6 tablespoons sugar	**2** Pour the mixture into a shallow, freezerproof pan. Place in the freezer.
Fresh fruit, such as blueberries, strawberries, kiwis, and pitted cherries	**3** After about 30 minutes, remove the pan from the freezer and, using a fork, scrape back and forth over the ice, eventually reaching the bottom of the container. Return the mixture to the freezer.
	4 Repeat Step 3 again after 20 minutes, again after another 15 minutes, and a final time after another 15 minutes. After you're finished, you shouldn't see any big chunks of ice.
	5 Serve in chilled bowls, with fresh fruits around it, or serve with cookies and garnish with an edible flower such as a pansy or violet.

Per serving (without fruit): Calories 56 (From Fat 0); Fat 0g (Saturated 0g); Cholesterol 0mg; Sodium 0mg; Carbohydrate 15g (Dietary Fiber 0g); Protein 0g.

Tip: When making granités, select the ripest fruit you can find; it can even be a tad overripe. You want as much flavor from the fruit as possible.

Vary It! You can make terrific granités with blueberries, strawberries, Concord grapes, watermelon, cantaloupe, apple juice, oranges, limes, and more. Just extract all of the juice either with a reamer (in the case of citrus) or by putting peeled and pitted fruit in a blender and then straining the juice into the saucepan along with the sugar and water. Fibrous fruits (mangoes, apricots, plums, figs, bananas, and papayas, for example) do not work as well for granités.

Peach-Blueberry Cobbler

Prep time: 35–40 min • **Cook time:** 45 min • **Yield:** 8 servings

Ingredients	*Directions*
2 pounds firm, ripe nectarines or peaches (or a combination of both)	*1* Preheat the oven to 375 degrees.
1 cup blueberries or blackberries, rinsed and stemmed	*2* Cut the nectarines or peaches in half and remove the pits. Cut each half into 4 to 5 wedges and place in a large mixing bowl.
⅓ cup (or more to taste) plus 2 tablespoons granulated sugar	*3* Add the berries, ⅓ cup of the granulated sugar, the light brown sugar, 2 tablespoons of the flour, cinnamon, and the grated lemon zest and juice. Toss to mix well. Taste the fruit and see if it's sweet enough. If necessary, add more sugar.
2 tablespoons light brown sugar, packed	
1½ cups plus 2 tablespoons all-purpose flour	
½ teaspoon cinnamon	*4* Turn the fruit mixture into a 2-quart baking dish that's 2 inches deep. Dot the top of the fruit with 1 tablespoon of the butter and bake for 10 minutes.
Grated zest and juice of ½ lemon	
7 tablespoons cold butter, cut into small pieces	*5* As the fruit bakes, prepare the dough. In a medium mixing bowl, mix the remaining 1½ cups flour, the remaining 2 tablespoons sugar, baking powder, and salt.
2 teaspoons baking powder	
½ teaspoon salt	
1 teaspoon fresh lemon juice	*6* Add the remaining 6 tablespoons butter and, using a pastry blender or two knives, cut the butter into the dry ingredients until the mixture resembles coarse bread crumbs. Sprinkle the mixture with the lemon juice.
8 to 10 tablespoons heavy cream or half-and-half	
¾ cup heavy cream, well chilled	
Confectioner's sugar	
½ teaspoon vanilla extract	

7 Using a fork, wooden spoon, or rubber spatula, gradually stir in just enough of the 8 to 10 tablespoons of heavy cream or half-and-half to moisten the dough so that it holds together and can be rolled or patted.

8 Gather the dough into a ball and place it on a lightly floured work surface. Roll out or pat the dough with your hands so it is about ½ inch thick and roughly matches the shape of the top of the baking dish.

9 Using a biscuit cutter, round cookie cutter, or knife, cut the dough into 2½-inch circles. (You should have 9 to 10 circles.)

10 After 10 minutes, remove the fruit from the oven. Place the dough on top of the fruit.

11 Return the cobbler to the oven and bake 30 to 35 minutes more, until the topping is golden brown and the fruit is bubbling around the edges.

12 As the cobbler bakes, make the sweetened whipped cream. Pour the ¾ cup heavy cream into a medium mixing bowl. Using an electric mixer, beat the cream just until it starts to thicken. Add the confectioner's sugar to taste and the vanilla and continue beating until soft peaks form. Refrigerate until ready to use.

13 To serve, put the warm cobbler into shallow bowls. Spoon some of the cream over each serving; drizzle some of the fruit juices over the cobbler and serve.

Per serving: Calories 355 (From Fat 146); Fat 16g (Saturated 10g); Cholesterol 47mg; Sodium 251mg; Carbohydrate 51g (Dietary Fiber 3g); Protein 4g.

Vary It! Substitute other summer fruits for the peaches and blueberries, such as plums, raspberries, or apricots. Add other spices, such as allspice, ginger, or nutmeg, or sprinkle fruit with a fruit liqueur. Substitute vanilla or lemon ice cream for the sweetened whipped cream.

Free-Form Fresh Fruit Tart

Prep time: About 30 min plus chill time • **Cook time:** 30–35 min • **Yield:** 6 servings

Ingredients	*Directions*
7 tablespoons butter, softened	**1** To make the pastry, in a medium mixing bowl, use a wooden spoon to blend 6 tablespoons of the butter, ¼ cup of the sugar, egg yolk, lemon zest, and vanilla extract. Add the flour and salt.
¼ cup plus 1½ tablespoons (or more to taste) sugar	
1 egg yolk	
Grated zest of ½ lemon	**2** Use your fingers or a pastry blender to lightly work the butter-egg mixture into the dry ingredients until they form a smooth dough. Press the dough into a ball; enclose in plastic wrap and chill for about 30 minutes.
¼ teaspoon vanilla extract	
1 cup all-purpose flour	
Pinch of salt	**3** Preheat the oven to 425 degrees. Butter a large, flat baking sheet, preferably nonstick.
Butter for the baking sheet	
4 to 6 ripe, medium peaches or nectarines, or a combination of both	**4** On a lightly floured counter, use a floured rolling pin to roll out the dough into a free-form rectangle, about 9 by 12 inches.
3 tablespoons apricot or peach jam	
1 tablespoon Cointreau or other fruit liqueur (optional)	**5** Carefully drape the dough over the rolling pin and transfer it to the buttered baking sheet. Fold up and lightly crimp the edges of the dough all around to form a neat rim. Set aside.
2 tablespoons finely chopped almonds	
¼ cup blueberries or raspberries, rinsed, drained, and stemmed	**6** Halve and pit the fruit; slice each half into 4 to 5 thin wedges.
Vanilla ice cream or whipped cream, optional	

7 Starting at one corner, arrange the fruit slices side by side on the dough, overlapping and fitting them snugly, until the surface of the pastry is completely covered.

8 In a small saucepan over low heat, combine the jam and the remaining 1 tablespoon butter, stirring. Cook a few minutes, stirring constantly, until the butter is melted and the jam is runny. Remove the saucepan from the heat and, if desired, stir in the Cointreau.

9 Using a pastry brush, coat the fruit slices with the jam-butter mixture.

10 In another small mixing bowl, combine the remaining 1½ tablespoons of the sugar and almonds.

11 Sprinkle the berries over the top of the fruit slices and then sprinkle the sugar-almond mixture evenly over the fruit. (Use a little more sugar to taste, if desired.)

12 Bake the tart for about 25 to 30 minutes until the dough is crisp and golden and the fruit is tender.

13 Cut the tart into 6 pieces. Using a metal spatula, transfer each piece to an individual serving plate. Serve warm or cold, with a little whipped cream or vanilla ice cream if desired.

Per serving: Calories 316 (From Fat 140); Fat 16g (Saturated 9g); Cholesterol 71mg; Sodium 31mg; Carbohydrate 42g (Dietary Fiber 2g); Protein 4g.

Tip: If baked ahead, the tart can be reheated in a 375-degree oven for about 10 to 15 minutes.

Vary It! Try substituting ripe plum slices for some of the peaches and/or nectarines.

Apple-Pear Crisp

Prep time: About 20 min • **Cook time:** 40–45 min • **Yield:** 6 servings

Ingredients	*Directions*
3 large Granny Smith apples 2 large firm, ripe pears	*1* Position a rack in the lower third of the oven. Preheat the oven to 375 degrees.
2 to 3 tablespoons brandy or dark rum (optional) ¾ cup flour	*2* Peel and core the apples and cut them into 1-inch chunks. Core the pears and cut them into 1-inch chunks. (You don't have to peel them.)
⅔ cup granulated sugar 2 tablespoons brown sugar, packed Grated zest of ½ lemon	*3* Spread the fruit evenly over the bottom of an unbuttered, shallow, 2-quart baking dish. If desired, sprinkle the fruit with the brandy or rum.
¼ teaspoon salt ½ teaspoon ground cinnamon ¼ teaspoon ground nutmeg ½ cup (1 stick) cold butter, cut into small pieces	*4* In a medium mixing bowl, combine the flour, granulated sugar, brown sugar, lemon zest, salt, cinnamon, and nutmeg. Using a pastry blender or two knives, cut the butter into the dry ingredients until the mixture resembles coarse bread crumbs. Mix in the chopped nuts.
½ cup toasted chopped almonds or pecans Vanilla ice cream or whipped cream (optional)	*5* Spread the topping evenly over the fruit. Bake for 40 to 45 minutes, or until the fruit is tender and the crust is lightly browned. Serve warm with vanilla ice cream or whipped cream if desired.

Per serving: Calories 445 (From Fat 184); Fat 21g (Saturated 10g); Cholesterol 41mg; Sodium 101mg; Carbohydrate 66g (Dietary Fiber 5g); Protein 4g.

Vary It! If desired, add ½ cup of fresh, rinsed cranberries to the apple-pear mixture before spreading on the sugar topping. Or, for a summer crisp, substitute peaches and nectarines for the apples and pears.

Old-Fashioned Chocolate Chip Cookies

Prep time: About 20 min • **Cook time:** 8–10 min per batch • **Yield:** About 36 cookies

Ingredients	*Directions*
1 cup plus 2 tablespoons all-purpose flour	*1* Preheat the oven to 375 degrees.
½ teaspoon baking powder	*2* In a medium mixing bowl, stir together the flour, baking powder, lemon zest, and salt.
½ teaspoon grated lemon zest	
¼ teaspoon salt	*3* Using an electric mixer at medium speed, cream the butter with the brown and granulated sugars, about 3 minutes. Beat in the egg, heavy cream, and vanilla until well blended.
½ cup (1 stick) butter, softened	
⅓ cup plus 2 tablespoons light brown sugar, packed	
⅓ cup plus 2 tablespoons granulated sugar	*4* Using a wooden spoon or a rubber spatula, stir the flour mixture into the butter mixture until well blended. Stir in the chocolate chips and, if desired, the nuts.
1 egg	
2 tablespoons heavy cream or half-and-half	*5* Drop heaping teaspoons of the batter onto a greased baking sheet, about 1 to 2 inches apart.
½ teaspoon vanilla extract	
1 cup (6-ounce package) semisweet chocolate chips	*6* Bake one sheet at a time, until the cookies are lightly golden on the top with slightly browned edges, about 8 to 10 minutes. Rotate the sheet 180 degrees halfway through baking to ensure even browning.
⅓ cup coarsely chopped walnuts or pecans (optional)	
	7 Remove the baking sheet to a wire rack and let the cookies cool for about 2 minutes. Using a metal spatula, carefully remove the cookies from the baking sheet and slide them onto a wire rack to cool completely.

Per cookie: Calories 84 (From Fat 40); Fat 4g (Saturated 3g); Cholesterol 14mg; Sodium 26mg; Carbohydrate 11g (Dietary Fiber 0g); Protein 1g.

Divine Brownies

Prep time: 25 min • **Cook time:** 20–25 min • **Yield:** 24 brownies

Ingredients	*Directions*
Butter and flour to prepare the baking pan	***1*** Preheat the oven to 375 degrees. Grease and flour a 9-x-13-inch baking pan.
1 cup (2 sticks) butter	
1 ounce (1 square) unsweetened chocolate, coarsely chopped	***2*** In a small, heavy saucepan, over very low heat, melt the butter and unsweetened chocolate, stirring occasionally until the mixture is smooth. Set the mixture aside to cool slightly.
2 cups sugar	
¾ cup unsweetened cocoa powder	***3*** In a large mixing bowl, combine the sugar and the cocoa powder; add the melted chocolate-butter mixture and stir well to combine.
4 eggs	
2 teaspoons vanilla extract	***4*** Add the eggs, one at a time, stirring with a wooden spoon or rubber spatula, only until well blended. Stir in the vanilla.
1⅓ cups flour	
½ cup chopped walnuts or pecans (optional)	***5*** Add the flour, in three batches, stirring after each addition, just until the ingredients are blended. If desired, stir in the walnuts. Do not overmix.
	6 Scrape the batter into the prepared pan, spreading it evenly and to the edges. Bake in the top half of the preheated oven for 20 to 25 minutes, until the center is firm to the touch when lightly pressed.
	7 Remove the pan to a rack and let stand until completely cool before cutting into squares.

Per brownie: Calories 182 (From Fat 86); Fat 10g (Saturated 6g); Cholesterol 56mg; Sodium 13mg; Carbohydrate 24g (Dietary Fiber 1g); Protein 3g.

Lemon Bars

Prep time: 15 min • **Cook time:** About 35 min • **Yield:** 24 bars

Ingredients	*Directions*
Butter for the foil lining	*1* Preheat the oven to 350 degrees.
½ cup butter, softened	*2* Line a 13-x-9-inch baking pan (nonstick is best) with aluminum foil. Butter the foil.
1½ cups plus 6 tablespoons sugar	
Grated zest of 1 lemon	*3* In a medium mixing bowl cream together the ½ cup butter, 6 tablespoons of the sugar, and half of the lemon zest, using an electric mixer. Gradually stir in 1½ cups of the flour to form a soft, crumbly dough.
1½ cups plus 3 tablespoons all-purpose flour	
4 eggs	
¼ teaspoon baking powder	*4* Turn the dough into the foil-lined pan and press it evenly into the bottom. Bake for 12 to 15 minutes or until the crust is firm and lightly browned.
¾ cup sweetened flaked coconut	
6 tablespoons freshly squeezed lemon juice (about 2 lemons)	*5* Prepare the filling as the crust bakes. In a large mixing bowl, use an electric mixer or a wire whisk to beat the eggs well. Add the remaining 1½ cups sugar, 3 tablespoons flour, and the baking powder, and beat well to combine. Stir or whisk in the coconut, the lemon juice, the remaining half of the lemon zest, and the vanilla, just until blended.
1 teaspoon vanilla extract	
	6 Using a rubber spatula, spread the filling over the hot, baked crust, being sure to evenly distribute the coconut throughout the filling.
	7 Return the pan to the oven and bake for about 20 minutes, or until the top is lightly golden and the filling is set.
	8 Set the pan on a wire rack to cool completely. Lift the foil by the ends to lift out the bar cookie; then set it on a cutting board. Gently loosen the foil along all the sides. With a long, sharp, wet knife, cut into squares. Refrigerate the squares until ready to serve.

Per bar: *Calories 151 (From Fat 49); Fat 5g (Saturated 3g); Cholesterol 46mg; Sodium 21mg; Carbohydrate 24g (Dietary Fiber 0g); Protein 2g.*

Tiramisù

Prep time: About 20 min plus chill time • **Yield:** 8 servings

Ingredients	Directions
3 heaping tablespoons instant coffee crystals or granules	*1* In a small bowl combine the instant coffee and granulated sugar. Bring the water to a boil and pour it over the coffee mixture, stirring. Set aside and let cool to room temperature.
3 tablespoons granulated sugar	
1 cup water	*2* Place about half of the ladyfingers on the bottom of a 9- or 10-inch square or round serving dish.
2 packages (6 ounces each) ladyfingers	
1 pint heavy cream, well chilled	*3* Using a tablespoon, drizzle half of the coffee mixture evenly over the ladyfingers in the serving dish. Set aside.
¼ cup confectioner's sugar	*4* In a bowl, combine the cream, confectioner's sugar, and vanilla. With a whisk or an electric mixer, whip the mixture until it forms soft peaks. Refrigerate for at least 1 hour.
2 teaspoons vanilla extract	
⅓ cup mascarpone cheese	
2 heaping tablespoons sour cream	*5* In another bowl, combine the mascarpone and sour cream. Using a wooden spoon, stir the mixture until smooth.
1 tablespoon unsweetened cocoa powder	*6* Fold half of the whipped cream mixture into the cheese and sour cream mixture until well blended. Then fold in the rest, being sure not to overmix.
	7 Using a metal spatula or spoon, spread half of the mixture over the ladyfingers, and place another layer of ladyfingers, curved side down, over it.
	8 Drizzle the ladyfingers with the remaining coffee and cover them with the other half of the cream mixture. Using a sieve, sprinkle the cocoa powder evenly over the top.
	9 Refrigerate for 2 hours before cutting into pieces to serve.

Per serving: Calories 450 (From Fat 281); Fat 31g (Saturated 18g); Cholesterol 251mg; Sodium 93mg; Carbohydrate 37g (Dietary Fiber 1g); Protein 7g.

Part IV
Now You're Cooking! Real Menus for Real Life

The 5th Wave   By Rich Tennant

©RICHTENNANT

"I'd get up, but I'm trying to soften a stick of butter to move dinner along."

In this part . . .

Just because you can cook and like to cook doesn't always mean you have the time, space, or energy to cook elaborate meals and gourmet cuisine. We all have to contend with limited time, ringing phones, leaking washing machines, traumatized tots, and begging dogs. What's an aspiring home cook to do?

In this part, we address the critical element of time. Recipes in this part are designed for real-life situations: cooking dinner with the fewest number of dishes, making more food for less money, cooking for multiple meals in one session, even entertaining company with ease and less stress. Finally, we talk you through how to throw a fun summer party, and even (are you ready for this?) *how to tackle holiday cooking duties!* Yes, you even learn how to roast a turkey. We kid you not! You can *do this* because now you've got the mad skills.

Chapter 16

Taking It Easy with One-Pot Meals

In This Chapter

▶ Simplifying your life with a slow cooker

▶ Baking your meal in a casserole dish

▶ Taking your one-pot meal to the stovetop

You can love to cook and hate to clean up. Who says all cooks think it's fun to do dishes and scrub out pots and pans? It's certainly not our favorite way to digest dinner. So why use two pots (or more) when one will do? If you're busy (and who isn't?), the concept of the one-pot meal is more than charming — it's indispensable.

A meal in one pot is an ancient concept. What could be more traditional than a big iron pot over a slow fire filled with a little meat, a lot of vegetables, herbs and spices, and water? A large enough pot could feed a small village.

Not every one-pot meal actually uses only one pot. Sometimes, you need a few other dishes to prepare individual ingredients to go into the final pot, such as a skillet to brown the ground beef or a pasta pot to pre-boil noodles. However, serving is a matter of putting the crock or casserole dish on the table and urging the family to dig in.

Whether you want to save time or just love the comfort-food appeal of one-pot meals, this chapter shows you how to become an expert at this delicious form of culinary minimalism.

Slow Cookers: Small Input, Big Output

Slow cookers, which consist of a ceramic crock with a lid that fits into an electric holder, cook food slowly over a period of 6 to 12 hours. Unlike with many other forms of cooking, you don't have to keep watching the food to save it from burning. You can even leave the house while the slow cooker does all the labor at a relaxed and steady pace.

The slow cooker, also known as the Crock-Pot, may seem so old-fashioned, but it's actually a miracle of modern technology. Fill it up in the morning with a roast and veggies; a yummy stew or chili; raw rice and broth; a layered casserole; or even a frozen chicken. Head off to work, and when you get home, voila! Dinner is served.

Slow cookers can also do many things besides prepare dinner: They can bake, make hot apple cider or cheese dip for a party, and even make gravy while your Thanksgiving turkey is resting.

While you can cook a lot of things in a slow cooker, they can't do absolutely everything (we're sorry to say). There are a few rules to remember:

- **Slow cookers can't brown ground meat.** Slow cookers don't get hot enough to cook ground meat safely. For dishes like chili or spaghetti sauce, brown ground meat in a skillet before putting it into the slow cooker. You can put steak, roasts, poultry, and fish into the slow cooker without cooking them first — you can even put them in frozen solid — but ground meat is the exception.

- **Slow cookers can't cook pasta.** They don't boil water, so the pasta won't cook properly. If a slow cooker recipe calls for pasta, cook it first according to package directions (in boiling water), and then add it to the slow cooker toward the end of cooking so it doesn't get mushy.

    Treat beans the same way as pasta: If your dish calls for canned beans (such as for chili or bean soup), add them toward the end of cooking so they doesn't turn to mush.

- **Slow cookers cook everything at the same pace.** For best results, cut vegetables into bite-sized pieces for even cooking. Vegetables that take longer to cook, like potatoes, should be in smaller pieces than vegetables that cook quickly, like tomatoes.

- **You should always follow the manufacturer's directions for your individual slow cooker.** Cookers vary, some running hotter or cooler than others.

Most slow cookers come with a recipe book to get you started, and you also can find some great recipes and general slow cooking tips in *Slow Cookers For Dummies* by Tom Lacalamita and Glenna Vance (published by Wiley). Also check out the video at www.dummies.com/go/slowcooking.

Later in the chapter, we offer a slow cooker recipe that we love: Ratatouille is a traditional French vegetable dish cooked until the vegetables form a rich, jammy blend. It makes a great side dish to meat, or you can serve it over rice as a meat-free main course. Ratatouille is a dish that benefits from long cooking, making it perfect for the slow cooker. Our Slow Cooker Ratatouille tastes even better the next day, so save the leftovers!

From Oven to Table: Simplicity in a Casserole Dish

Another great way to make a one-pot meal is with the good old-fashioned casserole dish. Load up the dish with ingredients, from chicken with potatoes to a layered lasagna, and let the oven do most of the work. There is something homey and comforting about dinner out of the oven. If you have kids who don't like their foods to touch each other, they may not appreciate the charm of the casserole, but for the rest of us, it's love in a dish.

Casserole dishes can contain everything from an old-style casserole to a piece of meat surrounded by potatoes and other vegetables to homey dessert like fruit baked with a crumbly topping, all in one dish. Later in the chapter, we offer some tasty recipes to bake in your oven:

- ✔ **Chicken and Biscuit Pot Pie:** You may remember those frozen chicken pot pies from childhood, but our version is made from scratch and oh-so-much tastier. The recipe takes a little time, but the end result is worth every warm, homey bite. We hope you'll try it.

- ✔ **Shepherd's Pie:** In Ireland, the classic Shepherd's Pie is made with beef, not lamb. We prefer the more distinctive flavor of lamb, so that's what our recipe uses. If you want to try it with beef, simply substitute the same amount of meat.

- ✔ **Taco Casserole:** Spicy, easy, filling, and delicious, this crowd pleaser (shown in the book's color section) may become a family favorite.

- ✔ **Hungry Family Lasagna:** An easy way to make your family happy, this layered meat-and-noodle dish is even easier if you use the lasagna noodles that don't need to be pre-boiled. Look for them in your store.

You can make lasagna unique by adding a variety of ingredients to the essential layers of noodles, cheese, and sauce. For example, combine ¼ to ⅓ cup cooked, chopped, drained, fresh or frozen spinach or broccoli with the cheese mixture. Or, sprinkle the layers with ⅓ to ½ pound cooked ground beef or cooked shredded chicken or turkey. Or, sprinkle the layers with 1 cup cooked chopped vegetables, such as mushrooms, zucchini, or carrots.

- ✔ **Homestyle Macaroni and Cheese:** You *could* make the stuff out of the box, but why do that when this easy recipe is so much creamier, cheesier, and more delicious? This is comfort food at its ultimate.

Simmering a Slow-Cooked Meal

Sometimes, your single pot will sit on the stove and contain everything you need for a meal. We're talking about everything from the classic pot roast to a savory stew to dishes that combine grains, meats, and vegetables.

Be sure to check out Chapter 7, where we feature recipes for Pot Roast with Vegetables, Old-Fashioned Beef Stew, and Mediterranean Seafood Stew, all of which are one-pot meals made on your stovetop. Another recipe to try is for savory and exotic Spanish Paella, coming up later in this chapter.

Slow Cooker Ratatouille

Prep time: About 20 min • **Cook time:** 6–8 hrs • **Yield:** 6 servings

Ingredients	*Directions*
3 tablespoons olive oil	*1* Heat the olive oil in a skillet over medium-high heat. Sauté the eggplant, zucchini, onion, red and green bell peppers, and garlic until the vegetables look golden but not dark brown, about 15 minutes.
1 medium eggplant, peeled and cut into 1-inch cubes	
1 medium zucchini, cut into 1-inch cubes	
1 medium red onion, chopped	*2* Put the cooked vegetable mixture, tomatoes, salt, basil, thyme, pepper, and bay leaf in the slow cooker. Turn on low and cook for 6 to 8 hours.
1 large red bell pepper, cored, seeded, and chopped	
1 large green bell pepper, cored, seeded, and chopped	*3* Remove the bay leaf and serve over rice. Garnish each serving with 1 tablespoon Parmesan cheese.
2 cloves garlic, minced	
2 cans (14 ounces each) whole tomatoes	
1 teaspoon salt	
2 teaspoons dried basil	
1 teaspoon dried thyme	
½ teaspoon black pepper	
1 bay leaf	
Hot cooked rice	
6 tablespoons grated Parmesan cheese	

Per serving: Calories 156 (From Fat 79); Fat 9g (Saturated 2g); Cholesterol 4mg; Sodium 682mg; Carbohydrate 17g (Dietary Fiber 5g); Protein 5g.

Chicken and Biscuit Pot Pie

Prep time: About 15 min • **Cook time:** About 1 hr 10 min • **Yield:** 8 servings

Ingredients	*Directions*
2 pounds skinless, boneless chicken breasts	*1* Combine the chicken breasts, broth, onion, celery, and garlic in a 4-quart pot. Add water to just cover the chicken and vegetables. Cover the pot and bring to a boil.
3 cups chicken broth	
1 medium yellow onion, chopped	*2* Uncover, reduce the heat, and simmer for 15 minutes. Remove the chicken, cut into bite-sized pieces, and return the pieces and any juice to the pot.
2 celery stalks, trimmed of leaves and diced	
2 cloves garlic, minced or put through a garlic press	*3* Add the carrots and potato to the pot. Bring the broth back to a boil and then lower the heat and simmer 15 minutes more, or until the chicken and vegetables are just tender. Let cool for about 5 minutes in the liquid.
3 carrots, trimmed, scraped, and sliced	
1 medium boiling potato, peeled and diced	*4* Carefully pour the broth with the chicken and vegetables into a large colander set over a larger pot (such as a Dutch oven) to catch and reserve the liquid. Put the pot with the liquid back on the stove over medium heat.
3 tablespoons butter	
1 tablespoon all-purpose flour	
¼ cup heavy cream	
¼ teaspoon ground nutmeg	
Salt and pepper	
1 cup fresh or frozen peas	
1 tablespoon sherry (optional)	
1 can (10 to 12 ounces) refrigerated biscuit dough (8 to 10 biscuits)	

5 Melt the butter in a pot or large saucepan over medium heat. (You can use the same pot that you used to make the stock.) Add the flour and cook, whisking constantly, for about 1 minute. Stir in the hot broth, whisking occasionally and cooking about 2 to 3 minutes until the sauce comes to a boil and thickens. Add the cream and nutmeg. Season with salt and pepper to taste.

6 Preheat the oven to 425 degrees.

7 Stir the chicken, vegetables, peas, and sherry (if desired) into the sauce. Spoon the mixture into a 3-quart or 9-x-13-inch shallow baking dish.

8 Arrange the refrigerated biscuits on top of the chicken mixture and bake for about 25 minutes, or until the biscuits are lightly browned. Serve immediately.

Per serving: Calories 371 (From Fat 146); Fat 16g (Saturated 7g); Cholesterol 86mg; Sodium 940mg; Carbohydrate 28g (Dietary Fiber 3g); Protein 28g.

Shepherd's Pie

Prep time: About 25 min • **Cook time:** About 1 hr 20 min • **Yield:** 6 servings

Ingredients	Directions
2½ pounds baking potatoes, peeled and quartered	**1** Preheat the oven to 350 degrees.
4 tablespoons butter	**2** Put the potatoes in a large pot of lightly salted water and bring to a boil. Cook, covered, until the potatoes are tender, about 20 minutes. Drain and return the potatoes to the pot.
About 1 cup milk	
Salt and pepper	
1 tablespoon vegetable oil	**3** Mash the potatoes along with 2 tablespoons of the butter and enough milk to make them smooth and fluffy. Season with the salt and pepper to taste and set aside.
1 medium yellow onion, chopped	
2 large cloves garlic, peeled and chopped	**4** Heat the oil in a large skillet over medium-low heat. Add the onion and garlic and cook, stirring often, until the onion is soft and wilted. (Don't let the garlic brown.)
1½ pounds cooked, chopped lamb (or raw, ground lamb)	
1 tablespoon all-purpose flour	**5** Turn up the heat to medium and add the lamb. Cook about 5 minutes, stirring. (If using raw ground lamb, cook about 10 minutes, stirring often, until browned.) Pour off and discard any fat in the pan.
½ cup homemade or canned beef or chicken stock	
1 tablespoon chopped thyme or sage, or 1 teaspoon dried thyme or sage	**6** Add the flour and cook, stirring often, for 2 to 3 minutes. Add the stock, thyme, rosemary, and nutmeg.
1 tablespoon chopped rosemary leaves, or 1 teaspoon dried rosemary	**7** Reduce the heat to low and simmer, stirring occasionally, for about 15 minutes. Remove from the heat and let cool slightly.
Dash of ground nutmeg	
	8 Transfer the lamb mixture to an oval gratin dish (about 13 inches long). Spread the mashed potatoes over everything. Dot with the remaining 2 tablespoons butter and bake for 45 minutes or until nicely browned. Let cool for 5 minutes before serving.

Per serving: Calories 474 (From Fat 173); Fat 19g (Saturated 9g); Cholesterol 125mg; Sodium 589mg; Carbohydrate 38g (Dietary Fiber 4g); Protein 37g.

Taco Casserole

Prep time: 10 min • **Cook time:** 35 min • **Yield:** 8 servings

Ingredients	*Directions*
2 pounds ground chuck or lean ground beef, or ground turkey	**1** Preheat the oven to 350 degrees.
½ medium yellow onion, chopped	**2** Put the ground meat and onion in a large skillet. Cook over medium heat until the meat is browned, about 10 minutes. Drain.
1 package taco seasoning mix	
1 can (8 ounces) tomato sauce	
1 can (14 ounces) crushed tomatoes	**3** Stir in the taco seasoning mix, tomato sauce, crushed tomatoes, green chiles, pinto beans, and 2 cups of the tortilla chips.
2 cans (4 ounces each) mild green chiles, drained and chopped, or ½ cup jarred jalapeño peppers, drained	**4** Put the mixture into a 3-quart casserole or 9-x-13-inch baking dish. Top with the cheese and the remaining 1 cup tortilla chips.
1 can (15 ounces) pinto beans, drained and rinsed	
3 cups slightly crushed tortilla chips	**5** Bake for 25 minutes, or until the cheese is melted and the casserole is bubbly. Serve immediately, garnishing each serving with salsa and sour cream sprinkled with green onions.
2 cups shredded cheddar cheese	
2 cups store-bought salsa	
½ cup sour cream	
2 green onions, chopped, including some of the green part	

Per serving: Calories 476 (From Fat 230); Fat 26g (Saturated 12g); Cholesterol 114mg; Sodium 1,154mg; Carbohydrate 28g (Dietary Fiber 6g); Protein 35g.

Hungry Family Lasagna

Prep time: About 20 min • **Cook time:** About 1 hr • **Yield:** 8 servings

Ingredients	Directions
12 lasagna noodles **1 pound mozzarella cheese (reduced-fat variety, if desired)** **2 cups (one 15-ounce container) ricotta cheese (reduced-fat variety, if desired)** **⅓ cup plus 2 tablespoons grated Parmesan or Romano cheese** **Salt and pepper** **5 cups (approx.) tomato sauce or jarred red pasta sauce (two 26-ounce jars)**	*1* Bring an 8-quart pot filled with about 6 quarts of lightly salted water to a boil over high heat. *2* Add the lasagna noodles a few at a time. Cover the pot to bring the water back to a boil and then cook uncovered, according to package directions, until barely tender, not soft. *3* As the noodles cook, preheat the oven to 375 degrees. *4* Cut the mozzarella cheese into ½-inch cubes. *5* In a small bowl, combine the ricotta, ⅓ cup of the Parmesan cheese, and 1 tablespoon of water taken from the boiling pasta pot. Season the mixture with salt and pepper to taste and set aside. *6* When the noodles are cooked, drain them in a colander and run cold water over them.

7 To assemble the lasagna, spread a heaping cup of the tomato sauce on the bottom of a 13-x-9-x-3-inch ovenproof pan. Place three noodles over the sauce so that they completely cover the bottom of the pan (they should touch but not overlap). Spread one-third of the ricotta mixture evenly over the noodles. Sprinkle one-third of the mozzarella cheese cubes over the ricotta. Spread a heaping cup of the sauce over this layer. Season, if desired, with salt and pepper.

8 Continue making layers, following the same order as Step 7 and ending with a thin layer of sauce. Sprinkle the top layer with the remaining 2 tablespoons Parmesan cheese.

9 Bake in the preheated oven, checking after 30 minutes. If the top layer appears to be dry, cover with foil. Bake for another 20 to 25 minutes, or until the lasagna is bubbly. Let stand, covered, for 15 minutes before cutting into squares and serving.

Per serving: Calories 464 (From Fat 216); Fat 24g (Saturated 13g); Cholesterol 73mg; Sodium 1,116mg; Carbohydrate 36g (Dietary Fiber 3g); Protein 27g.

Homestyle Macaroni and Cheese

Prep time: About 20 min • **Cook time:** About 35 min • **Yield:** 4 servings

Ingredients	*Directions*
2 cups elbow macaroni	*1* Preheat the oven to 350 degrees.
2½ cups milk	
5 tablespoons butter	*2* Bring a 4- or 5-quart pot of lightly salted water to a boil. Add the macaroni and cook for about 6 to 8 minutes, or until just tender.
3 tablespoons all-purpose flour	
½ teaspoon paprika	*3* As the macaroni cooks, make the cheese sauce. Heat the milk almost to the boiling point in a small saucepan over medium-low heat.
Generous dash of Tabasco sauce, to taste	
2 cups grated sharp cheddar cheese	*4* Melt 3 tablespoons of the butter in a large saucepan over medium heat. Add the flour and whisk constantly over low heat for 1 to 2 minutes. Do not let it brown.
Salt and pepper	
½ cup cubed Italian fontina cheese	*5* Gradually whisk in the hot milk and then add the paprika and Tabasco. Cook over medium heat for 2 to 3 minutes or until the sauce thickens, whisking occasionally. Whisk in the grated cheddar cheese and remove from the heat. Season with salt and pepper.
1 cup fresh white bread crumbs	

6 Drain the macaroni as soon as it is done, return it to the pot, and add the cheese sauce and the cubes of fontina cheese, stirring well to blend.

7 Use 1 tablespoon of butter to grease a deep, 2- to 3-quart casserole dish fitted with a lid. Add the macaroni and cheese mixture. Cover and bake for 20 to 25 minutes until hot.

8 Meanwhile, melt the last tablespoon of butter in a small skillet. Add the bread crumbs and sauté over low heat, stirring constantly, until they're moistened but not browned.

9 Remove the casserole from the oven and raise the temperature to broil. Spread the bread crumbs evenly over the macaroni and cheese. Return the dish to the oven, uncovered, and broil for 1 to 2 minutes, or until the crumbs are crisp and browned. Serve immediately.

Per serving: *Calories 732 (From Fat 392); Fat 44g (Saturated 27g); Cholesterol 134mg; Sodium 743mg; Carbohydrate 55g (Dietary Fiber 2g); Protein 30g.*

Spanish Paella

Prep time: About 15 min • **Cook time:** About 1 hr 10 min • **Yield:** 8 servings

Ingredients	Directions
¼ cup olive oil	**1** In a Dutch oven or large saucepan, heat the olive oil over medium-high heat.
1 chicken, cut into pieces (about 2 pounds)	
8 ounces kielbasa or other smoked sausage, sliced	**2** Add the chicken pieces and sauté, turning the chicken to cook all sides, for about 10 minutes.
1 large yellow onion, chopped	**3** Add the sausage, onion, garlic, and celery and continue to sauté until the chicken is golden brown and the vegetables are soft, about 10 additional minutes.
3 garlic cloves, peeled and minced	
2 stalks celery, minced, including some of the leaves	**4** Add the chicken broth, rice, and saffron. Stir to combine. Bring to a boil and then reduce the heat.
5 cups chicken broth	
2 cups raw white rice	**5** Add the peas and stir. Cover and simmer over medium-low until the rice is cooked through and has absorbed all the liquid and the chicken is no longer pink inside, about 45 minutes. (Check after the first 25 minutes of simmering; if the rice looks dry, add more broth.)
1 pinch of saffron threads	
1 cup frozen peas	
1 pound medium shrimp, shelled and deveined	**6** Stir in the shrimp and cook for an additional 3 to 4 minutes, or until the shrimp turns pink. Serve immediately.

Per serving: Calories 543 (From Fat 241); Fat 27g (Saturated 7g); Cholesterol 151mg; Sodium 1,104mg; Carbohydrate 41g (Dietary Fiber 4g); Protein 33g.

Tip: Find saffron threads with the herbs and spices at the grocery store.

Chapter 17

Making More (and Better) for Less

In This Chapter

▶ Making cheap eats that taste great

▶ Getting super deals with vegetables, beans, and rice

To understand how much money the average American shopper wastes every week, just stand around any supermarket checkout counter. Instead of flipping through the intellectual journals on sale ("Paris to Marry an Alien; Honeymoon on Pluto"), take an inventory of customers' shopping carts. Even discounting the usual junky snack food, you'll find that the average cart is loaded with high-priced (for what you get) frozen dinners, sugared-up prepared sauces, prebuttered garlic bread, precut vegetables, frozen pizzas, boxed croutons (stale bread, only $3.99 a box!), and more. (It's no surprise that America has the highest obesity rate in the world — and the personal debt to match it.)

You can definitely save money by making food from scratch, or even semi-scratch. In this chapter, we introduce you to the types of food that can help you feed a family for less — in many cases, far less. Frugality is no reason to forgo class, however, as the recipes in this chapter demonstrate.

Big Dishes for Small Bucks

Whether you're using inexpensive cuts of beef, stretching chicken with heaps of veggies and rice, or taking advantage of a weekly special at the supermarket, a little attention to detail and presentation can make any meal fit for a family — even one full of finicky eaters.

Here are a few guidelines for budget cooking:

✔ Rice, pasta, cornmeal, dried beans, and other grains cost far less than meat yet, if prepared creatively, can deliver as much or more protein. Serve smaller portions of meat along with any of these items.

✔ Soups and stews made with meat, veggies, and grains are great vehicles for getting the most out of relatively little.

✔ And don't forget salads! A big bowl of salad with a little meat (or cheese or egg) costs a lot less than a big plate of meat.

All the main dish recipes in this chapter also make delicious leftovers — a blessing for busy cooks.

Crowd-pleasing chili

Few words spark gastronomic brouhaha like *chili,* whether it's rich Texas-style chili con carne, fiery Arizona-style chili, or one of the myriad variations in between. Maybe it's not a glamorous meal, but chili is a real crowd pleaser, and you'll be surprised how festive you can make it look with some thought to presentation. Plus, you can feed your whole Little League team for about ten bucks.

You can turn up the heat on any chili recipe with extra red pepper flakes or chili powder. Be careful, though, because peppers intensify as they cook.

Later in the chapter, we present a recipe for Southwestern Chili. This classic recipe can easily be doubled or even tripled to serve 8 or 12 people. This dish is also great made with leftover lamb (as is Shepherd's Pie; see Chapter 16). If you have a plastic squeeze bottle (available in restaurant supply stores), you can squirt flavored sour cream on top of each bowl — maybe in the shape of Texas (or Cleveland).

Stir-fry for pennies

Stir-fry is great nutrition for the budget-conscious. Because of all the vegetables and the rich oil, you can stretch a little bit of meat for a lot of people. You don't need a wok to make stir-fry. Just be sure that the pan is hot, the oil is hot, and you cook the vegetables just long enough to be bright and crisp. You can whip up a stir-fry whenever you like, using beef, pork, chicken, fish, or whatever you have on hand, plus whatever fresh vegetables are waiting in your refrigerator. A little oil, a little sizzle, some spices, and you've got dinner. Serve stir-fry alone or over hot cooked rice or thin Chinese noodles (available in the Asian food section of your grocery store).

Be sure to check out our recipe for Pork and Noodle Stir-Fry in Chapter 19.

Super Sidekicks

Inviting side dishes are another great way to dress up your meals. Following are some inexpensive, tasty recipes.

Root vegetables

Root vegetables such as potatoes, carrots, turnips, and beets are hearty, filling, super-nutritious, and — you guessed it — cheap! Root vegetables make great side dishes, including the traditional (see the recipe for Homemade Mashed Potatoes in Chapter 5) and the unusual (raw julienned kohlrabi sticks, anyone?). Root vegetables stretch a soup, stew, or stir-fry, and they can also be good raw with a dip: Try mixing equal parts nonfat plain yogurt and sour cream with some minced garlic and dill, or just dip them in ranch dressing.

Potatoes can add creamy or thick texture to many dishes, and potato side dishes alone number in the dozens. See how they add heft and flavor to the Mixed Vegetables Italian Style recipe later in this chapter.

Seasonal vegetables

Root vegetables aren't the only vegetables that can help fill out a budget-conscious meal. Using seasonal produce in your cooking is not only economical but also follows the venerable tradition of European cooking.

Since this book was first published, in 1996, there has been an explosion of local farmers' markets. Chances are there is one within ten miles of your home. For the first time in many decades Americans can again purchase fresh, local, and seasonal food. This opens a world of possibilities for wholesome and inexpensive cooking. Take advantage of it!

Dried beans

We find it rather amazing that Americans don't cook more with dried beans, which are so inexpensive, healthful, and delicious. You can use dried beans in a side dish or as part of a main course. Whether or not you're cooking on a tight budget, becoming familiar with all kinds of legumes, each of which has a special texture and flavor, is definitely worthwhile. Table 17-1 lists several common types of dried beans.

Table 17-1	Dried Beans
Bean	*Description*
Black beans	Often used in South American and Caribbean dishes and mixed with rice and spices. Sweetish flavor.
Black-eyed peas	Traditional ingredient in the cooking of the American South — black-eyed peas and collard greens, black-eyed peas with ham. Earthy.
Borlotto beans	Large, speckled beans. Mostly puréed and turned into creamy dips.
Boston beans	See "White beans, small (navy and pea)."
Chickpeas	Large, semifirm beans sold dried and canned. Used in casseroles, soups, and stews. Puréed and seasoned in Middle Eastern cuisine. Also known as garbanzo beans.
Kidney beans/red beans	The traditional beans used in chili and other earthy casserole dishes and soups. A white kidney bean, called *cannellini*, is used in many northern Italian dishes. A staple in Mexican cooking as well. Faintly sweet.
Lentils	A tiny legume. Boiled with vegetables and other seasonings for side dishes, soups, and stews. No soaking is required before cooking.
Lima beans	Eaten as a side dish with mild seasonings. Also good in casseroles, especially with ham. Sweet flavor.
Pinto beans	The base of Mexican refried beans. Frequently used in highly spiced dishes. Earthy, mild flavor.

Bean	Description
Split peas	Often used in soups, especially with ham. Sweet. Like lentils, no soaking is required.
White beans, large	Used in stews and casseroles. Often simmered with ham bones or other flavorful stocks. Neutral flavor.
White beans, small (navy and pea)	Foundation of Boston baked beans and the French *cassoulet*. Neutral flavor.

Before cooking dried beans, sort and rinse them. Look over the beans carefully, picking out and discarding any that are withered. Rinse them thoroughly in cold water until the water runs clear, removing any beans or other substances that float to the surface.

Many cookbooks advise home cooks to soak dried beans overnight before cooking them, to reduce cooking time. We have consulted with some leading Mexican chefs and they maintain that this step is not necessary — in fact, soaking dried beans can leave them mushy. However, soaking them and discarding the soaking water does help with digestability.

Later in the chapter, we show you how to make two great bean dishes:

✔ **Lentils with Balsamic Vinegar:** The sweet edge of the balsamic vinegar performs magic on the nutty flavored lentils in this recipe. Lentils don't require soaking, and they boil tender in 20 to 25 minutes.

✔ **White Beans with Tomatoes and Thyme:** White beans are among the most likable of dried beans, appealing to almost everyone, even kids. This side dish relies on bacon, onions, garlic, tomatoes, and herbs to add panache.

Rice with some spice

As we show you in Chapter 13, rice is a terrific (and easy) addition to all kinds of meals. In this chapter, we offer a recipe for Spanish Rice that is a great accompaniment to taco casserole (see Chapter 16) or any south-of-the-border fare. Our rice recipe is pretty mild, but if you can't get enough fire, you can always stir in a few chopped jalapeño peppers or some hot red pepper flakes.

Money-saving kitchen tips

Being economical in the kitchen has nothing to do with cutting quality — in fact, just the contrary. Making every ounce count takes skill and respect for food. Here are some ways to begin:

✔ **Don't let leftovers ossify in the refrigerator.** Think ahead and use them the next day in omelets (see Chapter 11), chili, soups (see Chapter 12), stir-fries, casseroles like macaroni and cheese (see Chapter 16), and salads (see Chapter 12).

✔ **Don't use leftovers the same way you did the first time you served them.** Chop leftover roast chicken into a casserole or mix it with noodles in a soup. Toss leftover vegetables into a stir-fry or a pasta dish.

✔ **Develop knife skills.** Cutting up your own chicken and deboning your own meat save considerable money. (See www.dummies.com/go/deboning chicken for step-by-step instructions to debone a chicken.) Plus, you have bones for making homemade soup stock, another money saver. Whole vegetables are cheaper than cut-up ones, too, and heads of lettuce are less expensive than bagged salad mix.

✔ **Develop delicious recipes with high-protein dried beans and economical vegetables.** Try pairing red beans with collard greens, navy beans with winter squash, kidney beans with green beans, or garbanzo beans with mustard greens.

✔ **Use your freezer intelligently.** Take advantage of supermarket sales. Buy ground meat, chicken breasts, steaks, and chops in bulk. Wrap and save leftovers from large casseroles such as baked lasagna (see Chapter 16), meat from a roasted leg of lamb (see Chapter 8), or a baked ham. And date everything you put in the freezer. To discover some great ways of turning leftovers into delicious meals, see Chapter 19.

✔ **If possible, grow an herb garden, even in a window box.** So many packaged fresh herbs go to waste because you don't use them often enough. Plus, they're rather expensive, and the cost adds up over time. With an herb garden, you can cut just what you need, and the rest will stay fresh until you need more. Start with some popular herbs that are easy to cultivate: basil, thyme, rosemary, mint, parsley, and tarragon.

✔ **Make your own versions of foods that you routinely buy in the supermarket.** You'll spend less money and get better quality. Examples include salad dressings (see Chapter 12), garlic bread, pizza, and soup (see Chapter 12).

✔ **Buy less-expensive cuts of meat and learn to tenderize them by braising and stewing.** See Chapter 7.

✔ **Start a compost pile in the yard.** Recycle kitchen scraps and yard waste to make compost to improve the quality of soil in your home garden. Waste not, want not!

✔ **Send your kids to the neighbor's house for dinner.** Just kidding! But why not teach the kids to cook? The more help you have, the more time you have. Plus, you'll be teaching the kids lessons to last a lifetime: an appreciation for good food and some great cooking techniques.

Southwestern Chili

Prep time: About 25 min • **Cook time:** About 40 min • **Yield:** 4 servings

Ingredients	*Directions*
1 tablespoon olive oil	**1** Heat the oil in a large, deep pot or Dutch oven. Add the onion, green pepper, and garlic and cook for 2 to 3 minutes over medium heat, stirring occasionally.
1 large yellow onion, finely chopped	
1 small green bell pepper, seeded, cored, and finely chopped	**2** Add the ground beef and pork and cook for another 3 minutes or until browned, stirring to break up any lumps.
2 large cloves garlic, finely chopped	
½ pound lean ground beef	**3** Add the chili powder, cumin, and coriander. Stir well.
½ pound lean ground pork	
1 tablespoon chili powder, or to taste	**4** Stir in the tomatoes, beef stock, wine (or water), tomato paste, red pepper flakes, and salt and pepper to taste. Bring to a boil, reduce heat to a simmer, and then cook for 25 to 30 minutes, stirring often.
1 teaspoon ground cumin	
½ teaspoon ground coriander	
2 cups ripe, diced tomatoes, or 1 can (14½ ounces) diced tomatoes	**5** Add the kidney beans and cook 5 to 10 minutes more.
¾ cup homemade or canned beef stock	**6** If desired, serve over rice and garnish with sour cream and cilantro or parsley.
½ cup red wine or water	
2 teaspoons tomato paste	
¼ teaspoon red pepper flakes, or to taste	
Salt and black pepper	
1 can (15 ounces) red kidney beans, drained and rinsed	
4 cups cooked long-grain rice (optional)	
Sour cream (optional)	
Chopped cilantro or parsley (optional)	

Per serving: Calories 317 (From Fat 103); Fat 12g (Saturated 3g); Cholesterol 71mg; Sodium 358mg; Carbohydrate 23g (Dietary Fiber 7g); Protein 31g.

Mixed Vegetables Italian Style

Prep time: About 15 min • **Cook time:** 25–30 min • **Yield:** 6–8 servings

Ingredients	*Directions*
4 tablespoons olive oil	*1* Heat the oil in a large pot over medium heat and add the onions, garlic, and hot peppers (optional).
2 medium onions, coarsely chopped	
4 medium garlic cloves, chopped	*2* Meanwhile, boil the potatoes in salted water for about 10 minutes or until cooked through, not mealy.
Hot pepper flakes to taste (optional)	
2 medium white potatoes, cut into medium-sized cubes	*3* As the onions begin to turn golden, add the rosemary and tomatoes and cook, over medium high heat, stirring often, for about 2 minutes.
2 teaspoons chopped fresh rosemary, or 1 teaspoon dried	
3 ripe tomatoes, coarsely chopped (or 4 ripe plum tomatoes or 2 cups canned Italian chopped tomatoes)	*4* Drain the potatoes and add them to the pot along with the broccoli and red pepper. Season liberally with salt and pepper.
1 cup broccoli florets	*5* Cover and cook, turning gently several times, over medium-low heat until the potatoes and broccoli are tender, about 15 minutes. Taste for seasonings. Sprinkle each serving with parsley.
1 sweet red pepper, seeded, cored, coarsely chopped	
Salt and freshly ground black pepper to taste	
2 tablespoons chopped Italian parsley	

Per serving: *Calories 172 (From Fat 86); Fat 10g (Saturated 1g); Cholesterol 0mg; Sodium 115mg; Carbohydrate 21g; Dietary Fiber 4g; Protein 3g.*

Lentils with Balsamic Vinegar

Prep time: About 20 min • **Cook time:** About 30 min • **Yield:** 4 servings

Ingredients	Directions
1½ cups lentils, rinsed 1 quart water Salt	*1* Put the lentils in a large pot or saucepan. Add the water and salt to taste. Cover and bring to a boil over high heat.
2 cloves 2 small yellow onions 1 bay leaf 2 sprigs fresh thyme, or ½ teaspoon dried thyme	*2* Stick the cloves into one onion and chop the other onion finely. Add the onion with cloves to the pot, along with the bay leaf and thyme. Reduce the heat and simmer, partially covered, for about 20 minutes or until the lentils are tender.
1 tablespoon butter 1 tablespoon olive oil	*3* Carefully scoop out and reserve ½ cup of the cooking liquid. Drain the lentils. Remove and discard the onion with cloves, bay leaf, and thyme sprigs.
1 large carrot, peeled and finely diced 1 large clove garlic, finely chopped	*4* Heat the butter and olive oil in a large sauté pan or skillet over medium-high heat. Add the carrot, chopped onion, and garlic. Cook, stirring often, until the onion wilts, about 3 to 4 minutes. (Do not brown the garlic.)
1 tablespoon balsamic (or red wine) vinegar Pepper	*5* Add the vinegar and the reserved ½ cup cooking liquid to the skillet. Cover, reduce the heat, and simmer for about 5 minutes, or until the vegetables are tender.
	6 Stir the lentils into the vegetable mixture, cover, and cook over medium heat for about 2 minutes more, just to blend the flavors. Season with salt and pepper to taste and serve.

Per serving: Calories 309 (From Fat 63); Fat 7g (Saturated 2g); Cholesterol 8mg; Sodium 161mg; Carbohydrate 45g (Dietary Fiber 17g); Protein 19g.

White Beans with Tomatoes and Thyme

Prep time: About 20 min • **Cook time:** About 1 hr 10 min • **Yield:** 4 servings

Ingredients	Directions
2 whole cloves	*1* Stick the cloves into one of the onions and coarsely chop the other onion.
2 medium yellow onions	
1 cup dried white beans (such as Great Northern or navy beans), rinsed	*2* Place the beans in a large pot and add 1 quart water, the onion stuck with cloves, the bacon, carrot, bay leaf, and salt and pepper to taste.
1 quart water	
3 slices bacon	*3* Cover the pot and bring to a boil over high heat. Reduce the heat to medium-low and simmer, partially covered, for about one hour, or until the beans are tender.
1 large carrot, peeled and cut in half lengthwise	
1 bay leaf	*4* Remove the bacon strips and chop into small pieces.
Salt and pepper	
2 teaspoons butter or oil	*5* Heat the butter or oil in a large skillet over medium heat and sauté the bacon until golden brown, stirring.
1 large clove garlic, minced	
1 teaspoon fresh chopped thyme, or ½ teaspoon dried thyme	*6* Add the chopped onion, garlic, and thyme to the skillet and cook for about 2 to 3 minutes, or until the onions wilt.
1 can (14½ ounces) diced tomatoes, drained	*7* Add the tomatoes to the skillet and cook for 2 to 3 minutes, stirring frequently. Remove from the heat.
2 tablespoons chopped parsley	*8* Remove and discard the carrot, onion with cloves, and bay leaf from the pot of beans. Carefully scoop out and reserve half of the bean liquid and drain the beans.
	9 Add the beans to the tomato mixture and stir gently. If the mixture seems dry, add a little of the reserved liquid. Adjust seasoning with salt and pepper. Serve the beans hot, sprinkled with the parsley.

Per serving: Calories 194 (From Fat 43); Fat 5g (Saturated 2g); Cholesterol 9mg; Sodium 315mg; Carbohydrate 28g (Dietary Fiber 9g); Protein 12g.

Tip: If you prefer to soak the beans to aid with digestability, cover them with cold water and soak overnight, or boil them for 2 minutes and let stand for 1 hour. Drain and replace water to cook.

Spanish Rice

Prep time: About 10 min • **Cook time:** About 30 min • **Yield:** 10 servings

Ingredients	*Directions*
1 tablespoon olive oil	*1* In a large nonstick saucepan or Dutch oven, heat the olive oil over medium-high heat. Add the rice, onion, garlic, oregano, thyme, and bay leaves. Sauté until the rice is coated and onions are translucent, about 5 minutes.
2 cups converted rice	
½ medium yellow onion, chopped	
2 cloves garlic, peeled and minced	*2* Add the tomatoes, salt, and chicken broth. Bring the mixture to a boil.
1 teaspoon oregano	
½ teaspoon thyme	*3* Reduce the heat to medium-low, cover, and simmer until all the broth is absorbed, about 20 minutes. Add more broth if the rice looks dry. Remove the bay leaves and serve hot.
2 bay leaves	
1 can (14 ounces) diced tomatoes	
1 teaspoon salt	
4 cups chicken broth	

Per serving: *Calories 175 (From Fat 27); Fat 3g (Saturated 1g); Cholesterol 2mg; Sodium 683mg; Carbohydrate 33g (Dietary Fiber 1g); Protein 4g.*

Chapter 18

When You Want to Impress

In This Chapter

▶ Planning a menu when you have all day

▶ Getting it together in an hour or two

*P*reparing a special meal for friends and family is both a challenge and a joy. After all, you have spent months memorizing this book, so it's time to flaunt your knowledge! Sometimes you have all day to get it together, and sometimes you have only a couple of hours — or even less. No matter the time frame, your goal is to stay organized and not lose your nerve. In this chapter, we show you how to pull off an extraordinary meal no matter how fast the clock is ticking.

If You Have All Day

If you have all day, you'll probably sleep late, so you really don't have all day. Still, there should be enough time to try something different, even classy.

We're not suggesting a foie-gras-and-black-truffles terrine, nor Peking duck (for which, yes, you do need a bicycle pump). Maybe you try just a creative twist on a dish you have made before. Generally speaking, entertaining is not the time to experiment. While it may seem obvious, write out a comprehensive shopping list (and go to the store the day before if possible so you can return later for the things you forgot). The French term *mise en place* means having all your ingredients ready to go (chopped, peeled, trimmed, whatever) before cooking commences. That's your goal.

Classy hors d'oeuvres

We like to serve appetizers that involve marinating. Their acidic freshness primes the palate for what's to follow.

A great option is the spectacular Salmon Marinated in Ginger and Cilantro recipe later in the chapter. It can be prepared several hours in advance and has a tangy, herbaceous flavor that teases the palate without filling the stomach. Elsewhere in the book, we suggest using a dried herb if the fresh is not available. However, such substitutions don't always work. For example, you can't substitute powdered ginger for fresh gingerroot in this recipe; the same goes for the cilantro. The fresh ingredient tastes entirely different. (Dried parsley is another herb that has its limitations. Always use fresh, chopped parsley when sprinkling it on a dish as a garnish.)

Marinating fish can be tricky business. The acid in the marinade — which comes from the lime and vinegar — actually "cooks" the surface of the fish. Be sure to leave the fish in the marinade only as long as the recipe indicates (4 to 5 hours, in this case).

A simple and attractive appetizer we also love is braised endive with sautéed walnuts. Endive is a leafy vegetable with a lovely tart and peppery edge that makes it a titillating starter. All you need to do is trim away any discolored outside leaves and place the endive in a large skillet (two leaves per person). Add a tablespoon of butter, a bit of salt, a little sugar, and water to nearly cover the leaves. Simmer for about 25 minutes or until tender. Drain well and press out excess moisture, and then sauté the endive in butter until it's golden brown all over. For a novel touch, brown some chopped walnuts in butter and sprinkle over the endive.

Sometimes it's fun to serve guests something they rarely if ever prepare at home. One such appetizer is leeks vinaigrette. *Leeks* look like oversized scallions and carry hints of garlic and onion. The preparation is easy. First cut off the roots and most of the green leaves from four large leeks (or eight small ones). Remove any tough outer leaves. Slice the leeks lengthwise, stopping just above the root, and rinse them very well in running water. Simmer them in chicken stock or water for 10 to 15 minutes; don't overcook them or they'll get mushy. Drain, cool, and press the leeks to extract the liquid. Cut them crosswise, arrange them on plates, and drizzle them with vinaigrette dressing (which you can make from our recipe in Chapter 12).

Here are a few other ideas for hors d'oeuvres:

- ✔ Bell Pepper–Rice Salad (see Chapter 12)
- ✔ French Onion Soup (see Chapter 12)
- ✔ Grilled Vegetable Platter with Fresh Pesto (see Chapter 12)
- ✔ Warm Artichoke-Spinach Dip (see Chapter 21)

Enticing entrees

Okay, you've survived the appetizer course — which is to say, your guests are not anxiously glancing at their wristwatches. So you want to follow with a surefire winner. Osso Buco, a traditional Italian winter dish, melds succulent braised veal shank with garlic and vegetables. An essential garnish that adds a bright flavor and looks great on the plate is called Gremolata, a combination of minced parsley, lemon peel, and garlic. And while it may be inauthentic, we like to add a bit of minced rosemary to the mix. We provide recipes for both Osso Buco and Gremolata later in the chapter.

One traditional ingredient in Osso Buco is anchovies. Their intense saltiness, when added in moderation, adds a special depth to the flavor of the dish. If you're one of those people who pick anchovies off pizza as if they were road kill, simply omit them.

Osso Buco can be prepared a day or two in advance, chilled, and then reheated — the flavors meld and intensify that way.

Here are more suggestions for show-off dishes.

- ✔ Glazed Leg of Lamb with Pan Gravy and Red Currant Glaze (see Chapter 8)
- ✔ Poached Salmon Steaks with Béarnaise Sauce (see Chapter 5)
- ✔ Roasted Chicken (see Chapter 8)
- ✔ Roasted Fillet of Beef (see Chapter 8)
- ✔ Roast Loin of Pork (see Chapter 8)
- ✔ Shepherd's Pie (see Chapter 16)

Suave side dishes

A perfect side dish for all roasts is mashed potatoes. Chefs today like to call them "puréed potatoes," or worse, "pommes puree," as if they are something more sophisticated. You can jazz up mashed potatoes (see the recipe in Chapter 5) in many ways. Try adding mashed parsnips, carrots, baked garlic, turnips, chopped green onions, minced yellow onions, or fresh herbs.

If mashed potatoes aren't your thing, consider cabbage. Our recipe for Braised Cabbage with Apples and Caraway later in this chapter brings to life this cheap and often neglected vegetable.

Here are some other side dishes that go well with any of the main courses suggested in this chapter:

✔ Basic Wild Rice (see Chapter 13)

✔ Crispy Roasted Root Vegetables (see Chapter 8)

✔ Risotto (see Chapter 13)

✔ Sautéed Skillet Potatoes (see Chapter 6)

✔ White Beans with Tomatoes and Thyme (see Chapter 17)

Finishing touches: Desserts

You can make plenty of easy desserts that are winners for entertaining. Later in the chapter, you find an easy-to-make treat that will blow them off their chairs: a Lemon and Chocolate Tart. For lots of other great dessert ideas — from lemon granité to tiramisù — be sure to check out Chapter 15.

If You Have An Hour or Two

One to two hours is a good chunk of time in which to put together a fine meal — that is, if you are organized, have all the shopping done, and declare the kitchen a no-fly zone for children and pets!

Getting started: Quickie appetizers

You can take a lot of heat off the situation by starting with a good mixed salad, like the Avocado and Tomato Salad we present later in the chapter. This simple, colorful starter is a cinch to prepare.

Another of our favorite starters is called Tuscan Bread Salad. Originating in — duh — Tuscany, it can be presented as either a starter in small portions or as a more generous side dish. We provide the recipe later in the chapter.

Looking for other quickie start ideas? Try one of these, if you have only an hour or so:

✔ Carrot Soup with Dill (see Chapter 12)

✔ Garlic-Grilled Portobello Mushrooms (see Chapter 9)

✔ Layered Cheese and Vegetable Salad (see Chapter 12)

You can also assemble open-face sandwiches (called *tartines* in France) topped with cheese, meats, smoked fish, or herbed bean purees. Or, go south of the border and use the same technique on tortillas cut into wedges, or warmed in the microwave for 10 seconds and rolled up with meat, cheese, and greens and then sliced. We offer a simple recipe for Fresh Tomato Quesadillas later in the chapter.

The art of antipasto

When you barely have time to shop, much less prepare a full meal, knowing how to assemble various foods into an attractive spread is an invaluable skill. As a source of inspiration, we recommend an Italian approach that calls for serving an array of cheeses, meats, breads, olives, and vegetables on a large platter.

Assembling an Italian antipasto is 50 percent presentation. Think about how the tastes and colors contrast. Antipasto is traditionally served as the appetizer course, but there's no reason you can't make a meal of it. Here is a sampling of choices for an antipasto platter.

✔ Mozzarella, provolone, fontina, Parmesan, or goat cheese (cubed or thinly sliced)

✔ Thinly sliced ham, prosciutto, and Genoa salami

✔ Rounds of pepperoni or sopressata salami

✔ Thin slices of *mortadella* (a garlic-flavored bologna) or capicola (made from cured pork)

✔ Cooked shrimp (which is best if tossed in a vinaigrette dressing)

✔ Canned anchovies, sardines, or tuna packed in olive oil

✔ Canned chickpeas tossed in vinaigrette dressing

✔ Sun-dried tomatoes in oil

✔ Marinated artichoke hearts, roasted red peppers, and capers

✔ Assorted black and green olives

✔ Assorted fresh vegetables, including radishes with tops; carrot, celery, cucumber, and pepper sticks; pieces of fennel; green onions; and whole red or yellow cherry tomatoes

✔ Arugula, basil leaves, and radicchio for garnishing

✔ Sliced ripe pears, melon, figs, or small bunches of grapes

✔ Flavored breads, breadsticks, and flatbreads

Another appetizer option is to serve *antipasto*, which is an assembly of meats, cheeses, and fresh and marinated vegetables you arrange on a platter. Obviously, you use whatever you have on hand, unless you can squeeze in a quick trip to the market. For shopping ideas, check out the sidebar "The art of antipasto."

If you still haven't found the perfect appetizer, we have even more suggestions! With practice, you can knock off these appetizers in minutes:

✔ **Guacamole:** Mash in a small bowl the flesh from 2 medium, ripe avocados. Add 1 small finely chopped onion; 1 ripe finely chopped tomato; 2 tablespoons chopped cilantro; half a jalapeño chili, seeded and minced; and the juice and grated zest of half a lemon. Season with salt and pepper and serve with blue or white corn chips.

✔ **Hummus Dip:** Whirl in a blender until smooth a 16-ounce can of drained chickpeas, 1 clove garlic, ¼ cup sesame seeds, the juice and grated zest of 1 lemon, ½ cup water, with salt and pepper to taste. Serve on triangles of toasted pita or with assorted raw vegetables.

✔ **Seasoned Smoked Chicken Slices:** You can buy smoked chicken and slice it into bite-sized strips, serving the strips over thin slices of French or Italian bread. Brush with a basic vinaigrette seasoned with chopped cilantro and, if you like, a dash of Tabasco sauce.

✔ **Spicy Shrimp Kebabs:** Thread medium or large shrimp and chunks of sweet onions on skewers (preferably metal, which, unlike wooden skewers, don't require presoaking); grill or broil about 2 minutes a side or until done, brushing at the last minute with ¼ cup melted butter mixed with ½ teaspoon hot pepper flakes. Serve hot.

✔ **Sun-Dried Tomato Spread:** Whirl sun-dried tomatoes, garlic, and onions in a food processor or blender container with enough oil to moisten into a coarse spread. Season with white pepper. Serve on Melba toast rounds.

Entrée: The short version

Plenty of impressive entrees cook up quickly. Our Broiled Skirt Steak, Cajun Style recipe later in the chapter will get you started . . . because the clock is ticking! This zesty skirt steak dish, featured in the book's color section, is an alternative to flank steak and has a down-by-the-bayou kick. Adjust the seasonings — less if you like it a little less spicy, or more if you want to crank up the heat.

When time is short, you may also want to try our recipe for Snapper Fillets with Tomatoes. Fish cooks quickly, so it's great for a quick but fancy dinner. This classy main course has some unusual tastes, such as fennel (which you find in your produce aisle). The optional addition of anise-flavored liqueur will keep your guests guessing the secret. Our recipe calls for using a leek; check out Figure 18-1 for how to clean and trim it.

Cleaning & Trimming Leeks

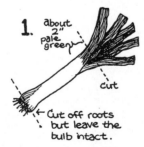

Figure 18-1:
Cleaning and trimming leeks.

Skirt steak: Fashionable fare

Skirt steak, formerly unknown to home cooks, has become a fashionable cut of meat in restaurants, particularly because it works so well in fajitas. Skirt steak is cut from the beef flank, and it can be tough if you don't know how to cook it. It has tons of flavor and is inexpensive.

Because skirt steak contains a lot of moisture, it should be cooked very fast over high heat to sear. For that reason, you should let the steak reach room temperature before broiling or grilling. Also let the cooked steak sit for several minutes before slicing, so the juices can settle. Cut the steak on a bias across the fibrous muscle on a cutting board that can catch the runoff. (*Cutting on a bias* means slicing the meat at about a 45-degree angle to the cutting board. Doing so gives you a larger, thinner slice for each portion.) Pour the juice back over the steak when serving, or use it in your sauce.

When you have only an hour or so, here are other main dishes to try:

✔ Grilled Shrimp Skewers (see Chapter 9)

✔ Penne with Parmesan Cheese and Basil (see Chapter 13)

✔ The Perfect Steak (see Chapter 9)

✔ Sautéed Chicken Breasts with Tomatoes and Thyme (see Chapter 6)

✔ Spaghetti with Quick Fresh Tomato Sauce (see Chapter 13)

✔ Steak au Poivre (see Chapter 6)

✔ Tuna Steaks with Ginger-Chili Glaze (see Chapter 6)

Super-quick side dishes

Try the Indian Rice with Ginger, Walnuts, and Raisins recipe later in the chapter — it's an exotic-tasting rice that goes well with any steak or poultry dish as long as the sauce doesn't contain the same seasonings. Or try one of the following super-quick side dishes to jump-start your dinner preparation:

✔ Green Beans with Shallots (see Chapter 21)

✔ Polenta with Herbs (see Chapter 13)

✔ Sautéed Skillet Potatoes (see Chapter 6)

✔ Steamed Broccoli with Lemon Butter (Chapter 5)

✔ Tabbouleh Salad (see Chapter 13)

Desserts on the double

A homemade sauce lends a special touch to ice cream or even store-bought pound cake. Try our Warm Blueberry Sauce recipe later in the chapter, and your guests will feel like you really went to a lot of trouble. (The technique works with all sorts of berries.) Or check out our recipe for Fresh Strawberry Sauce in Chapter 14.

The Caramel Sauce and Cracklin' Hot Fudge Sauce from Chapter 14 are also great with ice cream. And it doesn't take too long to assemble the Tiramisù in Chapter 15, which can add real class to a quick dinner. You can skip the two hours of chilling time, and the dessert will still be tasty!

Salmon Marinated in Ginger and Cilantro

Prep time: About 15 min plus marinate time • **Yield:** 8 servings

Ingredients	Directions
2 pounds skinless, boneless salmon fillets	*1* Slice the salmon thinly (¼ inch or less) widthwise, leaving strips about 2 inches long. Place the strips in a large bowl.
½ cup fresh lime juice	
1 large yellow onion, thinly sliced	*2* Add the lime juice, onion, vinegar, oil, cilantro, gingerroot, red pepper flakes, and salt and pepper to taste. Stir gently and cover with plastic wrap. Refrigerate for 4 to 5 hours.
3 tablespoons white wine vinegar	
3 tablespoons olive oil	
2 tablespoons chopped fresh cilantro	*3* Taste for seasoning. If you need more salt, blend it in thoroughly.
1 tablespoon grated fresh gingerroot	*4* Line small serving plates with the lettuce of your choice and place a serving of salmon over the lettuce. Discard the onion-marinade mix.
¼ teaspoon red pepper flakes	
Salt and black pepper	
Lettuce for garnish	

Per serving: Calories 174 (From Fat 76); Fat 9g (Saturated 1g); Cholesterol 62mg; Sodium 68mg; Carbohydrate 0g (Dietary Fiber 0g); Protein 23g.

Tip: If your salmon pieces have any small bones, use a pair of tweezers or your fingers to remove them before starting to prepare this dish.

Osso Buco

Prep time: About 40 min • **Cook time:** 1 hr 30 min • **Yield:** 4 servings

Ingredients	*Directions*
4 meaty slices of veal shanks cut across the bones (each about 2 inches thick), about 3½ pounds total	*1* Sprinkle the veal shanks with salt and pepper to taste. Roll them in the flour to give them a light coating, patting to remove excess flour.
Salt and pepper	
½ cup all-purpose flour for dredging	*2* Heat the oil over medium-high heat in a heavy Dutch oven large enough to hold the veal shanks in one layer with the bones upright. Brown the veal all around, turning often, about 10 minutes. Remove the shanks from the pan and reserve them on a plate.
2 tablespoons olive oil	
1 large yellow onion, finely chopped	*3* Lower the heat to medium and add the onion, carrots, and celery to the pan. Cook, stirring often, until the onions wilt, about 2 or 3 minutes.
2 to 3 large carrots, peeled and chopped	
1 stalk celery, chopped	*4* Add the garlic, mashed anchovies (if desired), marjoram, and thyme. Stir and add the tomatoes, wine, bay leaf, and salt and pepper to taste.
3 large cloves garlic, finely chopped	
4 canned anchovy fillets, drained and mashed with a fork (optional)	*5* Return the veal shanks to the pan with any juices that have accumulated in the plate. Cover, reduce the heat to low, and simmer for about 1 hour, or until the meat is tender. (The meat should easily separate from the bone when prodded with a fork.)
½ teaspoon dried marjoram	
2 sprigs fresh thyme, or 1 teaspoon dried thyme	
1½ cups canned crushed tomatoes	*6* Remove the veal from the pan and scoop some of the vegetable mixture onto each serving plate. Sprinkle with lemon and orange zest. Place a veal shank on top of each serving, and sprinkle Gremolata over it (see the next recipe).
1 cup dry white wine or white grape juice	
1 bay leaf	
1 teaspoon finely grated lemon peel	
1 teaspoon finely grated orange peel	

Per serving: Calories 447 (From Fat 125); Fat 14g (Saturated 3g); Cholesterol 195mg; Sodium 378mg; Carbohydrate 24g (Dietary Fiber 4g); Protein 54g.

Gremolata

Prep time: About 10 min • **Yield:** 3½ tablespoons

Ingredients	Directions
5 teaspoons grated or minced lemon peel (without the bitter white pith) 2 teaspoons finely chopped Italian parsley 1 teaspoon finely chopped garlic 1 teaspoon finely chopped rosemary (optional)	Combine all ingredients in a bowl.

Per serving: Calories 10 (From Fat 1); Fat 0g (Saturated 0g); Cholesterol 0mg; Sodium 3mg; Carbohydrate 3g (Dietary Fiber 1g); Protein 0g.

Tip: Tightly covered, this topping will last several days in the refrigerator.

Braised Cabbage with Apples and Caraway

Prep time: About 25 min • **Cook time:** About 25 min • **Yield:** 4 servings

Ingredients	*Directions*
3 tablespoons vegetable oil	*1* Heat the oil in a large skillet or sauté pan over medium heat. Add the onion and garlic and cook, stirring often, until the onion is wilted, about 2 to 3 minutes. (Do not brown the garlic.) Remove from the heat.
1 medium yellow onion, coarsely chopped	
1 large clove garlic, minced	
1 small head green cabbage (about 1½ pounds)	*2* Cut the cabbage in half, remove its core, and coarsely shred it. Peel, core, and cut the apple into thin slices.
1 medium apple	
½ cup homemade or canned chicken or vegetable stock	*3* Add the cabbage, apple, stock, vinegar, caraway seeds, and salt and pepper to taste to the skillet and return it to the stove.
1 tablespoon white vinegar	
1 teaspoon caraway seeds	*4* On high heat, bring the mixture to a boil. Cover, reduce the heat to low, and simmer for 15 to 20 minutes, or until the cabbage is crisp-tender, stirring occasionally.
Salt and pepper	
	5 Uncover. If a lot of liquid is still in the pan, raise the heat to high and cook, stirring, for about 1 to 2 minutes or until most of the liquid is evaporated.

Per serving: Calories 163 (From Fat 97); Fat 11g (Saturated 1g); Cholesterol 0mg; Sodium 254mg; Carbohydrate 16g (Dietary Fiber 5g); Protein 3g.

Lemon and Chocolate Tart

Prep time: About 15 min plus cool time • **Cook time:** 35–40 min • **Yield:** 6–10 servings

Ingredients	Directions
1 frozen 8-inch pie shell	**1** Preheat oven to 350 degrees.
¼ pound unsweetened chocolate, chopped very fine	**2** Grease a sheet of aluminum foil and place it, greased side down, over the pie shell. Put dried beans or rice on the foil (to weigh the shell down) and bake the shell for 15 to 20 minutes, until golden. Let it cool.
3 large eggs	
¾ cup sugar	**3** Remove the foil and scatter chopped chocolate over the bottom of the pie shell. Set aside.
½ teaspoon finely grated lemon rind	**4** Break the eggs into a metal mixing bowl. Add the sugar and mix by hand or with an electric mixer until light and fluffy. Beat in the lemon rind and lemon juice.
½ cup freshly squeezed lemon juice	
6 tablespoons cold, unsalted butter cut into medium cubes	**5** Select a saucepan large enough to hold your mixing bowl without the bottom of the bowl touching the bottom of the pan. In the saucepan, bring a quart of water to a boil.
Sweetened whipped cream	**6** Place the mixing bowl in the saucepan so it's over the water — not touching the water. Cook, stirring constantly, until the sauce thickens, about 5 minutes.
	7 Remove the mixing bowl from the heat and beat in the butter. Let stand at room temperature for 15 minutes.
	8 Pour the lemon cream over the chocolate in the tart crust, smoothing it with a spatula.
	9 Bake for 15 minutes; let cool to room temperature before serving. Top with sweetened whipped cream if desired.

Per serving: Calories 448 (From Fat 281); Fat 31g (Saturated 16g); Cholesterol 137mg; Sodium 174mg; Carbohydrate 43g (Dietary Fiber 3g); Protein 6g.

Avocado and Tomato Salad

Prep time: About 25 min • **Yield:** 4 servings

Ingredients	*Directions*
2 ripe avocados	*1* Halve and pit the avocados. Peel away the skin. Cut each half into 4 lengthwise slices and then across into large cubes.
4 ripe plum tomatoes	
2 hard-cooked eggs, peeled and quartered (optional)	
1 small red onion, thinly sliced	*2* Core the tomatoes and cut them into 1-inch cubes.
¼ cup coarsely chopped cilantro	*3* Toss the cubes of avocado and tomato with the eggs (if desired), onion, cilantro, garlic, olive oil, vinegar, cumin, and salt and pepper to taste in a salad bowl and serve.
2 large cloves garlic, finely chopped	
6 tablespoons olive oil	
2 tablespoons red wine vinegar	
½ teaspoon ground cumin	
Salt and pepper	

Per serving: Calories 338 (From Fat 297); Fat 33g (Saturated 5g); Cholesterol 0mg; Sodium 152mg; Carbohydrate 12g (Dietary Fiber 9g); Protein 3g.

Tuscan Bread Salad

Prep time: 15 min plus marinate time • **Yield:** 4 servings

Ingredients	*Directions*
1 country loaf of bread (or 1½ baguettes), sliced thinly and left out overnight	**1** Tear the bread roughly and soak it in ¼ cup of the vinegar mixed with enough water to soak it through. After 2 minutes, place the bread in a paper towel and press to squeeze out as much liquid as possible.
½ cup red wine vinegar	
4 scallions, trimmed and chopped (including green part)	**2** Place the bread in a large bowl with the scallions, cucumber, bell pepper, tomatoes, basil, anchovies (if desired), and tuna.
1 cucumber, peeled and sliced crosswise (⅛ inch thick)	
1 red or yellow bell pepper, cored, seeded, and sliced into thin strips	**3** In a separate bowl, combine the olive oil, the remaining ¼ cup vinegar, salt, and pepper. Stir to combine well.
3 tomatoes, halved and chopped	
20 fresh basil leaves, sliced thinly, or 1 teaspoon dried basil	**4** Add the dressing to the vegetable-bread mixture and toss well. Let sit for 30 minutes at room temperature.
8 to 12 anchovy fillets, rinsed and chopped (optional)	**5** Sprinkle the marjoram over the top and serve.
6 ounces canned tuna (in oil), drained and flaked	
6 tablespoons olive oil	
1½ teaspoons salt	
1½ teaspoons black pepper	
1 teaspoon chopped fresh marjoram (or ½ teaspoon dried marjoram)	

Per serving: Calories 559 (From Fat 240); Fat 27g (Saturated 3g); Cholesterol 11mg; Sodium 1,597mg; Carbohydrate 67g (Dietary Fiber 9g); Protein 20g.

Tip: Basil is very fragile. Shortly after you chop it, the pieces start to darken — the flavor is still there, but the appearance is off-putting. Always chop basil just before using it.

Fresh Tomato Quesadillas

Prep time: About 5 min • **Cook time:** About 15 min • **Yield:** 8 servings

Ingredients	Directions
2 teaspoons olive oil 4 flour tortillas, about 8 inches in diameter 1 cup grated Monterey Jack cheese 1 ripe tomato, cored, seeded, and chopped ½ cup chopped fresh cilantro plus extra for garnish	**1** In a skillet, heat 1 teaspoon of the olive oil over medium heat. Put one tortilla in the skillet. Top with ¼ cup cheese, half the tomatoes, half the cilantro, another ¼ cup cheese, and the second tortilla. **2** When the bottom tortilla is golden and crisp (use a spatula to check), flip it over and cook the other side until golden. Remove to paper towels to absorb any extra oil. **3** Repeat with the other 2 tortillas and remaining ingredients, adding more olive oil if necessary. **4** Cut each quesadilla into 8 wedges. Garnish with extra cilantro leaves.

Per serving: Calories 140 (From Fat 63); Fat 7g (Saturated 3g); Cholesterol 13mg; Sodium 202mg; Carbohydrate 14g (Dietary Fiber 0g); Protein 6g.

Vary It! You can vary quesadillas to include whatever you have in the refrigerator. Try adding cooked chicken or beef, different kinds of cheeses, or leftover cooked vegetables.

Broiled Skirt Steak, Cajun Style

Prep time: About 5 min plus marinate time • **Cook time:** About 6 min • **Yield:** 4 servings

Ingredients	*Directions*
4 skirt steaks, ½ pound each	*1* A half hour before broiling or grilling, sprinkle the steaks with salt to taste. In a small bowl, combine the oil, chili powder, cumin, thyme, cayenne, and black pepper and stir well to mix. Brush this mixture all over the steaks. Cover the steaks with plastic wrap but do not refrigerate.
Salt	
2 tablespoons olive oil	
1 teaspoon chili powder	
½ teaspoon ground cumin	*2* Preheat the broiler or set a charcoal or gas grill to medium-high.
½ teaspoon dried thyme	
¼ teaspoon cayenne pepper	*3* If broiling, arrange the steaks on a rack and place under the broiler about 6 inches from the heat source. Broil for 3 minutes with the door partly open. Turn the steaks and continue broiling with the door partly open. Broil about 3 minutes more for medium-rare, or to the desired degree of doneness.
¼ teaspoon black pepper	
2 tablespoons butter	
2 tablespoons finely chopped fresh parsley	
	If grilling, put the steaks on a medium hot, oiled grill and cover. Cook for 3 minutes. Turn the steaks, cover, and cook about 3 minutes more for medium-rare, or to the desired degree of doneness.
	4 Transfer the steaks to a hot platter and dot with butter. Let them stand in a warm place for 5 minutes to redistribute the internal juices, which accumulate as the steaks stand.
	5 Sprinkle with parsley and serve with the accumulated butter sauce.

Per serving: Calories 487 (From Fat 278); Fat 31g (Saturated 12g); Cholesterol 122mg; Sodium 292mg; Carbohydrate 1g (Dietary Fiber 1g); Protein 49g.

Tip: To check for doneness, make a small incision with a sharp knife into the center or thickest part of the steak.

Indian Rice with Ginger, Walnuts, and Raisins

Prep time: About 15 min • **Cook time:** About 25 min • **Yield:** 4 servings

Ingredients	Directions
1¾ cups homemade or canned chicken or vegetable stock	**1** Heat the stock to just below boiling. Keep it hot.
2 tablespoons butter	**2** Melt the butter in a saucepan over medium heat. Add the onion and cook, stirring often, until the onion is wilted, about 2 to 3 minutes.
¼ cup finely chopped yellow onion	
1 cup chopped walnuts	**3** Add the walnuts, gingerroot, cinnamon, and pepper flakes to the onion. Cook, stirring constantly, for about 30 seconds.
1 teaspoon grated fresh gingerroot	
½ teaspoon cinnamon	
¼ teaspoon red pepper flakes, or to taste	**4** Stir the rice into the onion mixture, coating the grains in the melted butter, and cook for 1 more minute, stirring constantly.
1 cup raw converted rice	
2 tablespoons brandy or orange juice	**5** Carefully add the hot stock to the rice mixture. Cover and simmer over low heat for 20 minutes, or until the rice is tender and all the liquid is absorbed.
½ cup raisins	
3 tablespoons finely chopped cilantro or parsley	**6** While the rice is cooking, pour the brandy or orange juice over the raisins and let them soak.
Salt (optional)	**7** When the rice is done, stir in the raisins, any remaining brandy or orange juice, and cilantro or parsley. Add salt if necessary, and serve.

Per serving: Calories 492 (From Fat 229); Fat 26g (Saturated 5g); Cholesterol 15mg; Sodium 279mg; Carbohydrate 60g (Dietary Fiber 4g); Protein 11g.

Warm Blueberry Sauce

Prep time: About 10 min • **Cook time:** About 6 min • **Yield:** 4 servings

Ingredients	*Directions*
⅓ **cup granulated sugar**	*1* In a saucepan, thoroughly combine the sugar, cornstarch, and salt. Add the water and lemon juice and cook over medium-high heat, stirring frequently, until the mixture thickens, about 3 to 5 minutes.
1 tablespoon cornstarch	
Pinch of salt	
¾ **cup water**	
2 teaspoons fresh lemon juice	*2* Add the blueberries and lower the heat to medium, stirring frequently, for 1 minute.
1 cup ripe blueberries, rinsed and stems removed	
2 tablespoons butter, softened	*3* Remove the pan from the heat and add the butter and cinnamon. Stir well. Keep warm in a double boiler until ready to serve. Stir well before serving.
¼ **teaspoon ground cinnamon, or to taste**	

Per serving: Calories 142 (From Fat 52); Fat 6g (Saturated 4g); Cholesterol 15mg; Sodium 38mg; Carbohydrate 24g (Dietary Fiber 1g); Protein 0g.

Snapper Fillets with Tomatoes

Prep time: About 15 min • **Cook time:** About 15 min • **Yield:** 4 servings

Ingredients	*Directions*
2 tablespoons olive oil	*1* In a medium saucepan over medium heat, combine 1 tablespoon of the olive oil and the tomatoes, leeks, fennel, garlic, and turmeric. Season with salt and pepper to taste. Cook, stirring often, about 3 minutes.
5 plum tomatoes, peeled, seeded, and chopped	
1 large leek, white and light green part only, finely chopped	*2* Add the wine, stock, bay leaf, thyme, and Tabasco. Bring to a boil, reduce heat, and simmer for 5 minutes.
½ cup chopped fennel bulb	
2 large cloves garlic, finely chopped	*3* In a large sauté pan, add the remaining tablespoon of oil and arrange the fillets of fish in one layer, skin side down. Season with salt and pepper to taste.
1 teaspoon turmeric	
Salt and pepper	*4* Pour the leek-tomato mixture evenly over the fish fillets. Sprinkle on the Ricard or Pernod, if desired, cover, and cook over medium heat for about 5 minutes, until the fish is opaque in the center.
½ cup dry white wine or white grape juice	
½ cup fish stock or bottled clam juice	
1 bay leaf	*5* Discard the bay leaf and sprinkle with the basil or parsley before serving.
4 sprigs fresh thyme, or 1 teaspoon dried thyme	
⅛ teaspoon Tabasco sauce	
4 snapper fillets with skin on, or other white-fleshed fish, about 6 ounces each	
2 tablespoons Ricard, Pernod, or other anise-flavored liqueur (optional)	
2 tablespoons chopped basil or parsley	

Per serving: Calories 264 (From Fat 85); Fat 9g (Saturated 1g); Cholesterol 61mg; Sodium 302mg; Carbohydrate 9g (Dietary Fiber 2g); Protein 35g.

Chapter 19

Would I Serve You Leftovers?
This Is My Latest Creation!

In This Chapter

▶ Main courses — pork, lamb, and chicken — that keep on giving

▶ A little stir frying goes a long way

*N*o matter how crazy you are about cooking as a result of this book, at times you'll be too busy to execute a meal from scratch every day. This chapter emphasizes one basic concept: It's possible to prepare one sizeable meal and use that as a resource for two more distinctive repasts. It's all about the inspired use of leftovers — leftovers so resourcefully put to use that nobody notices they are attending encore performances.

Improvising with Leftovers

Leftovers typically revolve around meat or poultry. The temptation may be to recreate the original dinner, but that is not only boring but unadventurous. Let's start with the most basic options for meat and poultry:

✔ Serve pieces of leftover cold meat or fish, from beef to chicken to salmon, in a salad.

✔ Slice leftover cold ingredients for sandwiches, or arrange them on an appetizer platter with several dipping sauces: mustard and dill, basil and sour cream, sesame oil and fresh coriander, and so on.

✔ Make a wrap. (Perfect. They won't know what they're eating.)

✔ Prepare appetizers of cold meat on crispy crackers or baguette slices spread with a thin layer of cream cheese. Top with a bit of watercress, lettuce, or a fresh cilantro leaf.

Leftover terminology

The term *leftover* is unfortunate. Its unsavory connotation — something you "left," like your briefcase — hardly does justice to foods that can be just as good, or better, the next day. We invite you to join our campaign to find a new term for *leftovers*. Possibilities include

✔ Previously prepared

✔ Vintage

✔ Tested

✔ Golden oldie

✔ Broken in

Looking for a hot meal that uses leftover meat or poultry?

✔ Mix it with pasta.

✔ Bake it into a strata (see Chapter 11).

✔ Fry it with rice and vegetables.

✔ Scramble it into eggs (see Chapter 1).

✔ Fold it into an omelet (see Chapter 11).

Any of these options go for leftover veggies, too.

Making the Most of a Pork Shoulder

The first group of meals we discuss is based on the inexpensive and versatile cut of meat called *smoked shoulder of pork.* You may be familiar with pork roast and pork tenderloin but not this delicious cut. Pork shoulder (also called pork "butt" even though it is far from the hog's butt — probably a practical joke) is the upper part of a hog's shoulder. Its firm, rosy, and well-marbled meat is used in pâtés and sausages. Pork shoulder is usually sold trimmed and tied to hold its shape while cooking. Buy it smoked, and you have a delicious flavor cooked right in. Believe us, it's a winner.

In this chapter we provide three recipes that feature pork shoulder. Here's the plan:

✔ **Meal 1: Smoked Pork with Winter Vegetables:** This recipe can be a dinner for four, so if there are only two of you at the table, you have plenty of leftovers to make the two follow-up dishes we recommend.

✔ **Meal 2: Smoked Pork Hash:** After you've served the Smoked Pork with Winter Vegetables, you can use most of the leftovers to make this tempting meal, which stands on its own as a light supper, perhaps with a green salad and bread. It also makes a great country breakfast with the addition of fried eggs and toasted cornbread muffins.

✔ **Meal 3: Pasta and Bean Soup:** Few kitchen tasks are more satisfying to a home cook (or a professional chef, for that matter) than making a delicious soup that uses rich, homemade broth derived from another dish. The smoked pork butt adds just the right salty, meaty tones to this soup's broth. Pasta and Bean Soup is one dish that tastes even better the next day. You can find different versions of a soup like this all over Italy, where it is called *pasta e fagioli* (yep, "pasta with beans").

On the Lamb: Serving It Three Ways

Lamb is another great meat that has the stamina to last for three meals. In this section, we give you three great dishes based on a roasted leg of lamb:

✔ **Meal 1: Roasted Leg of Lamb:** The recipe is in Chapter 8, called Glazed Leg of Lamb with Pan Gravy and Red Currant Glaze. You can make it with or without a glaze. A large roasted leg of lamb often has lots of meat left around the bone, which you can use the make the Lamb Curry.

✔ **Meal 2: Lamb Curry:** Check out our recipe later in the chapter. The flavors in this curry intensify if it's refrigerated overnight. It also freezes well.

✔ **Meal 3: Sliced lamb sandwiches with Red Onion and Mango Chutney:** Leftover cold lamb makes delicious sandwiches, especially when slathered with mango chutney, which we provide the recipe for later in the chapter. A good chutney tastes both sweet and savory at the same time, with flavors more complex than a jam or jelly. A mixture of fruits, onions, sugar, and vinegar, chutney makes a great sandwich condiment for strong-tasting meats like pork or beef tenderloin, lamb, or a grilled hamburger. The ingredients for chutney are extremely flexible. In this recipe, you can substitute firm peaches for the mangoes, or add dark raisins or chopped green pepper, if you like.

If you stick with the mangoes recommended in the recipe, be sure to check out Figure 19-1, which shows how to peel and cube them.

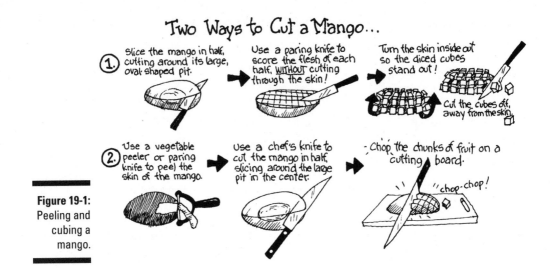

Two Ways to Cut a Mango...

① Slice the mango in half, cutting around its large, oval-shaped pit.

Use a paring knife to score the flesh of each half, WITHOUT cutting through the skin!

Turn the skin inside out so the diced cubes stand out!

Cut the cubes off, away from the skin.

② Use a vegetable peeler or paring knife to peel the skin of the mango.

Use a chef's knife to cut the mango in half, slicing around the large pit in the center.

Chop the chunks of fruit on a cutting board.

"chop-chop!"

Figure 19-1:
Peeling and cubing a mango.

Chicken Dinner Times Three

If you roast a large chicken (for example, 4 or 5 pounds), you'll have enough leftovers to make additional recipes. You may even want to roast two chickens while you're at it! Here's our three-day chicken plan:

✔ **Meal 1: Roasted Chicken:** You find the recipe in Chapter 8.

✔ **Meal 2: Chicken and Grilled Vegetable Wrap:** A *wrap* is a sandwich made with flatbreads, such as flour tortillas, that roll around a filling of vegetables, poultry, meat, or fish. Unlike a sandwich, the fillings in a wrap are usually diced, shredded, or thinly sliced. In this recipe, provided later in the chapter, we designed a wrap that uses leftover cooked chicken, grilled vegetables, and a sour cream–yogurt dressing. Because you're already grilling the vegetables, you can also use raw chicken breasts for this recipe and cook the chicken along with the veggies. If your grill is too small to hold all the vegetables we suggest, you can cook them in two batches instead.

✔ **Meal 3: Chicken, Avocado, and Red Onion Salad:** This chicken salad, which we provide the recipe for later in the chapter, uses leftover roasted chicken. However, if you don't have 3 cups of leftover chicken, simmer a whole chicken breast (or more depending on what you need) in chicken broth (or in water seasoned with salt, pepper, and lemon juice) for about 10 minutes or until the chicken is fully cooked (the center is not pink).

A good avocado is key to this salad. When buying one, feel the skin; it should be slightly soft but not mushy. If you want to ripen the avocado quickly, place it in a paper bag along with an apple or orange, close the bag, and let it sit overnight.

The dressing for this salad is first used as a marinade for the cooked, diced chicken. You can reuse it because the chicken it touched was never raw. (Never reuse marinade that has touched raw meat, unless you boil it first.)

Wok This Way: Stir-Frying

Stir-frying is an easy technique to master and is the perfect way to use up leftover meat, poultry, or vegetables, although uncooked meat can also work. When stir-frying, the oil should be very hot before adding the ingredients, but not so hot that it begins to smoke. You don't need a *wok* (a concave, bowl-shaped pan, traditional to Chinese cooking) to stir-fry — a large skillet will do, particularly cast iron. But if you do have a wok and are looking for more ways to use it, check out *Chinese Cooking For Dummies,* by Martin Yan (published by Wiley).

Before you start stir-frying, have all your ingredients cleaned, chopped, and ready to go. Measure and organize your ingredients, and set them up right next to the range before you heat the oil. Use two large forks or two large wooden spoons to toss the shredded ingredients in the hot oil. The tossing doesn't have to be constant, but tossing thoroughly and often exposes all the ingredients to the hot oil and causes them to cook quickly. To speed up the cooking, you can cover the wok or skillet immediately after adding the vegetables and pork to the oil, but remove the cover after about 45 seconds so you can watch the mixture to keep it from scorching.

Later in the chapter, we provide a recipe for Pork and Noodle Stir-Fry. You can make it with pork as we describe, or substitute leftover chicken or beef. Using light soy sauce, as the recipe calls for, adds a subtle salt flavor, but if you prefer a more intense flavor, use regular soy sauce instead. If you prefer, substitute 3 to 4 cups of cooked rice for the noodles. But don't toss the rice into the stir-fry; use it as a bed on which to place the pork and vegetable mixture. In other words, don't feel bound to the recipe! The whole point is to use up your leftovers in a delicious way.

Stir-fry greens

Greens are an essential part of traditional stir-fry. Besides being super-nutritious, greens add texture, crunch, and a pleasingly bitter bite to an otherwise rich stir-fry. The following greens are the ones most often used in stir-fry and most traditional to Chinese cooking.

Bok choy, with its long white stem and dark, ribbed leaves, resembles Romaine lettuce in shape. A staple in Chinese cooking, bok choy has a very mild flavor and comes in different sizes. The smaller bok choy is best for stir-frying, while the larger ones are best used in soups. Bok choy is available year-round in well-stocked groceries and Asian markets.

Napa cabbage is a laid-back term for common Chinese cabbage. It comes in two varieties. One variety is stout, with a thick core and wide leaves; the other is longer and narrower, with tall, clinging leaves. The flavor of both is more subtle than that of round cabbage, which makes it excellent for stir-frying. Napa cabbage is widely available in supermarkets.

Smoked Pork with Winter Vegetables

Prep time: 10 min plus soak time • **Cook time:** About 1 hr 30 min • **Yield:** 4 servings

Ingredients	*Directions*
3 to 4 pounds boneless smoked pork shoulder	*1* Remove the netting from the pork shoulder and soak the meat in warm water for about 5 minutes to remove excess salt.
1 large yellow onion, peeled and halved	
2 bay leaves	*2* Place the pork, onion, bay leaves, and peppercorns in a large pot; add cold water to cover. Cover the pot and bring the water to a boil.
10 black peppercorns	
6 carrots, peeled and quartered crosswise	*3* Reduce the heat and simmer for 1 hour and 10 minutes, adding more water if necessary to keep the pork immersed in the liquid.
6 medium baking potatoes, peeled and quartered	
3 large parsnips, peeled and quartered crosswise	*4* Remove the onion and bay leaves with a slotted spoon and discard. Add the carrots, potatoes, and parsnips and bring the liquid to a boil again. Reduce the heat and simmer for 10 minutes.
½ head green cabbage, cut into 3 to 4 wedges	
¼ cup chopped parsley	*5* Add the cabbage and return to a boil. Reduce the heat and simmer for another 10 to 15 minutes, or until the pork and vegetables are tender.
Salt and pepper	
1 stick softened butter	*6* Remove the meat from the simmering liquid and slice it into serving portions; arrange the slices on a serving platter. Remove the vegetables with a slotted spoon and arrange them around the meat. (Reserve the cooking liquid to make the Pasta and Bean Soup.)
Dijon-style mustard	
	7 Sprinkle the meat and vegetables with parsley. Season the vegetables with salt and pepper to taste. Serve with small bowls of butter, to mash into the steaming vegetables, and the mustard, for the pork.

Per serving: Calories 634 (From Fat 373); Fat 42g (Saturated 18g); Cholesterol 128mg; Sodium 2,100mg; Carbohydrate 43g (Dietary Fiber 8g); Protein 28g.

Vary It! If you can't find smoked pork shoulder (also called pork butt) in your supermarket, you can make this recipe with a 3-pound boneless smoked ham.

Smoked Pork Hash

Prep time: About 10 min • **Cook time:** About 15 min • **Yield:** 4 servings

Ingredients	*Directions*
3 tablespoons vegetable oil 1 cup chopped yellow onion 2 cups cubed cooked smoked pork shoulder, trimmed of excess fat 2 to 3 cups drained, cubed, leftover vegetables (excluding the cabbage) from Smoked Pork with Winter Vegetables Salt and pepper 3 tablespoons chopped parsley	*1* In a large skillet, heat the oil over medium heat; add the onion and cook, stirring often, until translucent, about 2 to 3 minutes. *2* Gently stir in the cooked pork and the vegetables so they're well mixed; season to taste with salt and pepper. *3* Using a metal spatula, press down on the hash to compress it against the bottom of the skillet. Cook, without stirring, until the bottom is well browned, 10 to 15 minutes. *4* If desired, place the skillet under the broiler, about 6 inches from the heat, for 3 to 4 minutes, to brown the top. *5* Using a metal spatula, lift and invert the hash onto individual serving plates. Garnish with the parsley.

Per serving: Calories 318 (From Fat 209); Fat 23g (Saturated 5g); Cholesterol 41mg; Sodium 1,081mg; Carbohydrate 19g (Dietary Fiber 3g); Protein 11g.

Tip: A well-seasoned cast-iron skillet gives hash a deep brown crust. You can use a nonstick skillet and reduce the oil to 2 tablespoons, but the crust on the hash will be lighter.

Vary It! Add 1 to 2 chopped, seeded, jalapeño or other chile peppers or 1 large seeded and chopped green or red bell pepper along with the onions. Add 1 cup of cooked frozen or canned corn or 1 tablespoon chopped fresh herbs, such as rosemary, thyme, or marjoram, with the cooked vegetables. Sprinkle some hot sauce, such as Tabasco, over the cooking vegetables.

Go-With: Round out this great meal by pairing the hash with Scrambled Eggs (see Chapter 1) or a simple green salad with vinaigrette dressing.

Pasta and Bean Soup

Prep time: 10 min • **Cook time:** 45 min • **Yield:** 8 servings

Ingredients	*Directions*
¼ cup olive oil	*1* In a large, heavy-bottomed soup pot or saucepan, heat the oil over medium setting. Add the onion and cook, stirring occasionally, until wilted, about 5 minutes. Stir in the carrots, celery, and garlic and cook over medium-high heat another 5 minutes, or until the vegetables are softened, stirring often.
1 medium yellow onion, peeled and chopped	
2 carrots, peeled and diced	
1 stalk celery, diced	
1 large clove garlic, peeled and chopped	*2* Add the tomatoes with their juice, 7 cups of the broth, the basil, and thyme. Cover the pot, bring to a boil, and then reduce the heat and simmer gently for 20 minutes.
1 can (14½ ounces) diced tomatoes	
7 to 8 cups broth saved from Smoked Pork with Winter Vegetables	*3* Carefully ladle 1½ to 2 cups of the soup into a blender container; pulse for just a few seconds. Stir the mixture back into the soup.
1 tablespoon chopped fresh basil, or 1 teaspoon dried basil	*4* Add the beans and the bay leaf; cover the pot and simmer another 5 minutes.
1 teaspoon chopped fresh thyme, or ½ teaspoon dried thyme	*5* Add the pasta and cook, partially covered, until al dente — about 10 minutes; stir occasionally.
1 can (15 ounces) cannellini or red kidney beans, rinsed and drained	
1 bay leaf	*6* If too much of the liquid evaporates and the soup seems too thick, add enough remaining broth to thin to a desired consistency.
1 cup small dried pasta, such as elbow macaroni	
Salt and pepper	*7* Remove the bay leaf. Adjust seasoning with salt and pepper to taste. Ladle the soup into bowls; sprinkle each with the grated cheese.
Grated Parmesan cheese (for garnish)	

Per serving: Calories 195 (From Fat 73); Fat 8g (Saturated 1g); Cholesterol 0mg; Sodium 515mg; Carbohydrate 23g (Dietary Fiber 4g); Protein 23g.

Lamb Curry

Prep time: About 15 min • **Cook time:** About 45 min • **Yield:** 4 servings

Ingredients

1 tablespoon olive oil

½ tablespoon butter

1 large yellow onion, chopped

1 medium red bell pepper, cored, seeded, and diced

2 teaspoons seeded and minced jalapeño or other hot chile pepper (optional)

1 clove garlic, minced

1 tablespoon peeled, grated fresh gingerroot

1 tablespoon curry powder

½ teaspoon ground cumin

1½ cups homemade or canned beef stock

¼ cup plus 2 tablespoons canned coconut milk

1 tablespoon tomato paste

2½ to 3 cups 1-inch cubed cooked lamb, trimmed of excess fat

⅓ cup golden raisins

Salt and black pepper

4 cups cooked long-grain rice

Optional accompaniments: mango chutney, chopped dry-roasted peanuts, chopped parsley or cilantro

Directions

1 In a large, deep saucepan, heat the oil and butter over medium-high heat. Add the onion, red pepper, jalapeño pepper (if desired), and garlic, and cook for about 4 to 5 minutes, stirring often, until the vegetables begin to soften.

2 Stir in the gingerroot, curry powder, and cumin; cook about 1 minute, stirring.

3 Stir in the beef stock, coconut milk, and tomato paste; bring to a boil.

4 Stir in the lamb. Reduce the heat, cover, and simmer for 20 minutes.

5 Add the raisins and simmer for another 20 minutes. Season to taste with salt and pepper. Serve over rice with suggested accompaniments, if desired.

Per serving: Calories 545 (From Fat 156); Fat 17g (Saturated 8g); Cholesterol 83mg; Sodium 252mg; Carbohydrate 62g (Dietary Fiber 3g); Protein 33g.

Go-With: Lamb curry is an assertive dish, packed with flavor, so pair it with something mild, such as a Cucumber-Dill Salad (see Chapter 12) or Converted Rice (see Chapter 13).

Red Onion and Mango Chutney

Prep time: About 20 min • **Cook time:** 25–30 min • **Yield:** 6 servings

Ingredients	Directions
2 tablespoons vegetable oil	**1** In a medium saucepan, heat the oil over medium setting; add the onion and sauté for 4 to 5 minutes, or until slightly browned, stirring often.
1 cup chopped red onion	
1 to 2 (or to taste) jalapeño peppers, or other hot chile pepper, seeded and minced	**2** Add the jalapeño, gingerroot, and garlic, and cook for 1 minute more, stirring. (Do not let the garlic brown.)
2 teaspoons peeled, minced fresh gingerroot	**3** Remove the saucepan from the heat. Stir in the brown sugar and vinegar. Return the saucepan to the heat and bring the mixture to a boil.
1 clove garlic, minced	
½ cup plus 2 tablespoons packed brown sugar	**4** Reduce the heat and simmer for 3 to 4 minutes. Stir in the mangoes.
½ cup cider vinegar	
2 large ripe mangoes, peeled and cut into ¼-inch cubes	**5** Raise the heat and bring the mixture to a boil. Reduce the heat and simmer, partially covered, for 15 to 20 minutes, or until the mango is tender. Taste and adjust seasoning, if desired, with salt and pepper.
Salt and black pepper (optional)	
	6 Chill and serve as a condiment on lamb sandwiches.

Per serving: Calories 187 (From Fat 44); Fat 5g (Saturated 0g); Cholesterol 0mg; Sodium 12mg; Carbohydrate 38g (Dietary Fiber 2g); Protein 1g.

Tip: A ripe mango is slightly soft to the touch, with at least half of its otherwise green skin tinged with orange, yellow, or red coloring.

Go With: This chutney also goes well with grilled chicken or beef.

Chicken and Grilled Vegetable Wrap

Prep time: About 15 min • **Cook time:** 25 min • **Yield:** 4 servings

Ingredients	Directions
Oil for coating the grill and vegetables	*1* Brush the grill grate with oil. Prepare a medium-hot fire in a charcoal or gas grill.
1 red, yellow, or green bell pepper, cored, seeded, and quartered	*2* Brush the vegetables with oil, coating all sides.
1 large portobello mushroom cap	*3* Place the vegetables on the grill grate. Also place the raw chicken, if using, on the grill grate. Grill, turning often, until the vegetables are lightly browned on both sides and the chicken is cooked through, about 25 minutes.
1 medium red or yellow onion, cut into ½-inch slices	
1 small zucchini, quartered lengthwise to make 4 long strips	
2 cups cooked chicken, cut into ½-inch cubes, or 2 chicken breasts, raw	*4* Remove the vegetables and chicken to a baking sheet and let them stand until they're cool enough to handle.
¼ cup chopped basil or parsley	*5* Chop all the vegetables into ½-inch-thick pieces. Chop the chicken, if just cooked.
Salt and black pepper	
¾ cup sour cream	
¼ cup lowfat yogurt	
4 flour tortillas (8 to 9 inches)	

6 Transfer the vegetables to a large mixing bowl; add the chicken and 2 tablespoons of the chopped basil or parsley. Toss well. Season to taste with salt and pepper.

7 In a blender container, combine the sour cream, yogurt, and the remaining 2 tablespoons of the basil or parsley. Blend a few seconds until they're well incorporated; season to taste with salt and pepper.

8 Divide the chicken-vegetable mixture among the tortillas, leaving a 1- to 2-inch border. Drizzle 1 to 2 tablespoons of the sour cream–yogurt dressing over the filling. Transfer the remaining dressing to a small pitcher.

9 On 2 opposite sides of the tortilla, fold the tortilla ½ inch over the filling; then take one of the unfolded sides and start rolling to the end. Serve with the remaining sour cream–yogurt dressing.

Per serving: Calories 418 (From Fat 170); Fat 19g (Saturated 8g); Cholesterol 82mg; Sodium 491mg; Carbohydrate 34g (Dietary Fiber 2g); Protein 28g.

Tip: Warming the tortillas in the microwave for about 30 seconds just before you use them makes the tortillas easier to work with.

Chicken, Avocado, and Red Onion Salad

Prep time: 20–25 min plus chill time • **Yield:** 4 servings

Ingredients	*Directions*
2 tablespoons cider vinegar 2 tablespoons fresh lemon juice 1 teaspoon Dijon mustard ½ cup olive oil 2 tablespoons chopped fresh herbs, such as basil, tarragon, and/or marjoram (or 2 teaspoons dried herbs) 2 cloves garlic, minced Salt and pepper	*1* In a medium mixing bowl, whisk together the vinegar, lemon juice, and mustard. Slowly add the olive oil, whisking constantly to incorporate it. Stir in the herbs, garlic, and salt and pepper to taste.
3 cups cubed cooked chicken	*2* Add the chicken and toss well. Refrigerate for at least 30 minutes.
6 cups spinach, rinsed and torn into bite-size pieces 2 cups Boston lettuce, rinsed and torn into bite-size pieces	*3* Divide the spinach and lettuce among 4 plates. Place equal amounts of the chicken on top of the greens. Reserve any vinaigrette that remains in the bottom of the mixing bowl.
2 ripe avocados, peeled, pitted, and cut into ½-inch cubes ½ cup crumbled blue cheese (or other favorite cheese) 8 slices bacon, cooked and broken into small pieces 16 cherry tomatoes, stemmed and halved 1 small red onion, chopped	*4* Arrange an equal amount of the avocados, blue cheese, bacon, cherry tomatoes, and red onion around the chicken on each plate; drizzle the remaining marinade over everything.
	5 If desired, adjust seasoning with salt and pepper; serve immediately.

Per serving: Calories 747 (From Fat 531); Fat 59g (Saturated 14g); Cholesterol 117mg; Sodium 749mg; Carbohydrate 16g (Dietary Fiber 10g); Protein 43g.

Vary It! You can substitute pitted black olives for the cherry tomatoes. You can also add four chopped, hard-cooked eggs to the base of the greens.

Pork and Noodle Stir-Fry

Prep time: About 15 min • **Cook time:** About 15 min • **Yield:** 4 servings

Ingredients	*Directions*
½ **pound dried Chinese noodles, or thin spaghetti or linguine (broken in half)**	*1* Bring a large pot of lightly salted water to a boil; add the noodles and cook according to package directions. Drain and rinse noodles under cold water; drain again.
2 **teaspoons sesame oil**	
3 **tablespoons light soy sauce**	*2* Transfer the noodles to a medium mixing bowl; toss them with the sesame oil. Set aside.
1 **tablespoon dry or medium-dry sherry**	
2 **teaspoons cornstarch**	*3* In a medium mixing bowl, stir together 2 tablespoons of the soy sauce, the sherry, cornstarch, and brown sugar; add the pork and toss to mix well. Set aside.
1 **teaspoon packed brown sugar**	
2 **cups thinly sliced cooked pork (or raw pork)**	
2 **tablespoons vegetable oil**	*4* Place a wok or large skillet over high heat. Add the vegetable oil and heat until oil is hot but not smoking.
1 **tablespoon peeled and grated gingerroot**	*5* Add the gingerroot to the wok and stir just a few seconds, or until it browns lightly. Add the cabbage, carrots, chicken stock, green onions, garlic, jalapeño pepper (if desired), and pork with all of the marinade.
3 **cups thinly sliced napa cabbage, bok choy, or green cabbage**	
1 **cup thinly sliced or shredded carrot**	
½ **cup homemade or canned chicken stock**	*6* Cook, tossing the ingredients often, for 3 to 5 minutes, or until the vegetables are crisp-tender.
3 **thinly sliced green onions (white and green parts)**	*7* Remove the wok from the heat; add the noodles and toss thoroughly. Stir in the remaining tablespoon of soy sauce. Season to taste with salt and pepper. Sprinkle with the cilantro before serving.
1 **large clove garlic, peeled and minced**	
½ **jalapeño or red chile pepper, seeded and chopped (optional)**	
Salt and black pepper	
3 **tablespoons chopped cilantro**	

Per serving: *Calories 444 (From Fat 134); Fat 15g (Saturated 2g); Cholesterol 56mg; Sodium 813mg; Carbohydrate 53g (Dietary Fiber 10g); Protein 29g.*

Chapter 20

Summertime Soirees

*T*anktop and shorts: check. Bathing suit: check. Suntan lotion and bug spray: check. Charcoal and lighter fluid: check. Flip flops, boombox, and the big cooler filled with ice: check, check, and check!

Summer practically *means* party. Backyard barbecues, beach volleyball bonanzas, revelry around the pool . . . from Memorial Day to Labor Day, summer is filled with opportunities for outdoor gatherings and rife with the fixins to make them pop. Whether you're celebrating a national holiday or surrounding yourself with family and friends just for the fun of it, we have the perfect menu for a summer soiree in this chapter. So sit back and relax with a tall glass of lemonade, and leave the planning to us. (We're invited, right?)

Planning the Menu

Planning a party can sometimes overwhelm even the most experienced host, but here's a secret: *It's all about the menu.* Figure out what your menu will look like and when to make what, and everything else falls into place. That's because the menu is the heart of a party. It sets the tone and sometimes even the theme of the entire affair. While you may have some great ideas of your own, here's a perfect summertime menu to get you started. Of course you can tweak it for any theme you prefer:

✔ **The Perfect Hamburger:** Juicy, meat, and moist, these simple, savory burgers are sure to be a hit at your party. See Chapter 9 for the recipe.

✔ **Barbecued Chicken:** The smoky-sweet tang of the barbeque sauce is the perfect foil for other summer foods like mellow corn, creamy salads, and sweet fruit. See Chapter 9 for the recipe (and the color section for a photo).

✔ **Summer Veggie Burger:** This is a yummy treat for the vegetarians in the crowd or those who just want to keep it light. Tasty and toothsome with black beans and vegetables, this hearty burger will satisfy any appetite without a speck of meat. Make burgers no more than one inch thick and grill them for just a few minutes for crispy veggie perfection.

✔ **Perfect Corn on the Cob:** How hard can it be to cook the perfect ear of corn? Not so hard if you follow a few simple tips:

- Buy corn still in its husk, if possible, rather than the plastic-wrapped, fully shucked kind you often see in the store. It will taste fresher.

- Do not shuck the corn until close to cooking time. The silk and husk help keep the kernels moist. If you have to store corn, put it in a plastic bag and refrigerate.

- Don't overcook your corn. About 5 to 6 minutes, just until the corn is heated through, is plenty for young, tender ears. Older ears may take up to 10 minutes.

Our recipe calls for one ear of corn per person, but if you have more guests or you think your guests may eat more than one ear each, just add more to the pot. The cooking time remains the same.

✔ **All-American Coleslaw:** Not a huge coleslaw fan? Maybe that's because you think of coleslaw as the gloppy, overly sweetened stuff so often served at the delicatessen. Give this recipe a try. Our homemade coleslaw is not heavily coated with mayonnaise, which means that the flavors of the cabbage and other vegetables shine through.

To shred the cabbage, you may choose to use a tool called a *mandoline*. We explain what a mandoline is — and show you an illustration of how it works — in Chapter 4.

✔ **A few of your favorite quick salads and dips with chips:** Here are some suggestions that highlight summer's bounty; the recipes all appear in a list in Chapter 12:

- Tomato, Red Onion, and Basil Salad

- Cucumber-Dill Salad

- Cherry Tomato and Feta Cheese Salad

- Pasta Medley Salad

- Layered Cheese and Vegetable Salad

- Grilled Vegetable Platter with Fresh Pesto

- Fruit Salsa

- Three-Berry Dessert Salad

As American as . . . corn?

Americans in particular have always fancied themselves as corn connoisseurs. Every summer, on picnic tables across the land, culinary Olympic judges rate the current crop as if it were a high-dive competition. "This is pretty good — I give it an eight. But it's not like the ones we had last Labor Day." Soil, sun, and freshness are critical in producing superior corn. True corn-on-the-cob aficionados say that fresh corn should be picked as close to cooking time as possible. The sugar in corn quickly converts to starch after picking, making it lose its sweetness. However, the corn industry has made a lot of progress in recent years to develop strains of corn that hold their sweetness for several days.

Corn comes in colors ranging from almost white to deep yellow, and the ears and individual kernels can be big or small. Size and color have nothing to do with flavor. Corn in a store or market should look fresh. The husks should be green with no sign of dryness or splotching. The silk at the tip of the husk can be dark, but the silk inside should be moist.

✔ **Red, White, and Blue Berry Shortcake:** With its strawberries, blueberries, and whipped cream, this patriotic cake is especially well suited for a Memorial Day or Fourth of July celebration. Not only does it look patriotic (see the photo in the color section), but it's a light, refreshing dessert that won't make everybody feel weighed down in the heat of summer. You can make all the components of this cake — the berry mixture, the cream, and even the biscuits — a few hours before serving and then assemble them while someone is whisking the dinner dishes off the table. To make this recipe even easier, use easy-bake biscuits that come in a tube in the refrigerated section of the grocery store. (We won't tell.)

Mixing Fruity Drinks for Thirsty Crowds

Summer heat makes party guests thirsty! Every party needs some beverages, and if you're serving beer, wine, or fruity umbrella drinks, you also want some delicious drinks for kids and people who prefer nonalcoholic beverages.

Here are three great options that we provide recipes for in this chapter:

✔ **Strawberry Lemonade:** Classic lemonade becomes even more exciting when flavored with other fruit purées like strawberry and watermelon. Don't feel limited by the "strawberry" in the title. This lemonade, which is shown in the color section, tastes great made with any kind of fresh berry, or even without berries in its unadorned, homemade goodness. People can tell that this is the real thing, not something you mixed up from a powder, so expect this recipe to be popular. Lucky for you that it's so easy to make more! (For seconds, just skip the chilling stage and serve over plenty of ice.)

✔ **Summer Berry Smoothie:** Smoothies look great in a margarita glass and are just thick enough to hold that little paper umbrella. Smoothies can also be a meal in themselves. Thick and nutritious, smoothies use the whole fruit, not just the juice, so you get all the benefits of the fiber as well as the vitamins. They're filling and a great way to cool off in the middle of a hot summer day. They can also stand in for daiquiris, margaritas, piña coladas, or any other blender drink — or skip the yogurt and add the booze, if it's *that* kind of party! (But make a pitcher of virgin smoothies for those who choose to abstain.)

Using frozen fruit keeps the smoothie thick and creamy and doesn't dilute the drink the way a lot of ice would. Buy a bunch of bananas, peel them, and store them in individual plastic bags in the freezer so you can whip up smoothies anytime, or keep frozen strawberries handy. If you don't have any frozen fruit, use fresh fruit and add two cups of ice to the blender (instead of the specified one cup). Or, use frozen yogurt instead of regular yogurt. Our recipe later in the chapter makes four small servings as before-dinner drinks or a dessert. For nonparty times, when your smoothie is your entire meal (it makes a great breakfast, hold the liquor!), this recipe serves two.

✔ **Sparkling Sangria:** Good red wine and juicy fruits plus a little sparkle make for the perfect grown-up summer treat. Mix this up ahead of time and add the ginger ale at the last minute for a refreshing and sophisticated offering.

Preparing in Advance for a Stress-Free Party

For the menu in this chapter, you can (and should) do a lot of the work before the party starts. That way, when the guests arrive, you can actually visit and enjoy yourself — at least for a few minutes at a time. Here, we walk you through how to handle the menu in this chapter.

Two or three days before the party:

✔ Collect all your recipes. Figure out how many people you are likely to have at your party and how much of each recipe you will need to make. For example, if a salad serves 4 and you expect 16 people, you will quadruple the recipe. If you expect 12 people, how many burgers or pieces of chicken will they probably eat? (It's always best to overestimate just a little — you won't run out of food and, at worst, you'll have tasty leftovers.)

✔ Make your food shopping list based on your calculations, going through each recipe and checking to see which ingredients you need to buy.

✔ Decide what you need for beverages. Do you have enough pitchers, or a punch bowl? Will you supplement your homemade beverages with sodas, juice, or beer in a cooler? Will you serve drinks in glass or plastic? Will you need fruity garnishes for your drinks? What about little paper umbrellas?

✔ Consider your theme. What kind of décor would work? Think of a good centerpiece for the table — flowers and flags? Glitter and poppers? A big bowl of tropical fruit? Coconuts? Make a shopping list for decorations, as well as party favors (if you decide they're in order).

✔ Decide if you want music at your party, what to play, and how to play it. Make a playlist. Old-time rock 'n' roll? Calypso music? Reggae? Cool jazz? Disco? The music sets the mood.

✔ Clean out your refrigerator so you have room for all the party food.

✔ Go shopping and purchase everything you need: food, party supplies, décor. Don't forget ice!

The day before the party:

✔ Make the All-American Coleslaw. Cover and refrigerate.

✔ Make the Summer Veggie Burger mixture (but wait to shape it into patties). Cover and refrigerate.

✔ Make the Strawberry Lemonade and the Sparkling Sangria (minus the ginger ale). Cover and refrigerate.

✔ Make the biscuits for the shortcake. Cover.

The morning of your party:

✔ Assemble all the salads except the Grilled Vegetable Platter with Fresh Pesto. (You can make the pesto, but the grilled vegetables have to wait.) Cover and refrigerate.

✔ Cut the vegetables for the Grilled Vegetable Platter with Fresh Pesto.

✔ Husk the corn.

✔ Clean and core the fruit for the shortcakes.

✔ Decorate the house, yard, and/or food table for the party.

One hour before the party:

- ✔ Take your meat out of the refrigerator and prepare it for grilling.
- ✔ Form the Summer Veggie Burger patties.
- ✔ Put cans and bottles of drinks in a cooler full of ice.
- ✔ Set out the following items on the party table: Bags of chips, platters, plates, silverware, napkins, and the centerpiece.

As guests arrive:

- ✔ Fire up the grill.
- ✔ Turn on the music!
- ✔ Set out the salads, burger buns, and condiments for the burgers.
- ✔ Put up the water to boil the corn. Drop in the corn and set out the salt, pepper, and butter.
- ✔ Grill the vegetables for the Grilled Vegetable Platter first, and then grill the meat and veggie burgers.
- ✔ Assemble the Grilled Vegetable Platter with Fresh Pesto.

Right before serving:

- ✔ Put out the pitchers of beverages, glasses, and a big bowl of ice with tongs.
- ✔ Make the whipped cream and assemble the shortcakes.

Throughout the party:

- ✔ Keep an eye on the table and see what needs to be replenished — Chips? Fruit? Silverware? People's drinks?
- ✔ Smile, greet people, and have fun. It's your party, too!

Summer Veggie Burger

Prep time: About 25 min • **Cook time:** About 8 min • **Yield:** 4 servings

Ingredients	*Directions*
1 15-ounce can drained and rinsed black or white beans	*1* Put the beans in a mixing bowl and mash them thoroughly with a fork. Stir in all the remaining ingredients except the olive oil, combining well. Let the mixture sit for 5 minutes.
1 medium yellow onion, peeled and minced	
½ cup grated zucchini or yellow summer squash	*2* Get your hands wet and form the mixture into 4 patties. Put them on a plate and let them sit for 3 or 4 more minutes while you heat the skillet.
½ cup breadcrumbs	
1 egg, lightly beaten	*3* Heat the skillet on medium and add the olive oil. Put the patties in the skillet and cook for 5 minutes. Carefully flip them with a hard spatula and cook for 3 more minutes, or until the surface is golden brown and crispy. Serve warm on whole grain buns.
¼ cup ketchup	
1 clove garlic, peeled and minced	
1 tablespoon minced fresh basil or cilantro	
1 tablespoon chili powder	
1 teaspoon minced jalapeno pepper (optional)	
1 teaspoon mustard	
½ teaspoon salt	
¼ teaspoon black pepper	
1 tablespoon olive oil	
Whole grain buns, for serving	

Per serving: Calories 311 (From Fat 76); Fat 9g (Saturated 1g); Cholesterol 53mg; Sodium 989mg; Carbohydrate 49g (Dietary Fiber 9g); Protein 12g.

Tip: After Step 1, you can put the mixture, covered, in the refrigerator up to 24 hours. Bring the mixture back to room temperature before cooking.

Perfect Corn on the Cob

Prep time: 5 min • **Cook time:** 5 to 6 min • **Yield:** 8 servings

Ingredients	Directions
8 ears fresh sweet corn	**1** Bring a large pot of water to a boil. While waiting for the water to boil, husk the corn.
Salt and pepper	
½ cup (1 stick) butter	**2** When the water boils, carefully drop the ears, one at a time, into the pot. Cover and boil for 5 to 6 minutes.
	3 Using tongs, remove the ears from the water and set them on a plate to drain. Serve immediately with salt, pepper, and 1 tablespoon of butter per ear.

Per serving: Calories 178 (From Fat 112); Fat 12g (Saturated 7g); Cholesterol 31mg; Sodium 88mg; Carbohydrate 17g (Dietary Fiber 2g); Protein 3g.

Vary It! Flavor the butter with assorted spices and herbs. For example, you can soften the butter to room temperature and mix in a little lemon or lime juice, chopped cilantro or chervil, or chopped fresh basil.

All-American Coleslaw

Prep time: 15 to 20 min plus chill time • **Yield:** 8 servings

Ingredients	*Directions*
1 medium head green cabbage (about 2 pounds), tough outer leaves removed	*1* Using a large chef's knife, halve the cabbage crosswise; cut out the hard, solid core; and then quarter the remaining chunks of leaves.
4 carrots, peeled and grated	*2* Slice the cabbage, starting at one end, as thinly as possible. Then chop the slices crosswise to make short lengths. (Or chop cabbage in a food processor using the shredding blade, or with a mandoline.)
2 red bell peppers, cored, seeded, and diced	
1 medium yellow onion, diced	*3* Place the cabbage, carrots, bell peppers, and onion in a large bowl.
1⅓ cups mayonnaise, or to taste	
⅓ cup sugar	*4* In a small bowl, using a wire whisk or fork to blend, combine the mayonnaise, sugar, vinegar, and salt and black pepper to taste.
⅓ cup cider vinegar	
Salt and black pepper	
	5 Pour the dressing over the cabbage mixture and toss thoroughly to coat. Taste to see whether it needs more salt and pepper.
	6 Cover the bowl with plastic wrap and refrigerate for 2 to 3 hours before serving to blend the flavors, stirring occasionally.

Per serving: Calories 360 (From Fat 263); Fat 29g (Saturated 4g); Cholesterol 22mg; Sodium 329mg; Carbohydrate 23g (Dietary Fiber 5g); Protein 3g.

Tip: Try using lowfat or nonfat mayonnaise to lower the calorie and fat content of this recipe.

Red, White, and Blue Berry Shortcake

Prep time: 40 min • **Cook time:** About 15 min • **Yield:** 8 servings

Ingredients	Directions
2 pints strawberries, rinsed and hulled	*1* Preheat the oven to 400 degrees.
2 cups blueberries, rinsed and drained	*2* Set aside the 8 best strawberries for garnish. Crush half of the remaining strawberries with a fork or the back of a spoon; cut the rest in half the long way, from core to tip.
1⁄3 cup (or more, to taste) plus 3½ tablespoons granulated sugar	
1 tablespoon Cointreau (optional)	*3* In a medium mixing bowl, combine the sliced and crushed strawberries, blueberries, 1⁄3 cup granulated sugar, and, if desired, the Cointreau. Taste the fruit mixture and add more sugar if necessary. Refrigerate until ready to assemble the shortcake.
1¼ cups heavy cream	
2 tablespoons confectioner's sugar (or more, to taste)	
½ teaspoon vanilla extract	*4* In a bowl, using an electric mixer, whip the cream with the confectioner's sugar and vanilla until stiff. Cover and refrigerate until you're ready to assemble the shortcake.
2⅔ cups self-rising cake flour	
¼ teaspoon salt	
10 tablespoons chilled butter, cut into small pieces	*5* In a large mixing bowl, combine the flour, the remaining 3½ tablespoons granulated sugar, and salt. Cut the butter into the flour mixture, using two knives or a pastry blender, until the mixture resembles coarse breadcrumbs. Work quickly so the butter doesn't melt.
1 cup plus 1 to 2 tablespoons milk	

6 Make a well in the center of the flour mixture and add 1 cup milk. Mix gently with a fork, rubber spatula, or wooden spoon just until most of the dry ingredients are moistened. Do not overmix.

7 Drop the dough, in eight equal portions 1 to 2 inches apart, onto an ungreased baking sheet. Lightly brush the tops of the rounds with the remaining 1 to 2 table-spoons of milk.

8 Bake the biscuits on the center rack of the oven for 15 to 17 minutes, or until golden brown. Transfer to a wire rack to cool. Finished shortcakes may be served warm or cold.

9 Using a serrated knife, carefully slice the shortcakes in half crosswise. Transfer each bottom half to an individual serving plate. Spread a generous dollop of whipped cream over the bottom of each biscuit; top with about ⅓ cup of the fruit mixture. Cover with the other half of the shortcakes. Spoon over more cream and berries, and drizzle with any berry juices that have accumulated. Garnish each serving with a reserved whole strawberry. Serve immediately.

Per serving: Calories 522 (From Fat 269); Fat 30g (Saturated 18g); Cholesterol 94mg; Sodium 621mg; Carbohydrate 59g (Dietary Fiber 4g); Protein 7g.

Strawberry Lemonade

Prep time: 10 to 15 min plus chill time • **Yield:** 8 servings

Ingredients	Directions
1½ cups fresh lemon juice, strained of pits (9 to 10 large lemons)	*1* Combine the lemon juice, sugar, and water in a large pitcher. Stir well.
1½ cups sugar 6 cups water 1 pint strawberries, rinsed and hulled	*2* Place the hulled strawberries in a blender or food processor; add a little of the lemonade from the pitcher, and blend until smooth.
Lemon slices for garnish (optional)	*3* Pour the strawberries into the lemonade, stir, and chill for 2 hours. Stir well before serving.
Mint sprigs for garnish (optional)	*4* Pour into ice-filled glasses, garnishing each, if desired, with a lemon slice or a sprig of fresh mint.

Per serving: Calories 168 (From Fat 1); Fat 0g (Saturated 0g); Cholesterol 0mg; Sodium 1mg; Carbohydrate 44g (Dietary Fiber 1g); Protein 0g.

Vary It! To make classic lemonade, simply omit the strawberries. Or try other fruit flavors, such as watermelon (use 3 cups of watermelon chunks with seeds removed) or peaches (use 2 cups of fresh peach slices).

Summer Berry Smoothie

Prep time: About 15 min • **Yield:** 4 servings

Ingredients	*Directions*
1 cup fresh (or frozen) berries, such as strawberries, blueberries, raspberries, or blackberries	*1* Combine all the ingredients in a blender.
1 fresh or frozen peeled banana	*2* Blend on high until smooth. Add more liquid if the smoothie is too thick. Serve immediately.
1 cup vanilla yogurt (nonfat, lowfat, or regular)	
1 cup ice	
½ cup orange juice, lemonade, or milk, plus more for thinning if necessary	

Per serving: Calories 118 (From Fat 3); Fat 0g (Saturated 0g); Cholesterol 1mg; Sodium 44mg; Carbohydrate 26g (Dietary Fiber 2g); Protein 4g.

Vary It! Try adding a teaspoon of instant coffee, a dash of cinnamon, 2 tablespoons of chocolate or maple syrup, or some crushed peppermint leaves. If daiquiris and margaritas are more your style, eliminate the banana and yogurt, increase the orange juice or lemonade to 1 cup (don't use milk), and add 1/2 cup (or so) of white rum, tequila, or vodka and a squeeze of fresh lime juice. Serve in wine glasses or margarita/daiquiri glasses. Now it's a party!

Sparkling Sangria

Prep time: About 5 min plus chill time • **Yield:** 6 to 8 servings

Ingredients	*Directions*
1 bottle red wine	**1** In a pitcher, combine wine and orange, lemon, and lime slices, and berries. Chill overnight in the refrigerator.
1 orange, sliced	
1 lemon, sliced	
1 lime, sliced	**2** Just before serving, stir in ginger ale and orange liqueur or brandy. Pour into wine glasses and garnish with a slice of orange.
1 cup any kind of fresh or frozen berries	
2 cups ginger ale	
¼ cup orange liqueur (such as Grand Marnier, Cointreau, or triple sec) or brandy	
Orange slices for garnish	

Per serving: Calories 175 (From Fat 1); Fat 0g (Saturated 0g); Cholesterol 0mg; Sodium 14mg; Carbohydrate 20g (Dietary Fiber 2g); Protein 1g.

Vary It! Sangria doesn't have to be made with red wine; you can also make it with your favorite white wine or sparkling wine. If you choose red, consider a Spanish wine, such as Tempranillo, Garnacha, or something from Rioja. But any red wine you enjoy will do!

Chapter 21

Feeding Holiday Hordes: Festive Winter Menus

In This Chapter

▶ Previewing your holiday menu
▶ Starting out with delicious dips
▶ Roasting the perfect holiday turkey
▶ Serving up stuffing and veggies
▶ Sweet ending: Praline pumpkin pie

*I*t's easy to lose your cool when a mob of salivating relatives comes marching your way for a holiday dinner. Don't panic. Take this approach: Rustle up only dishes you have made before (even better, several times); have on hand a generous selection of libations; and serve the meal 45 minutes late — by then they'll have lowered their threshold of satisfaction.

The challenging part of holiday entertainment is not so much the quantity of food you have to churn out, but the variety. When you consider several appetizers, four or five side dishes, a main course (in this case turkey), and a couple desserts, it can be intimidating to say the least.

If you try to do everything at once, you're courting a disaster. Thankfully, many of the dishes in our suggested menu can be assembled beforehand. In this chapter, we show you how to tackle a holiday menu.

Planning the Menu

Just as you would not serve sorbet with juicy tenderloin of beef, you should not pair clashing recipes at the holiday meal. Think heavy with light, full flavored with refreshing, starchy with crisp, even sweet with sharp. Pairing foods the right way is easier than it sounds, even with a sprawling holiday spread. Here is just one suggestion for a winning menu:

- Warm Artichoke-Spinach Dip
- Apple Curry Dip
- Roasted Turkey with Cornbread, Sausage, and Apple Stuffing
- Madeira Pan Gravy
- Fresh Cranberry-Orange Relish with Walnuts
- Green Beans with Shallot Butter
- Homemade Mashed Potatoes
- Rum-Baked Sweet Potatoes
- Praline Pumpkin Pie
- Eggnog
- Warm Red Wine and Orange Punch

Except for the Homemade Mashed Potatoes, which you find in Chapter 5, the recipes for the rest of this menu appear in this chapter.

Getting Yourself Organized

Two days of preparation should be plenty to pull off this menu, provided you don't watch too much daytime TV. Most items can be prepared in advance. In this section, we walk you through what to do, and when, so you aren't too stressed when guests start arriving.

For starters, here are four items you can prepare either two or three days in advance of your holiday meal:

- Cornbread for the stuffing
- Fresh Cranberry-Orange Relish with Walnuts (but wait to stir in the walnuts until just before serving)
- Rum-Baked Sweet Potatoes
- Praline Pumpkin Pie

The day before your big meal, do these tasks:

- ✔ Wash and trim the green beans, wrap them in a paper towel, and seal them in a plastic bag.
- ✔ Make the shallot butter for the green bean recipe.
- ✔ Make and chill the dips.

On the morning of the dinner do the following:

- ✔ Make the Cornbread, Sausage, and Apple Stuffing.
- ✔ Roast the turkey.
- ✔ Peel the potatoes for your Homemade Mashed Potatoes and cover them with cold water.

Two hours before guests arrive, do this:

- ✔ Make the Eggnog.
- ✔ Make the Warm Red Wine and Orange Punch.
- ✔ Whip the cream for the pie.

After you remove the turkey from the oven, let it rest, covered with aluminum foil, and tackle the final tasks:

- ✔ Make the Madeira Pan Gravy.
- ✔ Cook the Green Beans with Shallots.
- ✔ Make the mashed potatoes.

All about Turkey

Turkey is an ideal main course for entertaining a crowd, but how do you choose the right one, and what's the best method for cooking it? Here are some important turkey tips:

- ✔ Most supermarket turkeys are frozen; fresh ones are better, so it's worth finding one. Here's why: When a turkey is frozen, its juices turn to ice crystals; when thawed, these crystals disrupt the protein cell membranes in the flesh and cause some of the juices to leak out — that's the reddish stuff you see in the packaging when you open it. A frozen turkey is never as moist as a fresh one, which is why many frozen turkeys are injected with a broth/sugar solution to replace the lost moisture.
- ✔ If you buy a frozen turkey, let it defrost in the refrigerator; allow about 24 hours for every 4 to 5 pounds.

✔ When you're trying to decide what size turkey to buy, consider that an 18- to 20-pound bird feeds 14 or more. A 25-pound bird could easily serve 20 or more. (Think roughly 1 pound of turkey per person.) Also, consider the dimensions of your oven so you don't find yourself charging the bird with a kitchen stool attempting to force it inside.

✔ Basting a turkey during roasting gives the bird a nice golden skin; it does not, however, permeate the meat nor does it create a crisp skin.

✔ If your turkey starts to get too brown during cooking, cover it loosely with aluminum foil.

✔ Check out Table 21-1 for roasting times for a fresh or thawed turkey at 325 degrees. These times are approximate and should be used only as a guide; factors that can alter cooking time include the accuracy of your oven, the temperature of the bird when it goes into the oven, and the number of times the oven door is opened during roasting. Always use a meat thermometer to be sure of the temperature.

✔ If you don't want to stuff your turkey, you can cook the stuffing in a casserole dish in the oven. Doing so decreases the turkey's cooking time and diminishes the chance of salmonella bacteria growing in the cavity. If you want to stuff the bird, be sure to keep the turkey well chilled before stuffing. Add the stuffing just before baking.

✔ Another stuffing tip: Pack it loosely in the turkey cavity for quicker cooking and better texture.

✔ Always test the stuffing for doneness. It should register 160 degrees on an instant-read thermometer. If the bird is done but your stuffing is not, remove the turkey from the oven, spoon the stuffing into a buttered casserole dish, and continue to bake it (as the bird rests).

Table 21-1	Turkey Roasting Chart	
Weight	**Cooking Time (Unstuffed)**	**Cooking Time (Stuffed)**
8 to 12 pounds	2¾ to 3 hours	3 to 3½ hours
12 to 14 pounds	3 to 3¾ hours	3¼ to 4 hours
14 to 18 pounds	3¾ to 4¼ hours	4 to 4½ hours
20 to 24 pounds	4½ to 5 hours	4¾ to 5¼ hours

You can season a turkey in all sorts of ways to add flavor and color to the skin. For example, mix 2 tablespoons molasses or maple syrup with 2 tablespoons reduced-sodium soy sauce; baste the turkey with this mixture, along with the pan juices, during the last hour of cooking — but no sooner! Never baste a turkey with a sugar-based mixture for more than an hour or the sugar will burn.

Turkey roasting resources

The following organizations are available to provide information about turkey roasting — in case you need a little help around the holidays:

✔ **The National Turkey Federation:** Visit www.eatturkey.com for lots of recipes, as well as information about purchasing, storing, and cooking a turkey. The site even gives tips for using leftovers.

✔ **The USDA Meat and Poultry Hotline:** Visit the USDA on the Web at www.fsis.

usda.gov for food and safety tips about meat, poultry, and eggs. You can also call toll-free at 1-888-674-6854.

✔ **Butterball Turkey:** Visit Butterball online at www.butterball.com for recipes, tips, and a list of the ten most frequently asked questions, along with the answers, of course! Or you can call 1-800-BUTTERBALL (800-288-8372).

Of course, roasting a turkey means you have to carve it — a potential source of confusion for some people. Check out our illustrated instructions in Chapter 4, which walk you through the carving process, or visit www.dummies. com/go/carvingturkey to find a helpful video.

Turkey meat, especially the dryer parts from the breast, calls for a great gravy. We offer a recipe later in the chapter for Madeira Pan Gravy. *Madeira* is an earthy sweet wine from the island of the same name, which is part of Portugal. If you don't have the wine, you can substitute chicken broth.

For an attractive presentation, garnish your turkey platter with fruits and other produce. Try a heap of fresh cranberries, piles of leafy greens or fresh herbs (such as tarragon and thyme branches), a few kumquats or orange slices, or red and green grapes dusted in sugar.

Teasing the Palate with Fresh Dips

As a rule, you don't serve filling hors d'oeuvres, like aged cheeses or puff pastries filled with meat, before a big meal. We favor light, tasty starters like fresh raw vegetables and dips. Later in the chapter, we present recipes for two dips that can be jazzed up in many ways.

✔ **Warm Artichoke-Spinach Dip:** This classic dip is perfect to tantalize everyone's palate for the big meal. Serve it in hollowed-out round sourdough bread. Or use tortilla chips, good crackers, or thin toasted slices of French bread.

✔ **Apple Curry Dip:** This unusual dip packs a surprising combination of flavors: the tart sweetness of green apples and the exotic spiciness of curry powder. Serve it with good crackers or raw vegetables such as carrots, celery, and cucumber slices.

Scrumptious Stuffings and Sides

Some people like stuffing even better than the turkey. Here's some advice:

✔ **Whenever making stuffing for your roasted turkey, make sure that the bread you use is very dry, even stale.** Two-day-old bread (left out uncovered) yields the best result; fresh, moist bread can create gummy stuffing. Just be sure to slice the bread before you dry it, or it can get too hard to work with.

To dry out fresh bread, place slices or cubes on a baking sheet and leave them uncovered a day or two, turning them now and then. Or dry out the bread on a baking sheet in a 200-degree oven, turning frequently.

✔ **You need about ¾ to 1 cup of stuffing per pound of bird.** This amount also leaves you with delicious leftovers.

✔ **When making stuffing, over mixing and packing it too densely into the bird's cavity can cause it to cook more slowly and crumble when served.** If you're not baking it inside the bird's cavity, bake your stuffing in a well-buttered, covered baking dish for about 45 minutes. (You can remove the cover for the last ten minutes of baking to give it a crisp crust.) Try to time the cooking so that the stuffing comes out of the oven as the bird is being carved.

✔ **Drizzle a little chicken stock, white wine, or turkey pan drippings over the stuffing for extra flavor and moisture.**

In our recipe for Cornbread, Sausage, and Apple Stuffing later in the chapter, we use *poultry seasoning,* which is a commercial blend of ground sage, rosemary, thyme, marjoram, savory, and salt. However, you can experiment and substitute any of your favorite herbs. Be sure the poultry seasoning — or any seasoning in a jar for that matter — is not over-the-hill. One telltale sign is a faded label with a promotional quote like "Eleanor Roosevelt's favorite!" Dried spices can lose potency within a year of opening.

Stuffing cooked separately from the turkey may need a little extra moisture. The stuffing in our recipe is kept moist with pork sausage, eggs, and an assortment of fruits and vegetables. However, if after 30 minutes in the oven the stuffing becomes a little dry, simply add a little more chicken stock or warm water and return it to the oven to finish baking.

Cornbread mixes and cornbread muffins are often too moist and sweet to use as a base for turkey stuffing. Our Cornbread for Stuffing recipe later in the chapter holds its shape when combined with the other ingredients. You can make it ahead of time and freeze it, or wrap it and keep it in the refrigerator for a few days.

Looking for another accompaniment to your roasted turkey? Be sure to check out our recipe for Fresh Cranberry-Orange Relish with Walnuts. We jazz it up by adding some Cointreau or Grand Marnier (sweet orange-flavored liqueurs), but they're optional. So are the walnuts, but they add interesting texture.

Don't forget the mashed potatoes (see Chapter 5) so you can use that delicious gravy. Here are two other favorites that round out the meal nicely:

- ✔ **Green Beans with Shallots:** This recipe is simple and elegant; it also lends a nice green color to your menu, which is dominated by shades of orange. And while several of the other side dishes are sweet, this bean dish is savory. You can make it at the last minute provided you have already trimmed the beans and minced the shallots.

- ✔ **Rum-Baked Sweet Potatoes:** Remember that bottle of dark rum you bought at the duty-free store in Barbados? If you're like us, that bottle is sitting, unopened, somewhere around the house. Well, go find it! You finally have an excuse to taste it.

  These terrific sweet potatoes can be baked very quickly — you can put them in the oven as you're removing the turkey to rest. The sweet potatoes are first parboiled (which softens them slightly and makes the second cooking much quicker) for about 15 minutes, and then baked for about 20 minutes. (These potatoes are particularly tasty accompanied by a frosty Mai Tai.)

Last Man Standing: Holiday Desserts

One American dessert that is fitting from the first blush of autumn through the chills of Christmas is pumpkin pie. On the difficulty meter, it comes in low. The most common failing is having the cooked center collapse. This simply means your pie filling was not thick enough. If your pumpkin mix looks too thin, beef it up by stirring in a tablespoon or more of cornstarch.

In this chapter we offer a great variation on this classic: Praline Pumpkin Pie. It features a pecan layer on top of the crust that is a nice contrast to the semisweet pumpkin filling. To make this recipe, you first need a crust, of course! You have two options: Make one yourself by following our recipe and illustrated instructions in Chapter 10, or buy a frozen shell. A deep-dish pie plate is best for this recipe because the filling comes right to the top of a regular pie plate (and you want to avoid spillage). So you're better off taking the time to make your own crust.

If your dinner is for 10 or more people, we suggest making two pies. Perhaps make one pumpkin and one apple; for a homemade apple pie recipe, see Chapter 10. If your family likes a wider variety of desserts, you can find plenty of choices in Chapters 10 and 15 or in *Desserts For Dummies,* by Bill Yosses, Alison Yates, and Bryan Miller, or *Baking For Dummies,* by Emily Nolan (both published by Wiley).

Warming Up with Holiday Libations

You're trashing your diet for the holidays anyway, so why not really blow it off with a rich, rum-laced eggnog? As you'll see in our recipe later in the chapter, eggnog can be made delightfully frothy by folding in beaten egg whites — without adding significant calories.

Eggnog is traditionally made with raw eggs. Because of widespread concerns over possible salmonella poisoning, we give you a great recipe for eggnog made with eggs that are cooked long enough to eliminate the problem but not the flavor. This recipe is adapted from one created by Alton Brown of the television Food Network.

It's a good idea to pair a rich, cool drink like eggnog with something lighter and warmer, such as our terrific Warm Red Wine and Orange Punch in this section. It could not be easier, and the combination of fruity red wine, orange, cinnamon, and clove makes for a sure holiday winner. You can serve it warm, or mix it a couple of hours in advance and chill until serving.

Warm Artichoke-Spinach Dip

Prep time: About 15 min • **Cook time:** About 20 min • **Yield:** 12 servings

Ingredients	Directions
2 boxes (10 ounces each) frozen spinach, thawed	**1** Preheat the oven to 350 degrees.
2 tablespoons butter	**2** Put the thawed spinach in a colander and cover with paper towels. Squeeze to remove as much moisture as possible. Set aside.
¼ medium yellow onion, minced	
2 cloves garlic, peeled and minced	**3** In a medium saucepan, melt the butter over medium-high heat. Sauté the onion and garlic until the onion is soft and translucent but not brown, about 5 minutes.
2 tablespoons flour	
1½ cups whole milk or half-and-half	
3 tablespoons canned chicken broth	**4** Add the flour and cook, stirring, for 2 minutes.
1 teaspoon freshly squeezed lemon juice	**5** Slowly whisk in the milk or half-and-half and the chicken broth. Bring to a boil and then remove from the heat. Immediately add the lemon juice, Tabasco sauce, salt, and Romano cheese. Stir to combine and then set aside.
½ teaspoon Tabasco sauce	
¼ teaspoon salt	
½ cup grated Romano cheese	**6** Combine the sour cream, Monterey Jack cheese, tomato, artichokes, and spinach. Fold into the warm cream mixture and pour the dip into an ovenproof casserole dish.
⅓ cup lowfat sour cream	
⅔ cup shredded Monterey Jack cheese	
1 large ripe plum tomato, cored, seeded, and chopped	**7** Bake in the oven for 10 minutes, or until warmed through but not browned. Serve immediately.
1 can (12 ounces) artichoke hearts (not marinated), drained and coarsely chopped	

Per serving: Calories 96 (From Fat 55); Fat 6g (Saturated 4g); Cholesterol 19mg; Sodium 231mg; Carbohydrate 6g (Dietary Fiber 2g); Protein 5g.

Vary It! Add more spice to this dish by upping the amount of Tabasco sauce, or make it milder by eliminating the Tabasco altogether. If you do the latter, try adding ½ teaspoon dried dill or 1 tablespoon fresh, chopped cilantro leaves.

Apple Curry Dip

Prep time: 10 min • **Yield:** 4 servings

Ingredients	Directions
1 Granny Smith apple, peeled, cored, and grated	**1** In a bowl, stir together the apple, mayonnaise, yogurt, curry powder, and salt and pepper to taste.
½ cup mayonnaise	
½ cup lowfat plain yogurt	**2** Transfer the mixture to a small serving bowl and chill until served. Garnish with the parsley before serving.
2 to 3 teaspoons curry powder, according to taste	
Salt and pepper	
2 tablespoons chopped parsley (as a garnish)	

Per serving: Calories 239 (From Fat 204); Fat 23g (Saturated 4g); Cholesterol 18mg; Sodium 324mg; Carbohydrate 8g (Dietary Fiber 1g); Protein 2g.

Vary It! Not a big fan of curry? You can make a sweeter version of this dip. Use 1 cup yogurt instead of using half mayonnaise. Replace the curry powder with ½ teaspoon ground cinnamon, ¼ teaspoon ground nutmeg, and 2 tablespoons honey. Skip the salt, pepper, and parsley, and garnish with a drizzle of honey and a few cinnamon sticks. Serve with slices of fruit and sticks of carrots and celery.

Roasted Turkey

Prep time: 15 min • **Cook time:** About 3 hr • **Yield:** 12 servings

Ingredients	*Directions*
1 fresh or thawed frozen turkey (about 12 pounds) **1 medium yellow onion, quartered** **2 carrots, peeled and quartered** **2 large cloves garlic, crushed** **2 tablespoons vegetable oil** **Salt and pepper**	*1* Preheat the oven to 325 degrees, with the oven rack on the lowest rung. Set a wire roasting rack in a large roasting pan. *2* Remove the giblets and neck from the turkey cavity and reserve for gravy (see the next recipe). Discard the liver. Remove any excess fat from the turkey. Rinse the turkey inside and out with cold water and pat dry. *3* Place in the turkey cavity the onion, carrots, and garlic. Tie the legs together with kitchen string. If desired, bend the wing tips back and fold them underneath the turkey. *4* Set the turkey, breast side up, on the roasting rack. Rub the turkey all over with the oil. Season generously with salt and pepper. *5* Add 1 cup of water to the roasting pan. If using a meat thermometer, insert it into the thickest part of the thigh, close to the body, without touching any bone. *6* Roast for about 3 to 3¼ hours, or until the thigh temperature registers 180 degrees. Add another ½ cup water to the roasting pan if it gets dry. To brown the turkey evenly, turn the pan laterally midway through the roasting. Check for doneness during the last 30 minutes of roasting, and baste with the pan drippings 2 to 3 times during the last hour. *7* Remove the turkey from the oven, transfer it to a carving board, and cover loosely with aluminum foil, letting it rest for 20 minutes while you make gravy. *8* Remove the vegetables from the cavity and discard. Carve the turkey and serve with the Madeira Pan Gravy.

Per serving (without gravy): *Calories 404 (From Fat 122); Fat 14g (Saturated 4g); Cholesterol 171mg; Sodium 206mg; Carbohydrate 0g (Dietary Fiber 0g); Protein 66g.*

Madeira Pan Gravy

Prep time: 10–15 min • **Cook time:** About 35 min • **Yield:** 12 servings

Ingredients

4 cups canned chicken broth

Turkey giblets (liver discarded) and neck

1 medium yellow onion, peeled and quartered

2 carrots, quartered

2 stalks celery, quartered

1 bay leaf

Turkey pan drippings

½ cup Madeira (optional)

3 tablespoons flour

Salt and pepper

Directions

1 In a medium saucepan, combine the chicken broth, turkey giblets and neck, onion, carrots, celery, and bay leaf. Cover and bring to a boil. Reduce the heat to low and simmer, partially covered, for 30 minutes.

2 Strain the stock through cheesecloth or a fine sieve into a large measuring cup. You should have 1½ to 2 cups. If you have less, add water or chicken broth. Refrigerate.

3 When the broth is chilled, skim and discard any fat that rises to the surface.

4 Pour the drippings from the turkey roasting pan into a 2-cup glass measuring cup or a degreaser. Spoon off and discard all but 3 tablespoons of fat from the drippings. Reserve the fat in a small cup.

5 Strain the skimmed drippings through a fine sieve into a second 2-cup glass measuring cup or bowl. Set aside.

6 Add the Madeira to the roasting pan and cook over medium-high heat, stirring and scraping the bottom for about 1 minute; strain this into the cup holding the skimmed pan drippings.

7 Add the 3 tablespoons of reserved fat to the roasting pan. Set two burners to medium heat under the pan and heat the fat. Add the flour to the pan and stir constantly with a wire whisk, about 1 to 2 minutes, to blend the flour into the fat. The mixture should turn golden brown.

8 Slowly whisk in the Madeira pan drippings; whisk for about 1 minute, stirring and scraping the bottom of the pan. Continue whisking and gradually add the turkey stock, 1 cup at a time. Use only enough stock to reach a gravy consistency. Season to taste with salt and pepper.

Per serving: Calories 102 (From Fat 52); Fat 6g (Saturated 2g); Cholesterol 32mg; Sodium 392mg; Carbohydrate 2g (Dietary Fiber 0g); Protein 10g.

Cornbread, Sausage, and Apple Stuffing

Prep time: 20 min • **Cook time:** About 1 hr • **Yield:** 12 servings

Ingredients	*Directions*
7 to 8 tablespoons butter	**1** In a large skillet, melt 2 tablespoons of the butter over medium-high heat. Add the sausage and cook until browned, about 5 minutes, stirring frequently to break it up. Using a slotted spoon, remove the sausage to a large mixing bowl.
1 pound bulk pork sausage (mild or hot, to taste)	
1 large yellow onion, diced	
1 cup diced celery	**2** Add to the skillet 4 more tablespoons of the butter with the onion, celery, red bell pepper, and, if desired, the hot peppers. Cook, stirring occasionally, about 4 to 5 minutes, or until the vegetables are cooked but still a little firm. Stir the vegetables into the sausage.
1 large red bell pepper, cored, seeded, and diced	
2 hot chile peppers or jalapeño peppers, seeded and diced (optional)	
8 cups cornbread cubes (see the next recipe)	**3** Add the cornbread and French bread cubes, apples, parsley, poultry seasoning, sugar, and salt and pepper to taste; toss well.
4 cups stale French bread, cut into ⅓- to ½-inch cubes	
2 Golden Delicious apples, peeled, cored, and cut into small cubes	**4** In a small bowl, whisk together the chicken stock and eggs; add this to the stuffing, about 1 cup at a time, stirring well. Add enough egg-broth mixture to moisten the stuffing so that it holds together when lightly pressed between the palms of your hands.
⅓ cup chopped parsley	
2 teaspoons poultry seasoning, or to taste	**5** Transfer the stuffing into a well-buttered baking dish with a lid; dot with the remaining 1 to 2 tablespoons of butter. Cover and bake at 325 degrees for 45 to 55 minutes, or until heated through.
1 teaspoon sugar	
Salt and black pepper	
1 can (14½ ounces) chicken stock, or 2 cups homemade stock	
2 eggs, lightly beaten	

Per serving: Calories 360 (From Fat 204); Fat 23g (Saturated 8g); Cholesterol 86mg; Sodium 675mg; Carbohydrate 31g (Dietary Fiber 2g); Protein 9g.

Tip: If you can't find bulk pork sausage, purchase sausage links and remove the casings.

Vary It! You can substitute some white wine for some of the chicken stock to add more flavor. Instead of using poultry seasoning, substitute 2 to 3 tablespoons fresh chopped herbs, such as sage, marjoram, thyme, or any combination.

Cornbread for Stuffing

Prep time: 5 min • **Cook time:** 20 min • **Yield:** 8 cups of cubes

Ingredients	*Directions*
1 cup yellow cornmeal	*1* Preheat the oven to 425 degrees.
1 cup flour	
1 tablespoon plus 1 teaspoon baking powder	*2* In a large bowl, combine the cornmeal, flour, baking powder, sugar, and salt; stir to mix.
2 teaspoons sugar	*3* With a wire whisk, stir in the buttermilk, egg, and oil; beat just until the mixture is combined — do not overmix.
½ teaspoon salt	
1 cup buttermilk	
1 egg	*4* Spread the batter in a buttered 8- or 9-inch square baking pan. Bake for 20 minutes, or until the top of the bread springs back when touched. Cool in the pan on a wire rack.
⅓ cup corn oil or vegetable oil	
	5 If you're not using the cornbread right away, cut the bread into big pieces, wrap tightly, and refrigerate until ready to make the stuffing. Slice the cornbread into ¼- to ½-inch cubes for turkey stuffing.

Per serving: Calories 227 (From Fat 95); Fat 11g (Saturated 1g); Cholesterol 28mg; Sodium 376mg; Carbohydrate 28g (Dietary Fiber 2g); Protein 5g per cup.

Fresh Cranberry-Orange Relish with Walnuts

Prep time: 10 min plus chill time • **Yield:** 12 servings

Ingredients	*Directions*
1 navel orange	*1* Starting at the stem end of the orange, remove the peel, working in a spiral fashion with a sharp paring knife. Take care to leave behind the bitter pith (the white layer beneath the orange peel). Set the orange peel aside.
1 package (12 ounces) fresh or frozen cranberries	
1 cup sugar	*2* Peel away and discard the white pith from the orange; coarsely chop the fruit.
2 teaspoons Cointreau, Grand Marnier, brandy, or other orange liqueur (optional)	
½ cup chopped walnuts (optional)	*3* Put the orange pieces, the orange peel, and the cranberries into the bowl of a food processor. Pulse 4 or 5 times, or until the fruit is coarsely chopped.
	4 Transfer the cranberry-orange mixture to a bowl or a glass serving container. Stir in the sugar and, if desired, the brandy or orange liqueur and the walnuts. Chill until ready to serve.

Per serving: Calories 85 (From Fat 0); Fat 0g (Saturated 0g); Cholesterol 0mg; Sodium 0mg; Carbohydrate 22g (Dietary Fiber 1g); Protein 0g.

Green Beans with Shallots

Prep time: 15 min • **Cook time:** About 20 min • **Yield:** 12 servings

Ingredients	Directions
3 pounds fresh green beans, rinsed and trimmed 6 tablespoons butter 1 cup shallots, sliced crosswise into thin rounds 2 teaspoons fresh lemon juice (optional) Salt and pepper	*1* Place the beans in a large pot. Add cold salted water to cover. Cover the pot and bring to a boil over medium-high heat. Cook until just tender but still firm, about 10 to 15 minutes. Check for doneness after about 8 minutes. *2* As the beans cook, melt the butter in a large skillet. Add the shallots and cook over medium heat for 3 to 4 minutes, stirring often, until golden. Set aside. *3* Drain the beans well and add them to the skillet with the shallots. Stir to combine and heat briefly just before serving. If desired, stir in the lemon juice. Season to taste with salt and pepper.

Per serving: *Calories 99 (From Fat 54); Fat 6g (Saturated 4g); Cholesterol 15mg; Sodium 54mg; Carbohydrate 11g (Dietary Fiber 4g); Protein 3g.*

Vary It! An elegant alternative for this dish is thin, French string beans, called haricot verts. If making this variation, reduce the cooking time to 4 to 6 minutes, or until tender.

Rum-Baked Sweet Potatoes

Prep time: 5–10 min • **Cook time:** About 45 min • **Yield:** 12 servings

Ingredients	Directions
6 medium sweet potatoes (about 3½ pounds), peeled	**1** Preheat the oven to 350 degrees.
⅓ cup butter	**2** Place the potatoes in a large pot of lightly salted boiling water. Cover and boil for 15 to 20 minutes, or until still slightly firm when pierced with a fork.
1½ cups packed dark brown sugar	
⅔ cup dark rum	**3** Drain and cut each sweet potato in half lengthwise and then widthwise into quarters. Place the potatoes in a single layer in a 9-x-13-inch baking pan or ceramic dish. Set aside.
⅓ cup fresh orange juice	
¾ teaspoon ground allspice	
Salt and pepper	**4** In a large skillet, melt the butter over medium heat; add the brown sugar, rum, and orange juice. Bring to a boil, stirring occasionally to break up any lumps of sugar.
	5 Reduce the heat and simmer for 7 to 8 minutes, stirring occasionally, until the sauce is thickened and slightly caramelized. Stir in the allspice.
	6 Drizzle the rum mixture over the sweet potatoes. Gently turn the potatoes in the glaze to coat all sides. Season the potatoes well with salt and pepper. Bake for 20 to 25 minutes, or until the sauce is bubbly and the potatoes are heated through and tender.

Per serving: Calories 261 (From Fat 48); Fat 5g (Saturated 3g); Cholesterol 14mg; Sodium 73mg; Carbohydrate 53g (Dietary Fiber 2g); Protein 2g.

Vary It! Instead of rum, you can use ⅓ cup molasses mixed with ⅓ cup pineapple juice and ¼ teaspoon almond extract or rum extract.

Praline Pumpkin Pie

Prep time: 15 min plus chill time • **Cook time:** 50 min • **Yield:** 8 servings

Ingredients	*Directions*
One 9-inch pie crust (preferably deep dish), unbaked	*1* Preheat the oven to 375 degrees.
1 cup packed light brown sugar	*2* Place a piece of foil over the bottom of the pie crust and weight it down with uncooked rice or beans. Bake the crust for 20 minutes, and let it cool. Remove foil.
3 tablespoons butter	
⅔ cup coarsely chopped, lightly toasted pecans	*3* In a small pan, combine ⅓ cup of the brown sugar with the 3 tablespoons butter. Cook over medium heat for a few minutes, stirring constantly until the butter is melted and the brown sugar is dissolved. Stir in the pecans.
1½ cups canned pumpkin	
3 eggs, lightly beaten	
1 tablespoon granulated sugar	*4* With a spatula or spoon, spread this hot mixture over the bottom of the cooled pie shell; set aside to cool to room temperature.
1 teaspoon ground ginger	
1 teaspoon ground cinnamon	
½ teaspoon ground nutmeg	*5* In a large mixing bowl, combine the pumpkin with the remaining ⅔ cup brown sugar. Add the eggs, granulated sugar, ginger, cinnamon, and nutmeg and beat lightly with a whisk or hand-held mixer on low speed until well blended.
1 can (5 ounces) evaporated milk	
¼ cup whole milk	
2 teaspoons vanilla extract	*6* Whisk or beat in the evaporated milk, whole milk, and vanilla extract, blending well. Pour the filling over the cooled pecan mixture in the pie shell.
1 cup lightly sweetened whipped cream (optional)	
	7 Cover the top edge of the pie crust with foil (to prevent over-browning). Bake the pie for 30 minutes. Remove the foil and bake for another 15 to 20 minutes, until a knife inserted into the center comes out clean. Cool on a wire rack.
	8 Cover and refrigerate until ready to serve. If desired, spoon lightly sweetened whipped cream over each portion before serving.

Per serving: Calories 432 (From Fat 222); Fat 25g (Saturated 9g); Cholesterol 110mg; Sodium 168mg; Carbohydrate 48g (Dietary Fiber 4g); Protein 7g.

380

Part IV: Now You're Cooking! Real Menus for Real Life

Eggnog

Prep time: About 5 min plus chill time • **Cook time:** 10–15 min • **Yield:** 6–8 servings

Ingredients	Directions
4 egg yolks	**1** In the bowl of a stand-up mixer, whip the egg yolks until they lighten in color. (You can also do this step by hand with a whisk.) Slowly pour in the sugar while mixing until it is thoroughly incorporated. Set aside.
1/3 cup sugar	
1 pint whole milk	
1 cup heavy cream	**2** In a medium saucepan over medium-high heat, combine the milk, heavy cream, vanilla extract, and nutmeg, stirring frequently. Bring just to a boil and quickly remove from the heat.
1½ tablespoons vanilla extract	
1 teaspoon freshly grated nutmeg	
3–4 ounces dark rum	**3** Very slowly whisk a cup of the milk mixture into the egg yolks. Add remaining milk mixture, whisking.
4 egg whites (optional)	
	4 Return mixture to a pot over medium-high heat until it registers 160 degrees on a liquid thermometer. Remove from the heat and stir in the rum. Chill thoroughly.
	5 To give the eggnog a lighter texture, beat egg whites until they form stiff peaks. Fold them into eggnog and whisk for a minute before serving.

Per serving: Calories 304 (From Fat 187); Fat 21g (Saturated 12g); Cholesterol 207mg; Sodium 60mg; Carbohydrate 16g (Dietary Fiber 0g); Protein 5g.

Warm Red Wine and Orange Punch

Prep time: 5 min • **Cook time:** About 30 min • **Yield:** 6 servings

Ingredients	*Directions*
¾ **cup water** ¾ **cup granulated sugar** **1 cinnamon stick** **One orange** **8 whole cloves** **1 bottle (750 milliliters) red wine (such as Merlot or Pinot noir)**	*1* In a saucepan, combine water, sugar, and cinnamon stick. Bring to a boil, lower heat, and simmer for 30 minutes. *2* Quarter the orange and squeeze the juice into the saucepan. Pierce the orange peels with the cloves and add to the pan. Stir the ingredients until syrupy. *3* Pour in the wine and heat to just below simmering, Remove oranges. Let cool for 10 to 15 minutes before serving in mugs. (Fragile glass may shatter.)

Per serving: *Calories 197 (From Fat 0); Fat 0g (Saturated 0g); Cholesterol 0mg; Sodium 7mg; Carbohydrate 30g (Dietary Fiber 1g); Protein 1g.*

Part V
The Part of Tens

"This is a wonderful rub. We use it on everything — fish, chicken, calluses..."

In this part . . .

Think of this part as a cheat sheet to use after finishing your own personal cooking course. You can refer to these lists for specific reminders or just for fun. (We had fun writing them, anyway.)

Here, you find information about common kitchen disasters and how to avoid them (they happen to the best of us!). You discover how to think like a chef by absorbing some classic cooking wisdom (you probably already know more than you think). You also get some tips for eating for good health, including how to reduce fat, sugar, and salt in your diet without reducing taste, and how to cook for special diets, whether vegetarian, vegan, or gluten-free.

Chapter 22

Ten Common Cooking Disasters and How to Deal with Them

In This Chapter

▶ Preventing and putting out fires

▶ Preventing and treating burns and cuts

▶ Rescuing a recipe from ruin

▶ Stretching a meal to feed more people

▶ Saving your kitchen counter

*N*o matter how careful you are and how experienced a home cook you are, you're bound to encounter the occasional kitchen disaster. It happens to the best of us! Whether your stovetop is aflame or you just burned that special birthday cake, we feel your pain. And so do you if your disaster involves a scalding, a cut, a scrape, or a hot apple pie dropped on your foot!

That's why we devote this chapter to ten common cooking disasters, and what you can do to a) deal with the disaster, and fast; and b) prevent it from happening again (or preferably, prevent it from happening in the first place!).

You Started a Fire

Why oh why did you put the roll of paper towels on the stovetop? Why did you forget to watch the pot? Why did you put that gold-rimmed bowl in the microwave? Why oh why didn't you spring for the *whistling* teapot!

When you have a flare-up in the kitchen, you need to act fast to keep the fire from getting out of control. But how you act depends on what kind of fire you have and where it is. Most small fires don't require a call to the fire department, let alone a fire extinguisher, but just in case, always have an ABC-certified fire extinguisher handy! These fire extinguishers can put out fires caused by electrical appliances as well as grease fires.

If you do have a kitchen fire, don't panic. Instead, memorize these instructions for putting out kitchen fires:

- ✔ If you have a fire in the oven, shut the door and turn off the oven. The lack of oxygen will douse the flames. If your oven continues to smoke as if a fire is still going on in there, call the fire department.

- ✔ If you have a fire in a cooking pan and you can safely put the lid on the pan, do so. Use an oven mitt, clap on the lid, move the pan off the burner, and turn off the stove. The lack of oxygen will douse the flames in a pot just like it will when you shut the oven door. If you can't safely put the lid on a flaming pan or you don't have a lid for the pan, use that fire extinguisher! That's what it's there for.

- ✔ To use a fire extinguisher, pull out the pin, hold the fire extinguisher firmly with one hand, point the nozzle at the fire, squeeze the trigger, and sweep the spray back and forth over the fire.

- ✔ Don't use water to put out grease fires; the old wives' tale "Oil and water do not mix" happens to be true. Water repels grease and can spread the fire by splattering the grease. Instead, smother the fire with a wet towel or use that fire extinguisher. If you're closer to the pantry than the fire extinguisher, throw a few handfuls of baking soda or salt on the fire to cut off its oxygen supply while you get the extinguisher.

- ✔ If the fire is spreading and you can't control it, get out of the house and call 911! Make sure everybody in your family knows how to get out of the house safely in case of a fire. Practice your fire escape route. Kids, especially, should practice how to get out of the house safely on their own, in case of fire.

You can do a lot to prevent kitchen fires in the first place:

- ✔ Keep your appliances serviced, clean, and in good repair. Dump the crumb tray and clean out the toaster crumbs periodically from the toaster or toaster oven. Wipe out the microwave. Clean the oven. If the waffle maker starts sparking or the coffee maker makes strange crackling noises, unplug them and have them repaired or replaced.

- ✔ Install a smoke detector near, but not in, the kitchen. (You don't want the small amount of smoke sometimes generated from cooking to constantly trigger the alarm.)

- ✔ Use caution when lighting the pilot light or burner on a gas stove. Follow the manufacturer's instructions.

- ✔ Don't use metal in the microwave. The sparks can turn into fire or can seriously damage your microwave.

- ✔ Don't overfill pots or pans with oil or grease. Wipe up spills and don't cook on a dirty stove.

✔ Always roll up long sleeves and tie back long hair when cooking. You don't need your beautiful flowing silk sleeves trailing in the spaghetti sauce, and you certainly don't need to catch on fire!

You Burned Yourself

Maybe you accidentally touch a hot burner, pick up a hot pot handle without an oven mitt, or burn the back of your hand on the oven coils when taking a pie out of the oven. Always keep a first aid kit in the kitchen that contains antibiotic ointment and/or burn cream and adhesive bandages, as well as gauze pads.

Treat burns by running cold water over them for five minutes. If your skin is seriously blistering, see a doctor. Otherwise, follow up your cold-water rinse with an ice pack for pain and, when the pain eases, apply antibiotic and/or burn cream and an adhesive bandage. For larger burns or burns that aren't healing quickly, look inflamed or infected, or ooze fluid, please see your doctor for treatment.

Prevent burns by following these tips:

✔ Always use oven mitts when taking things out of the oven or removing things from the stove. The large, heavy mitten-types are good because they protect the backs of your hands, too.

✔ Never touch or put anything other than pots and pans on the stovetop, especially if you aren't sure whether the burners are still hot.

✔ Stand back from hot pans when you remove the lid, to avoid steam burns.

✔ Be very careful when draining hot pasta or pouring hot liquids like soup from a pot into a bowl or a blender. A splatter of boiling water, hot soup, or hot oil can burn you.

✔ Never mix hot liquids in a blender. They can explode out of the blender container, even with the lid on. Allow liquids to cool to lukewarm before blending.

✔ Stand back from spattering grease (such as when you are cooking bacon or deep-fat frying) and vigorously boiling liquids, including water, which can also spatter and burn you.

✔ Keep pot handles turned inward, not out over the edge of the stove where someone could bump them and send a pan full of hot food flying.

✔ Teach kids to stay away from the stove, oven, and microwave, and to never touch anything on the stove or in the oven.

You Cut Yourself

Knives can be very dangerous, whether they're super sharp or too dull. Very sharp knives can easily cut skin, and dull knives can slip instead of easily cutting through food, putting you at risk for losing control and getting cut.

Always keep your knives sharp (see Chapter 4 for instructions), but keep them out of reach of children! Use them carefully and always keep your fingers curled under when chopping with a knife. Better to ding a knuckle than slice a fingertip!

Also use caution with steak knives, and please don't lick the cream cheese off that butter knife! It really can cut your tongue. Also use caution when handling mandolines, cheese graters, food processor and blender blades, and coffee and spice grinder blades. To secure your cutting board if it doesn't have rubber feet, put a wet towel under it when cutting. Also, don't ever slice things freehand over the sink. Slice that raw carrot on the cutting board, not against your own hand!

If you do cut yourself, wash the cut and apply pressure to stop the bleeding. Fingertip cuts can bleed a lot. Raise your hand above your head as you press on the cut with a cloth or paper towel until the bleeding stops. Then put antibiotic cream on the cut and bandage it. If the cut won't stop bleeding after a few minutes or if it is very deep, see your doctor or an emergency care facility; you may need stitches.

You Burned the Food

The best way to avoid burning food is, of course, to keep an eye on it! When the recipe says to stir the sauce *constantly,* that's what it means. When the recipe says to bake the cookies for 12 minutes, that doesn't mean 18 minutes. Use meat thermometers, candy thermometers, and deep-fat frying thermometers, and watch them carefully. Buy and use a kitchen timer instead of believing you'll remember when the pizza is done. Many microwaves, stoves, and ovens come with kitchen timers built right in, including digital ones with loud beepers. Let technology help you prevent a kitchen disaster! But if you do overcook something, here are a few suggestions:

- ✔ If you burn a large piece of meat, you may be able to cut off the burned sections and save the rest. Or cut off the burned sections, chop up the rest of the meat, and stick it in a nice soup. Will anyone know the difference? Probably not (unless you then proceed to burn the soup!).

- ✔ If you burn soup, pour the unburned soup into a separate pot, removing any blackened pieces, and reheat.

✔ As for your poor burned pots and pans, a good soaking and some elbow grease along with a steel wool scrubber (if it's safe to use on your particular type of cookware) can go a long way toward rescuing them, but sometimes, you can't do much other than buy a new pan. If your roaster looks like it has been lined in black, shiny volcanic rock, you probably need a new roaster. Just be thankful you didn't start a fire!

Your Barbecue Is Ablaze

Just because you're cooking outside instead of inside is no guarantee that you won't experience culinary misfortune. Especially with charcoal grills, controlling the flame height and the heat of the fire can be difficult, so grilling does take a little bit of practice. Here are a few tips for keeping your outdoor cooking experiences safe, sound, and savory:

✔ Before lighting the grill, make sure it's a safe distance (4 feet or more) from deck railings, roof eaves, patio umbrellas . . . anything that could catch on fire.

✔ Use extreme caution when using lighter fluid to soak briquettes. Never let children use lighter fluid.

✔ Keep matches and lighters out of the reach of children.

✔ If the grill fire gets too high, cover the grill and close the vents to smother the flame.

✔ Always know where the fire extinguisher is, just in case the flames get out of control.

✔ Always follow the manufacturer's instructions for grill usage, especially for gas grills and propane tanks.

✔ Use long-handled tongs, spatulas, and other grill tools rather than the regular tools you use in the kitchen. Grills can get much hotter than indoor stoves, and those long handles on grill tools keep your hands farther away from the heat.

✔ Don't overcook food on the grill. Charred food could pose a health risk, and it certainly doesn't taste very good!

Your Recipe Misses the Mark

Sometimes, no matter how closely you follow the recipe, the food you cook just doesn't taste very good. Maybe the recipe wasn't a very good one, or your ingredients weren't great. But food that doesn't taste good can sometimes be made to taste better. Here are some tips:

✔ **Too bland:** If your food is bland, it's usually under-seasoned. Just add salt (a little at a time, tasting after each addition). Salt perks up just about everything, from a boring soup or piece of meat to a tasteless tomato or slice of watermelon.

Add herbs and spices to any savory dish. Herbs and spices can add interesting flavor to bland casseroles, meats, fish, egg dishes, soups, stews, and salads. Try adding Italian-inspired combinations like oregano, basil, and thyme to tomato-based or egg dishes. Creamy soups can taste great with some dill, marjoram, or tarragon. To meaty dishes, add chili powder, cumin, paprika, or some of the hotter spices like cayenne pepper or hot pepper flakes, for some jazz. (See Chapter 3 for more ideas on using herbs and spices.)

For boring soup, stew, casserole, sauce, or gravy, enhance the flavor and make the texture silkier by stirring in any of the following: 2 tablespoons butter or olive oil or ¼ cup cream.

✔ **Too salty:** If a soup or stew is too salty, the simplest solution is to add water. Or, try adding paper-thin slices of potato. Cook them until translucent — they tend to soak up salt like little sponges. Leave them in the dish if that's appropriate, or fish them out with a fork and discard them. Tomatoes, either fresh or canned (but unsalted!), do the same thing. You can't always save a dish that's overly salted, but you can try.

✔ **Flat-tasting fruit:** Sugar does wonders for fruit. If you were planning a fruit-based creation but the fruit leaves something to be desired, sprinkle it with sugar and let it sit for a few minutes. Sugar will do lovely things for berries, melons, or orchard fruits. Or drizzle fruit with honey or cream. A squeeze of lemon or lime juice can also perk up bland or boring fruit.

✔ **Uninspiring desserts:** Here are tips for trying to enliven a dull dessert:

- If it seems appropriate, add some cinnamon, nutmeg, or a tiny pinch of cloves.

- If your cookies are ho-hum, perk them up with frosting or jam. Try making them into sandwiches with peanut butter filling or dipping them in melted chocolate and letting it harden.

- If your cake is too dry, poke tiny holes all over it with a toothpick or a skewer and soak each layer with a quarter cup of sweet liqueur such as Kahlúa, amaretto, Kirsch, or Grand Marnier. For a nonalcoholic version, drizzle with a little warmed honey, chocolate syrup, or strong coffee. Add some homemade whipped cream (see Chapter 14), and suddenly you have a very special dessert.

You're Out of an Ingredient

If you suddenly realize that you're out of an ingredient you need for a recipe, think twice before substituting something else. Sometimes, substitutes work great — soy milk for regular milk, yogurt for sour cream, strawberries for blue-berries, chicken for pork. However, substitutions don't always work. Ounce for ounce, baking soda and baking powder are not the same thing. Flour and cornstarch are not the same thing. Neither are wine and vinegar, eggs and mayo-nnaise, condensed milk and evaporated milk, or brown sugar and white sugar. Your idea *might* work, but we're not going to take out an insurance policy on it.

The safest way to go about substituting ingredients is to check reliable cooking resources. For advice on smart substitutions, check out Appendix B.

You Have Too Many Mouths to Feed

What do you do when the good food you have prepared, or are in the process of preparing, doesn't quite stretch? Try these tricks for making your dinner stretch to feed a few more mouths:

✔ **Transform your menu.** If you planned to serve each guest a chicken breast or steak, cut the meat into bite-size portions and mix with rice or pasta and lots of veggies sautéed in butter or olive oil. Suddenly, your dinner for 6 will serve 12 . . . or more! Or, put everything into a wok with hot oil for a delicious stir-fry.

✔ **Soup it up.** Throw meat and rice into a soup pot with some canned chicken broth. Get out all your fresh veggies, sauté them in a little butter, and add them to the pot. Let it all simmer for 30 to 45 minutes and serve. See Chapter 12 for some easy soup recipes.

✔ **Add a course.** Serve smaller portions of the entrée and add a big salad, a simple soup, a dish of pasta with butter and herbs or a simple sauce, a bowl of creamy risotto (see Chapter 13), or a stir-fry of fresh vegetables. Cut up some fruit, and you've got significantly more food.

✔ **Set up a buffet instead of serving everyone at the table.** Put out the dishes you had planned to serve and then fill out the meal with more items you already have on hand: a bowl of fruit cut into bite-sized pieces, chips and salsa, or a salad mix topped with a quick homemade vinaigrette dressing (like the one in Chapter 12).

You Damaged Your Kitchen Counter

If you accidentally scorch, scratch, knick, or otherwise mar your kitchen counter, don't despair. Some of these goofs can be repaired. You can also do a lot to prevent wrecking your kitchen counter. Here are some tips:

✔ Always use a cutting board when cutting with a knife, pizza cutter, or other sharp utensil, to prevent nicks and scratches.

✔ Clean up spills immediately to prevent stains. Foods that contains food coloring or that naturally have lots of color (such as tomato sauce or berries) can quickly stain a counter. If you do get a stain, try a bleach-water solution, a bleach pen, or vinegar. Certain enzyme-based stain-removing products can also work well.

✔ You can place a ripping hot pot or roasting pan on a slab of granite or on a countertop made of ceramic tile. But when you place hot pots and pans on most other countertops, including those made of expensive Corian (a synthetic, solid-surface material), they can scorch. As a general rule, set hot pots and pans on your stovetop or on a heat-resistant ceramic or metal trivet.

✔ If your countertop does seem irreparably damaged, consult a countertop repair specialist to see whether the countertop can be refinished or repainted, or whether it needs to be replaced. Every surface is different, so it pays to have a specialist advise you, but get several estimates so you can best assess what needs to be done. In the meantime, maybe your canister of flour or your coffee pot could sit right *there*.

You Have to Do All the Cooking

Okay, maybe this isn't such a huge disaster. If everybody clamors for your famous brownies or your to-die-for lasagna; if your children beg and plead for you to make dinner "because it's always so good"; or if the dinner parties always end up at your house, we don't feel too sorry for you. But here are a few tips to make sure you don't spend *all* your time in the kitchen:

✔ **Plan your meals a week in advance.** If you already know what you're going to cook and you shop accordingly, you won't waste time trying to decide what to make or running to the market at the last minute to pick up the necessary ingredients.

✔ **Enlist others to help.** Even the most kitchen-challenged person can tear lettuce leaves, chop veggies, or fetch meat from the freezer.

✔ **Share cleanup chores.** Shouldn't all the people who benefited from your fantastic meal help clean up the mess after dinner? We think so.

✔ **Take a break now and then.** Just because you *can* cook doesn't mean you always *must* cook. There is no shame in the occasional take-out or a visit from the pizza delivery guy. Everyone does it.

Chapter 23

Ten Ways to Think Like a Chef

. . . .

In This Chapter

▶ It's all in your head: techniques for success

▶ Save those chicken bones!

▶ Build dishes from the bottom up

. . . .

*I*n observing and interviewing many chefs, we found a consensus among them about how to progress as a cook. The ten points in this chapter reflect their thoughts.

Know the Basic Techniques

Cooking is so much more fun — and successful — when you approach it with confidence. Chefs say that confidence arises from knowing your techniques so well that they're second nature. Part II is chock full of information about the basic techniques you need to know.

Use Only the Freshest Ingredients

Use only the freshest ingredients and buy in-season fresh fruits and vegetables. Seasonal produce offers the highest quality at the lowest price. Why make an apple pie in the summer from mealy fruit held in storage all year when you can make a pie with fresh, ripe peaches or juicy plums? Let what's fresh and available at the market help you spontaneously decide what's for dinner. And definitely seek out farmers' markets in your area.

Get It Together

So much of cooking, even for professionals, is preparation — slicing, peeling, dicing, and so on.

The French call this preparation *mise en place,* which translates to "everything in its place." Get the chopping, mincing, deboning, and washing chores out of the way in order to create an even, efficient flow of cooking steps. Also have in front of you all the seasonings you need for the dish. That way, when the butter or oil is hot and sizzling in the skillet, you don't need to lurch over to the cutting board to peel and mince onions.

With This Basil, I Thee Wed

Learn about herbs, both fresh and dried, so that you can season without always relying on a recipe. (Chapter 3 is a great place to start your education.) Chefs base some of the world's great cuisines on the combination of a few simple herbs and spices.

All the Plate's a Stage

Some cooks expend much effort preparing a fine meal only to diminish it by heaping ingredients onto plates chuck wagon–style. There is no excuse for doing so.

Think how food looks — its colors, its textures, its shapes — and make the most of it. This is not to say you should recreate Machu Picchu with your mashed potatoes, just that you give some thought to aesthetics. It can be as simple as fanning thin slices of steak over the plate instead of serving it in one big slab; garnishing with fresh herbs or citrus; spooning a sauce onto the plate and then arranging meat, poultry, or seafood over it; or packing cooked rice into a small cup and inverting it over the plate. When you begin thinking this way, the options will seem endless.

Plan Your Menus in Advance

Spend some time up front figuring out what a whole meal is going to look like. If the appetizer is a salad of grilled portobello mushrooms, featuring mushrooms in the entree is not an interesting choice. Keep the courses balanced, and don't overtax yourself. If you serve a time-consuming and complex appetizer, serve a simple entree or one that needs only reheating.

Be Thrifty

Throw out nothing (unless, of course, it's spoiled). Nearly every morsel of food is usable for soups, stocks, salads, and so on. You can sometimes make great meals from leftovers (flip to Chapter 19 to see what we mean).

Learn about different cuts of meat and how to cook them so that you don't have to rely on more expensive cuts. Hone your knife skills so that you can save money by purchasing whole chickens, meats on the bone, fish, and so on and then cutting them up yourself — a huge discount.

Don't Be a Slave to Recipes

Use a good, basic recipe that you like as a starting point, but don't consider it written in stone. One of the great chefs of his generation and a close friend of ours, the late Pierre Franey, had one mantra: Taste, Taste, Taste! Don't assume that the cookbook is infallible. Even if it is, each kitchen is different, ingredients vary, and so on. As you cook, continually taste.

(Oh yes, he had another axiom: "Don't brown the garlic!")

Simplify

Too many spices spoil the broth. If you stick to two or three basic flavors in a dish, they work together to provide complexity, yet each flavor maintains its individuality. Don't load up your dishes with everything you can find. Sometimes the most perfect, delicious creations are the simplest.

Above All, Have Fun

Take a cooking course, buy a cookbook, or make a new dish that you've always wanted to try. Cooking, like monster wave surfing, should be exhilarating — something you look forward to. So what if you wipe out once in a while? It's all part of the challenge. Bon appétit!

Chapter 24

Ten Ways to Cook for Good Health

. . . .

In This Chapter

▶ Cooking more: An automatic health boost!

▶ Buying better ingredients

▶ Making allowances for special diets

▶ Transforming "healthful" into "healthful and tasty"

. . . .

*F*ood is good. We love food. We can eat it all day long. And food is an important component of good health. You know what they say . . . you are what you eat. So what are you: a slim carrot, a juicy tomato, a burly beefsteak, a curvy peach, or a lumpy bag of fried cheese puffs?

Because you're learning how to cook, you've already got a big advantage. Home-cooked food is almost always better for you than the processed stuff in a package. And you can take lots of steps to make your diet even better, keeping you full of energy and muscle tone. Isn't that better than constant fatigue and an extra layer of fat? In this chapter, we present ten ways to make your meals even better for your health.

Cooking at Home

Buying fresh ingredients and preparing them at home automatically gives you a leg up because your home-cooked creations don't require heavy doses of preservatives, fillers, artificial colors, or more salt than you've got in your salt shaker right now. Cook more, from scratch, and you'll do yourself and your family a big favor. If you're the type who finds cooking calming, you'll be reducing your stress levels, too. It's win–win.

Choosing Great Ingredients

Should you splurge on the extra virgin olive oil, the sea salt, the wild-caught fish? Yes! Should you buy the local vegetables picked fresh this morning, rather than the ones shipped from hundreds of miles away? Yes! Higher quality ingredients usually taste better and are better for you, whether they retain more vitamins and minerals due to freshness or contain fewer additives because of how they were made or raised. For example, farmed salmon may be dyed pink, but wild-caught salmon isn't. Fruit shipped from far away may be dyed or waxed to make it look appealing, but local fruit probably isn't.

A natural sea salt or Himalayan pink salt may contain more minerals than processed rock salt. Extra virgin olive oil may contain fewer impurities than regular olive oil and a more favorable essential fatty acid profile than other vegetable oils. Local vegetables may retain more vitamin C.

But sometimes, quality is just as much about taste as nutrition. Imagine a dish made with the best artisanal cheese and a gourmet pasta from Italy, served with a freshly baked loaf of sourdough bread and a salad of fresh crisp baby greens and homemade vinaigrette. Now imagine a dish of cheap pasta with processed American cheese, a slice of white bread, and a salad of iceberg lettuce and bottled dressing. Either one offers basic sustenance, but which one would you prefer? If the first meal just sounds better, know that selecting better ingredients is key both to improving your health and satisfying your taste buds.

If you've ever visited Europe, particularly Italy, France, or Spain, you may have recognized an entirely different attitude about food. Meals aren't something to rush through so you can get back to work. They are meant to be savored, and cooks take great pride in using the very best ingredients. It's a good lesson for us in-a-hurry Americans. We could all stand to slow down and get a bit choosier about what goes into our recipes and into our stomachs. Eating higher quality food and enjoying meals more will always be good for your health.

Going Organic

The jury is still out on whether organic food is actually more nutritious. Some studies say it is. Some studies say it isn't. However, most experts agree that organic food is better for you just because of what it *doesn't* contain: chemical residue from conventional farming.

Organic food costs more than conventionally grown food because it costs more to produce. To label a food organic, legally, it must be produced according to certain standards. The farmer may not use conventional chemical fertilizers, pesticides, herbicides, insecticides, or drugs, including antibiotics and hormones (in the case of organic meat or dairy products). Crops also cannot be treated with any fossil-fuel or sewage-based fertilizer and cannot be grown from genetically modified seeds.

The food must also be produced in a way that is considered most beneficial to the environment in terms of minimizing pollution and preserving soil fertility and water quality. Animals raised organically must be treated according to certain humane standards, such as being allowed to graze outside. They must also be fed food that is organic.

Some past studies have shown very little difference from a purely nutritional standpoint between organic and non-organic produce, but a few recent studies suggest that there are superior nutritional components to some organic foods. However, that may not be the main reason to go organic.

The fact is that when your food contains fewer chemicals, and when your environment is cleaner because of organic farming, you are likely to be a healthier person. When you pay extra for organic, you may or may not be investing in an insurance policy against future disease, but you will be voting with your dollars for an agricultural system that is less detrimental to the planet.

Finally, there's that good ol' matter of taste. Sometimes, organic produce just tastes better, and some people say it tastes more like food "used to taste." (To others, conventional produce tastes better because it tends to stay fresher longer.)

When you buy local food, you may be buying organic without realizing it. Official organic certification is pricey, and not all small farmers can afford it. If you buy your vegetables from the local farm stand or farmer's market, ask about the grower's methods. It's always nice to know your farmer and understand how your food was grown.

In general, we recommend a moderate approach. We think that meat, milk, and coffee are better when organic, not just for our own health but for the health of the people who work to produce these foods and the health of the environment. But we don't always buy them organic, every single time.

We also prefer, in general, to buy organic versions of the fruits and vegetables on the widely published Dirty Dozen list — the foods most likely to be harmfully tainted in their non-organic form. We worry less about the Clean 15, the conventional foods least likely to contain high levels of pesticides and other chemicals.

Dirty Dozen: We recommend organic versions of these items:

✔ Apples	✔ Kale
✔ Bell peppers	✔ Nectarines
✔ Blueberries	✔ Peaches
✔ Celery	✔ Potatoes
✔ Cherries	✔ Spinach
✔ Grapes	✔ Strawberries

Clean 15: Don't worry so much about finding organic versions of these foods:

✔ Asparagus	✔ Papaya
✔ Avocadoes	✔ Pineapple
✔ Broccoli	✔ Sweet corn
✔ Cabbage	✔ Sweet peas
✔ Eggplant	✔ Sweet potato
✔ Kiwi	✔ Tomato
✔ Mango	✔ Watermelon
✔ Onions	

So this one's up to you. Not everybody thinks that organic is better, but if you do, go for it when you can. It won't hurt you, and it may even make you healthier.

Managing Fat, Sugar, and Salt

What makes food taste good? Let's be frank: It's usually the fat, sugar, and/or salt. Fat gives food a rich mouth feel. Sugar is sweet. Salt adds savory flavor. Cooking is, in many ways, a matter of learning how to manipulate the taste of good ingredients by adding varying amounts of fat, sugar, and/or salt. We sauté in fat, we salt meat and vegetables, we add sugar to fruits and chocolate and desserts and even bread and the occasional stir-fry.

We will go so far as to say that fat, sugar, and salt are *necessary* for cooking and enjoying food. However, unless you live in a cave, you know that too much fat, sugar, and salt are not good for your health. In excess, they can cause obesity, high cholesterol, high blood pressure, out-of-control blood sugar and insulin levels, even heart disease and diabetes. Some doctors say that a poor diet — which usually means too much fat, sugar, and salt, at least in the United States — is second only to cigarette smoking as a cause of chronic disease.

Here's the thing: It's not that fat, sugar, and salt are so bad. The "too much" part is the problem. Eliminating these elements from your diet is likely to make you feel deprived, which can lead to further imbalances in the form of overindulgence, just when you were trying to cut back.

For good health, we recommend cutting back on fat, sugar, and salt without cutting them out entirely (unless your doctor has recommended that you do so). A sweet treat once a day is perfectly nice. A little fat for flavor is one thing, but deep-fat-fried food should probably be reserved for only the occasional indulgence. Salt brings out the flavor of your food, but you don't want to overwhelm it — and you need to taste your food at the table *before* salting it.

In general, when you cook at home, your fat, sugar, and salt consumption will probably be lower than if you eat mostly processed foods or go out to restaurants. Remember, practice moderation in all things, and managing fat, sugar, and salt won't seem so difficult.

Making Low-Fat Meals

To help you cut back on the fat without sacrificing flavor, here are some tips for making low-fat meals that still taste great. Try them, and if you can't tell the difference or you don't mind the difference, go for the lower-fat version. If you do mind the difference, cut back elsewhere. Feeling deprived will only make you eat more fat later:

- ✔ Sauté meat and vegetables in chicken broth or wine instead of butter or oil.

- ✔ Use cooking spray instead of butter or oil to grease skillets, griddles, and baking pans.

- ✔ Make salad dressing with a vinegar-to-oil ratio of 3:1.

- ✔ Don't eat the skin off your chicken or turkey.

- ✔ Eat less red meat and more fish. Fish contains fat, but it's the kind that is good for your heart.

- ✔ Slow-cook roasts, pork chops, and chicken; they'll be moist and tender without added fat.

- ✔ Broil, bake, grill, or steam food rather than sautéing or frying it. Roll chicken strips or pieces of fish in bread crumbs and bake them instead of frying. You can even bake strips of white or sweet potatoes into "fries" for a fraction of the fat you'll find in the deep-fat-fried kind.

- ✔ For scrambled eggs, use two egg whites for every whole egg. You won't even miss the extra yolks.

✔ Try lower fat cheese, milk, coffee creamer, cream cheese, sour cream, and yogurt.

✔ Blot the fat off pizza with paper towels.

✔ Drain the fat off cooked meat before serving.

✔ Try veggie "meats" made out of soy or wheat gluten (and sometimes with egg whites). If you like them, they'll save you a lot of fat when they replace traditional burgers and hot dogs.

✔ Make a vegetarian meal once or twice a week using beans, mushrooms, pasta, and/or tofu.

✔ When baking, substitute half the fat for apple sauce or canned pumpkin.

✔ Eat more brothy soup.

✔ Fill up on vegetables and fruit. You'll have less room for the fatty stuff.

Reducing Sugar

A little sugar is a sweet thing, and we would never want to cut it out of our diets entirely. But we also know it's all too easy to start eating cookies or movie candy or "just one more sliver" of cake and overdo it. Too much sugar isn't good for your body and can send your blood sugar and insulin levels soaring and crashing. For energy and good health, it's best to limit the sweet stuff. Here are some tricks for how to do that:

✔ **Get fruity.** Fruit is nature's candy, naturally sweet. Use raw chunks, fresh berries, or even applesauce to sweeten your oatmeal, smoothies, and desserts. Try jam that is naturally fruit-sweetened with no added sugar. Even if you just eat more raw fruit every day, you may not feel the desire for candy or baked goods.

If you crave sweet, chewy, fruity candy, try munching on dried fruit, such as raisins and dried apricots, cherries, or cranberries. You'll get fiber and minerals along with your sugar fix.

✔ **Drink less sweetened soda — or cut it out entirely.** Soda is probably the number-one source of added sugar in the American diet. It doesn't have one single nutritional benefit, and it wreaks havoc on your blood sugar. Switch to diet, or better yet, drink club soda with a splash of real juice. Your body will thank you.

✔ **Explore the dark.** Dark chocolate is full of healthful antioxidants. Plus, the darker the chocolate, the less sugar it contains. Darker chocolate also has more flavor, so you may be inclined to eat less. Look for chocolate that has 70 percent or more cacao content. Go ahead, have an ounce a day. Studies say it's good for you!

✔ **Add protein.** Protein will help you digest the sugar more slowly. Instead of a candy bar, put a few chocolate chips or jelly beans into vanilla yogurt, or spread peanut butter on a graham cracker and eat that with your square of chocolate.

✔ **Sweeten naturally, whenever possible.** Natural sweeteners contain more nutrients, and your body may digest them more slowly. They also have more flavor so you may not need to use as much. Instead of white sugar, try raw sugar — or better yet, honey, molasses, agave nectar, brown rice syrup, sorghum, or real maple syrup. Once you get used to these more complex sweeteners, you'll probably need a lot less sugar to make your life sweet.

Increasing Fiber

You need fiber so your body can keep everything, um . . . *moving right along.* Literally. Fiber comes in two types: insoluble and soluble. Both types are necessary for good digestion and — well, let's just say it — good elimination. When everything moves through unimpeded, your whole body works better and you feel good. *Without* laxatives.

Your best sources of fiber are whole grains, fruits, and vegetables. Avoid eating or drinking too many foods stripped of their natural fiber, such as juices and products made from white flour. Whenever you have a choice, go for the whole fruit, the whole vegetable, and the whole grain. The more whole foods you eat, the less room you'll have in your stomach for junk food that doesn't serve your health.

You can also add fiber to your favorite foods. Sprinkle wheat germ, oat bran, or ground flax seed into smoothies, on top of cereal, or into baked goods for an extra punch of fiber. You'll stay regular, and you'll feel like kicking up your heels.

Going Vegetarian or Vegan

Whether you decide to give up meat or just cut back, and whether it's for health reasons or environmental reasons or objections to animal cruelty, you may decide at some point in your life to give animal products the old heave-ho. Or maybe you're just veg-curious.

Vegetarians come in many guises:

✔ **"Regular" vegetarians** don't eat meat, poultry, or fish. Those who choose to eat eggs and dairy products sometimes call themselves *lacto-ovo vegetarians* (not the catchiest name ever, but nobody asked us).

- ✔ **Pescetarians** eat fish but no red meat or poultry.

- ✔ **Flexitarians** go vegetarian most of the time, but they aren't strict about it and may occasionally eat meat.

- ✔ **Vegans** eat no animal products at all, including eggs, dairy products, and in some cases even honey. Those who live the vegan lifestyle may also choose to shun all leather products and as many animal-derived products as they can.

Many nutritional studies suggest that vegetarians have lower body fat and lower incidence of chronic disease than meat eaters, although it's certainly easy to eat an unhealthy vegetarian diet if you exist on French fries and candy. Without careful planning, vegetarians can eat too many carbohydrates and not enough protein. Vegans may lack vitamin B-12 and calcium. Most nutritionists agree that if you decide to eliminate a major dietary category, you do have to take steps to make sure you get a balanced diet.

However, many vegetarians and vegans thrive, are in excellent health, and are at a sensible weight. Some are even highly competitive athletes.

It is beyond the scope of this book to explain how to go vegetarian or vegan. You may want to check out *Living Vegetarian For Dummies* and *Vegetarian Cooking For Dummies,* both by Suzanne Havala Hobbs, and *Living Vegan For Dummies* by Alexandra Jamieson (all published by Wiley). And if you want to cut back on meat and dip a toe into the veg lifestyle, here are a few hints to get you started:

- ✔ **Try tofu, tempeh, and seitan.** These protein staples of vegetarian and vegan diets can stand in for meat in almost any dish:

  - *Tofu* is bean curd, like cheese made from soybeans. It soaks up any marinade and has a chewy, meaty texture. It's also a ringer for scrambled eggs, with the right seasonings.

  - *Tempeh* is a fermented soy (or rice or both) product. You can cut it into strips and marinate it to make fake bacon, or toss it in a stir-fry. It's tasty and also soaks up the flavors of your dish. Some people like to steam it first to remove any bitterness leftover from the fermentation process.

  - *Seitan* is basically pure wheat protein, with a chewy texture not unlike chicken.

  If you find you like any or all of these protein sources, you'll have an easy time making the occasional (or frequent) meatless meal.

- ✔ **Sample milk alternatives.** It's easy not to drink milk these days. Most grocery stores stock a wide variety of alternatives, including soy milk, rice milk, almond milk, hemp milk, oat milk, hazelnut milk, coconut milk, and more. Good on cereal and perfectly acceptable in almost any recipe, these milk alternatives give cows a break. They're also great for people who are intolerant of lactose, the natural sugar in milk.

✔ **Just eat more vegetables.** Isn't that why they call it "vegetarian"? Nutritionists now know that plant foods are the most nutritious and health-bestowing foods on the planet. The more of them you eat, the better. Get in the habit of filling up at least half your plate with fresh vegetables, include a whole grain at every meal, and choose fruit for dessert. Do you even have room for anything else? When you begin to consider meat as more of a condiment than the main attraction, you're well on your way to a more flexitarian, if not vegetarian, if not *vegan* lifestyle.

Eliminating Gluten

For a small number of people, *gluten* — the protein in wheat and some other grains such as barley and rye — can actually be harmful. These people have celiac disease, a condition doctors are recognizing more often. People with celiac disease should never eat any gluten if they want to be healthy and avoid serious consequences.

But even those who don't suffer from celiac disease may choose not to eat wheat or not to eat gluten. Whether you have a wheat allergy, a wheat sensitivity, or you just want to cut back on something you've spent your life overeating, there are plenty of ways these days to eat happily gluten-free. Here are some tips:

✔ Get rid of all products made with wheat flour, including pasta. Also get rid of anything containing barley, rye, bulgur, couscous, durum, semolina, cream of wheat, emmer, spelt, kamut, graham flour, matzo, and of course, wheat gluten, including seitan. Although oats don't contain gluten, most brands in the United States are contaminated with gluten during processing, so avoid oats or get only those that state they are gluten-free.

✔ Replace all these grain products with those made from gluten-free grains:

- Rice, all types, including wild rice

- Buckwheat

- Quinoa

- Corn/cornmeal

- Any flour made from nuts or beans, such as almond flour, soy flour, or chickpea flour

- Any starch made from potato, arrowroot, or corn

✔ Learn to cook with gluten-free grains. Many grocery stores have gluten-free sections with pasta, flour, and baking mixes made from gluten-free grains.

✔ Invest in a good gluten-free cookbook to find reliable recipes (check out *Living Gluten-Free For Dummies* by Danna Korn [Wiley]). Because gluten gives bread and baked goods their springy texture, baking without it can be a particular challenge. However, there are some tricks you can learn, such as adding xanthan gum to simulate the action of gluten. Until you get very confident, always follow a reliable gluten-free recipe.

Making Healthful Food Taste Great

If we haven't made our point by now, we'll give it just one more go: Healthful food should taste great! *Don't* cut out all the fat, all the sugar, or all the salt. Include these taste-enhancing elements in moderate amounts. Cook with the highest quality ingredients. Include lots of fresh vegetables and fruits in your dishes and in your diet. Sniff, taste, and experiment with fresh herbs, dried herbs, and spices. Most of all, *enjoy* your food, *enjoy* cooking, and pay attention to what you are doing both during food preparation and food consumption.

The best foods are those made with the best ingredients, prepared with loving care at home, and enjoyed with friends and family (or in peaceful quiet, all on your own). That's how you cook and eat for good health without sacrificing even a fraction of good taste.

How's that for a diet plan you can get behind?

Appendix A

Glossary of 100 (Plus) Common Cooking Terms

• •

*C*ooking and recipe writing have their own distinct language. Before you roast a chicken, for example, you need to know what *trussing* means. To make a soufflé that rises above the rim of the dish, you need to understand *whipping* and *folding* egg whites. This appendix gives you a list of basic terms. Most of them are thoroughly described elsewhere in the book.

Al dente: An Italian phrase meaning "to the tooth" that describes the tender but still firm texture of perfectly cooked pasta. (See Chapter 13 for pasta recipes.)

Au gratin: A dish, usually topped with buttered bread crumbs, grated cheese, or both, that has been browned in the oven or under the broiler.

Bain-marie: A container partially filled with hot water that holds a smaller pan for gentle cooking.

Barbecue: Any food cooked on a charcoal or gas grill over an indirect fire (as opposed to grilling, which occurs directly over the fire). Also refers to the process of cooking foods in a pit or on a spit for a long time, or is a descriptive term for the particular spicy tomato-based sauce used to baste grilled meat.

Baste: To add flavor and moisture by brushing food with pan drippings, fat, or a seasoned liquid as it cooks.

Batter: An uncooked, semiliquid mixture usually containing beaten eggs, flour, liquid, and a leavening ingredient, such as baking soda or baking powder, that makes the batter rise when cooked.

Beat: To mix ingredients briskly in a circular motion so that they become smooth and creamy. A hundred hand-beaten strokes generally equal one minute with an electric mixer, if you're the type who counts these things. (See Chapter 10 for information about beating egg whites.)

Beurre manié: A butter-flour paste used to thicken soups and stews. (Turn to Chapter 12 for instructions for making this paste.)

Bind: To bring together a liquid mixture, such as a sauce, with a thickening ingredient, such as cream or butter.

Blanch: To plunge vegetables or fruits into boiling water for a short time to loosen their skin or preserve their color (see Chapter 5).

Blend: To mix or combine two or more ingredients with a spoon, whisk, spatula, or electric mixer.

Boil: To bring the temperature of a liquid to 212 degrees for water at sea level, causing bubbles to break at the surface (see Chapter 5).

Bone (or debone): To remove the bones from meat, fish, or poultry.

Bouquet garni: A package of mixed herbs (often tied in cheesecloth) that is used to season stocks, soups, and stews to impart flavor. A typical combination is parsley, thyme, and bay leaf.

Braise: To brown meat or vegetables in fat and then cook, covered, in a small quantity of liquid over low heat, usually for a long time. The long, slow cooking both tenderizes and flavors the food, especially tough cuts of meat. Braising can take place either on the stovetop or in the oven. (See Chapter 7 for braising and stewing recipes.)

Bread: To coat a piece of food with crackers or bread crumbs to seal in moisture and give it a crisp crust. The piece of fish, poultry, meat, or vegetable is usually first dipped into a liquid, such as beaten egg or milk, to make the crumbs adhere.

Broil: To cook food under a hot oven coil, as opposed to grilling, in which the heat is underneath (see Chapter 9).

Brown: To cook food briefly over high heat, usually in fat and on top of the stove, to impart a rich brown color to its skin or surface. Food also may be browned in a very hot oven or under the broiler.

Brush: To coat the surface of food with a liquid ingredient such as melted butter, egg, or fruit glaze.

Butterfly: To split food down the center (removing bones if necessary), leaving the two halves joined at the seam so that the food opens flat to resemble a butterfly.

Caramelize: To heat sugar until it melts into a liquid, syrupy state that ranges from golden to dark brown in color (320 degrees to 350 degrees on a candy thermometer). See Chapter 14 for a recipe for Caramel Sauce. Also, to cook onions and other vegetables until they become soft and brown (the sugars they contain caramelize).

Chill: To put food in a cool place, typically the refrigerator, to bring it to a cold (but not frozen) state.

Chop: To cut food into small pieces by using a knife or food processor.

Clarify: To make a cloudy liquid clear by removing the impurities. For example, you can clarify a stock or broth by simmering raw egg whites or eggshells in it for 10 to 15 minutes to attract impurities. You then very gently strain the liquid through a sieve lined with cheesecloth.

Compound butter: Butter that has been flavored with herbs or spices.

Confectioner's sugar: A fine powdered sugar cut with cornstarch that is used for cake icings or to powder cakes and cookies. Also called "powdered sugar."

Core: To cut out the core of a food, usually a fruit or vegetable such as an apple or pepper.

Coulis: A fruit or vegetable purée, used as a sauce.

Cream: To beat one ingredient, such as butter, with another, such as sugar, until soft and smooth.

Crimp: To press together with your fingers or a fork and seal the rim of a double-crust pie to form a double thickness of dough that you can then shape into a decorative pattern (see Chapter 10).

Crumble: To break up or crush food, such as dried herbs or crackers, into small pieces with your fingers.

Cube: To cut food into ½-inch square pieces. Cubed food is larger than diced food. See also *dice*.

Cure: To preserve food such as meat or fish by salting, drying, and/or smoking.

Cut in: To use two knives or a pastry cutter to mix hard fat (like butter) into dry ingredients (like flour). For example, "Cut the butter into the flour until it resembles coarse crumbs."

Dash: See *pinch*.

Deglaze: To add liquid, usually wine or broth, to a hot skillet or roasting pan and scrape up the browned bits clinging to the bottom of the pan that pieces of sautéed meat, fish, or poultry left behind. You then *reduce* and season the pan sauce. See Chapter 6 for recipes that use this technique.

Degrease: To skim the fat off the surface of a soup or gravy with a spoon. Also done by chilling the mixture, turning the liquid fat into a solid, which you can then easily lift off the surface.

Demi-glace: A rich brown sauce made by boiling down meat stock until it's reduced to a thick glaze that can coat a spoon.

Devein: To remove the vein from shrimp or other shellfish. (See Chapter 7 for illustrated instructions for cleaning shrimp.)

Devil: To season foods with hot and spicy ingredients such as Tabasco sauce, mustard, or red pepper flakes.

Dice: To cut into small (⅛-inch to ¼-inch) cubes.

Dilute: To thin a mixture by adding water or other liquid.

Disjoint: To sever a piece of meat at its joint, as when you separate a chicken leg from its thigh.

Drain: To remove the liquid from a food, often in a colander. Also, to pour off liquid fat from a pan after you brown a food (such as bacon or ground meat).

Dredge: To coat the surface of a food by dragging it through flour, cornmeal, or crumbs.

Drizzle: To pour a liquid such as melted butter, sauce, or syrup over a food in a thin, slow stream.

Dust: To give the surface of food a thin coating of flour or confectioner's sugar.

Emulsify: To combine two liquids that ordinarily would not meld on their own (water and oil, egg yolks and acid). This is achieved by combining small amounts of each while beating vigorously. Mayonnaise is one example.

Fillet: As a verb, to cut the flesh away from the bones of a piece of meat or fish. As a noun, a piece of meat, fish, or poultry that has the bones removed.

Flake: To peel off or form into flakes, usually with a fork, as in the process for determining if fish is done. (When you can flake the fish with a fork, it is cooked.)

Flambé: To ignite food that is drenched in alcohol so that it bursts into a dramatic flame just before serving.

Flute: To form into a decorative pleated groove, as in fluting a pie crust before baking.

Fold: To combine a light mixture, such as beaten egg whites or whipped cream, with a heavier mixture, such as sugared egg yolks or melted chocolate, by using a gentle mixing motion. (See Chapter 10 for illustrated instructions.)

Fricassee: A white stew in which meat or poultry is not browned before cooking.

Fry: To cook or sauté food in fat over high heat. Deep-fried foods are submerged in hot fat and cooked until crisp.

Fumet: A concentrated fish stock that is used as a flavoring base for sauces.

Garnish: An edible plate adornment, ranging from a simple wedge of lemon to a fancy chocolate leaf.

Glaze: To coat the surface of a food with syrup, melted jelly, an egg wash, or another thin, liquid mixture to give it a glossy shine.

Grate: To rub a large piece of food (such as a block of cheese) against the coarse, serrated holes of a grater.

Grease: To spread a thin layer of fat, usually butter, on the inside of a pan to prevent food from sticking as it cooks.

Grill: To cook food over a charcoal or gas grill, or to cook on an iron (or other) grill pan on the stovetop (see Chapter 9). Relatively high heat is used to sear food and add depth of flavor.

Hull: To trim strawberries by plucking out their green stems.

Julienne: To cut foods into thin (⅛ inch or less) strips; see Chapter 4.

Knead: The technique of pushing, folding, and pressing dough for yeast breads to give it a smooth, elastic texture. You can knead by hand, with an electric mixer equipped with a bread hook, or with a bread machine.

Macerate: To soak fruit in liquid — usually liqueur, wine, or sugar syrup.

Marinate: To soak or steep a food such as meat, poultry, fish, or vegetables in a liquid mixture that may be seasoned with spices and herbs in order to impart flavor to the food before it is cooked (see Chapter 9). The steeping liquid is called the marinade.

Mash: To press food, usually with a potato masher or ricer, into a soft pulp.

Mince: To cut food into tiny pieces.

Mirepoix: A combination of finely chopped sautéed vegetables, usually carrots, onions, and celery, that is used as a seasoning base for soups, stews, stuffings, and other dishes.

Parboil: To partially cook foods, such as rice or dense vegetables like carrots and potatoes, by plunging them briefly into boiling water (see Chapter 5).

Pare: To remove the skin from fruits or vegetables (see Chapter 4).

Pickle: To preserve food in a salty brine or vinegar solution.

Pinch or dash: A small amount of any dry ingredient (between $\frac{1}{16}$ and $\frac{1}{8}$ teaspoon) that can be grasped between the tips of the thumb and forefinger.

Poach: To cook foods in a simmering, not boiling, liquid (see Chapter 5).

Pound: To flatten food, especially chicken breasts or meat, with a meat mallet or the flat side of a large knife (such as a cleaver) to make it uniform in thickness. Has some tenderizing effect.

Powdered sugar: See *Confectioner's sugar.*

Preheat: To turn on the oven, grill, or broiler before cooking food to set the temperature to the degree required by the recipe.

Purée: To mash or grind food into a paste by forcing it through a food mill or sieve or by whirling it in a food processor or blender. Finely mashed food also is called a purée.

Ream: To extract the juice from fruit, especially citrus.

Reconstitute: To bring dehydrated food, such as dried milk or juice, back to a liquid state by adding water.

Reduce: The technique of rapidly boiling a liquid mixture, such as wine, stock, or sauce, to decrease its original volume so that it thickens and concentrates in flavor.

Refresh: To cool hot food (especially vegetables) quickly by plunging it in ice water or rinsing.

Render: To cook a piece of meat over low heat so that its fat melts away.

Roast: To cook in the dry heat of an oven (see Chapter 8).

Roux: A cooked paste of flour and fat such as oil or butter that is used to thicken soups, stews, and gumbos (see Chapter 14).

Sauté: To cook food quickly in a small amount of fat, usually butter or oil, over very high heat (see Chapter 6).

Scald: To heat milk to just below the boiling point when making custards and dessert sauces to shorten the cooking time and add flavor.

Score: To make shallow cuts (often in a crisscross pattern) on the exterior of a food (such as meat, fish, or bread) so that it cooks more evenly.

Sear: To brown quickly in a pan, under the broiler, or in a very hot oven (see Chapter 8).

Shred: To reduce food to thin strips, usually by rubbing it against a grater.

Shuck: To remove shells from shellfish, such as clams, oysters, and mussels, or to remove husks from fresh corn.

Sift: To shake dry ingredients, such as flour or confectioner's sugar, through a fine mesh sifter to incorporate air and make them lighter.

Simmer: To gently cook food in a liquid just below the boiling point or just until tiny bubbles begin to break the surface — at about 185 degrees (see Chapter 5).

Skim: To remove the fat and bits of food that rise to the surface of a soup or stock with a spoon (see Chapter 12).

Sous vide: A method of cooking (used primarily by the food industry and restaurants) in which ingredients or entire meals are cooked in vacuum-packed pouches for a long time at low temperatures, then chilled. They can be reheated and served or frozen for up to 18 months.

Steam: To cook over a small amount of simmering or boiling water in a covered pan so that the steam trapped in the pan cooks the food (see Chapter 5).

Steep: To soak dry ingredients like herbs and spices to infuse the liquid with flavor.

Stew: To simmer food for a long time in a tightly covered pot with just enough liquid to cover. The term *stew* also can describe a cooked dish (see Chapter 7).

Stiff peaks: A term describing whipped egg whites at the stage when they form stiff, upstanding peaks that stay erect when the beater is lifted out of the egg whites.

Stir-fry: The Asian cooking technique of quickly frying small pieces of food in a wok with a small amount of fat over very high heat while constantly tossing and stirring the ingredients. The term stir-fry also can refer to a dish prepared this way.

Stock: The strained, flavorful liquid that is produced by cooking meat, fish, poultry, vegetables, seasonings, or other ingredients in water.

Strain: To separate liquids from solids by passing a mixture through a sieve.

Tenderize: To soften the connective tissue of meat by pounding or cooking very slowly for a long time. See also *braise*.

Toss: To turn over food a number of times to mix thoroughly, as when a green salad is mixed and coated with dressing.

Truss: To tie meat or poultry with string and/or skewers to maintain its shape during roasting (see Chapter 8).

Whip: To beat air into ingredients such as eggs or cream with a whisk or electric beater to make them light and fluffy (see Chapter 10).

Whisk: A hand-held wire kitchen utensil used to whip ingredients like eggs, cream, and sauces. When used as a verb, the term *whisk* describes the process of whipping or blending ingredients together with a wire whisk.

Zest: As a noun, the colored, grated outer peel (the colored portion only) of citrus fruit that is used as a flavoring ingredient in dressings, stews, desserts, and so on. As a verb, the process of removing the colored, grated outer peel.

Common Substitutions, Abbreviations, and Equivalents

. . . .

*I*n this appendix, we list all kinds of ingredients to substitute for ingredients you need but don't have, we decode the most common cooking abbreviations, and we give you a list of English to metric equivalencies.

Substituting in a Pinch

Say that you're making a vinaigrette dressing for a salad and suddenly realize that you're out of vinegar. But you do have lemons. Can you use them? (Yes!) You may not have whole milk for a gratin dish, but you do have skim milk. Is skim milk okay? (Yes, but the taste won't be as rich.) Situations like these are what this section is all about.

Some ingredients are almost always interchangeable. For example, you can substitute vegetable or olive oil in most cases for butter when sautéing or pan frying; lemon juice for vinegar in salad dressings and marinades; almonds for walnuts in baked breads and muffins; vegetable stock for beef or chicken stock in soups, stews, or sauces; and light cream or even whole milk for half-and-half in almost anything.

But sometimes there is no acceptable substitution for an ingredient. Other times, the substitution is very exact and specific. This is most often the case for baked goods, where you need to follow a formula to produce a cake, soufflé, pastry, or bread with the perfect height, density, and texture.

Here are some reliable substitutions for thickening soups, stews, and sauces:

- ✔ 1 tablespoon cornstarch or potato flour = 2 tablespoons all-purpose flour. Make sure to cook the dish for at least 10 minutes after adding flour, to get rid of the raw flour taste.

- ✔ 1 tablespoon arrowroot = 2½ tablespoons all-purpose flour. See the preceding note about cooking the dish.

Different flours have different protein contents. These substitutions aren't ideal, but they'll work:

- 1 cup minus 2 tablespoons sifted all-purpose flour = 1 cup sifted cake flour

- 1 cup plus 2 tablespoons sifted cake flour = 1 cup sifted all-purpose flour

- 1 cup sifted self-rising flour = 1 cup sifted all-purpose flour plus 1¼ teaspoons baking powder and a pinch of salt

For leavening agents in baked goods:

- ¼ teaspoon baking soda plus ½ teaspoon cream of tartar = 1 teaspoon double-acting baking powder

- ¼ teaspoon baking soda plus ½ cup buttermilk or yogurt = 1 teaspoon double-acting baking powder in liquid mixtures only; reduce liquid in recipe by ½ cup

For dairy products:

- 1 cup whole milk = ½ cup unsweetened evaporated milk plus ½ cup water

  or 1 cup skim milk plus 2 teaspoons melted butter

  or 1 cup water plus ⅓ cup powdered milk

  or 1 cup soy, rice, coconut, or other non-dairy milk

  or 1 cup buttermilk plus ½ teaspoon baking soda

- ¾ cup whole milk plus ⅓ cup melted butter = 1 cup heavy cream (but not for making whipped cream)

- 1 cup skim milk =1 cup water plus ¼ cup nonfat powdered milk, or ½ cup evaporated skim milk plus ½ cup water

- 1 cup sour milk = 1 cup buttermilk or plain yogurt

  or 1 cup minus 1 tablespoon milk, plus 1 tablespoon lemon juice or white vinegar after standing 5 to 10 minutes

- 1 cup sour cream = 1 cup plain yogurt

For eggs:

- 2 egg yolks = 1 egg for thickening sauces and custards

- 4 extra large eggs = 5 large eggs or 6 small eggs

For sweetening:

> ✔ 1 cup sugar = 1 cup molasses (or honey) plus ½ teaspoon baking soda
>
> ✔ 1 cup brown sugar = 1 cup white sugar plus 1½ tablespoons molasses

Miscellaneous substitutions:

> ✔ 1 cup broth or stock = 1 bouillon cube dissolved in 1 cup boiling water
>
> ✔ 1 square (1 ounce) unsweetened chocolate = 3 tablespoons cocoa plus 1 tablespoon butter, margarine, or vegetable shortening
>
> ✔ 1 square (1 ounce) semisweet chocolate = 3 tablespoons cocoa plus 1 tablespoon butter, margarine, or vegetable shortening plus 2 tablespoons sugar
>
> ✔ 1 2- to 3-inch piece of vanilla bean = 1 teaspoon pure vanilla extract
>
> ✔ 1 tablespoon fresh chopped herbs = ¾ to 1 teaspoon dried herbs
>
> ✔ 1 medium garlic clove = ⅛ teaspoon garlic powder
>
> ✔ 1 cup red wine = 1 cup apple cider, cranberry juice, or beef broth
>
> ✔ 1 cup white wine = 1 cup apple juice, apple cider, white grape juice, or chicken broth

Taking a Quick Look at Abbreviations

Although we spell out measurements in this book, many cookbooks use abbreviations. Table B-1 lists common abbreviations and what they stand for.

Table B-1	Common Abbreviations
Abbreviation(s)	*What It Stands For*
C., c.	Cup
G, g	Gram
kg	Kilogram
L, l	Liter
lb.	Pound
mL, ml	Milliliter
oz.	Ounce
pt.	Pint
t., tsp.	Teaspoon
T., Tb., Tbsp.	Tablespoon

Looking Up Conversions and Metric Equivalents

Cookbook writers have a penchant for practical jokes. Just when you're getting the hang of cups and tablespoons, they throw you a recipe in ounces or pounds or some other measurement. Tables B-2 and B-3 list common equivalent measures. All measurements are for level amounts.

Note: Some metric measurements are approximate. The recipes in this cookbook were not developed or tested using metric measures. There may be some variation in quality when converting to metric units.

Table B-2	Conversion Secrets	
This Measurement . . .	*. . . Equals This Measurement*	*. . . Equals This Metric Measurement*
Pinch or dash	less than ⅛ teaspoon	0.5 mL
3 teaspoons	1 tablespoon	15 mL
2 tablespoons	1 fluid ounce	30 mL
1 jigger	1½ fluid ounces	45 mL
4 tablespoons	¼ cup	50 mL
5 tablespoons plus 1 teaspoon	⅓ cup	75 mL
12 tablespoons	¾ cup	175 mL
16 tablespoons	1 cup	250 mL
1 cup	8 fluid ounces	250 mL
2 cups	1 pint or 16 fluid ounces	500 mL
2 pints	1 quart or 32 fluid ounces	1 L
4 quarts	1 gallon	4 L

Table B-3	Food Equivalents
This Measurement . . .	*. . . Equals This Measurement*
3 medium apples or bananas	about 1 pound
1 ounce baking chocolate	1 square
2 slices bread	about 1 cup fresh bread crumbs
1 pound brown sugar	2¼ cups packed

This Measurement . . .	. . . Equals This Measurement
4 tablespoons butter	½ stick
8 tablespoons butter	1 stick
4 sticks butter	1 pound
6 ounces chocolate chips	about 1 cup
1 pound confectioner's sugar	about 4½ cups sifted
1 pound granulated sugar	2 cups
½ pound hard cheese	about 2 cups grated
1 cup heavy whipping cream	2 cups whipped cream
1 medium lemon	3 tablespoons juice, 2 to 3 teaspoons grated zest
1 pound macaroni	4 cups raw, 8 cups cooked
4 ounces nuts	about ⅔ cup chopped
1 large onion	about 1 cup chopped
1 cup uncooked rice	4 cups cooked
1 pint strawberries	about 2 cups sliced
1 large tomato	about ¾ cup chopped
3 to 4 tomatoes	about 1 pound
1 pound all-purpose flour	about 4 cups sifted

Tables B-4 through B-6 show you metric conversions for volume, weight, and temperature. Use them if you need to convert a recipe, but remember that these are approximate and results could vary.

Table B-4	Volume	
U.S. Units	**Canadian Metric**	**Australian Metric**
¼ teaspoon	1 milliliter	1 milliliter
½ teaspoon	2 milliliters	2 milliliters
1 teaspoon	5 milliliters	5 milliliters
1 tablespoon	15 milliliters	20 milliliters
¼ cup	50 milliliters	60 milliliters
⅓ cup	75 milliliters	80 milliliters
½ cup	125 milliliters	125 milliliters
⅔ cup	150 milliliters	170 milliliters
¾ cup	175 milliliters	190 milliliters

(continued)

Table B-4 *(continued)*

U.S. Units	Canadian Metric	Australian Metric
1 cup	250 milliliters	250 milliliters
1 quart	1 liter	1 liter
2 quarts	2 liters	2 liters
3 quarts	3 liters	3 liters
4 quarts (1 gallon)	4 liters	4 liters

Table B-5 Weight

U.S. Units	Canadian Metric	Australian Metric
1 ounce	30 grams	30 grams
2 ounces	55 grams	60 grams
3 ounces	85 grams	90 grams
4 ounces (¼ pound)	115 grams	125 grams
8 ounces (½ pound)	225 grams	225 grams
16 ounces (1 pound)	455 grams	500 grams (½ kilogram)

Table B-6 Temperature (Degrees)

Fahrenheit	Celsius
32	0
212	100
250	120
275	140
300	150
325	160
350	180
375	190
400	200
425	220

Index

• D •

Apple & Macs

iPad For Dummies
978-0-470-58027-1

iPhone For Dummies,
4th Edition
978-0-470-87870-5

MacBook For Dummies, 3rd
Edition
978-0-470-76918-8

Mac OS X Snow Leopard For
Dummies
978-0-470-43543-4

Business

Bookkeeping For Dummies
978-0-7645-9848-7

Job Interviews
For Dummies,
3rd Edition
978-0-470-17748-8

Resumes For Dummies,
5th Edition
978-0-470-08037-5

Starting an
Online Business
For Dummies,
6th Edition
978-0-470-60210-2

Stock Investing
For Dummies,
3rd Edition
978-0-470-40114-9

Successful
Time Management
For Dummies
978-0-470-29034-7

Computer Hardware

BlackBerry
For Dummies,
4th Edition
978-0-470-60700-8

Computers For Seniors
For Dummies,
2nd Edition
978-0-470-53483-0

PCs For Dummies,
Windows
7 Edition
978-0-470-46542-4

Laptops For Dummies,
4th Edition
978-0-470-57829-2

Cooking & Entertaining

Cooking Basics
For Dummies,
3rd Edition
978-0-7645-7206-7

Wine For Dummies,
4th Edition
978-0-470-04579-4

Diet & Nutrition

Dieting For Dummies,
2nd Edition
978-0-7645-4149-0

Nutrition For Dummies,
4th Edition
978-0-471-79868-2

Weight Training
For Dummies,
3rd Edition
978-0-471-76845-6

Digital Photography

Digital SLR Cameras &
Photography For Dummies,
3rd Edition
978-0-470-46606-3

Photoshop Elements 8
For Dummies
978-0-470-52967-6

Gardening

Gardening Basics
For Dummies
978-0-470-03749-2

Organic Gardening
For Dummies,
2nd Edition
978-0-470-43067-5

Green/Sustainable

Raising Chickens
For Dummies
978-0-470-46544-8

Green Cleaning
For Dummies
978-0-470-39106-8

Health

Diabetes For Dummies,
3rd Edition
978-0-470-27086-8

Food Allergies
For Dummies
978-0-470-09584-3

Living Gluten-Free
For Dummies,
2nd Edition
978-0-470-58589-4

Hobbies/General

Chess For Dummies,
2nd Edition
978-0-7645-8404-6

Drawing
Cartoons & Comics
For Dummies
978-0-470-42683-8

Knitting For Dummies,
2nd Edition
978-0-470-28747-7

Organizing
For Dummies
978-0-7645-5300-4

Su Doku For Dummies
978-0-470-01892-7

Home Improvement

Home Maintenance
For Dummies,
2nd Edition
978-0-470-43063-7

Home Theater
For Dummies,
3rd Edition
978-0-470-41189-6

Living the
Country Lifestyle
All-in-One
For Dummies
978-0-470-43061-3

Solar Power Your Home
For Dummies,
2nd Edition
978-0-470-59678-4

Internet

Blogging For Dummies,
3rd Edition
978-0-470-61996-4

eBay For Dummies,
6th Edition
978-0-470-49741-8

Facebook For Dummies,
3rd Edition
978-0-470-87804-0

Web Marketing
For Dummies,
2nd Edition
978-0-470-37181-7

WordPress
For Dummies,
3rd Edition
978-0-470-59274-8

Language & Foreign Language

French For Dummies
978-0-7645-5193-2

Italian Phrases
For Dummies
978-0-7645-7203-6

Spanish For Dummies,
2nd Edition
978-0-470-87855-2

Spanish
For Dummies,
Audio Set
978-0-470-09585-0

Math & Science

Algebra I
For Dummies,
2nd Edition
978-0-470-55964-2

Biology For Dummies,
2nd Edition
978-0-470-59875-7

Calculus For Dummies
978-0-7645-2498-1

Chemistry For Dummies
978-0-7645-5430-8

Microsoft Office

Excel 2010 For Dummies
978-0-470-48953-6

Office 2010 All-in-One
For Dummies
978-0-470-49748-7

Office 2010 For Dummies,
Book + DVD Bundle
978-0-470-62698-6

Word 2010 For Dummies
978-0-470-48772-3

Music

Guitar For Dummies,
2nd Edition
978-0-7645-9904-0

iPod & iTunes For
Dummies, 8th Edition
978-0-470-87871-2

Piano Exercises
For Dummies
978-0-470-38765-8

Parenting & Education

Parenting For Dummies,
2nd Edition
978-0-7645-5418-6

Type 1 Diabetes
For Dummies
978-0-470-17811-9

Pets

Cats For Dummies,
2nd Edition
978-0-7645-5275-5

Dog Training For Dummies,
3rd Edition
978-0-470-60029-0

Puppies For Dummies,
2nd Edition
978-0-470-03717-1

Religion & Inspiration

The Bible For Dummies
978-0-7645-5296-0

Catholicism For Dummies
978-0-7645-5391-2

Women in the Bible
For Dummies
978-0-7645-8475-6

Self-Help & Relationship

Anger Management
For Dummies
978-0-470-03715-7

Overcoming Anxiety
For Dummies,
2nd Edition
978-0-470-57441-6

Sports

Baseball
For Dummies,
3rd Edition
978-0-7645-7537-2

Basketball
For Dummies,
2nd Edition
978-0-7645-5248-9

Golf For Dummies,
3rd Edition
978-0-471-76871-5

Web Development

Web Design
All-in-One
For Dummies
978-0-470-41796-6

Web Sites
Do-It-Yourself
For Dummies,
2nd Edition
978-0-470-56520-9

Windows 7

Windows 7
For Dummies
978-0-470-49743-2

Windows 7
For Dummies,
Book + DVD Bundle
978-0-470-52398-8

Windows 7 All-in-One
For Dummies
978-0-470-48763-1

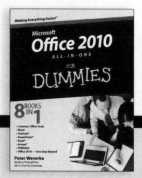